BOTTOM LINE'S

SECRETS OF THE SAVVY CONSUMER

INSIDER TIPS TO SAVING MONEY ON EVERYTHING

Secrets of the Savvy Consumer

10 9 8 7 6 5 4 3 2 1

ISBN 0-88723-779-7

Bottom Line Books® publishes the opinions of expert authorities in many fields. The use of a book is not a substitute for legal, accounting, investment, health or any other professional services. Consult competent professionals for answers to your specific questions.

Offers, prices, rates, addresses, telephone numbers and websites listed in this book are accurate at the time of publication, but they are subject to frequent change.

Bottom Line Books® is a registered trademark of Bottom Line Inc.,
3 Landmark Square, Suite 201, Stamford, CT 06901

BottomLineInc.com

Bottom Line Books is an imprint of Bottom Line Inc., publisher of print periodicals, e-letters and books. We are dedicated to bringing you the best information from the most knowledgeable sources in the world. Our goal is to help you gain greater wealth, better health, more wisdom, extra time and increased happiness.

Printed in the United States of America

Contents

Introduction

There are two types of consumers: those who buy, and those who are sold. This book is for that first type—the small group of people who keep the power on their side of the table when they negotiate a purchase.

It is my goal in life to live well beyond my means. I am not talking about going into debt. Instead, I have learned hundreds of ways to get more for my dollars. I am convinced that those of us who know the tricks and strategies of being a savvy consumer are subsidized at every turn by the vast majority of shoppers who don't know how to buy.

One of the keys to being a savvy consumer is to recognize that when you buy a car, a house, a vacuum cleaner, an airline ticket, or most anything else, you are taking part in a deal. The same applies when you engage the services of a doctor, a roofer, or a landscaper.

How can you live beyond your means?

- **Spend thousands of dollars less on a vacation.** Do you know the best time to buy an airline ticket? How can you beat the one-way ticket rip-off? How do you compare cruise lines? When is "free" a bad deal? How can you save big bucks by arranging your own tours? When does it make sense to hire an agent or buy a travel package?

- **Become smarter than your computer when you shop on the internet.** Do you know how to methodically compare prices? Can you get an internet price at a local retail store? Do you know the sometimes-secret path to speaking with a live human being behind the screen of an online store? What can you do to lower costs, obtain a price match, or otherwise adjust your deal from an internet seller?

- **Understand the relative advantages and disadvantages of computers, tablets, and smartphones.** What are the most important product specifications to understand? Which bells and whistles are worth paying for, and which are just background noise? And what about internet access: cable modems, cellular service providers, and WiFi access points?

- **Figure out the best way to pay for items.** How will you pay—cash, credit, debit, or perhaps points? You'll learn why some items should always go on your credit card (if you've got the right type) and why sometimes it is to your advantage to pay cash.

- **Make the most of warranties, guarantees, price matches, and rebates.** Why should you keep shopping even after you make a purchase? How can you get an extended warranty for free? If you are considering paying for an extended warranty, I'll help you decide between the deals and the duds.
- **Cut the cost of certain prescriptions in half.** Together we'll also explore ways to work with your doctors and your insurance companies to keep medical bills in check.
- **Save tens or hundreds of thousands of dollars on a mortgage with very little pain.** About two-thirds of us live in a home or dwelling we own (or share ownership with the bank). We'll explore updates and improvements that add value to your home, and I'll warn you against those that do not. And if you're in the market, I'll tell you the savvy consumer's advice on how to buy or sell a house or apartment. Who does the real estate agent work for? When is the highest offer not the best offer?
- **Get the best price on a new or used car.** I'll help you make what is most people's second-largest purchase. We'll begin with the difference between a want and a need, and then answer questions like these: When is the best time to buy? What is the best way to pay? And I'll tell you why you should call your insurance company *before* you buy a car, not afterward.

Who Should Read This Book

Some people happily pay thousands more than they should for a car, or buy flat-screen TVs and computers at list price, or pay twice as much as the people across the aisle on an airliner or across the passageway on a cruise ship. And there are those who don't think twice (or even once) about unnecessarily paying hundreds of dollars on credit debt or tens of thousands (or even more) to pay off a home mortgage.

These may well be the same people who don't worry at all about squandering their income with wasteful computer purchases, driving up costs with poorly chosen automobile and travel-insurance policies, and who happily pay bonuses to their local electric, gas, and water utilities.

These are not the people who are reading these words. Or if they are, they're not going to continue to be happy doing business the way they had become accustomed.

The readers of this book are the people who hate to waste money. They want to know the secrets of savvy consumers and the inside story from the people who sell them insurance, cars, houses, vacation and business travel, and even food, entertainment, household items, and office equipment.

This is not a book for cheapskates or penny pinchers. I'm not going to advise you to root through other peoples' garbage (Dumpster Diving) for cast-off food and clothing. You won't find 100 recipes for cooking weeds. Not found here are instructions for do-it-yourself funerals. (These are all actual ideas from some sensationally useless tip books.)

Instead, I'm devoted to providing real-world suggestions on how to maximize your lifestyle. Whether your annual income is $30,000 or $300,000, you can find ways to get more bang for your bucks in almost everything you do.

Here are some of the subjects we explore…

- **How to put your car-buying business out to competitive bid.**
- **How to get the best deal and the best coverage on home and auto insurance.**

- How to travel first class on an economy budget.
- How to buy almost anything on the internet while saving money and time and protecting yourself against fraud.
- How to hire a real-estate agent and how to negotiate the commission you pay.
- How to select the best mortgage and keep it up to date with changing rates and conditions.
- How to outfit your house with the latest and greatest appliances, which use less electricity and do a better job.
- How to maximize your chances of getting the most financial aid for your children when they head off to college.
- How to do your bank a favor by giving it your business...on your terms.

About the Author

I've made my career out of explaining the complexities of consumer topics, business, travel, and computers in more than 300 books. Beginning as a Gannett Newspapers and Associated Press newsman and columnist, I also served as the first executive editor of *PC Magazine*, one of the magazine industry's greatest success stories.

I've appeared on NBC's *Today Show*, CNN, ABC, National Public Radio's *Fresh Air*, the Travel Channel, and dozens of local radio and television shows. I've been the subject of many newspaper and magazine articles.

These days, in addition to writing books, I also work for one of the world's top luxury cruise lines, traveling the world giving lectures on ports of call, history, art, music, and more.

Over the years, my wife and I have purchased four homes (and gone through about a dozen mortgages and refinances when it was to our advantage), bought and sold about two dozen cars (with the most recent five or six acquisitions made by phone, internet, and email), and have traveled to more than one hundred countries around the world by plane, train, automobile, and ship.

Through it all, I am constantly on the hunt for better, bigger, and best deals. Living large and enjoying the ride.

The first version of this book was published twenty years ago and though much has changed, the strategies have remained the same. I've gone back and updated and rewritten nearly every negotiation.

And I'd love to hear from you with suggestions of your own. You can write to me through the contact page on my website at CoreySandler.com.

PART I

Don't Be Sold

CHAPTER 1

Training for Buying Savvy

Buy. Don't be sold.

That is the key to success for the savvy consumer.

A buyer has done his or her homework before setting foot in a store or visiting a website.

A buyer never pays for unnecessary features or services when a better alternative is available.

A buyer knows the best way to pay each time: cash, credit, check, points, miles.

And most importantly, a buyer remembers that until the contract is signed or the payment is made, all the power resides on his or her side of the table.

My lovely wife, a very capable shopper herself, has learned that I am not at all impressed when she comes to me and says something like, "This dress was on sale for $200 less than retail price." She is quite familiar, after all these years, with my response: "I'm not interested in how much the price was discounted. Is the dress worth the price you paid, and is that the best price possible?"

You've got the power...because you've got the money. In most every purchase you make, you have options...

- **You can ask for a better deal.**
- **You can buy from someone else.**
- **You can buy somewhere else.**
- **You can buy something else.**
- **You can choose not to wait for a better deal.**

In this chapter, I'll start by discussing how to shop for the right store before you shop in a store, as well as help you find the right salesperson. Then it's on to insider information about the best time of the year to buy particular products and a few quick lessons on markups and markdowns.

You'll learn some valuable information about when it's to your best advantage to use a credit card, or when you might be better off paying cash or points or miles. I'll explore the value of a good warranty and then talk about buying strategies where you can cut your costs by accepting items that are already less than perfect. And finally, I'll explore buying situations where you can become directly involved in the economic laws of supply and demand—buyer's cooperatives, wholesale stores, and auctions.

Secret Customer Service

How do you break through the computer screen to talk to a human being at an online store? What if you have a question or need help and the seller lists only an email address? First, I tend to stay away from sellers who hide their address or phone number. Second, *there are ways to obtain a number.* Start by entering the company's name (not its web address) into a search engine on the internet. For example, enter *Amazon* but not *Amazon.com.* You just might be rewarded with a customer service number.

Several websites offer help contacting sellers. One is GetHuman.com, which offers to sell you their services in disputing a purchase but also—a few clicks into the site—has a list of phone numbers for you to use.

Anyhow, here are some numbers you might need to use someday...

- **Apple Store's customer service:** 800-692-7753
- **Amazon's customer service:** 866-216-1072 or 888-280-3321
- **Staples' customer service:** 800-333-3330

- **Shop for the right store.**
- **Shop for the right salesperson.**
- **Ask the right questions.**
- **Buy at the right time.**
- **Understand a retailer's markup strategy.**
- **Get familiar with the gray market.**
- **Know when to use a credit card.**
- **Here's when you might pay by check.**
- **Here's when you might pay cash.**
- **Debit cards.**
- **Examine outlet malls.**
- **Learn how to shop in foreign countries.**
- **Study sales tax laws for fun and profit.**
- **Turn back freebies for fun and profit.**
- **Buy scratch-and-dent.**
- **Consider joining a warehouse club.**
- **Join or create a buying cooperative.**
- **Know how to raise your hand at an auction house.**

Shop for the Right Store

As a savvy consumer, you should be just as careful choosing the places *where* you spend your money as what and how much you spend it on.

Here's what I want in a store...

- **A wide variety of quality merchandise.**
- **Prices that represent a good deal for the buyer.**
- **The customer-friendliest return and warranty policies.**

Does this sound like an impossible dream? It's not. Many places fit the bill.

It may be a huge national retail operation or a local mom-and-pop retailer. It may be a major internet seller or a traditional brick-and-mortar store's internet outpost. Ask yourself—and anyone you know who buys the same things—if you should deal with a different seller. Consider warehouse stores, builders' supply houses, catalog stores, and internet vendors.

You can spend hours or days trapped in a car dealership office in an endurance match with a salesperson who has been trained to wheedle, prevaricate, and otherwise inflate profit, or you can put your business out for bids online or over the phone, insisting that sellers justify every penny of the deal before you arrive for a brief ceremonial contract signing.

You can subject yourself to the nearly opaque process of buying eyeglass frames and lenses from the thinly concealed oligopoly of retail stores, or you can shop online at a safe and clarifying distance.

You can accept an insurance quote handed to you by an agent, or you can educate yourself on what you are seeking to buy and then be very specific—and cost-conscious—in your shopping with an agent or online.

Don't make assumptions about sales policies based on the size of the operation. Many major discount-store chains advertise "price guarantees" promising they will not be "undersold." A small local store, where the owner or manager is behind the counter, may be quite willing to match or beat a major competitor even if there's no advertisement about that policy. Either way, these businesses are smart enough to realize that it's better to make a small profit than no profit at all.

Major internet sellers may offer spectacular bargains on a wide range of items, but one way or another you're going to have to pay for shipping. The differences may be negligible when we're talking about clothing or other lightweight items. Buying an appliance or a gallon of laundry detergent by internet may or may not be the best deal. I'll talk about "free" shipping, "prime" or "club" shipping, and other sometimes hidden costs later on in this book.

You're almost certain to need your own group of stores: the best place to buy hardware, the best place to buy appliances, the best place to buy clothing, and so on. Don't concentrate solely on finding the best price, however, unless you're talking about a basic and known commodity you will consume immediately. Instead, be on the lookout for a place that will deliver your product on time, in good condition, with setup or technical support if necessary, and one that will stand behind its products after the sale.

Ask a lot of questions, and push—gently and politely—for any reasonable concessions on price or service.

Remember this important lesson that many people have learned from difficult situations: If a store is difficult to deal with *before* you buy from them, they will not be easier to work with *after* they have your money.

Shop for the Right Salesperson

Here's what I want in a salesperson…

- **Someone who knows the product at least as well as I do.**
- **Someone who knows that there are other places selling this product or service.**
- **Someone who knows that I'm a savvy buyer who is willing to pay a fair price for a good product** backed by excellent service (but not an inflated price that has a "you're on your own from here" sales policy).
- **Someone who is unimpressed by sales, marketing ploys, and high-pressure tactics.**

The greatest possible savings may come when you decide not to buy something because the price is wrong, the product is wrong, or the seller or manufacturer does not fully stand behind the product or service.

Here's a buying tip for certain large items like appliances and cars that may sound counterintuitive: You may get the best deal by buying from a commissioned salesperson rather than from a salaried order taker.

Here's why: A person who earns his or her income on the basis of a commission has a greater personal interest in seeing that you make a purchase, even if they have to cut the price to make you loosen your grip on your wallet. A smaller commission is better than no commission at all. A salaried sales force often doesn't care whether the customer is happy or not, unless a supervisor is watching.

If you know that a particular store uses a commissioned sales force, you might try shopping there at the end of the month in hopes of taking advantage of sales contests and sales quotas that manufacturers and stores use to incentivize its staff. I'll discuss that in more detail in the chapter about buying a new car.

And if you find a particularly accommodating commissioned salesperson, ask him or her for advice on upcoming sales and special events. Make the salesperson your partner in savvy consumption. Then pass along your compliments about the salesperson to the manager.

Not All Salespeople Are Evil

Now, please don't misunderstand. I'm not saying that every salesperson, agent, or seller of services will attempt to rob you blind. In fact, most salespeople are pretty close to honest in their dealings. It's just that in any free economy, sellers will always try to get as much money for their goods and services as possible. *To the seller, making more profit is better than making less...*

- **Most real estate agents (including those who are escorting buyers) are paid by the seller,** not the buyer. The higher the price, the greater their commission.
- **Some of the most maddening games are baked into the formula for sales of new cars.** Things that should be real, like the invoice price, the list price and rebates are almost all elements of a game. Make it your goal to pry out the facts from the fictions.
- **Hotels, airlines, and cruise lines set their prices as high as they can** and hold on until as late as possible—then most will cut sharply to avoid an unsold night.
- **Even small local retailers are smart enough to realize that a small sale is better than no sale at all.** In this book, you'll learn how to buy from megastores and mom-and-pop stores.

Honest businesspeople and well-run businesses deserve to make a reasonable profit. I hope you will support the best sellers and let them know why. In this book, though, it is your bottom line I seek to protect. It is your family I want to preserve. It is your retirement I hope to make comfortable.

Ask the Right Questions

One of the most important skills you need to develop as a savvy consumer is the ability to speak for yourself. Almost everything is negotiable in our free-enterprise society. Remember that except for the motor-vehicle bureau and other fine government agencies, businesses know you can take your money elsewhere.

Ask your bank to give you a checking account without a service fee or to lower your minimum-balance requirements. You know and they know that there is always another bank. The institution that currently has your account doesn't want to lose your deposit and the money it has invested in setting up and managing that account. You can make yourself even more appealing to your bank by directly depositing your paycheck or Social Security check, accepting a credit card that they issue, or telling the bank officer that you are in the market for a mortgage loan and will consider applying there. (That said, don't use the credit card or apply for a mortgage unless the rates and charges are reasonable, and don't hesitate to negotiate for a better deal on loans. Interest rates are negotiable!)

Even if you have insurance of one form or another (private, employer-provided, Medicare, or Medicaid), educate yourself on deductibles and copays for services, treatments, and medications. Your number-one goal, of course, is to take care of yourself and your family. You have the right to ask why a doctor has ordered a particular test or suggested a specific medication.

As one example, I was prescribed an ointment for a minor skin irritation. A much larger irritation came when I went to the pharmacy to pick up the order and found the price—even with my health insurance—to be outrageously expensive. I asked the pharmacist about it, and he suggested two considerably less painful alternatives. I called the doctor and, after she told me that she'd had no idea of the price, received a new prescription.

Various federal laws, including the Health Insurance Portability and Accountability Act of 1996 (known as HIPAA), give you the right to access your own medical records and to have your records sent (by mail or electronically) to another provider. Again, don't endanger your health, but if you change doctors or hospitals it may not be necessary to retake a test you've already had done and paid for (as a copay or part of your deductible). At least ask these questions: "Have you received my medical records? Do you need me to request them? Is this test necessary? How is it different from the one I had last week at another doctor?"

Ask a restaurant for a discount for a large group. Ask your credit card company to reduce the interest rate they charge for unpaid balances. (Tell them you're about to accept an offer from another card company that offers a lower rate. You may find they'd rather keep you at a lower rate than lose your business.)

Ask your cellphone or cable television company to cut your monthly bill. Don't hesitate to ask them to match or beat a competitor's offer. The carriers know full well that you can easily change your affiliation. They need you more than you need them. The quickest way to go up the ladder to someone who can offer a special price is to politely begin talking about canceling your service. You can always change your mind, but chances are you will end up speaking with someone whose job is to retain customers.

Ask a supermarket or a furniture store or a home-improvement service for a better deal when you make a larger purchase. Ask a college admissions officer for a bit more scholarship money or guaranteed loans. They usually have some additional funds for contingencies, but *you have to ask*.

Am I Getting a Fair Markup for This Product?

A well-informed buyer has an idea what price a dealer paid for an item. With this knowledge, you can change the direction of any price discussion during negotiation. Instead of asking, "What kind of discount can I get off the list price?" you can ask the seller, "What is a fair markup from your cost?" This sort of negotiating strategy is well suited to expensive purchases such as cars, boats, and furniture. For more information, read "Understand a Retailer's Markup Strategy" later in this chapter.

Will You Pay Me the Difference, Since You Lowered Just After I Made My Purchase?

Many stores have price guarantees, which spell out policies to protect you from bad timing. Even if the store doesn't have a policy, you can create your own short-term guarantee. Go back to the store within its returns period and ask for a rebate because of a change in price. If they balk, tell them you are prepared to return the item. You can always repurchase it at the lower price.

As an example, while I was writing the edition of the book that's in your hands, I took a quick break to purchase a laptop computer as a gift for my adult son, who was about to enroll in graduate school for an advanced degree. (The Bank of Mom and Dad never closes.) I got a good price on the laptop and two days later I received an email telling me that the computer had been shipped. The very next day I got another email from the same computer company announcing a very special sale for the same laptop. It was a relatively small reduction in price, but I could not take that sort of insult sitting down. I called the company and spoke to customer service and politely offered them two choices: return the difference in price back to my credit card or instruct FedEx to return the laptop to their warehouse. I got the refund. My son got his laptop.

Here are some tips that will work for a period within the store's return or price-protection period…

- **Be sure you understand a store's return policy.** Just in case, take good care of all packing materials and paperwork for a couple of weeks after a major purchase. Don't send in warranty cards until you are certain you will keep the item.
- **See if the store has a price-protection guarantee or something similar.** These pledges are usually aimed at promising that a competitor won't offer the same item at a lower price within a particular time period. However, most also apply if the price is lowered at the store where you made your purchase.
- **Get a refund or return (and re-buy) it.** If the store does *not* offer a price-protection plan, but you are still within the return period, go back to the store with your paperwork and ask to speak with a manager. Ask for a cash refund (or if it suits you, a store credit) for the price difference. If they resist, you have an ace in the hole: Return the item for the price you paid for it. If you still feel like shopping at a store that forces you to such extremes, you can then repurchase the same item at the sale price. The same principle can also be applied to airline tickets. Say you bought a ticket for $500 with a $100 reticketing fee, and the airline drops the cost of the flight to $300 before you fly. Call and ask to be reticketed at the lower rate and pay the fee. In this case, you'll still be ahead by $100.

What Does This Term Mean, Exactly?

Do you know the difference between a "full warranty" and a "limited warranty"? When is a "free" cellphone truly an expensive purchase? These distinctions can make a real difference in the value of an item or service you purchase. *Here's how to find out…*

- **Talk to friends and acquaintances who have had the same experience or bought the same item,** browse a company's online comment sections, and always read a contract's fine print.
- **Research online.** We live in an age when it is very easy to consult the internet to find the definition of a technical, medical, or legal term. Always consider the source, though. Some information is accurate and unbiased, and some sites or people offer just the opposite. Ensure you're getting information from a professional organization or another unbiased source.
- **Ask a salesperson to explain specifications or the difference between products.** Remember, however, that someone trying to sell something may not always have your best interests in mind. Verify any claims by going to a different source (such as the manufacturer's website).

When it comes to claims about a product's capabilities, return policies, or warranties, make sure everything you are told is also in the sales literature, the packaging, or the receipt. If you are promised something beyond that, ask for it in writing. It can be a signed note on the receipt or a separate memo. That extra bit of paper may be the key to success if you need proof to get a refund or services after the sale. If a salesperson refuses to give you this assurance before the sale, do not rely on it. Nothing verbal is guaranteed.

How Do I Get the Best Price Performance Ratio?

For most products, the pace of innovation works like this: The latest and greatest product is faster/lighter/more durable or otherwise improved and it costs a bit (or a lot) more than the previous hot product. It may be that the newest version is worth the extra money, but it is also often true that you'll get the most for your money by buying a product that is one step behind the latest and greatest. This is especially true for high-tech devices including personal and tablet computers, digital cameras, smartphones, and audio equipment. (You'll usually get a better price on the previous year's car model when the new models begin arriving on the lot, although its depreciated value will be less. That becomes all but insignificant once you've used a vehicle for four or five years.) After listening to the sales pitch for the newest product, ask about prices on any leftovers and closely compare their features and costs to those of the latest and greatest.

Buy at the Right Time

For many products, the best time to buy is when there is more product than shoppers. Don't go looking for a snow blower as the first winter storm arrives. You can, though, expect a better price on a snow blower in July. The timing mentioned here applies whether you're buying in a store or online.

Ski and Snowboard Equipment and Winter Apparel

By early spring, most skiers and boarders have made their major purchases and have begun shopping for bathing suits and beach umbrellas. As winter departs, retailers want to clear out their inventory to make room for bicycles, tennis rackets, and kayaks. Or they may be ready to close for the season and watch their bank accounts dwindle as they pay interest on winter items no one is buying.

Look for major sales to begin around late March, after spring break, and build toward even better deals later in the season.

Some of the best deals are at the stores at ski resorts. Many of these locations are far away from major metropolitan areas and operate only seasonally.

And don't overlook rental shops. When my hotdog daughter was first learning to ski—and outgrowing her original equipment—I equipped her with well-maintained skis and boots from a ski resort at a fraction of the cost of brand new gear. And yes, the time to shop is at the tail end of the season.

Charcoal Grills, Swimming Pools, and Lawnmowers

Buy a grill after Labor Day and put it in the garage until next season. (Or use it all winter...a charbroiled steak or chicken tastes just as good at Christmas as it does on the Fourth of July.)

Prefabricated backyard swimming pools are hot items in the stores in the summer and sit around gathering dust from about Labor Day through May. Offer to help out your local dealer with an off-season purchase.

Lawnmowers start to gather dust by the Fourth of July. Go in and make your best offer while you are still blessed with a few months to go in mowing season. Or offer to buy one in September and put it away in your garage until spring.

Swimwear

Prices start to plunge soon after customers head to the beach for the summer. The largest discounts are likely late in the summer—assuming there are any suits in your size still on the shelves. If you're planning a wintertime defrost in the Caribbean or other hotspots, you'll probably get the best deal by planning ahead and shopping the summer before.

Bicycles

Shop in October and November for the best prices on closeouts from the summer past. Most dealers place orders for next season in September, and they'll be anxious to clear some space in the warehouse and on the floor.

If you live, as I do, in a resort area, check with stores that rent bicycles to tourists. Many such shops clear out some or all of their rental fleet every fall, offering good prices on generally well-maintained bikes.

Heating Systems and Insulation Upgrades

When the temperature starts to fall, heating contractors do their winter dance of joy and insulation and winterization companies bring their tools out of the back shed.

If you want to negotiate a better deal—and probably a quicker and more efficient delivery and installation—go forth and buy sometime between May and September.

And by the way, check with your local electric, gas, or fuel oil company for available rebates or incentives for upgrading heating systems or insulation. Some of these rebates are limited, and the early savvy consumer is often rewarded.

Air Conditioners

Buy summer merchandise after Labor Day. Shop for an air conditioner for Christmas. Offer to buy a leftover unit from last season, sealed in its box, with a full warranty. Ask a salesperson or a manager about units that are in storage, waiting for next season. Many retailers also can order items from distributors who are happy to unload an off-season model instead of carrying its expense until next year. Just ask.

Another good time to buy may be in the dead of winter when stores place their orders for summer merchandise. Help the dealer clear out last year's models or buy this year's new model as soon as it arrives and before the dealer has had to spend any money on storage and interest.

Carpeting, Furniture, and Appliances

In the trade, large appliances like clothes washers, dryers, ovens, and refrigerators are called white goods. The origin of the term comes from the fact that these big boxes used to be available in any color you wanted as long as it was white.

Most buyers have their minds on less substantial purchases between Thanksgiving and Christmas. That's a good time to offer to buy white goods. The appliance store just might throw in a turkey with the deal.

The same goes for things like carpeting, flooring, furniture, and other large items not intended as family gifts.

Tools

The two biggest sales periods for consumer hand and power tools are the days leading up to Christmas and Father's Day. Check for sale prices then or hold out and shop the leftovers just after those holidays, in January and late June.

Automobiles

The best time to buy a car may well be at the end of the day at the end of the month at the end of a selling season. Even better is if that particular day is blessed with a howling rainstorm or a colossal snowstorm.

Let's go over those specifications in more detail…

- **The end of the day.** Salespeople have families and softball leagues, and they get tired, too. And the sales manager may be breathing down their necks, pushing for the sales staff and the dealership to meet its planned sales. Come in an hour or so before the store closes with all of your numbers, ready to make a deal.

- **The end of the month.** Carmakers and dealers, like many other sales organizations, are big on sales quotas and competitions, and they usually run by calendar month. Come in during the last few days of the month to put some of that pressure to work for you. The salesperson may be willing to accept less of a commission for a car if another sale will bring him or her a bonus. The dealership may be willing to sell the car for less to qualify for additional incentives from the manufacturer, such as promises of more attractive allocations of cars from the factory in coming months or a free trip to Hawaii for the boss. If you're ready to pounce, come in on the very last day of the month with your financing all lined up and your pencil freshly sharpened.

- **The end of the selling season.** New car models generally begin to arrive in the second half of each year, with many manufacturers aiming for September. When the new models start to arrive, both the dealership and the manufacturer will want to clear out "old" cars. You will be in an especially good position if the new cars do not have much of a price increase—the manufacturer will want to place some distance between this year's model and last year's. The downside to buying a car at the end of the selling season is that the value of the car for resale purposes is immediately reduced. That makes the most difference if you expect to sell off your new car within the first three to five years after purchase. For older cars, the number of miles on the odometer takes on greater importance, and you may regain some or all of the value you lost by buying an older model year.
- **A rainy or snowy day.** Think of it: You might be the only customer to walk through the door all day. Tell them you are willing to make a deal today (although you know that you are willing to walk away if the price is not right). They just might pay you to take a car off their hands. You don't have to go to the dealership to negotiate. Begin by calling or sending an email. Don't accept vague promises of a "great deal" when you come to the store. Get a firm price, with the vehicle's details (including the VIN to nail down a specific car), and make it clear you will not accept any attempt to raise the price when you arrive.
- **Any other day when traffic is going to be lighter than usual.** The day before Christmas is usually when buyers have other things on their minds. Is it homecoming day for the local football team? Shop on a sleepy Tuesday rather than a frantic Saturday. In general, Saturday is the busiest day at most car dealerships. That makes it the worst day to strike a hard bargain. If that coincides with the end of the month, come in the day before. Put the calendar to work for you.

Computers

PC prices have headed south while equipment speed and capabilities have improved. I was one of the pioneers of personal computer magazines, serving as the first executive editor of *PC Magazine* in the early 1980s. My first IBM PC cost nearly $5,000 and possessed a tiny fraction of the computing power found in my current smartphone.

Today's desktop, laptop, and tablet computers can be had for as little as $150 to $200, with a top-end model available for about $1,500. And all of them are faster, with huge amounts of internal memory, hard drives, or flash memory storage of prodigious capacity, and the ability to communicate with the internet and with other devices.

I'll be talking more about computers in Chapter 17. Let's consider here the shopping calendar for computers and other similar electronic devices.

Now that this sort of equipment has moved from high-end luxury to everyday commodity, nearly every seller offers sales and discounts throughout the year. But you will generally find the best deals in the weeks leading up to Labor Day, which is when parents and students prepare for school. There's usually another sales spike in consumer-oriented equipment before Christmas.

Another time to go shopping is soon after Microsoft or Apple introduces any major new operating system or when a new line of microprocessors arrives from Intel or AMD.

Here's why that makes sense: Computer makers will offer promotions for the new systems at the same time as they are trying to clear out the inventory of the previous machines.

The best buys are usually found by buying one generation behind the latest and greatest machines. Buy the PCs that have suddenly been relegated to yesterday's news.

Some associations (AAA, AARP, college alumni groups) offer discounts you can use when directly purchasing from some computer makers. And some wholesale clubs (Costco, Sam's Club, BJ's Wholesale) offer specials on computers sold at their stores, although they may be offering models that are specially configured or named just for them, which makes it difficult to compare prices.

If you buy from one of these wholesale clubs, study the specifications carefully and compare them to direct offerings from computer makers.

Theater Tickets

Your best chance for a good deal on theater tickets may come during previews, before the opening for a promising show, and at the end of a run. The worst possible time is immediately after a new show opens to good reviews. If you happen to be in New York, you can try Broadway Box (BroadwayBox.com), which sells discounted on- and off-Broadway theater—in addition to concert and event—tickets.

If the show you are seeking to see is sold out, call the box office and ask whether they release house seats on the day of the performance. These are seats that are held back from regular sale to accommodate VIPs and financial backers. The theater may also have some tickets that have been returned from various sources. In some situations, the last-minute house seats are sold at discount.

Reject the MSRP and MAP

A savvy consumer will go to great lengths to avoid paying an item's list price. The *list price* is the amount a manufacturer or distributor would like you to pay for its product. Just as importantly, it is the perceived value the maker would like buyers to have of their product.

Auto manufacturers have a similar concept. The *MSRP* (Manufacturer's Suggested Retail Price) tells the list price for the car before optional equipment, fees, taxes, and other charges are added. It's also referred to as the *sticker price* since it is printed on the paper you'll find on the side window of a new car. As you will learn in the chapter about buying a car, unless you are seeking to buy a car in great demand and short supply (not a likely way to get a discount) the MSRP is the unofficial starting line for one style of negotiation.

And then you have the *MAP* (Manufacturer's Advertised Price), which is a set price below which a seller is not supposed to venture. Some retailers point to that price as their *floor*, saying they are bound not to violate the sanctity of that number. But we are not talking about any sort of legal barrier here. Go forth and ask for a lower price or free cushions or free delivery or anything else you feel is reasonable. And this same MAP is the reason some internet sellers will show you a product but say, "Put this in your cart to see the real price." The extra step lets a seller work around agreements it may have about "advertised prices" while allowing them to add a discount to your benefit.

Understand a Retailer's Markup Strategy

Another important way to keep the power on your side of the table is to have some idea of a retailer's markup. Some products—cars and personal computers among them—have relatively small markups from wholesale to retail price. Other items, such as certain types of furniture and designer clothing, have very large profit margins. Jewelry can carry huge markups, which is why jewelers can claim huge markdowns and sales and still make a nice profit.

Think of markups as the percentage of the asking price that goes to the seller. (It's not all profit, though. The store has to pay overhead, including rent, utilities, advertising, and salaries.) As a buyer, having some idea of the wholesale cost of a product gives you an informed starting point in figuring the sort of discount you can ask for. *The following sections reveal some general markup ranges...*

- **Appliances.** Dealers mark up larger devices such as refrigerators and washing machines about 15 percent. Smaller items such as televisions and microwave ovens are usually marked up about 25 percent. Be on the lookout for rebates offered by the manufacturers for certain models. They may be advertised by the dealer or you may have to search for them on the makers' websites.

- **Automobiles.** Big-ticket vehicles have small markups, typically in the range of 5 to 12 percent. Vehicles with a lower MSRP may have a smaller range of 8 to 10 percent markup. As you'll find in the chapter about automobiles, though, car dealers have a number of other ways to squeeze more cash out of customers (and have a range of hidden kickbacks and incentives from the manufacturer).

- **Books.** The selling price for most books represents a markup of 50 to 100 percent.

One inside note: Most booksellers stock their shelves on a consignment basis, meaning that they can send back unsold copies to the publisher for credit or sell books at deep discounts if they choose. You may be able to purchase used copies of books from internet and retail sources, and that is certainly a way to save some money.

And please, allow me as an author to point out that buying a used book means that not one penny goes to the author or the publisher. The long-term ramifications of that could be fewer new books and fewer publishers. Buying a used car also does not directly benefit the manufacturer, but repairs and maintenance do help support dealers and factories.

- **Clothing.** Name-brand fashion is usually marked up about 50 percent, although manufacturers often strike special deals with major retailers to reduce prices to move out older product as seasons and styles change.

- **Furniture.** A furniture or department store usually marks up its wares 50 to 100 percent or even more. Discount operations work closer to the wholesale price. And this is another sales channel where the *list price* is usually a fiction. You might see a sofa selling for $500, supposedly marked down from a list price of $1,000. The only thing that matters is the selling price.

Furniture makers also commonly employ MAP, which is supposed to be the minimum price a store is allowed to sell the item. There is nothing to stop you from asking for a price lower than MAP (or asking for a free ottoman or box spring or dinner for four at your favorite steakhouse).

Some dealers pay salespeople a full commission on items sold at or near MSRP and reduce the commission rate if the price drops below a particular markup. As much as I care about the family and mortgage payment of the salesperson, it's my bottom line, not theirs, that is my focus. I can always head for the exit door…slowly…and see if the store is willing to accept less profit instead of no profit at all.

• **Personal Computers.** The highly competitive PC market usually prices hardware about 10 to 25 percent above cost. However, products become outdated by new technologies quickly. Look for discounts and sales on devices one step behind today's latest and greatest.

• **Travel Agents.** The role of travel agents has diminished greatly in the past decade. Nearly everyone buys airline tickets directly from the websites of airline companies or from online comparison sites like Orbitz, Travelocity, Expedia, Priceline, Kayak, and Booking. Airlines now pay travel agents little or no commission, and some agents even charge a fee for procuring tickets for you.

The online sites—and there are dozens of them—allow you to compare prices across dozens of airlines and in various combinations of carriers. Many sites can put together a package of air, hotel, car rental, and other services that may amount to a discount.

Inside info: Orbitz, Travelocity, and Expedia are all part of the same company now. Kayak and Booking are part of the Priceline Group. That doesn't mean you won't see an occasional difference in price on one site or the other. If you've got the time, check several. I also like the internet travel portal of American Express, which has some special services for cardholders and allows you to earn or redeem credit card miles for some or all of the cost.

A travel agency may be helpful to you in two areas…

- Booking a cruise
- Booking a specialty tour that involves many flights, hotels, and other services

Although a travel agent is most likely unable to discount any particular cruise, airline, hotel, or car rental, he or she may be able to reward customers in other ways, such as upgrades or rebates in the form of customer loyalty clubs.

Agents typically are paid between 10 and 15 percent in commission on hotel, cruise, and package deals. Car rental companies pay less. You can do the math: If you are booking a $10,000 trip through a travel agent, the commission to the agency is typically at least $1,000. Can you ask for a rebate or upgrade or something of value that represents a portion of the commission? Of course you can. And if one agency won't accommodate you, another one might.

Get Familiar with the Gray Market

How can one merchant sell a camera, a watch, or home electronics for dozens or even hundreds of dollars less than the next guy? Although it is possible that some dealers simply offer much better prices, sometimes the answer is that the products are gray market goods. *Gray market items* are imported from unusual sources, such as a foreign distributor or a dealer who bought the item from that same offshore source. A product sold in the gray market economy is in most instances not illegal. However, you may find that the products do not include the same warranties and guarantees offered by official importers and resellers.

In some instances, gray market products may be slightly different from those designed for the domestic market and may come with or require different accessories or spare parts. You may find instruction manuals in a foreign language or pidgin English. This doesn't mean you should avoid gray market products. But make certain you understand the bona fides of any product you are about to buy.

Ask specifically, "Does this product come with a US warranty?" If there is *not* a US warranty, find out what sort of protection the seller will offer. If you risk a gray market product, decide for yourself if the difference in price is worth whatever risk you must take. Repairs that are not under warranty can be very expensive.

Know When to Use a Credit Card

For a careful consumer, a credit card is usually the safest way to buy something. I use my credit card for almost everything I buy, making sure to pay off the full balance when it is due. Today it is easy to set up your credit card account for autopay, which deducts the balance from your checking account on or before the due date.

Note that in endorsing the use of a credit card, I am *not* suggesting you run up a loan balance. If you must borrow money, there are less expensive loans.

Here are the top reasons to use a credit card...

• **Nearly every credit card**—and especially American Express, Visa, and MasterCard—offers a range of protections against fraud. You can dispute a charge and even stop payment to a merchant in many situations.

• **Most credit cards, and in particular those at premium levels**—silver, gold, platinum, plum, and other colorful categories—offer built-in protection such as extended warranties, short-term insurance against theft or breakage, and other valuable features.

• **Nearly every credit card now offers users some form of rebate or bonus**—cash back as a percentage of spending, points that can be applied to travel or other expenses as if they were cash, or miles that can be used in airline frequent flyer programs.

• **Putting all of your expenses on one or more credit cards is a great way to help you analyze how you spend your money and organize records for tax season.** If you operate a business, it is probably preferable to have separate cards for business and personal expenses.

Nearby you will find a sidebar in which I pose the question, "Can a merchant charge a fee for the use of a credit card?" If you find yourself in a situation where there is a fee of a few percentage points, ask yourself whether the extra cost is worth the benefit. I would pay a bit more for an extended warranty, but would not pay more for a meal or a tank of gas that will each be gone long before the monthly bill arrives.

Here's when to use your credit card...

• **When you buy over the internet, by telephone, or place an order at a retail store for future delivery.** In this sort of transaction, you are authorizing a charge to your credit card before you receive the product or get the chance to check out its quality. That's the scary part. But the good news is this: Though you have authorized a charge to be put on your account, you hold on to your money for the moment. If the seller does not deliver the goods, if what you receive is not what you contracted for, or if the amount you are billed does not match the receipt you received at time of purchase, you can contact the credit card company and dispute the charge. You'll have the federal Fair Credit Billing Act on your side of the table, which allows you to refuse to pay for a purchase and any finance charges while you make good faith efforts to resolve a dispute. And your credit card company will also get involved on your behalf in contacting the merchant. Be sure to follow the rules for disputing a credit card bill. They're generally listed on the back of your monthly statement. You can also discuss them with the customer service department of the credit card company.

• **When you are traveling abroad and are paying local currency.** Your credit card company will convert the bill into dollars at the bank rate, which is usually better than the local merchant or money-changing outlets will offer. In recent years, some credit card companies have eliminated fees for this service. You merely pay the converted price at the bank's foreign exchange rate.

By the way, when you use your card, be sure to check that the credit slip is marked in local currency. If you have agreed to pay 1,000 Croatian Kuna for a pair of shoes, make certain the merchant hasn't "accidentally" marked the bill as 1,000 US dollars. You'll have a hard time convincing your credit card issuer that this was an $850 mistake.

• **When you want to receive airline or travel points when you spend.** If you use your credit card fairly heavily—several hundred to several thousand dollars per month—you should consider using a card that accrues points in an airline frequent-flyer program. Some are offered with an affiliation with a particular airline or group of companies, while others allow you to bank points that can be applied to any air ticket of a certain class.

Here's what you need to be a savvy consumer of this type of card: First of all, check out the annual fee (usually a bit higher than other cards and certainly more expensive than a free card) and compare it against the value of a ticket. If it costs you $100 per year for the card and it takes you three years to

TIP

ATMs Abroad

If you need some walking-around cash in a foreign country, ATMs almost always have the best exchange rates. Be sure you understand any fees your credit card issuer applies for use of a foreign ATM. I use a debit card linked to an account with Charles Schwab Bank. In return for keeping a few thousand dollars on deposit in an online checking account, they give me a debit card that includes a rebate for any domestic or international ATM card fees.

TIP

Primary Coverage

Some credit card issuers, including American Express, will sell you a Premium Car Rental Policy that is *primary coverage* (meaning you do not have to first seek payment from your personal auto policy) and has higher limits for other types of coverage. You can put the premium policy in force so that it kicks in every time you rent a car, or you can add it to your account only when you decide you want to upgrade coverage.

build up enough miles to obtain a ticket worth $300, this is no deal at all. Also compare the frequent-flyer programs of the various airlines that offer cards. You don't want to accrue miles on an airline that doesn't serve an airport near you or a destination where you want to fly. Plus, some airlines give away tickets at a much lower point level or may have fewer blackout periods for tickets.

- **When you want to earn a cash rebate on an account.** Rebate cards, available from nearly every card issuer, promise you a rebate of all charges at the end of the year. The amount is relatively small—usually one or two percentage points. A rebate is a good thing, but be sure you are not paying too much for the privilege in the form of a higher-than-average annual fee or interest rate. If you spend $10,000 per year and receive 2 percent back, that will return $200 to your wallet.

- **When you want to apply a credit card's extended warranty to your purchase.** Some credit cards offer special insurance policies that extend the warranty for certain purchases. These limited warranties have numerous exclusions, including normal wear and tear and abuse, but can be valuable for items such as cameras, cellphones, televisions, and other appliances. Read the small print carefully and be sure to keep hold of all sales slips and manufacturer's warranties. You do, of course, have to make the original purchase with the credit card, and you must maintain the account in good standing to make a claim.

- **When you want to use your credit card's auto insurance coverage when you rent a car.** Many credit cards offer special auto insurance coverage for rentals made using the card. Be sure to read the fine print from the credit card company, and don't hesitate to call customer service for clarification before you use the card to rent a car.

The insurance coverage usually has exceptions that exclude luxury cars and trucks. And the issuer may also withhold payment if it determines that an accident was due to driver negligence. Finally, some credit card companies do not extend coverage to rentals in some or all foreign countries. In most instances, the coverage is *secondary*, meaning that you will have to put in a claim with your personal auto insurance carrier first and then the credit card insurance will reimburse you for deductibles and certain other charges not otherwise covered. If you do not have personal auto insurance coverage, discuss this with your card issuer. I also suggest you consider purchasing a renter's auto insurance policy, usually priced at a fraction of the cost of a policy tied to a vehicle you own.

- **When you want free worldwide travel accident insurance on tickets purchased with your credit card.** Many credit cards, including the Citi Platinum Select card I just added to my wallet, includes up to one million dollars in worldwide travel accident insurance if you die or are very seriously injured on board a common carrier (airlines, railroads, buses, cruise ships, and ferries included). Understand that this is not medical insurance (that's a separate policy you should consider purchasing when you travel internationally) but functions as a form of short-term coverage that may provide for immediate care or help returning you home for medical care. You will need to pay the full cost of any covered form of travel with the credit card that offers the benefit in order to be covered in this way.

Special insurance coverage for airline flights, purchased from an airport kiosk or machine or directly from an insurance company, is generally not a good deal. You're better off buying and maintaining proper health, life, and travel insurance or taking advantage of coverage included by some credit card companies on trips you paid for with their card.

> **TIP**
>
> **Charging You for Using Your Charge Card**
>
> Can a merchant charge you for using your credit card? Maybe.
>
> In most of the US, a merchant may charge a fee up to but not exceeding the percentage that the credit card company collects. However, MasterCard and Visa prevent merchants from adding a surcharge. American Express generally does not permit the practice. Some states have laws prohibiting surcharges on credit card use.
>
> Now turn to the other side of the coin. In most of the US, there is no prohibition against offering a discount for payment in cash, check, or debit card. In any case, there is no requirement that a merchant accept a credit card at all. And some merchants may choose to accept one type of card but not another. Practices differ in foreign countries, although in much of Europe there is more widespread use of plastic for any and every purchase.

Here's When You Might Pay by Check

If the merchant is willing to offer you a lower rate for cash and you are willing to give up the protections of using a credit card, you can write a check. You'll have a bit of protection against fraud from your bank, but nothing like the benefits of most credit cards.

If you are negotiating a deal, you may be able to reduce the price of a major purchase or service by a few percentage points by offering a check. Be sure to obtain a detailed receipt and statement of warranty if you do business in this way.

Here's When You Might Pay Cash

For small purchases, where issues of warranties and taxes are not important, cash is still king. According to a 2015 study by the Federal Reserve, a bit more than 26% of purchases were still made in cash, with something close to 50% cash involved in small retail purchases. The percentage goes up for older people and less affluent people, who may not have the option of a credit or debit card.

So why might you prefer to use cash? It may save a few seconds or minutes at the checkout line. There are some who fear that using plastic or checks opens privacy concerns since records are kept of names and purchases.

And in certain circumstances, you might receive a discount for using cash. Let's give most sellers the benefit of the doubt here and say they are seeking to avoid paying a percentage to a credit card issuer (but it is also true that some sellers might be looking for ways to avoid reporting some part of their income to federal and state tax agencies). For example, some gas stations charge more for credit purchases. This detail is often poorly advertised, with the lower cash price appearing in the forefront. If you adopt a general rule to always pay cash at the gas pump, you don't have to worry about reading the fine print.

If we're talking about paying for a cup of coffee, pay any way you want. But for something more substantial, consider this: What protections do you have against faulty product or service?

Speaking for myself, I use cash so rarely that the interior of my wallet has a colony of moths living within, but studies by MIT professors Drazen Prelec and Duncan Simester and others contend you are more likely to spend more money if you pay with credit cards (http://nyti.ms/2vpuy27). Remember that when you're buying the next round at happy hour. Having to count out a few hundred dollars from your wallet, or having to go to the bank or an ATM, may help some buyers keep their budget in line.

Debit Cards

Debit cards lie somewhere in between. Some merchants may be happier to accept a debit card because the fee they must pay is usually slightly lower than that on a credit card purchase. As a consumer, you should consult with the bank (or whoever issued your debit card) to see what consumer protection they offer for purchases. In general, debit cards do not have the same extended warranty or price protection that upper-tier credit cards have, although there are some worthy exceptions. And remember that funds for purchases made with a debit card are almost immediately withdrawn from your bank account or from a prepaid balance.

Examine Outlet Malls

There is no disputing that a true factory outlet—a store operated directly by a manufacturer—is often a place where savvy consumers can obtain great bargains. However, many manufacturers don't want to undercut the stores that sell the bulk of their products, and in that case the outlet may actually be selling items at prices equal to or higher than what you'll find at a discount store.

The best deals at a factory outlet are usually in the closeout or irregular bins. These are items that are not in competition with retail stores and often at significant reductions in price. I'll comment further on irregular items in a moment.

There is also another type of outlet store—an operation that sells a particular brand of clothing or other merchandise. These outlets may or may not be directly related to the manufacturer. Often, they sell items that are made especially for them and are unavailable in retail stores.

The bottom line: You've got to know the territory. What price would you pay at a discount store? How irregular can a product be before it is unacceptable?

Here are some of the things you may find at an outlet store…

- **Closeouts.** Some of the best deals are on leftovers from seasons past, overruns of special products made for particular customers, and product lines that just plain failed to sell. You may see breakfast cereals that were test marketed unsuccessfully, clothing in last year's colors, or sneakers with last season's sports stars.
- **Irregulars or seconds.** Quality clothing manufacturers are very picky about the products they sell to retail outlets. They may classify as irregular any item with small flaws including minor marks, broken stitches, or tiny holes. Ask yourself if the damage is more than the clothing would receive after a few cycles through your clothes washer. If you're looking at hardware, consider the fact that the first time you use the tool you're likely to put your own marks on the product. What you don't want to buy is something that is damaged in a way that will make it unusable before its time.
- **Remanufactured items.** Have you ever wondered what happens to computers or bicycles that are returned to a store because of a broken part, or because the buyer just decided not to keep the item? In many cases, retail stores send returned products back to the manufacturer for credit. The factory then repairs or repackages the item and tries to sell it again. In many cases, a remanufactured item is perfectly good to use. Make sure the outlet offers a full warranty and the right to return the item.
- **Outlet specials.** Some manufacturers make a line of products just for sale at outlet shops. The products may be very similar to retail lines, or they may be a different quality or design. Make sure you understand the outlet's return policy. Find out if you can return items by mail or to a retail outlet. Sign up for email coupons and sale alerts. And if the outlet is big enough to attract bus tours of avid shoppers, ask the manager whether you can get a copy of any special coupon books or special offers made to bus customers. A polite request might be rewarded with some significant discounts.

Learn How to Shop in Foreign Countries

Shopping in the Caribbean or Europe or most anywhere else in the world is an exciting adventure, with products and prices you may not see at your neighborhood mega-mall. One other thing you're unlikely to see is the full range of consumer protections offered to Americans shopping at home.

Coupon Know-How

The savvy consumer is not blinded by sales or coupon discounts. Start by knowing the ordinary selling price of items. In some cases, a store will raise prices before a sale or before a major coupon is published. That might be illegal in certain situations and locations, although difficult to prove. If you've got a discount coupon, consider holding on to the discount until near its expiration to see if an inflated price comes back down to its presale level.

Do you know enough about the product to know if you're being offered the real thing? Stores around the world are stocked with brand name counterfeits. Some are good quality and others are junk. In some parts of the world there is widespread illegal copying of computer software, music CDs, movie DVDs, and watches. You may find that the real manufacturers have lodged complaints with US Customs authorities that could result in seizure of the item when you return from your trip. Among the brands most commonly copied—and possibly more likely to catch the eye of an officer at the border—are Chanel, Gucci, Louis Vuitton, Prada, and Rolex.

Some items, real as they are, are simply illegal to remove from some countries or import into others. Be sure you understand the law on antiques, furs, and exotic foods before you make a purchase.

Be sure you understand all the terms of sale before you buy something outside the country. *Here are a few critical questions...*

- **Have you been charged the proper price?** If you are paying in US dollars, has the conversion from local currency been made properly?

- **Do you have any right to return or exchange the item?** If so, where? Is there any warranty offered by the seller or the manufacturer? Make sure any verbal promises are converted to written form on the receipt. That might or might not help, but it can't hurt.

- **If you are not taking the items with you, be sure you understand shipping arrangements.** How and when will the product be shipped? Who pays for shipping? Who pays customs fees? Will the shipment be insured? Be sure you obtain all details in writing. Here is another instance where paying by credit card should protect you from fraud.

- **Does the price include a charge for Value Added Tax (VAT) or its equivalent?** As a tourist, are you eligible for a refund of all or part of that tax? Do you have proper documentation to apply for the refund? In some countries, the merchant can process the refund. Elsewhere the process can sometimes be done at the airport. If you are buying within the European Union, any claim for refund of VAT has to be made at the airport or border where you are leaving the EU. If you miss that opportunity, you miss your chance.

• **Does the receipt properly match the actual product?** Any discrepancy could cause difficulties when you pass through customs. Keep any certificates of authenticity, appraisals, and receipts with you. Don't ship them with items or pack them in your suitcase.

Study Sales Tax Laws for Fun and Profit

In my experience, there are three types of buyers when it comes to state sales taxes—those who ignore them, those who curse them, and those who include them in their savvy shopping strategies.

I do want to point out that sales and other taxes are essential support for schools, roads, emergency services including police and fire, and much more. No one wants to endorse waste and abuse, but taxes are not in and of themselves evil.

Here are some ways to save money on taxable purchases…

• **Shop where the tax is less.** If you are within a short commute to a neighboring state, take into account differing tax rates when you make major purchases. Obviously, you don't want to spend more money on gasoline and other expenses than you will save on taxes. It would certainly seem worthwhile to cross a state line to save money on an expensive and easily transportable item such as jewelry, camera, and many appliances.

In a number of states, sales tax does not apply to clothing priced below a certain level. A number of states, New York and Massachusetts among them, have experimented with occasional tax "holidays" to boost the local economy. Some retailers—inside or outside of the holiday state—have offered discounts equal to or exceeding the sales tax rate. It may be possible to cross a state line to buy an automobile in a tax-free or low-tax state. Check with your department of motor vehicles about any regulations that might force you to pay the tax when you register the car.

• **Look for companies that do not charge sales tax in your state.** In general, this applies to operations that do not have a physical location in your state. This is becoming more difficult. As an example, in mid-2017, Amazon began collecting sales tax in all states where one is levied. But you will still find some online retailers who promise tax-free sales. They usually ship from a distribution center in a state that does not levy sales tax.

Turn Back Freebies for Fun and Profit

Everything costs something, and there is no reason to pay for something you don't need. It annoys the heck out of me when, for example, my cable television company tells me they are adding a "free" set of channels that I know I will never watch. Actually, almost everything my cable television company does annoys me.

Here are some ways to turn back freebies…

• **If an appliance or mattress store promises "free delivery," ask for a discount**—$50 sounds reasonable to me—if you'll be loading your purchase into your own vehicle.

• **Refuse the offer of "free rails" at a bedding store if you're replacing an existing mattress.** Ask for $20 off the price.

• **If you're buying a suit or outfit that includes "free alterations" you don't need,** ask for $25 off for your perfect body.

• **Call a car dealer's bluff if the dealer advertises something like "free undercoating worth $250."** Pass on the undercoating and ask for the $250. You may not get it, but you will put the salesperson on notice that you're going to demand a very sharp deal.

Buy Scratch-and-Dent

You can save money—from a few dollars to hundreds—by buying a dented or scratched but otherwise new product. The trick is to find an item where the scratch doesn't matter, or where a perfect version would end up scratched very soon in any case. *Some examples…*

• **Appliances.** A minor dent or scratch in the side of a clothes washer that is headed for the basement or utility closet sounds like a deal too good to pass up. Be sure the device is fully covered by warranty.

• **Casual furniture.** Is the damage in an area that will face the wall?

• **Luggage.** A mark on a suitcase may disqualify it from sale as a perfect item, but you can be sure that the case will have dozens of stains and scratches after its first trip through the baggage belts at an airport. Don't buy a suitcase with damage to a zipper or other closure.

• **Sporting goods.** A fielder's or catcher's mitt with a mark on the leather (not a tear) will look identical to a new mitt after a few innings. You can improve the look and feel of leather goods with a rub-in oil.

In some towns you'll find dealers specializing in scratch-and-dent products (one old name for this type of store: *railroad salvage*). You may also find these items in the back of the warehouse at a regular dealer. Ask the salesperson for a tour. Put the dent against the wall and the cash in your pocket.

Consider Joining a Warehouse Club

Well, first, you're reading a book by a guy who has a closet filled with several dozen boxes of his family's favorite breakfast cereal, a chest freezer in the basement with several hundred dollars' worth of frozen fish, turkey, and vegetables, and kitchen cabinets stocked with enough salad dressing, bread mix, and sauces to open a small supermarket of his own.

Warehouse stores offer discount prices on large-quantity packages, sometimes in sizes or numbers not offered at supermarkets. You'll also find commercial-size or -quality food and supplies at reduced prices. Leaders in this segment include Costco, Sam's Club (a division of Walmart), and BJ's Wholesale.

But that doesn't mean I recommend everyone shop at a warehouse store. You'll still need to be a careful shopper: When a supermarket puts something on sale, the price is often considerably lower than regular prices at a warehouse store. It is also important to note that some warehouse stores don't accept discount coupons. And then there is one other important issue: If you buy something in large quantity, you had better hope that you actually like the food and that it doesn't spoil before you finish it. Finally, although warehouse stores often stock some unusual items, they generally offer a much smaller number of food products than does a large supermarket. If you're looking for tomato paste, you'll find one brand—in a huge can—instead of the half dozen or more you might find at a market.

A good reason to join a club is for nonperishable items, from television sets to furniture to hardware to home supplies. Don't expect much in the way of service or advice, though. Do your research before you enter the store.

Most warehouse clubs charge an annual fee, typically about $50. In fact, some industry analysts say that the stores make the bulk of their profit on the sale of the membership. A basic membership at most clubs includes a second card for a family member. Similarly, you can usually add a second card without extra charge to a membership that is in a business name. A savvy consumer can figure out ways to share that benefit.

You may find an occasional offer that allows you to shop at a warehouse store on a visitor's pass, in which case you have to pay a surcharge of as much as 5 percent, which may negate much of the savings.

Join or Create a Buying Cooperative

You're so proud of your 150-pound St. Bernard named Tiny that you've joined a club of large-dog owners. At meetings, you sit around and discuss the fact that you go through a 50-pound sack of dry dog food each week.

Stop, think: Don't you think a pet store—or even better, a pet-food wholesaler—would be happy to send a truck full of food to one address at a deep discount? Start a dog-food cooperative.

The concept of a buying cooperative can extend to major purchases, too. Gather four friends together and seek a fleet discount on a group of car purchases or leases. No auto dealer worth his hairpiece is going to balk at giving an extra-special deal to a bulk purchase.

You should also investigate food-buying cooperatives that purchase from restaurant supply houses or wholesale grocers. Ask around at social-service agencies, churches, and alternative merchants such as health-food stores.

And if you have friends or family you are willing to travel with, consider renting a multi-bedroom house or condo instead of a group of hotel rooms at your destination. You'll save money, get more space, and have the option to eat some of your meals at your home away from home instead of at a restaurant.

Call for Customer Service

One of the most famous—and amusingly accurate—cartoons about the internet appeared in *The New Yorker* all the way back in 1993. Cartoonist Peter Steiner pictured a canine at the keyboard, informing another friend with a tail, "On the Internet, nobody knows you're a dog."

When you make a purchase from an online store, how do you know a company is legitimate? You can check elsewhere on the internet by entering the company's name and looking for comments by previous customers. You can also check Yelp.com for ratings. When I am about to make a large purchase—a camera or computer equipment, for example—I do my research on the internet and prepare my cart for purchase—but before I click Buy, I call the store and ask a question or two.

Why make a phone call? Because I want to see how I am treated. If the store is rude and difficult before they have my money, why should I expect them to be helpful if I have a problem after they have my money?

Know How to Raise Your Hand at an Auction House

Private and commercial auctions are exciting places to pick up tremendous bargains and one-of-a-kind items for a collection. They are also an easy way to go to the cleaners without benefit of a laundry tag. They are also places where the incautious or uninformed can make an expensive mistake with the twitch of a finger. As a consumer, you are basically buying an item retail that you may have to dispose of at wholesale prices later on.

The best advice for auctiongoers is this: Bid only on items you know very well, and have a firm and unbreakable maximum price in mind for any item. *Here are some more tips...*

- **Know the bottom line before you make a bid.** Many auction houses add a commission fee—often as much as 15 percent—on top of the sales price. The buyer, not the sellers, pays the fee. And in many states, the buyer also must pay sales tax. Together, these two charges can add 20 percent or more to the price.

- **Understand the auction process.** Most auction houses have an agreement with the seller that sets a minimum price for an item. If bids do not reach to that level, the auction house may withdraw the item for sale.

You should also be aware that in many states it is legal for the auctioneer to fake the bidding process up to the seller's minimum price. For example, the owner of a fabulous collection of plastic-cup coasters may set a minimum acceptable price of $1,000. The auctioneer can start the bidding at $1,000 or can accept bids from confederates or even phantom bids up to $1,000.

Is this ethical? You might argue that it is not. But in any case, it shouldn't matter. You should still set your own maximum price for an item. If the plastic coasters are worth $1,200 to you, that should be the most you bid. If they are worth $500 to you and the auctioneer starts above that level, stay out of the market.

- **Try buying something after the sale.** If an item you want to buy does not fall to the gavel, don't hesitate to approach the auctioneer or the private seller after the day is over with a private offer at the price you are willing to pay. Insiders say the best deals at many auctions can be had in this after-sale market.

CHAPTER 2

Knowing Your Rights as a Buyer

Earlier I explained the most important starting point for negotiating a purchase: The buyer has the advantage because he or she has the money.

The power begins to shift as soon as you hand over the cash (or the credit card or the signed contract) to the seller.

The scariest situation is to pay in advance for a product or service and then wait for its delivery. And yet we do it all the time: We purchase airline tickets weeks or months ahead of a flight... we put down a deposit on a special-order item...and we reveal our credit-card information over the internet or by phone to stores near and far.

The good news is that consumers are protected by a web of state and federal laws and regulations. Add to that policies of credit-card companies and the sellers themselves, and you have a pretty good consumer safety net. The trick, though, is to know your rights...and demand that they be honored.

- **Send it back.**
- **Cool off a mistake purchase.**
- **Search for a good warranty and understand its terms.**
- **Protect yourself when you shop in foreign places.**
- **Protect your privacy online.**
- **Understand shipping costs and procedures.**
- **Know the ins and outs of layaway plans.**

Send It Back

In most situations you have the right to cancel a deal and receive your money back because of nonperformance, unacceptable quality, and even a limited right to merely change your mind. I once sent back a house I had purchased, for instance. (I'll explain that in a moment.) When you purchase from most retail or online stores, you have the right to return the item within a reasonable period for any reason—a 30-day period for no-questions-asked returns is common. There are reasonable exceptions intended to protect businesses.

As a consumer, include in your calculations the nature of the return policy. For example, if I'm choosing between two stores with the same (or reasonably close) prices, I'll buy from the one with the better return policy. Will the seller refund your money in full, or charge a restocking fee? Will you get your money back, or just store credit to spend on other products at the same store? And some online retailers will pay to pick up returned items, while others require you to pay for return shipping.

As this book goes to press, the online megastore Amazon has one of the most liberal return policies for most items it sells directly—but watch out for differing policies for items purchased *through* Amazon but fulfilled by the third-party marketplace it promotes. Some online sellers, including Jet.com (purchased by Walmart in 2016), have experimented with a choice of prices that include varying return policies. You pay less for lesser return policies.

Read the return policy of sellers before buying something. *Here is a sample policy, drawn from rules of various large internet sellers…*

- **New desktop, laptop, or tablet computers that are dead on arrival, damaged when received** (perhaps someone dropped the box on the way to your porch?), or still in an unopened box can be returned with all parts for a full refund within 30 days of purchase. The company reserves the right to test returned computers and impose a customer fee equal to 15% of the sales price if it determines you misrepresented the product's condition. If the device has been damaged by customer misuse, you may not be able to return it at all, although I have seen lenient return policies that impose a higher-than-usual restocking fee for such items.

- **Major appliances, including televisions, can only be returned if they are new and in unopened shipping boxes.** Some sellers will refer you to the manufacturer for repairs of malfunctioning new appliances. You can order certain devices with *enhanced delivery,* which allows return of like-new devices subject to the terms of that form of shipment.

- **In general, do not accept a package that has obvious damage to its packaging.** Refuse delivery or contact the seller for their instructions.

- **New, used, and refurbished products purchased from a website but sold by third-party vendors are subject to the returns policy of the *individual vendor.*** That is an important distinction. It is one reason to tread carefully when you shop from a major internet seller. On Amazon.com, as one example, you have to look carefully to see if the item is being sold and shipped by Amazon or by another company that is essentially renting space on the site. Amazon calls this the Marketplace.

- **Unless you see a notice to the contrary, you can't return downloaded games, software, music, or video.**

Again, before you buy something, study the details of a store's return policy. If Store A sells a widget for $75 but proclaims that "all sales are final," while Store B offers the same widget for the same price and allows returns for 30 days after the sale, you should take your business to Store B. In fact, it may be worth paying a bit more for a product if you feel more comfortable with return policies at the higher-priced store.

Get It in Writing

When you pay for a repair on your car or a fix to your leaky plumbing, you have the right to expect that the problem be fixed. Read the fine print on a service agreement before the work is done and be sure you understand it and agree with it. If the repair service makes an oral promise to you ("It'll be as good as new," or "We won't charge you a penny if we can't fix it"), have that written into the contract.

If you have a contract, read it carefully and make sure it protects you properly. If there is no written contract, as a consumer (in almost every situation) you have an implied warranty that is set by state law. If you pay to have your furnace repaired, you are entitled to a working furnace.

Not every tradesperson will offer a written contract, but you have the right to ask for one. If a plumber or an electrician does not provide a written contract, ask what will happen if he or she can't make a full repair. Make notes on what you are told. If you are starting an expensive process, you might want to reconsider whether you want to work with someone who does not offer a written promise,

The same implied warranty goes with products. A toaster should toast; a watch will tell time. Know the terms of sale: a merchant should make them clear, and if they are not, or if they are not acceptable, take your business elsewhere.

When you order a meal at a restaurant, you are making a deal with the management based on the specifications laid out in the menu as well as a general expectation that the food will be of acceptable quality. If you order a steak and are given chicken instead, send it back. If you order a steak cooked rare and receive it one step short of incinerated or in any other way unacceptable, send it back.

Some deals are less formal but still valuable to you as a consumer. If you order a meal and receive what you ordered but find it not to your liking, politely inform the waiter or waitress or speak with the manager. I've never heard of a restaurant failing to make an effort to accommodate a diner. A smart business is well aware of the value of customer goodwill.

Keep your receipts from all major purchases for at least as long as the item is under warranty or has enough value that you might file a homeowner's or renter's insurance claim for theft or damage. And don't throw away receipts until you

Record of Receipt

Receipts can become unwieldy. You might organize them by using a scanner to make copies to store on your computer. If you don't have a scanner, use your smartphone's camera to take pictures of the receipt. (In fact, use your smartphone camera to photograph all receipts, warranties, and items you purchase of great value.)

Store one copy on your smartphone. Store a second copy in the cloud using one of many available services. Your phone may come with a cloud service that automatically stores all photos, or you can use a service like Microsoft's OneDrive or similar services like Dropbox. Most cloud storage services offer a basic level of free storage and reasonably priced annual plans for more storage. One of the beauties of using a computer to store scans or smartphone photos of receipts or warranties is that they will automatically be sortable by date or by name, and you can switch the organizational scheme any time you want.

What if you need a receipt that you don't have a copy of? If you have established an account with major internet sellers, they will have online records of your purchases. That will help if you need to retrieve a receipt for a warranty claim. The same applies for most credit-card companies, many of which have added a feature that allows you to upload a copy of receipts that they will store, along with your monthly statement.

throw away the item they reference. You might need the receipt if you ever need to make an insurance claim for a lost or stolen item.

About that house I sent back. I suppose it is not exactly accurate to say I *sent it back* since we never moved it from where it stood. My wife and I had made an offer on a fix-me-up summer cottage, and the owner had accepted the deal. But then we got cold feet. There was just too much fixing up to be done, and a second look at the cost of the house and the needed repairs convinced us we would be better off spending more money on a property in better condition. Although we had, in theory, a binding contract for purchase of the house, there were enough loopholes in the agreement to drive a motor home through. And so we sent back the house (and got back our deposit).

Cool Off a Mistake Purchase

"We've got a special deal, but you've got to sign up for it right now, right here!"

Watch out! Don't let a deal that sounds too good to be true override your good judgment. Sometimes the deals are indeed good, but sometimes they are too good to be true. This is one of the tactics of high-pressure sales, a situation that has brought many a buyer to grief when the bill came due.

We can thank the Federal Trade Commission (FTC) for something called the Cooling-Off Rule, intended to protect buyers who sign on the bottom line in situations that are outside normal business settings. Any time you buy an item costing more than $25 in your home or priced at more than $130 at a location that is not the seller's permanent place of business, you have the right to cancel the deal and obtain a full refund until midnight of the third business day after the sale.

The Cooling-Off Rule applies to sales at the buyer's home, workplace, or dormitory, or at facilities rented by the seller on a temporary or short-term basis, such as hotel or motel rooms, convention centers, fairgrounds, and restaurants. An important benefit: The rule applies even if you invited the salesperson to make a presentation in your home.

Here's what the FTC requires of salespersons in an environment outside their place of business…

- **They must tell you about your cancellation rights at the time of sale.**
- **They must give you two copies of a cancellation form** (one to keep and one to send).
- **They must give you a copy of your contract or receipt,** and it must show the date and seller's name and address, and it must explain your right to cancel. The contract or receipt must be in the same language used in the sales presentation.

Alas, there are some exceptions to the Cooling-Off Rule. *Sales not covered by the regulation include…*

- **Real estate, insurance, or securities.**
- **Automobiles, vans, trucks, or other motor vehicles sold at temporary locations** (provided the seller has at least one permanent place of business).
- **Arts or crafts sold at fairs or locations such as shopping malls, civic centers, and schools.**

- **Goods or services not primarily intended for personal, family, or household purposes.**
- **Sales made by mail or telephone.**
- **Deals that are the result of prior negotiations that were done at the permanent business location where the goods are regularly sold.**
- **Items purchased for an emergency need,** such as plumbing or pest control. (You may be asked to waive your rights to a cooling-off period in such a situation.)

Here's how to cancel…

- **Sign and date one copy of the cancellation form.** Mail it to the address given for cancellation, making sure the envelope is postmarked before midnight of the third business day after the contract date. (Saturday is considered a business day; Sundays and federal holidays are not.)

Because proof of the mailing date and proof of receipt are important, you may want to take the letter to the post office and obtain a hand cancellation of the letter. To be even more careful, send the cancellation form by certified mail and obtain a return receipt. Or, consider hand delivering the cancellation notice before midnight of the third business day and ask for a written receipt for the cancellation notice, including the name of the person who accepted it. Keep the other copy of the cancellation form for your records.

- **If the seller did not provide a cancellation form or if you cannot find the one given you, write your own.** Be specific about what you are calling off and include the date of the contract and the date of the cancellation. You do not have to give a reason for canceling your purchase.

If you cancel your purchase, the seller has 10 days to cancel and return any promissory note or other negotiable instrument you signed, refund all your money, arrange for the pickup of any product you still have, and return any trade-in. Within 20 days, the seller must either pick up the items left with you or reimburse you for mailing expenses if you agree to send back the items. If you received any goods from the seller, you must make them available to the seller in the same condition as when you received them. If you do not make the items available to the seller, or if you agree to return the items but fail to, you remain obligated under the contract.

Some state laws provide you even more rights than the FTC rule. Search online for *attorney general + Your State* and use that website to find out more information.

Search for a Good Warranty and Understand Its Terms

There is no law that requires a manufacturer to offer a warranty on its products. Instead, it is the pressure of the marketplace that convinces a maker to promise things about the quality or longevity of its offerings. As a savvy consumer, you should include consideration of the type and length of warranty as part of your buying decision. All things being equal, buy the product with the better warranty. If a product with a better warranty costs more, weigh that cost against possible expenses down the road for the lower-priced product.

If a company does offer a written warranty, though, its provisions must follow several federal laws, including elements of the Magnuson-Moss Warranty Act and regulations put forth by the FTC. An important distinction to look for in a written warranty is whether it is full or limited.

• **A *full warranty* means that the maker promises to repair or replace malfunctioning parts at no cost for the length of time promised.** This sort of broad warranty is relatively rare.

• **A *limited warranty* typically promises protection against defects in material and workmanship with certain specified exceptions, and therein lie some major differences from one warranty to another.** For example, a limited warranty might say that coverage does not extend to problems caused by abuse or accident, or failure to follow maintenance procedures outlined in the instruction manual; some makers will not honor a warranty if an unauthorized service provider has altered the system, and other companies will exclude items that wear out through ordinary use such as automobile tires and lawnmower blades. A limited warranty may also say that its promises apply only to the original owner, or set restrictions on how warranties are transferred if the product is resold.

A written warranty must include details of how service is to be provided. *Read the terms carefully to find out…*

• **Where the repairs are done.**

• **Whether the owner is responsible for paying any shipping costs in one or both directions.**

On some products, including major appliances and computers, repairs may be offered in your home or office. If you live in a remote location, find out beforehand whether your area is excluded in some way.

What if the manufacturer or seller does not offer a written warranty? You're not completely out of luck, although you're going to have to be your own best advocate. State laws establish the outlines for implied warranties for products. Two common types for these protections are an *implied warranty of merchantability* and an *implied warranty of fitness for a particular purpose.* State law may set a time limit or place other limitations on implied warranties.

• ***Merchantability* means that a product must perform as it obviously should.** A washing machine must wash clothes, a computer must compute, and a tennis ball must bounce. There is no promise that the washing machine do its job particularly well or quickly, that the computer do the same, or that the tennis ball bounce to a particular height or help you beat Andy Murray in the Wimbledon Finals. The definition of merchantability, though, can be extended to include any promises made in packaging or advertising.

• ***Fitness* for a particular purpose is related to any discussions you have with the seller and any promises made to you in return.** For example, if you tell a computer seller that you need a particular piece of software to manage an office of 12 power users and the seller knows you are relying on his or her recommendation, the product is warranted to be fit for that purpose. If you tell an appliance salesperson you need a microwave that can be in almost constant use in a restaurant, this is a similar situation where the product is warranted to be fit for such a situation.

If you want to make a claim based on an implied warranty, you had better be prepared to back up your assertion with anything you received in writing and any notes you made at the time of sale. Consult your state or local consumer protection agency for assistance. In an online search engine, search *consumer protection agency + Your State*.

One possible exception to an implied warranty: an as-is sale, which indicates that the seller is making no representations at all about the product. So long as the buyer understands the full terms of the sale, in many instances there is nothing wrong with this sort of transaction. Some states put limits on the concept of as-is sales. For example, a car that cannot pass a necessary inspection might not qualify. And some states say the as-is sale language must be specific, along these lines: "As is, including known defects disclosed by the seller such as the fact that the alternator, tires, and brakes need to be replaced and the fuzzy dice on the rearview mirror are hanging by their last thread." (Remember that in Chapter 1 I tell you how to use extended warranties that are offered for many purchases made with many types of credit cards.)

Protect Yourself When You Shop in Foreign Places

Here are some other concerns about buying any product in foreign places…

• **Warranties.** The camera or smartphone you purchase at a great price in Montenegro may come with a warranty limited to that country. If you need repairs, you might have to pay to ship the device back to Estonia, or you might have to pay the full cost of repairs at a service center in the United States or Canada.

• **Voltage and other standards.** If what you bought requires connection to wall current, remember that not every part of the world uses the same 110-volt, 60-cycle AC current offered in the US Many modern devices, such as laptop computers and video cameras, are capable of switching back and forth between 110 and 240 volts, but you'll need adapters to plug foreign items into US electrical outlets. And there are more than a dozen designs of electrical plugs in use around the world.

• **Video standards.** Half a dozen different video standards are in use around the world. Television sets manufactured for the US market are for use only in countries that use the same protocols. It may be possible to use some of the most advanced non-US standard TVs on a digital cable box, but consult with your cable or satellite television provider first.

• **Video DVDs purchased outside the US may not work on US DVD players.** That's because commercially produced DVDs are assigned a particular country code for copyright and copy protection purposes; they should tell you that on the label. Region 1 is intended for use in the US and Canada. Region 2 is intended for use in Western Europe, Japan, South Africa, the Middle East, and Greenland. A DVD made by a non-commercial source (including street vendors) might have the wrong country code or might be assigned Region 0, which will work around the world but might employ the European PAL video standard rather than the standard used in the US and Canada, known as NTSC.

Music CDs, thankfully, are universal. You can buy music on a CD anywhere and have a reasonable expectation that it will play back properly when you get home.

Protect Your Privacy Online

Among the beauties of shopping online is the fact you can do it in your jammies, any time of day or night. But beware: Some stretches of the electronic superhighway are just as fraught with danger as the retail alleyways of the downtown shopping district.

The internet is not quite a fully private den. *There are three points of vulnerability…*

• **Your PC, tablet, or smartphone,** where you may have stored passwords, credit-card numbers, bank information, your calendar, and the details of all your contacts.

• **The computer at the other end of the connection,** where the merchant records your name, address, phone number, purchase history, and in many instances your credit-card or banking information.

• **The internet itself,** over which your financial and personal information travel.

Here's how to protect yourself in online commerce…

• **Use a secure browser that includes data encryption facilities.** Most major browsers, including Apple's Safari and Google's Chrome, have a secure mode. That feature is initiated by the business at the other end. You'll know you are in secure mode when you see the start of the web address change from "http" to "https." The secure (https) mode has a small padlock icon on the address bar to tell you it's there.

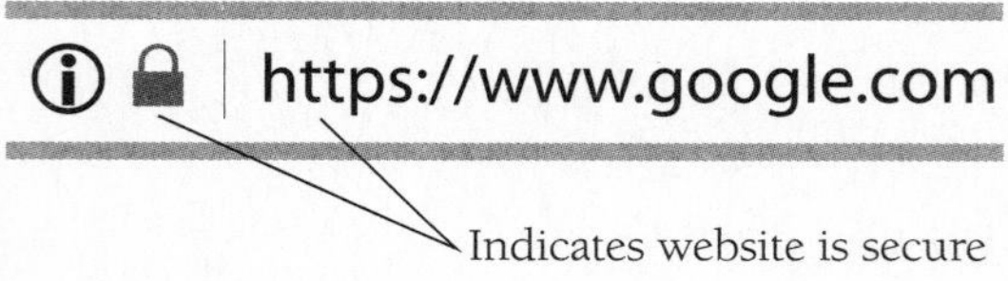

TIP

Pick Passwords Wisely

The most commonly used passwords on the internet are ridiculously simple for a human or machine to guess. According to industry sources, number one on the password list is *password* followed closely by *123456*. There's also *qwerty*, the first six characters of the computer keyboard used in the US and Canada.

How do you concoct a difficult-to-hack password? Start by making sure it does not contain publicly available information about you. Don't use the names of your children or pets, your favorite sports team, or your birthday. Give me a few minutes on your Facebook page and I would almost certainly have all that information.

Here's a better scheme: Pick a name or a phone number that has no direct connection to you and pair it with a place or an address that makes sense only to you. Let me make up an example: You recently watched a television series called "The Man in the High Tower" and in 1968 you stayed at the old Hotel Delano in Miami Beach. A difficult password that includes upper- and lowercase letters and special characters, would be *Hightower+1968_Delano*. You could, if you must, write down an indirect reminder like, "That TV show about a man who lived above, plus the year I stayed in the hotel in Miami Beach."

And then six months later, change it to something else.

Another option is to install and use a password vault program on your computer, tablet, or phone. You create one very, very complex password to keep the vault locked, and then you let the program generate completely nonsensical and complex passwords that you don't need to memorize. The only password you must remember is the vault password.

There are password vault programs from companies including Symantec (including its Norton security products) and other sources. They generally all work well, assuming you apply a complex set of letters and numbers as the master password.

• **Use the technologies offered by many credit-card companies that allow you to enhance security.** One system generates a temporary code that is good for only one transaction; your purchase goes through but anyone intercepting the data will be unable to make further purchases.

• **Use two-step authorization.** When you enter your credit-card number, the card issuer texts a one-time PIN code to your cell phone; you'll have to provide the code to complete the purchase. Online sites that offer two-step authorization will display that option when you establish or update your account.

• **Use a complex password for your accounts, and change it often.**

Understand Shipping Costs and Procedures

Is there truly such a thing as free shipping? I suppose the answer depends upon your definition of *free*.

When a seller promises free shipping, ask yourself these questions…

• **Can you buy the item elsewhere for a lower price even with added shipping costs?**

• **Is fast shipping worth the extra cost?** If I am purchasing staples—reams of paper, boxes of paper towels, a few dozen pair of socks on sale—I don't need to pay extra for overnight shipping. If I need a book or a piece of electronics in a hurry, then quick shipping has real value to me.

• **Will the seller give you a discount if you decline free shipping?** Sellers both large and small will sometimes offer a deal here.

• **Is the free shipping one-way only?** How much will it cost to send back an item you decide not to keep? Will the seller pay for the return if the item is defective? Will you be charged if you simply decide (within the published time limit) not to keep the item?

• **Be on the lookout for *handling charges*, which are nothing more than added profit.** There is a cost to any seller for stocking, packing, and shipping an item. As a buyer, I am

Be Stingy with Info

Facebook, Google+, LinkedIn, and dozens of other social media sites each have their particular lure for many computer users. They are great ways to keep in touch with friends and current or former co-workers, as well as ways to connect with political, social, and other causes of importance to you. But each requires you to disclose somewhere between a little and a great deal of personal information about yourself: address or hometown, birthplace, birthday, former and current employers, educational institutions, and more. Compound that with the fact that many users purposely or inadvertently disclose other tidbits about themselves, including the names of their children, pets, favorite sports team, and the like.

Sad to say, seemingly harmless bits of information disclosed on these sites are exactly what hackers and identity thieves are looking for.

Start by resisting, as best you can, requests for information that are unnecessary for a transaction or membership. A good rule of thumb: Don't respond to any question online if it is one you would not expect to be asked if you were buying an item in a brick-and-mortar store.

I am at heart an honest guy, but I will tell you that I have at times constructed a fictional doppelgänger with a different birthdate, hometown, education, and workplace. I have done this to protect real information and as an alert to fraudulent emails and phone calls. It is surprising—and saddening—to see how often the false information pops up in appeals for my money.

Returning Things

Be sure you understand a seller's return policies, including any fees for shipping an item back to the warehouse. Some sites, including Amazon, have a Return button on their website for customers with an account; click the button to initiate the process and print out a shipping label. Other companies include a return label in the box you receive.

More expensive and complex items may require prearrangement with the seller, usually involving obtaining a magic code, commonly called an RMA, which stands for Return Merchandise Authorization. It works like this: You call customer service and explain your predicament. If there is a problem with how the item works, a support person may try to help you fix the problem, but if the decision—yours or theirs—is to return the item, a file is opened at the shipper with all the information. You are assigned an RMA that you'll need to feature prominently on the outside of the package. They do this to help track incoming shipments, and it makes sense. Some manufacturers refuse any returned products that don't have the RMA in place.

One last point: If you are using the return label provided by the shipper, it includes tracking and insurance. But if you are responsible for arranging for shipping yourself, consider paying for insurance and tracking (which allows you to watch the package's progress and confirm its delivery). Most shipping companies include a basic level of insurance, perhaps coverage up to $50, but if the item is worth considerably more than that, pay for extra coverage.

FedEx, UPS, and most other package shipping companies routinely include tracking. You can enter the tracking number on the company's website or as a search phrase in Google, Bing, or another web browser. One tracking gap shows up when shippers use programs that use private carriers like FedEx and UPS for long-distance shipping but use the US Postal Service for final delivery. You may only be able to track the package as far as the USPS.

Keep all your receipts and shipping information until you receive full credit for your returned item.

interested in one thing only: the bottom-line cost. If an added handling charge takes the price above another company's price, I take my business elsewhere.

Under federal laws and FTC regulations, companies should ship orders within the time promised in advertising or on their website. If no time is promised, the company should ship your order within 30 days after receiving it, or give you an *option notice*. This notice gives you the choice of agreeing to a delay or canceling your order and receiving a prompt refund.

If a seller places a charge on your credit-card account but delays shipping, contact the seller to find your options, including canceling the order. There is no hard and fast rule that states when a charge can be applied for a preordered item, but credit-card companies will allow you to refuse payment for an item not received on terms promised by the seller.

Know the Ins and Outs of Layaway Plans

Layaway plans are ways to reserve merchandise and pay in installments before taking it home. Less common now than in years past, layaways are in some ways like credit-card purchases in reverse: You are paying for an item before you take possession.

Why would you use this sort of service? It's all a matter of cash flow. If you want to buy something now because it is on sale or in short supply but do not have the full amount of money available, a layaway is one option. You could use a credit card, of course, but you will have to pay the bill—or accrue interest on the balance—by the time your next statement is due. Layaway is more popular with people who do not have a credit card.

Some layaway plans apply a *service charge*, which is supposed to recompense the seller for the costs of storage and other expenses while it waits for full payment. Some stores charge a cancellation fee if you decide not to complete the purchase. If that is the case, you will get back any money you paid, minus the charge. Some states do not allow a cancellation fee.

Make sure you understand a store's layaway policy before using the service. Remember that you are giving your money to someone else without receiving something of substance until the end of the contract. If you have any doubts about the store's likelihood of staying in business, you probably should stay away.

Keep all your paperwork, including a full description of the layaway policy as well as receipts for all payments you make. The agreement should fully identify the item you are purchasing: model number, color, and sale price. And understand what happens if the item you want to purchase goes on sale at a lower price. Can you convert your contract to the new price? If not, do the math. Is it worth paying the cancellation fee and then buying the item at the reduced price?

CHAPTER 3

Shopping Online with Savvy

Just as you shouldn't walk down a dark street along the waterfront with cash in your hand and a fancy watch on your arm, you wouldn't buy something online without knowing the rules of the road.

I was present at the creation of the internet, serving as the first executive editor of *PC Magazine* in the early 1980s. In its very early years, it emerged as a complex and limited extension of ARPANET. (ARPA, as in the Advanced Research Projects Agency of the United States Department of Defense.) The intent was to link academic, military, and government networks. From that came a rudimentary and disorganized collection of chat rooms that mimicked, in some ways, a much more prevalent form of communication at the time—Citizens Band radio. (It's funny to look back at some of the early few years of *PC Magazine* and see all early computer products being offered for sale by mail-order catalog, telephone sale, and brick-and-mortar stores.)

Someone figured out that it might be possible to make some money on the network, and operators of some of the chat rooms began establishing the equivalent of internet flea markets. Although it was not the first major store on the internet, the establishment of Amazon in 1994 opened the door to what is now the world's largest online seller. eBay was started a year later as an auction version of a flea market. Both companies have gone on to become massive operations, expanding in just about every which way.

The appeal of shopping online: tremendous convenience and, usually, lower prices than can be found at brick-and-mortar stores. It is easy to search for and learn a great deal about products without venturing from your den or office. Similarly, it is very easy to compare prices between sellers. You can do this by jumping from one site to another or by using the services of a price-comparison site. PriceGrabber (PriceGrabber.com) and Google Shopping (Google.com/shopping) are popular options.

Be sure to include the cost of shipping in any comparison. Sometimes the least expensive price can yield the most expensive bottom line when you add shipping and other fees. And don't overlook the value of good customer service and refund policies in making your decision.

Earlier in this book I gave a general recommendation that the best way to protect yourself in shopping online (and in most other situations) is to use a credit card. As far as I am concerned, the only possible downside of using plastic is the propensity of some buyers to spend more money when using a card.

- **Take online reviews with a grain of salt.**
- **Be a tough cookie online.**
- **Raise your hand at online auctions.**
- **Clip online coupons.**
- **Pay extra for Prime or club shipping.**

Take Online Reviews with a Grain of Salt

Says who? A real purchaser who has no connection whatsoever to the manufacturer or the seller? The nephew of the owner of the website who posts great reviews from his bedroom in return for payment? Someone who has received a free tool from the manufacturer with the understanding that she will make positive comments on every website?

Most online sellers now offer comments and reviews about products they sell. I'd like to believe that the respondents are posting out of honest desire to help—or warn—fellow consumers. It's just that I don't fully believe that.

There have been numerous documented cases of false reviews, or paid endorsements on many websites. And there are those that are just plain dumb: "I haven't used this hedge trimmer yet, but it looks great and I give it five stars." Or, just as useless: "I am opposed to the whole idea of trimming hedges, and would never buy this device. Zero stars."

That said, I do take a spin through the ratings on many products before making a buying decision. *Here is what I look for…*

- **Patterns of problems.** Do I see multiple instances where a previous buyer reports a particular failure or shortcoming, like parts that break or motors that burn out after the first 30 minutes of use? One complaint might mean nothing, but I do take seriously eight or 10 or dozens with the same report.
- **Reports of bad customer service.** If many buyers write in to complain that the manufacturer (or the seller) did not stand behind the product in case of a problem, I will either look for an alternate product or call the manufacturer to discuss before I make a purchase.
- **Irrelevant comments.** Be on the lookout for comments like this: "This slow cooker was too large for the little cabinet beneath my kitchen cabinet." Or, "I didn't buy this cooker, but I think it probably is not fast enough for me." Like it or not, everyone gets a vote and the right to comment, even when they are of no use whatsoever.

Be a Tough Cookie Online

When you walk into a Home Depot and pay cash for a hammer, there's little or nothing in the transaction that threatens your privacy. (Yes, I know there are video cameras overhead; alas, that's the world we live in.)

Website Red Flags

Stay away from sites that...

• **List great prices for items they don't have in inventory.** It is possible that an item is temporarily out of stock; some sites will tell you when products are due in the warehouse. But some less-than-wonderful sites may be trying to lure you to buy something other than what you first wanted.

• **Don't give a phone number or physical address.** There are not many more helpless feelings than firing off a series of emails for help or inquiries about a missing delivery and getting no response. Then again, if you paid by credit card, you can contact the issuer and contest a charge that has become less than satisfactory.

Contrast that with a purchase made on the Home Depot website, just as an example. You have to enter your name and address (your real name and real address, since they have to match the information on record with the credit card company). And you have to enter some version of your credit card number (the actual number).

If you establish an ongoing relationship with the store, you'll be asked to enter an email address.

Think that's the end of it? Perhaps not. Many websites will also place a cookie on your computer's hard drive or in your tablet's or phone's memory. Most of the information is benign. Most cookies merely track what sites you've visited and what specific pages you've looked at. (If you've ever wondered how the next time you return to a site it presents you offers similar to whatever you looked at last time, now you know.)

But some sites might want to put a cookie on your device that collects other information, like where you went next on the web or your physical location. They're not supposed to share that with others without your permission, but how exactly would you know?

Note that internet browsers generally allow you to prevent websites from placing cookies on your device. That said, if you turn off cookies, some websites may refuse you entrance or make it impossible to maintain a shopping cart.

And finally, watch out for pirated websites. You may think you have properly entered the name of a store or other site in the search engine, but being off by just one letter might send you to (in the best case) a site that tries to sell you something else or (in the worst case) a site that imitates the real thing and steals some of your personal information, starting with your username and password.

Raise Your Hand at Online Auctions

If you know what you want, and know what it's worth, an online auction may be a great place to shop. That is, if the seller is honest about the nature of the product and then ships the product to you as promised. When you participate in an online auction, the computers do all the work, tracking the bids and listing the current high price. After a specified period of time, the auction is closed, and the buyer and seller communicate by email through the auction site to arrange for payment and shipment.

You'll find an astounding collection of strange stuff for sale on auction sites, but there are also more than a few gems among the junk. This sort of website is a meeting ground for buyers and sellers of just about anything, from automobiles and artwork to Barbie dolls and matchbook collections. The online auctions are, for the most part, exercises in pure capitalism. Some guy somewhere in East Overshoe advertises that he's got a one-of-a-kind ashtray constructed out of old Moxie bottle caps and then he sits back and watches collectors from around the world place increasingly larger bids for it.

Before you engage in an auction, make sure you know what you are proposing to buy…

- **Do you have all the information you need before making a bid?** Can you obtain a UPC code, model number, or other information so you can compare it to the same item sold elsewhere?
- **Is the product new or used?** If the package has been opened, are all of the parts, instruction manuals, and warranties included? Are warranties still in effect, and can they be transferred to a new owner?
- **What are the terms of sale?** Is the item sold as is, with no right to return it to the seller? If so, how does the auction site protect you against fraud or misrepresentation?
- **Do you understand the insurance or guarantees against fraud offered by the auction site?**

As with any other mail order or online purchase, the safest way to buy is to use a credit card. PayPal is another reasonably safe option, acting as an intermediary between your source of funds and a seller. PayPal offers fraud monitoring, but it doesn't offer warranty protection. If you do not receive a product or service paid for through PayPal or if it was not as described, they promise to protect you. If you used a credit card to send funds with PayPal as the middleman, you might also be able to enlist the credit card company in obtaining a refund to your account in certain circumstances, but I prefer certainty; I use credit cards in almost all purchases I make.

eBay

eBay, as the leader in this segment of the market, has become very good at requiring sellers to disclose a great deal of information about items, as well as photos and condition. eBay, to its credit, has gone to great lengths to stand behind its business model with various guarantees about the nature of products sold on its site and a promise that you will actually receive something you purchase or get your money back. (It is worth noting that not all the products sold on eBay are sold at auction; a large portion of them are sold at a fixed price.) For common products, the seller often uses predefined templates that include all the specifications and details of products like smartphones, cameras, and other consumer items.

eBay has been generally recognized as a well-run company and its guarantees do protect most buyers in all situations. If you are using a different auction site, be careful—especially if the seller is in a foreign country. Check with your credit-card issuer to find out what, if any, protection

Different Types of Auction

Most of us are familiar with a *Yankee auction*, also known as an *English auction*, where the product is sold to the highest bidder except when the seller has set a secret reserve price. If a reserve price has been set and the bidding does not reach that level, the sale is canceled. Some online auction sites will tell you when the reserve price has not been met.

When a seller has more than one identical item for sale, the process is sometimes conducted as a *Dutch auction*. Here, the lowest winning bid determines the price for all other high bidders. For example, if there are five DVD players available and the fifth-highest bid is $200, all five will be sold at that price—even if other bidders offered more.

In a *reverse auction*, the seller sets a price and bidders make offers they hope the seller will accept. In most cases, the successful bid will be less than the buyer's set price but in some cases, demand pushes the price above the offering price.

you have for purchases from a foreign seller. This is a situation when it is valuable to closely examine comments from previous buyers posted on the website. If you see more than a few complaints of bad product or bad customer service, I suggest seeking a different seller.

Although few individuals accept cards in online auctions, eBay allows buyers to pay with credit or debit cards, or by other methods if the seller permits. On eBay, some sellers will post the price they want, along with an onscreen button that reads Make Offer. There's no guarantee the seller will accept your offer, but I have had good luck making an offer 5% to 10% below the asking price.

eBay is by far the largest online auction site, and it generally receives high marks from reviewers and users. Smaller auction sites may be appropriate for highly specialized products and collectible items; look for comments from users on the internet before making any major buys or sells on these sites.

Other Sites

eBay dominates the market, but you might also want to check out online estate sales, which are held auction style, and government auctions of surplus items, where you can find all manner of items, from tools to fire trucks. You generally have to arrange for pickup or shipment of items purchased (versus them being delivered to you). The General Services Administration operates at GSAauctions.gov. Goodwill runs a popular auction site at ShopGoodwill.com. And finally, if you want to give the IRS even more of your money, try their auctions at Treasury.gov/auctions/irs.

Clip Online Coupons

Getting a good deal is exciting. Finding a way to improve the deal is even more of a thrill. That's why I am regularly on the hunt for rebates, coupons, and special offers. If you're about to buy an appliance, check the equipment manufacturer's website to see if they have any specials and then contact sellers to make sure they will honor the deal.

If you sign up for an online account with most sites, you are likely to receive emails offering discounts and specials. My inbox fills with offers from car rental companies, office supply sellers, travel websites, and just about every other site with which I do business.

But how do you know if you are somehow missing a special deal? You might want to visit one of a number of websites that collect coupons and special offers and pass them along to readers. (Most make their income by selling ads or by receiving fees paid by the websites to which they link.) My favorites are Coupons.com and RetailMeNot.com. Or simply Google the retailer's website and the words "promo code" to find extra sales reductions.

Pay Extra for Prime or Club Shipping

Amazon, perhaps the most successful and certainly the most innovative online seller, is constantly experimenting with new ways to lure customers, keep them loyal, and (not unrelatedly) boost their own bottom line.

One of the more interesting efforts by Amazon is the Prime program, which allows customers to receive two-day (or otherwise expedited) shipping on listed as being in the Prime inventory.. Members must pay an annual fee to join the Prime club; as this book went to press the fee was $99 per year. But wait, there's more...Prime members also get the right to stream a fairly large library of movies and television shows to a wide range of devices including TVs, computers, laptops, and smartphones. Many of the shows are part of your membership, including some award-winning shows produced by Amazon. There is also Prime Music, which includes similar enticements for music. Some people might find the $99 fee worth paying just for the video and audio. Others may enjoy the ability to order a $3 tool and receive it in two days without a shipping charge.

Amazon also allows you to share your Prime account with another adult who lives in the same household, and who agrees to share payment methods. Understand that this other

Jet to Walmart

The online site Jet.com began with dreams of approaching Amazon's market share. Jet experimented with increased discounts based on the number of items ordered as well as price reductions based on the buyer's willingness to share some of the burden of business.

For example, I priced a tool on Jet at $79.05 as a starting price for a one-item order. Or, I could have paid $78.07 if I opted out of free returns; I could still return an item but would have to pay a $5.99 shipping cost plus a 5% restocking fee. Next down the pricing tree was $77.86 if I paid with a debit card instead of credit card; free returns were restored. And the lowest price for a single-item order was $76.90 if I opted out of free returns and paid by debit card. In my opinion, the small amount of extra cost for using a credit card is worth the option to return an item for free.

In late 2016, Jet agreed to sell itself to another company you may have heard of, Walmart, which has hopes of zooming to a larger internet presence.

person will be able to place orders and use any credit card stored as part of the account. Set up an Amazon Household within your account for this purpose.

Or you could give someone your username and password and allow them to order things as if they were you, although I'm not comfortable with that option.

Now a word of advice: Only products marked Prime are shipped for free, and in some cases you can buy the same product at a lower price without Prime shipping. You'll have to do the research yourself.

Amazon has another special program that gives you a discount on items you might buy monthly or several times a year: You get a lower price on your first offer and subsequent shipments are sent out automatically on the schedule you establish. Not a bad idea, but a study by *The New York Times* showed that the prices can sometimes get out of whack because Amazon is constantly adjusting prices—up or down—based on supply and demand and you may not notice the price change. You would almost certainly do better by shopping for the best price, including delivery, each and every time you buy something. One month, Amazon may be amazing; the next month Walmart may be more wonderful.

PART II

The Savvy Personal Shopper

CHAPTER 4

Saving on Clothing and Accessories

Some people spend a great deal of time (and money) on fashion and go way out of their way to regularly update and expand their wardrobe. And others say, "Shoes? I've got shoes: one pair each in black and brown. I'll go shopping for new ones, and maybe a belt, when the old ones fully disintegrate." I fall into the second category, although when I do go shopping, I am as determined as ever to get the most for my money. And if I can do it as quickly and painlessly as possible, that's a real bonus. My wife, on the other hand, falls into the other category of shopper. She has plenty more than two pairs of shoes and a clothing collection that occupies 90% of the closet space in our home.

But dressing well does not necessarily mean dressing extravagantly. If you've got unlimited funds and want to spend them on real gold threads in a diamond-encrusted cocktail dress, go right ahead. ("What? This old thing?") Most of the people reading this book get their thrills from paying a whole lot less for something that makes them look like a million.

Earlier I mentioned some of the varied markups for products. Let's get specific on apparel. Clothing is typically marked up about 100%, although some items, like designer clothing and boutique or designer jeans, may be marked up as much as 350%. If a store offers 25% or more off, it can still make a profit. Shoes also begin with a markup of about 100% for basic models. Again, shoe sales are common. Fancy brands (notice that I did not say *better quality*) may be marked up as much as 500%. Am I implying that a brand name or a product that bears a celebrity's name is not necessarily the highest quality? Yes, I am. Quality is usually apparent. Prices do not always follow suit.

We've already explored a shopping calendar. Clothing is a product category that is especially sensitive to the season. Buy winter clothing after Christmas...ski outfits around Easter...and summer wear after the Fourth of July. Prices for swimwear start to plunge soon after customers head to the beach in May and June.

- **Make sense of shoe sizes.**
- **Suit yourself with two pants at a time.**
- **Pay more to get a better warranty.**
- **Mix and match fibers.**
- **Learn the secrets of women's clothing.**
- **Keep your head at the milliner's.**

TIP

Try Every Pair

When I find a particularly comfortable pair of shoes, I sometimes order two or even three pair and put the extras in the closet until I need them. (Try them on before you store them away, though; sometimes shoes of the same design and size vary slightly in fit.) I use only one set of black, brown, and walking shoes at a time. Not simultaneously, of course.

- **Shop for haute couture hand-me-downs.**
- **Rent a bit of elegance.**

Make Sense of Shoe Sizes

When is a size 11 Medium not an 11 Medium? The answer: When you buy shoes. Unfortunately, shoe sizes are often not precise, especially when you move from type to type or brand to brand. If you're buying shoes at a retail store, you can try on shoes all day if you want. (Keep in mind that feet tend to swell by the end of the day. For some buyers, that is enough to warrant shopping for shoes in the afternoon rather than the morning.)

But how do you purchase shoes online? *Here are a few sizeable suggestions…*

• **Make sure the site offers returns.** Even better? Free returns.

• **If you have shoes of a particular style (work, casual, walking, hiking) from a particular brand, there is a fair likelihood that sizes within that style will be consistent.** So a 9.5 Medium Grasshoppers Stretch Lace walking shoe should be similar to others of that sort from the same maker. And if you do the research and know that Grasshoppers is part of the same family of shoes as Keds, Hush Puppies, Sebago, and half a dozen other brands, you have a reasonable expectation that sizes will be relatively consistent.

• **Pay attention to the fit ratings you will find on some online stores.** Once again, Amazon (or its subsidiary Zappos) is at the forefront, with a report on most shoes that allows you to compare the fit of a shoe you find on their website to a shoe you already own. And you can still return the shoes if you end up with a Cinderella story that doesn't fit.

Suit Yourself with Two Pants at a Time

One way to extend a suit's life is to buy a jacket with two pairs of pants. Trousers tend to wear out more quickly than jackets, and assuming you don't undergo a radical change in size, you should be able to get a few years of active wear with four legs' worth of pants.

To make the most of your purchase, try to give both pants an equal amount of wear and have all three pieces dry cleaned at the same time to keep their colors the same over time.

Pay More to Get a Better Warranty

I do not endorse paying extra just for the cachet of a particular brand name, but sometimes it pays to spend more to get more. For example, brand-name handbag manufacturers stand behind their products with extended warranties and repair facilities. For example, Dooney & Bourke bags come with a one-year warranty, but beyond that the company says it will repair any damaged or worn bag or accessory for a price that does not exceed half the current retail price of that particular style. If the bag is beyond repair, the owner can trade it in for a newer model at half price.

L.L. Bean offers a 100 percent satisfaction guarantee for products purchased directly from the company online or in one of its stores, excluding third-party resellers. Duluth Trading Company offers a No Bull unconditional guarantee that says if you're not satisfied with one of their products you can send it back for a refund.

Slightly less comprehensive but still valuable warranties come from brands like Saddleback Leather Company, which has a warranty against defects (but not damage) that extends 100 years from date of purchase. Depending upon your particular circumstances, that may or may not qualify as a lifetime.

Take the time to read the warranty and return policies from any store before making a purchase, and consider whether a seller who has a slightly higher price but better customer service is more worthy of your business.

Mix and Match Fibers

Clothing made of pure cotton or pure wool has a certain cachet, and may suit you just fine. In many instances cotton shirts and pants may require special cleaning and ironing.

No-iron or wrinkle-resistant cotton shirts may be a giant leap for man- and womankind, but they are not quite the same as pure cotton. The resistance to wrinkling comes as the result of chemicals (including formaldehyde resin) that bond together molecules; the fabric is stiffer than untreated cotton.

Cotton blended with a relatively small percentage of synthetic fabric, perhaps a 90/10 or 80/20 blend, is an alternative. This fabric is wrinkle resistant and nearly as soft as pure cotton. But it may appear shiny, and may be warmer, which might be a disadvantage in the summer.

More about cotton: There is a wide range of fabric (called *shirting* when used for shirts) and your preferences and the balance in your checking account might move you in one direction or another. If you see specifications advertised for shirting, look for the yarn number. The lower the number, the coarser the yarn. A fabric made from yarn numbered in the 30s will be very coarse; a number of 80 to 100 is common in mass market stores, and some of the best cotton is number 200 or even higher.

There's also *thread count*, which is not the same thing as the yarn number in all fabrics. Though the world would be a much simpler place if thread count always meant the number of threads per square inch or centimeter, that's not the case. Fabrics can be woven tightly or loosely. In its technical sense, thread count is a measure of the number of hanks in one pound. It is still true that the higher the number, the finer the yarn. (Why a hank? A *hank* is an old measurement of the density of either cloth or yarn; a hank of cotton or silk is 840 yards in length, while a hank of worsted spun wool is 560 yards.)

But wait, there's more: the longer the fiber, the finer the cotton and the dressier the resulting shirt. Why? Because longer fiber, also called long staple cotton, has fewer tiny knots binding the yarn together. Some of the best cotton comes from Egypt or part of the Caribbean, with fibers as long as two inches. And then there is two-ply cotton, made of a pair of intertwined lengths of yarn. It is denser and thicker.

Back to wool: A quality-made 80/20 blend of wool and synthetic fiber should wear as well as 100 percent wool and is less likely to lose its shape. The same goes for stretch fabrics or elastic elements in clingy clothing, socks, and undergarments: they usually mean a longer useful life.

So what do you do with all this information? Use it to decipher the claims of quality and durability made by sellers or manufacturers. But, remember that when it comes to fashion, price and quality are not always the same thing.

Learn the Secrets of Women's Clothing

One of the great mysteries of the ages is why a woman's jacket, typically made with flimsy stitching and thin lining, can sell for so much more than a man's jacket with more material, better craftsmanship, and an overall higher quality. It has something to do with "fashion," but that does not deter many savvy women from shopping in the men's aisle or catalogs.

Now I expect I don't have to explain to you that men and women are constructed differently. *Leaving out the private parts, a few observations…*

- **Women tend to be wider in the hips than men, which means that equivalent waist sizes for pants do not directly translate into a comfortable fit.** For the same reason, this is why properly constructed shoes (especially ski boots) made for men are unlikely to fit a woman well.
- **Men are generally wider in the shoulders and narrower under the armpits than women, which affects the fit of shirts and jackets.**

Here is a conversion chart that roughly equates women's sizes to men's clothing; your experience may differ.

Men's size	XS	S	M	L
Women's size	S	M	L	XL
Women's dress size	6–8	10–12	14–16	18–20
Waist Size	26–28	29–31	32–34	36–38

An imperfect conversion of men's pants size (identified as a waist size) to women's sizes (expressed as a number) is to subtract 21 from the men's size—but pay attention to the cut and fit. In other words, a man's 33-inch waist pants is about equal to a woman's size 12.

Keep Your Head at the Milliner's

Some stylish people top off their outfits with a man's fedora or other headgear. Here is a chart that compares the three measures of hat sizes: size name, head size (circumference in inches), and hat size. Women's hat sizes can follow those for men, or, more commonly, be available in small, medium, or large sizes. And, of course, if you are putting a lot of hair beneath your hat, you may need a larger size.

Size	S	S	M	M	L	L	XL
Head size	21⅛	21½	21⅞	22¼	22⅝	23	23½
Hat size	6¾	6⅞	7	7⅛	7¼	7⅜	7½

Shop for Haute Couture Hand-Me-Downs

Does anyone really have to know that you bought your gorgeous wedding gown or tuxedo secondhand? Wedding gowns are expensive clothing that are usually worn just once...and carefully. Styles for tuxedos and other formal wear for men tend to change infrequently.

Look for outposts of a growing market: retail stores that sell high-quality secondhand clothing. If you're buying name-brand clothing, check the price of new items so you understand their original value. If you're shopping for an expensive piece of clothing (or jewelry, which is explained in detail in the next chapter), insist on the right to obtain an independent appraisal before you buy, or an iron-clad right to return for refund anything that is not appraised at the value you were promised.

The appraiser you use should be a professional who has no association with the seller. In fact, it is to your advantage not to disclose the seller's name. That way you reduce the chances of any collusion. Look for an appraiser with credentials from one of several organizations or societies, including the American Society of Appraisers (Appraisers.org), Appraisers Association of America (Appraisersassociation.org), or International Society of Appraisers (ISA-appraisers.org/home). You may want to ask friends or acquaintances for recommendations.

One other place to shop: pawnbrokers. Here you need an especially fine eye to pick the wheat from the chaff. And again, don't trust the seller's appraisal. Get your own for any expensive purchase.

And finally, you might think twice before trying on—or buying—a used hat or other article of clothing because of the remote chance of acquiring lice or bed bugs or other trespassers as part of the deal. In any case, inspect clothing carefully. To be really sure, you can throw washable items into water hotter than 140 degrees Fahrenheit for a washing or into a hot dryer for at least 15 minutes (according to the National Center for Biotechnology Information). Dry cleaning can take care of items—and any nasties living on them—that you can't wash (or dry) yourself.

Rent a Bit of Elegance

Who says you have to buy a fabulous gown for a formal occasion or a spectacular dress for your wedding? Look into renting a top-of-the-line outfit. Check bridal shops, high-end clothing shops, and online for leads. Find current well-reputed rentals at RentTheRunway.com and BagBorrowOrSteal.com. Your alterations for a rented piece of clothing are likely to be limited to "hemming" with removable tape.

When it comes to tuxedos, the decision may come down to this: Do you expect to need formal wear often, or is this something that will happen rarely? Tuxedos rent for something close to half the cost of purchasing a suit. (And be sure you understand the full cost, including necessary alterations and shipping or delivery.) In my line of work, I actually put on a penguin suit fairly regularly and so I purchased a tux. About two or three parties down the line I was ahead of the game.

If you are concerned about the possibility of the same gown appearing twice at an event, ask the renter. Chances are the store stocks just one of each outfit. There is nothing you can do about someone choosing the same outfit from another source, but you would run the same risk if you were buying the clothing from a retail store.

For more on weddings, see Chapter 10.

CHAPTER 5

Buying Jewelry

For most of us, shopping for jewelry is a labor of love performed mostly in the dark. The shopping, that is.

Do you know the difference between a karat of gold and a carat of diamond? Are you able to assess the luster of a pearl, or the purity of silver or platinum? And is that little bright chip really a valuable diamond? I assume that most of us have to put a great deal of trust in the honesty and accuracy of a seller about whom we know nothing.

What is the savvy consumer to do? Put the power back on his or her side of the table by taking three important steps:

1. **Before you check out a jewelry store's showcases or the pages of an online or catalog seller, check out the business's reputation.** Troll the internet for complaints or praise by past customers, reading carefully in hopes of weeding out improper bias for or against a company. Many jewelers are members of one trade organization or another; most have codes of ethics and business practices. Some—but not all—stores may also have a record with your local or national Better Business Bureau.

2. **Read this chapter so you can learn how to buy intelligently.**

3. **When the price rises above a casual level of comfort, put your credit card back into your wallet** and engage an independent appraiser to examine the quality and to gauge the piece's value.

- **Know jewelry prices.**
- **Buy a diamond.**
- **Buy other gemstones.**
- **Buy gold.**
- **Buy silver.**
- **Buy platinum.**
- **Buy pearls.**
- **Repair your jewelry.**
- **Know where to shop for jewelry.**

Know Jewelry Prices

If you purchased an original Picasso, the price would be based entirely on the appraised value of the work as a piece of art. You wouldn't pay for the quality of the canvas or paint.

Jewelry prices partly reflect the intrinsic value of the components. You could think of this as the breakup value: How much would the gold or silver or platinum be worth if melted down, and how much would the stones be worth if resold separately? The other part of the price is a valuation placed on the jewelry designer's and maker's artistry.

The markup on cut diamonds ranges between 50% and 200% of the wholesale price. Gold is typically marked up from 100% to 400%. As for finished products, a ring with stones in place, for example, is generally marked up between as little as 50% and as much as 400% (and sometimes even more). What does this mean to you? A jeweler can easily offer sales of 50% off and still make a profit. And you really don't know what the true original price was. It is very unlikely that you will be able to find an identical item to compare at competing jewelry stores.

Buy a Diamond

Do you really know the difference between a half-carat diamond and a 75-point stone? How about a Pavé versus a Tiffany setting? More to the point: How do you know the diamond ring in the jeweler's case really is worth $12,000? And is it worth that much money to you?

If you're like most people, myself included, you don't have a clue when it comes to diamonds. *Unless you're willing to go back to school for a degree in gemology, your best bets when it comes to buying a high-priced diamond follow...*

- **Learn as much as you can about diamonds and the diamond market before setting foot in a store.**

- **If the price is more than trivial to you, consider paying an independent appraiser to check the piece's quality and determine its value before you buy it.** (Sometimes you can specify a period after purchase during which you can return the piece for a refund. Be sure to obtain a written promise of your right to return a purchase.) A professional appraiser might charge in the range of $100 to $300 or more for a single item. Some appraisers have an hourly rate of about $100 to $500. More elaborate jewelry items with multiple stones and intricacies might require more time and a longer, costlier appraisal. Obviously, it does not make sense to pay hundreds of dollars to appraise an item that is selling for $50. In that case, go ahead and make the purchase...and never have it appraised. You'll be happier (and wealthier) that way.

- **Ask about guarantees the jeweler is willing to make about diamond quality or other elements, and get any such assertions in writing.** If the jeweler will not provide that information on the bill of sale, I suggest shopping elsewhere. If the diamond comes with a gemological certificate that spells out the qualities, get an original and keep it with your receipt. Make certain the receipt lists the diamond's quality to protect you in case of dispute or resale, and to help establish value for any insurance you might purchase.

• **When you examine a diamond, check these things...**

• How it looks against a white background. Black and colored backgrounds change the eye's color perception.

• The mounting quality. The more prongs holding a stone in place, the better. Channel settings are attractive but less secure and need to be checked often for loose stones. Ask the jeweler for recommendations here, and ask if the store provides free or reasonably priced maintenance for items they sell.

• Clasps, for sturdiness. They should be well attached and easy to open and close.

• Solder joints. They should be clean, neat and as close to invisible as possible.

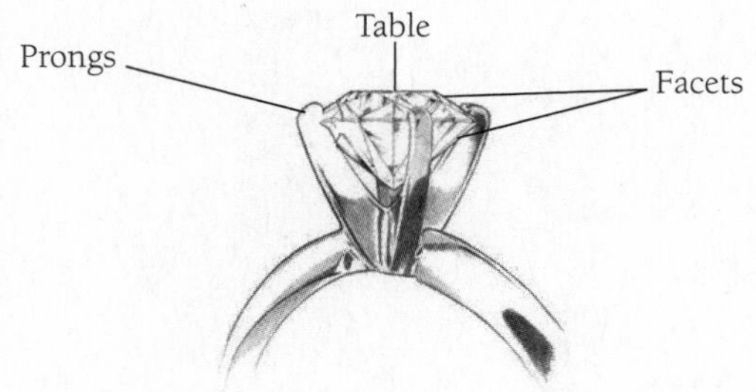

Diamond Quality

The experts on the arcane art of gemology say that there are four qualities that gauge the value of a diamond. They call them the four Cs: carat, color, clarity, and cut.

• **Carat.** A carat is a measurement of a stone's weight. One full carat is equal to 200 milligrams in metric measurement. If you want to compute in avoirdupois (16 ounces to the pound), there are 142 carats in an ounce. Carats are further divided into points, with 100 points in a carat. Therefore, a half-carat diamond is sometimes called a 50-point stone. Larger diamonds are more scarce than smaller ones, and therefore command a higher price per carat at an equivalent quality.

• **Color: White is the most popular color for diamonds, although the stones are found in nearly every hue.** The rarest and most expensive shade is a colorless, icy white. White diamonds are rated on how far they deviate from the purest white. Colorless stones are graded D to Z, with each subsequent letter of the alphabet representing a step toward yellow. Diamonds in other colors are called fancies, with shades including

Artificial Diamond Monopoly

Diamond buyers should know they are making a purchase in what is essentially an artificially manipulated monopoly market. Prices for rough-cut diamonds are greatly influenced by De Beers Consolidated Mines Corporation of South Africa. Up until about the start of the 21st century, about 80% of the world's production of rough diamonds went through that company's hands. Today, the monopoly on diamonds has been much reduced, although De Beers still handles, directly or indirectly, about 35% of rough diamonds, from sources in South Africa, Namibia, Botswana, and Canada.

red, blue, green, and brown. They are graded on their color depth, with 27 color hues with names like red, green-yellow, yellow-green, blue, violet, and purple, all the way to brown, gray, and black. Beyond that, there is a judgment regarding the saturation of these hues, on a scale from faint to light to fancy to vivid, and eventually fancy vivid.

• **Clarity: A diamond's clarity is an appraisal of the passage of light through the stone, including what we amateurs would call its sparkle.** Clarity can be reduced by irregularities on the stone's surface as well as internal imperfections such as spots, bubbles, or lines called inclusions. The fewer inclusions, the higher the value. Clarity is graded on a scale ranging from flawless (FL or IF) to imperfect (I). To be graded flawless, a diamond must have no visible inclusions under a 10X magnification. Diamonds with flaws are rated VVS (very, very slightly included), VS (very slightly included), SI (slightly included), and I (included and visible to the naked eye).

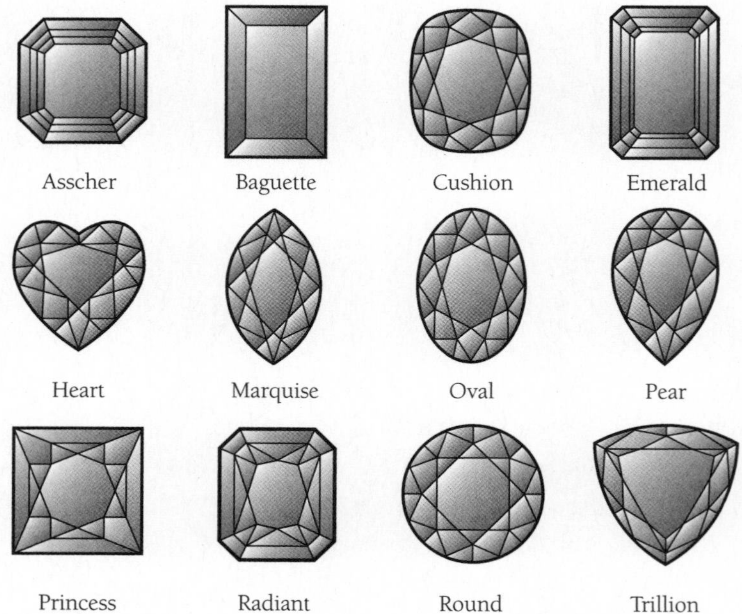

• **Cut: Diamonds are cut to a precise formula.** The most common cut is called a round brilliant and has 58 facets (small, flat, polished planes) to reflect light to the viewer. The reflection is called the stone's brilliance and is an important measure of its quality. A poorly cut diamond appears dull, and commands a markedly lower price.

Here are a few other terms you should know: On a brilliant cut diamond, there are 32 facets plus the table, the largest and the topmost facet, above the widest circumference of the stone, which is known as the girdle. Below the girdle, a brilliant cut diamond has 24 facets plus the cutlet, or point. (Here's the math: 32 facets plus the table equals 33 above the girdle. Then 24 facets plus the cutlet below the girdle, for a total of 25. Add 33 and 25 to reach the total of 58 facets in a brilliant stone.) In addition to the round brilliant, other popular cuts—classified as fancy cuts—include asscher, baguette, emerald, heart, marquis, pear, oval, and princess, among others. A baguette is a small, rectangular diamond often used to enhance a larger stone's setting.

Bezel, channel, Pavé, and Tiffany are four important diamond settings. In a bezel setting, the diamond is surrounded, like a picture frame, by a precious metal border. A channel setting is often used to mount rows of small, uniformly sized stones between two strips of metal, like a railroad track. A Pavé setting places stones so closely together the surface seems to be paved with stones. A Tiffany setting uses four or six finger-like prongs to hold the stone.

Altered Diamonds

One important question to ask is if the diamond has been treated or altered in any way. Diamonds can be colored, tinted, coated, irradiated, or heated to improve their appearance. In some processes, inclusions (imperfections) are removed with lasers, and external fractures filled with a plastic-like compound.

In addition to misleading the buyer about the stone's real value, some of these procedures are not permanent. Epoxies used in fracture-filled diamonds can melt if the stone is exposed to high temperature. You should only purchase an altered or enhanced diamond if you have been informed about its nature, if the price reflects its less-than-perfect construction, and if you are willing to pay for a less-than-natural stone. I'm calling these diamonds altered, and that is the term many reputable jewelers will use. Some will use the euphemism enhanced. If a jeweler tells you a stone is unaltered, ask for that promise in writing.

There is no hard-and-fast rule for how much of a discount you should expect for an altered stone versus an unaltered one. Shop around and compare prices for yourself.

Some diamond sources and some jewelers put tiny markers on their stones as a form of identification and sourcing. Forevermark, a brand of the De Beers Group, inscribes an icon and identification number invisible to the naked eye. If a jeweler offers such a stone, ask to see it through a loupe or video screen at the store.

Synthetic Diamonds

I have visited a bazaar in Kusadasi, Turkey, numerous times. The bazaar is semi-famous for a sign that hangs out front: "Genuine Fake Rolex Watches." You have to give them points for honesty. This brings me to genuine synthetic diamonds. They are not fakes, in that they are real diamonds almost indistinguishable from natural stones and, in some properties, actually superior.

Synthetic diamonds are manufactured in a laboratory using either a high-pressure high-temperature or a chemical-vapor deposition crystal formation process. They are made of carbon, the same material that constitutes a natural diamond. Laboratories can produce diamonds with greater hardness, thermal conductivity, and electrical conductivity than natural ones.

Synthetic diamonds are already in wide use in industrial applications and a small but potentially growing share of the gem-quality jewelry market. Yellow or bluish synthetic diamonds,

Sentimental Value

When I go out to sea as a destination and special-interest lecturer for a luxury cruise ship company, I often tell guests my theory about how to shop for pearls, jade, amber, gold, and silver jewelry offered to tourists in many ports around the world.

Here's what I say: "If you see something that looks good, and if the price does not cause personal pain, go ahead and bargain a bit for a good price. Then bring it home and show it off to friends and family as a souvenir of a great trip. But never have it appraised. The news could be good or it could be bad, but from a distance of thousands of miles it serves no purpose. Just enjoy it."

the color resulting from minor chemical impurities, are most common. White or colorless stones are tougher to come by.

The debate amongst gemologists (and customers) about synthetic diamonds are somewhat like arguments about bottled water that comes from a mountain stream or from a scientifically designed and maintained distillation or desalination plant. Water is water. Diamonds are diamonds. However, synthetic diamonds do not come from some parts of the world tainted by the violence of war and sometimes-awful working conditions for the miners.

At first, it was all but impossible to tell the difference between synthetic and natural diamonds but researchers—including those in the employ of De Beers and others with an economic stake in the market—have developed instruments that can detect minor impurities that are often present in synthetic stones.

Does it matter to you, the buyer? If the price on a synthetic stone—and its potential resale value—is to your advantage, in my opinion it is worth considering. On the other hand, if you are determined to go au naturel, insist on a statement of authenticity. A high-quality synthetic diamond can be as beautiful as a natural stone. And the selling price can be less than that for a natural diamond but sometimes nearly the same. Perhaps most importantly, a synthetic diamond's resale value may be considerably less than that of an equivalent real diamond.

Buy Other Gemstones

Diamonds are included in the term gemstone, although some people hold them to a separate class. The term precious stone is usually applied to diamonds, rubies, sapphires, and emeralds. The rest fall into the class called semi-precious.

The quality and value of colored gemstones is mostly in the eye of the beholder. There are thousands of varieties, but only about two dozen are commonly available in jewelry.

Common species and varieties include…

- **Beryl:** Emerald, aquamarine
- **Corundum:** Blue sapphire, ruby, star ruby, star sapphire
- **Quartz:** Amethyst, citrine, smoky quartz
- **Topaz:** Blue topaz
- **Tourmaline:** Green tourmaline

• **Zoisite:** Tanzanite

Rough colored gemstones (stones that are not in their final form for jewelry) are either faceted or cut en cabochon, meaning polished but not faceted. Faceted pieces are generally made from better quality rough stones, and usually offer better clarity and brilliance. Cabochon-cut gemstones are flat on the bottom and domed on the top, and are usually more translucent or opaque.

Some gemstones are treated to intensify color or to deal with internal flaws. Processes include heat treatments, fracture filling, and dyes, similar to the techniques used to enhance diamonds. Such treatments may be less than permanent; be sure to ask whether the stones have been treated, and obtain a written description of their quality on the receipt from the jeweler.

You may also run into assembled stones, which are gemstones, synthetic, and glass parts held together with colored glues. Synthetic gemstones have the same physical, chemical, and optical properties as natural stones, but usually sell for less. There is nothing wrong with such stones. You do, though, have the right to know if they are real or were manufactured in a laboratory. Some synthetic gemstones are marked CRTD, an arcane marking that stands for created.

Once again, it is not necessarily wrong to buy a treated stone, but it is certainly wrong for a store to sell such a stone without informing you of its history.

Buy Gold

Gold is relatively rare and extremely difficult to extract in large quantities. That's one element of its value. Another element is the quality of workmanship of jewelry fashioned from the metal. A third component is the intrinsic value of the gold itself. If a wedding ring is no longer of use, its value may be based on its appearance or on the value of the gold itself melted down for resale.

The price of a piece of gold jewelry is based on karatage, gram weight, design, and craftsmanship.

Karatage is a measure of the gold's purity. Pure gold is rated at 24 karats. Metal of that purity is considered too soft to be used in jewelry. In most uses, gold is mixed with other metals in an alloy to increase its strength. Two common alloys are 18 karats (18/24 or ¾, pure gold) or 14 karats (just over half pure gold).

Gold products sold in the United States are required to include a mark reporting its karatage as well as the trademark or name of the manufacturer, importer, or dealer of the item.

European jewelry is sometimes marked with a different scale, with 999 representing near pure. *Here's a conversion chart…*

Karat Marks	10K	14K	18K	24K
European	417	585	750	999
Percent Pure Gold	41.7	58.5	75	99.9

Any alloy less than 10 karats cannot be legally sold as gold jewelry in the United States.

The various alloys can create gold of many colors. Yellow gold is created by an alloy of gold, copper, and silver…gold and copper create pink gold…white gold contains platinum or palladium, zinc, and copper…green gold contains silver, copper, and zinc. Some people are allergic to certain metals, while others who have a high acid content may find that gold alloys turn their skin colors.

The next measure is the piece's gram weight. Intangible elements of value include construction and design.

Here are additional important steps you can take to protect yourself…

- **Pay special attention to fasteners or clasps.** The ideal is a closure that is secure but easy to use.
- **Backs of pins and earring posts should be firmly attached;** solder should not be visible on a fine piece.
- **Evaluate the quality of gold chain by laying the piece flat and making sure the links are not kinked.**

Very lightweight gold pieces may be hollow, making them more susceptible to damage. And that brings us to an important definition: Solid gold does not mean "pure gold." Instead, it means that the piece is not hollow. The gold's purity is an entirely different matter.

Protect yourself when you buy gold by ensuring that the jewelry is clearly marked with karat weight and the manufacturer's trademark, and make sure the karat weight is listed on the sales receipt.

One other thing: Gold-plating, or gilding, means applying a thin layer of gold to another metal, often silver and sometimes copper. The result can be a fine piece of jewelry, but it is not solid gold and should not be sold or priced as such.

Buy Silver

Silver has been used in jewelry for more than 5,000 years, back to at least ancient Egyptian times.

The highest quality form of the metal is sterling silver, which means the item contains at least 92.5% silver. Objects may be labeled as sterling or marked 925 to indicate the quality of the metal. (Sterling is short for Easterlings, a form of money used in 12th century England.)

Watch out for items marked as nickel silver or German silver. These alloys do not contain any silver; they are made from a mix of copper, zinc, and nickel. Silver items will tarnish over time, turning dark or black. You can clean tarnish with special solutions or polishes, or even with toothpaste.

Look for a sterling marking on jewelry, and make sure your sales receipt indicates the quality of the item. Various makers have their own markings, and you will find variations based on the country of origin.

Buy Platinum

Platinum is an attractive and extremely durable metal. It is often used to hold diamonds and is increasingly used to fashion jewelry by itself. It is relatively expensive because of the skill required to work with the metal. The prices of gold and platinum vary over time. As this book goes to press they are nearly equal in cost.

The most common marks for platinum are 900 PT, or 900 PLAT, or PT900, which indicate a metal of 90% purity. Some pieces bear markings like 900 Plat 100 Irid, which indicates a 90% platinum, 10% iridium alloy.

Be sure the item is stamped with its metal content and manufacturer, and that your sales receipt has platinum written in the description.

Buy Pearls

Pearls are a lovely piece of whimsy by Mother Nature, a shellfish's self-defense against an irritation within its armor. Natural pearls are created without human involvement. Cultured pearls are created by the injection of sand or a tiny bead into the shellfish. The resulting pearls are otherwise identical to natural ones.

As with diamonds, if you are shopping for a high-priced set of pearls, you should consider hiring an independent appraiser to help you determine true value. (See the Buy a Diamond section about appraisals, page 54.)

Experts assign pearl value on the basis of luster, surface, shape, color, size, and match.

- **Luster.** The assessment of a pearl's surface brilliance and the hard-to-quantify glow is its luster. A high-quality pearl has a bright luster. At the other end of the scale, pearls appear too white, dull, or chalky.
- **Surface.** The longer a pearl is cultivated in the oyster, the thicker the skin (also known as the nacre). Pearls with a thin skin may lose their luster through wear or as the result of exposure to strong perfume or hair spray. Blemishes on the surface of a pearl, including spots, bumps, pits, and cracks, reduce its value.
- **Shape.** Pearls come in various shapes, including round, oval, pear, and baroque (irregular). A perfectly round pearl is rare and generally most valuable.
- **Color.** Cultured pearls are in colors from white to off-pink to black.
- **Size.** A pearl's size is stated as the diameter in millimeters. The tiniest seed pearls can be as little as one millimeter, and large South Sea pearls as big as twenty millimeters—just over ¾ inches in diameter! The most popular size for cultured pearls is about seven millimeters (just over ¼ inches in diameter). Larger pearls, of equivalent quality, are worth considerably more than smaller ones.
- **Match.** If you're buying a strand of pearls, it's important that there be a good match of color, luster, size, shape, and surface. In some cases, pearl growers must search among several thousand oysters to find enough to match for a short strand.

Finally, there are many dozens of types of pearls. *Here are a few common varieties...*

- **Akoya.** These pearls, grown in pearl oysters in Japan and China, are the most common type used for necklaces. Colors are on the warm side.
- **Baroque.** A form of irregularly shaped pearl, baroque are also used in individual pieces of jewelry.

TIP

Land Pearls

A Mallorcan Pearl is one particular type of pearl-like object. It is not actually a pearl at all. They are manufactured from glass balls coated with pigmented lacquer.

That's not to say they are not pretty, but they have never seen the inside of an oyster.

- **Freshwater.** This form of pearl is cultivated in mussels in freshwater lakes and rivers in China, Japan, and the United States. They can be found in a wide range of shapes, including rice and spheres. They are more common and thus among the least expensive types of pearls.
- **Keshi or Seed.** These tiny pearls are as small as a grain of sand.
- **Mabe.** These half-round cultured pearls are grown inside oysters' shells rather than within their bodies. They are generally less valuable than round pearls, and are used in non-strand pieces, such as in rings, earrings, and brooches.
- **South Sea.** These large pearls come primarily from tropical and semi-tropical oysters in the South Seas and off Australia. They command premium prices because of their size. Colors are mostly in the range of silvery white to gold.
- **Tahitian Black.** This variety of large and relatively expensive pearls grow in black-lipped oysters in French Polynesia. And sure, they're black (or really, really dark gray, depending on how you look at it). But they can also be white, blue, and gold.

Finally, pay attention to the construction of jewelry that holds the pearls. Be sure any clasp is firmly attached and closes securely. On a strand, make sure the pearls are knotted individually to protect against loss if the strand breaks. Make sure the receipt from the jeweler fully describes the quality and source of the pearls.

Repair Your Jewelry

Yet another black hole for consumers—jewelry repair.

Let's start with just one troubling question: How do you know that the diamond in the ring you have come to retrieve is the same one you dropped off a week ago? It's not an easy question to answer.

If it is possible to make an appointment to have a repair done while you watch, that is one solution. Don't watch a ball game on the TV in the shop and try not to drink too much coffee while you wait. Keep your eyes on the prize.

Here are some alternatives if you must leave a piece behind…

• **For expensive pieces, have an independent appraiser examine the piece before it goes in for repair,** making notes on dimensions, cut, and any of the stone's notable external or internal features. Then, be prepared to return after repair to ask the appraiser's if you've been returned the same stone. Make arrangements—and know the cost—for this sort of double-check. The price should be less than twice the original inspection's cost.

• **Make certain you receive a receipt with your name and address from the jeweler,** stating in detail the quality and specifications of the item you have left behind. The receipt should also list the item's estimated value. If the jeweler's description of the item is different from what you believe it to be, put a halt to the exchange; one of you is wrong, and the issue should be resolved before you leave the item for repair. It is perfectly appropriate for the jeweler to perform tests to assure that any diamonds are real or that metals are properly classified.

• **Make certain the receipt itemizes exactly what repairs are to be done and the work's estimated cost.** It should also indicate when the item will be ready and give you a reasonable period of time in which to pick it up.

• **Make certain the store is properly insured against theft, loss, or damage.** Check with your own insurance agent about coverage of your own.

Know Where to Shop for Jewelry

My advice is to buy from the source with which you feel most comfortable. You might feel that a particular retail store offers the best quality and selection, or you might decide that you would rather purchase online from a major national jewelry company.

Either way, make sure you understand and accept the terms of sale. Before we were officially engaged, my girlfriend and I shopped in person at jewelry stores for her engagement and then for her wedding ring. Since then, across our four decades of marriage, I have bought many pieces of jewelry for my wife (not as many as she might like, I expect) from online companies without problem.

Most online jewelry shops offer a reasonable money-back guarantee, usually within 30 days, if the item you receive does not meet your expectations. Make sure you follow all instructions for returns. Retail shops are well aware they are in competition with online sellers, and most will come close on price and return policies.

In some situations, small local jewelry shops may offer good prices and customer service.

You may be tempted by the television and print ads for some of the national chains. Be aware that—as is the case with certain other industries—just a few major players control much of the market. As discussed, you must look for the best quality at the best price with the best warranty. Some brands or outlets may offer lower prices but if you are not comfortable with their customer service, consider shopping elsewhere.

• **Signet Jewelers,** a company based in the United Kingdom, has shops in United States, Canada, and elsewhere. Signet owns Kay Jewelers, Jared: The Galleria of Jewelry, J.B. Robinson, Marks & Morgan, Belden Jewelers, and a few other chains.

• **Zales Jewelers** began in 1924 in Texas and today has more than a thousand stores under various names including Zales, Zales Outlet, Gordon's Jewelers, Piercing Pagoda and, in Canada, Peoples Jewellers and Mappins Jewelers.

• **Ross-Simons,** very active in catalog and online sales as well as retail, began in Providence, Rhode Island, in 1952. They claim to send out 50 million catalogs per year, many of which seem to find their way to our home. The company also operates Sidney Thomas Jewelers for higher-end pieces.

• **The Goldenwest Diamond Corporation of Tustin, California,** is a major diamond importer and produces many of its own pieces sold at its stores, which are branded as The Jewelry Exchange.

CHAPTER 6

Going Grocery Shopping

We've all got to eat. We should do it well. Let's look at some of the inside secrets of the supermarket as well as take a guided tour of food labels and nutrition claims.

- **Make the most of grocery sales.**
- **Don't let your food spoil.**
- **Decide between fresh and frozen.**
- **Watch out for hidden price hikes.**
- **Create your own discount.**
- **Test your taste.**
- **Collect rain checks for sold-out items.**
- **Learn the true meaning of food-marketing terms.**
- **Send an SOS to food experts.**
- **Save on a cuppa Joe.**
- **Be a smart egg.**

Make the Most of Grocery Sales

In my family, we can go through several containers of breakfast cereal per week. And in case you hadn't noticed, those boxes of wheat, corn, and sugar have substantially risen in price. We also prefer bakery-style bread over mass-market loaves that taste about the same as the packaging in which they are delivered. And we eat a lot of chicken, fish, rice, and noodles.

And so we keep a close eye on supermarket flyers for sales. When something we consider a commodity goes on sale, we go out and pick up a few cases of cereal, six or eight loaves of bread, several cases of soda, and as many pounds of chicken or fish as we have room for. When fresh local corn is available, we might buy a few to test them out and then come back to purchase a bunch that we'll boil, strip from the cob, and pack away in the freezer. (However, as I'll explain in a moment, sometimes frozen food is of higher quality than "fresh" food that is weeks distant from the farm.)

We keep a large chest freezer in the basement, and it is home to the chicken, fish, bread, and other items. When turkeys go on sale in the run-up to Thanksgiving, we usually buy one for the holiday, and two or three wait their turn in the freezer for coming months. Here on our island, we can often get (relative) bargains on scallops, mussels, and lobster and they head for the freezer in raw or cooked form.

Here are some hints on making the most of sales…

• **Find out when the sale begins and, if the specials are particularly good, get there early.** Not all that long ago, back when Sunday newspapers were a big thing and came stuffed with colorful grocery ads, most supermarkets ran their sales beginning on that day. Nowadays, most supermarkets run their weekly sales starting on Wednesday or Thursday of each week. Saturday has become the busiest grocery shopping day of the week. As far as some of us are concerned, that is a great reason to shop on Thursday or Friday. I suggest going early in the morning or late in the day to avoid crowds and get the best pickings.

• **Shop early in the day for meat counter markdowns.** Many supermarkets or butchers start the day by taking a few dollars off meat and poultry that is at or near its sell-by date. The fact that you see markdowns on meat is a good sign, meaning that the butcher pays attention to the dates. That said, be careful not to buy products that are past the expiration date or that don't look fresh or have an inappropriate odor. And, be sure to cook and use the meat or poultry within a day of purchase. You can also cook and freeze marked-down meat. Once the food is cooked and frozen, you can keep it for an extended time.

• **Read the fine print carefully.** See if there are any limits on quantity, and be sure to exercise your rights to the fullest when the item is one you will use and can safely store. Take advantage of any rain checks offered if the store doesn't receive the special item or if someone else has cleaned them out. (Ask if the supermarket expects to be restocked with the item during the course of the sale.)

• **Don't buy more than you can use.** If you can freeze it, great. If you've got the room to store them before and after cooking, you'll get more for your money by purchasing the largest chickens and turkeys in the display case.

• **Experiment with store brands.** Almost always considerably less expensive than name brands, they are often manufactured by the same big-name companies. Check ingredients and the FDA nutrition labels for clues on identical products. On the other hand, some brands of packaged food are justly revered for high quality. Many consumers, myself included, make exceptions to buy certain brands of ketchup, mayonnaise, mustard, juice, peanut butter, and other products that are worth a bit more because of better ingredients.

• **Test a small quantity of something new before filling your pantry.** Brand name cheese in the gourmet section may be the same as, or very similar to, cheeses you'll find in the dairy section. Comparison shop within the store for the best price per pound.

• **Buy larger packages if you know you'll use it.** In most, but not all, cases larger cans or bottles cost less per ounce than smaller portions. Do the math or consult shelf labels that tell you the unit price. Watch out, though, for sales or special promotions that can sometimes make it cheaper to buy smaller packages.

Don't Let Your Food Spoil

Properly store nonperishable items such as paper goods, cleaning supplies, canned goods, bottled goods, and the like. Avoid damp places such as the basement and under the sink and hot spots such as the attic for most items. Use the backs of closets throughout the house.

Canned goods are generally good for one to two years, although there is always the possibility that they have been sitting on the store shelves for quite a while before you bring them home. Look for use-by dates. Buy the youngest cans you can find and don't plan on going too far beyond that date. The best place to store cans is in a relatively cool, dry place, such as in closets. Keep them away from heaters, stoves, and other warm spots.

Experts say most foods will last much longer than their stated shelf life, and in most cases spoiled food is obvious—an off odor, strange taste, discoloration, or a slimy appearance. I'm not recommending you eat food that sets off your personal alarm, but in most cases the worst that will happen will be temporary stomach distress. Do, though, avoid food that has mold on it, since the mold might produce toxins.

Some foods bear special spoil watch: "wet" deli meats (versus dry like salami), unpasteurized dairy products, and ready-to-eat refrigerated foods. Any of these can develop colonies of bacteria such as listeria, which can thrive even in refrigerated storage.

> **TIP**
>
> **Freezer Burn Funk**
>
> Food in the freezer stays tasty depending on what it is:
>
> - **Frozen meat generally keeps for six months to a year at zero degrees.** Keep an eye on chicken, though, since recent studies show that poultry products can lose flavor and texture after two months in the freezer. A package of frozen chicken parts is still safe to eat after two months, but it won't taste as good as fresh.
> - **Keep ground beef and processed food for fewer than six months.**
> - **Keep frozen fish for six to nine months.**
> - **Keep frozen vegetables for as long as a year.**

Decide Between Fresh and Frozen

It's hard to argue with an assertion that a fresh vegetable, hand selected from the farmer's market (or from your own plot) and properly cooked is the best way to dine. Or that buying a freshly filleted fish from the boat and delivered directly to your backyard barbecue is not an experience worthy of superlatives. A fresh cut of beef or lamb from the refrigerated display case of your local butcher would seem so…fresh.

But with a few exceptions, fresh food is not always the best deal (or the most nutritious).

Let's deconstruct my examples…

Mystery Date

What exactly does the date printed on most foods mean? There is no federal regulation that requires or defines the nature of this information; some state health or agriculture departments may have set regulations. In any case, you've got to read the inscription carefully.

Best if used by: This is a recommendation by the manufacturer or producer that indicates the point at which a product is expected to become stale or lose some flavor (for example, the expected point at which a loaf of bread will become stale).

Use by: The maker's recommendation for the date when a particular food item is at its last, best condition, which may or may not be same as "best if used by."

Expiration date: The point at which food's nutrients or texture are expected to be below standards, or a live product like milk or cheese may start to sour or otherwise change. You could think of this as the day after the use-by date.

Manufacture date: This is the date (and sometimes time and batch number) that a particular product was made. This information is useful when you call a company to complain about the quality of a product (and ask for a refund or coupons).

• **Fresh vegetables in a supermarket may have been picked weeks before and hundreds or thousands of miles away.** We have all grown used to seeing red tomatoes in the middle of winter and ripe bananas in places where a banana plant has never grown. The fact is that most vegetables and fruits are picked well before they reach ripeness (and peak levels of vitamins and other nutrients) and delivered far from the fields.

Contrast that with frozen vegetables, which are often picked when they are fully ripe and quickly parboiled and packaged. Nutritionists say that most frozen vegetables are equal to or superior to fresh vegetables when they are cooked properly. To get the most out of vegetables, steam them with as little water as possible and don't overcook them. Canned vegetables, with a few exceptions like tomatoes and pumpkins, lose much of their nutrient value in the packaging process and also are imbued with salt as a preservative.

• **How long has the "fresh" fish in the cooler been waiting for your arrival?** Was it caught several weeks ago and brought to the market in a refrigerated truck?

Think: How fresh is a tuna fillet in Indiana? On the other hand, most frozen fish is processed and flash frozen within hours of being brought in by fishing fleets or even frozen aboard factory ships out at sea. Again, unless you can go down to the docks and buy fish directly from the boat, frozen is likely in better condition and better for you than most offerings in your grocer's refrigerator section.

• **The same principle applies to "fresh" meat in the supermarket or at a butcher's shop.** You are not likely to buy meat that was on the hoof a few hours ago unless you live on a farm. Frozen meat, like frozen fish, is usually made very cold right at the processing plant. Frozen ground beef is also usually produced from very fresh meat. That is not the case for unfrozen ground meat packaged at the grocery, which may have been put through the grinder at the supermarket using meat that was at the stockyard weeks ago. Some fancy meats are aged under special conditions, a process that is supposed to tenderize them. Aged steaks are pricey and often hard to find on the retail level.

- **Buying a "fresh" turkey around Thanksgiving brings you the same problem; how long ago was the tom or hen running free?**

Now, with all this said: If you live near a farm and can buy fresh and ripe vegetables and fruit in season, go forth and shop. Even better is a little garden of your very own. That can be very economical, especially if you share seeds with others. (Check your local library for a seed collection.) The same goes for fresh fish for those of us who live near the water; buy from the boat and cook it immediately.

A Bum Steer

Over the years, some supermarkets have gotten into trouble by repackaging old perishables with new dates or by grinding up old cuts of steak into hamburger with a new sell-by date.

Another trick: Putting the older, grayer side of meat face down in packaging.

A related trick: Using reddish lighting in the meat section to improve the appearance of products there.

Don't hesitate to bring back to the store food you find unacceptable. Hold on to receipts and packaging when you can, and visit the customer service or manager's office with the evidence.

Watch Out for Hidden Price Hikes

When is a pound of pasta not worth its weight at the checkout counter? When the package has been stealthily downsized. I'm looking right now at two packages of pasta from the same major manufacturer. They are the same width and height, and only when you look closely do you see that one box has slightly less depth. And there on the front, visible but not exactly flashing a warning size is this: One box contains 16 ounces and the other 12 ounces by weight.

We've seen what was once a traditional ice cream package of a half-gallon (64 ounces) magically reappear as a 56-ounce or even 48-ounce container. Some changes have been more subtle, such as a reduced can of beans or sauce from 24 ounces to 23 ounces. Another way to do the same thing is to reduce the quantity—35 sticks of licorice in a package instead of 36. Now, there is nothing wrong with a manufacturer packaging a smaller size. The problem comes when the lesser offering is priced as if it were larger.

And there are insidious small changes like this one: A bag of packaged baked goods in our closet has the same number of cookies as the one we brought previously but we noticed that the package weight had shrunk from 12 ounces to 11.5 ounces, a sneaky price increase of 4.3% or about the equivalent of one fewer cookie in the bag.

The only protection against this particular form of pocket picking is to pay close attention to the quantity or weight of packaged food. If you're lucky, you will find an accurate calculation of prices per ounce. And look closely. I have seen hundreds of instances where the supermarket calculation is incorrect, often as the result of someone misunderstanding the difference between fluid ounces (32 to the quart) and ounces that measure weight (16 to the pound).

That's one area in which the metric system improves on the American systems of weight and measure; metric measures differentiate between grams for weight and liters for capacity.

Create Your Own Discount

Years ago we found an unusual packaged salad dressing, an Asian sesame-soy concoction, that was only occasionally available in markets. We bought them when we could find them. And then one day I was studying the packaging and saw that the manufacturer listed a phone number for comments and questions. My comment was: "We like your product." My question was: "Can we buy a box? At a discount, of course." A few weeks later, UPS showed up at our home with a case of 48 packets. The price, including shipping, was about half the price we would have paid at the market for that number of items.

But there's no reason to stop there. If you are planning a big party or wedding reception, visit your neighborhood liquor store and inquire about a quantity discount on wine and spirits. Our local liquor store gave us a discount off the top on our order and also agreed to buy back any unopened and undamaged bottles. In some states, sales of wine and liquor are so tightly regulated that this sort of special price might not be permitted. But they might be able to provide the equivalent of a discount by offering a special price on other items they sell.

Ask the supermarket about quantity prices on cases of soda and other packaged goods, and for a discount on a few dozen lobsters, steaks, or other party necessities. You will probably get a better deal if you place your order a few weeks ahead of time. It allows the store to ensure it is fully stocked. And remember that if one store says no, another might say yes. In my experience, you will receive a nice discount if you purchase by the case, crate, or whatever is the full amount the grocer gets right off the truck.

Test Your Taste

Does someone in your family insist on afflicting the family budget with a particular brand of ketchup, peanut butter, ice cream, or jam? In some cases, they may have a really good reason for their preference, but sometimes stubbornness gets in the way.

You can make a game out of it and possibly save some money along the way. Set up a family "blind taste test." Buy a few samples of particular types of food, including any family favorites as well as good-quality store brands and products by other makers, and prepare them in the same way. Keep track of which is which, and then challenge your picky eaters to choose their favorites. Speaking strictly for myself, I have found that brand-name ketchup and mustard are usually superior to no-name products, although some store brands are quite good. The worst that could happen following a taste test is no change to your budget.

The best: a change for the better in quality, taste, and perhaps price.

In recent years, many major supermarket chains have introduced their own high-quality food brands; the not-so-deep secret is that many of these items are manufactured by the same companies that sell the famous names.

Collect Rain Checks for Sold-Out Items

Super-Duper Sugar-Frosted Oatios with Walnut Clusters: $1.29 for a four-pound megabox! It's an offer to make a shopper's heart race—but, oh, the disappointment when you arrive to find a "sold out" sign on the empty shelf.

Here's the scoop: Under the unavailability clause that is part of the Federal Trade Commission (FTC) Retail Food Store Advertising and Marketing Practices Rule, stores that run out of advertised items must offer rain checks allowing purchase of the item at a later time, offer comparable products at comparable prices, or offer other compensation at least equal to the advertised value. The truck-sized loophole in the rule, though, is that if the ad clearly states that "quantities are limited" or advises that "products are available only at some stores," no rain check is required.

If your Oatios are out of stock, march up to the customer service counter and ask for an accommodation. Tell the manager that the FTC sent you.

Learn the True Meaning of Food-Marketing Terms

Free! Light! Reduced! Low fat! Suddenly, less is more in food marketing as most of us try to reduce our weight or maintain our health through careful eating.

The federal Food and Drug Administration, which sets the standards for the Nutrition Facts tag on packaged foods, has also assigned a set of quantities to qualitative labels. *Here are some of the terms, as they apply to the specified serving size for each product...*

Calorie-free. Fewer than 5 calories per serving.

Low calorie. Fewer than 40 calories per serving.

Reduced calorie. At least 25% fewer calories than a standard formulation.

Fat free. Less than .5 grams total fat per serving.

Saturated fat-free. Less than .5 grams saturated fat per serving.

Low fat. Fewer than 3 grams total fat per serving.

Low saturated fat. Less than 1 gram saturated fat per serving.

Reduced fat. At least 25% less total fat, or at least 25% less saturated fat, than a standard formulation.

Cholesterol-free. Less than 2 mg per serving.

Low cholesterol. Less than 20 mg per serving.

Sodium-free/Salt-free. Fewer than 5 mg per serving.

Very low sodium/salt. Fewer than 35 mg per serving.

Serving Size Matters

Details	
Serving Size: 32 grams (2 tbsp)	
Calories	190
Calories from Fat	140
Total Fat	16g
Saturated Fat	2g
Trans Fat	0g
Polyunsaturated Fat	5g
Monounsaturated Fat	8g
Sodium	100mg
Total Carbohydrates	7g
Protein	8g

In my opinion, one of the best things our Washington, DC, bureaucrats have provided for the national defense is the Nutrition Facts label on food. It is also, potentially, one of the most misleading and misunderstood indicators in our consumer society.

Here's an example: I love peanut butter (all-natural, no sugar, super chunky). I also try to safeguard my health by managing fat and caloric intake. The nutrition facts for my favorite brand, Teddie's (a New England treasure whose ingredients consist of peanuts and salt and nothing more, or peanuts alone for the no-salt version), can be seen in the box on the left.

These numbers don't sound too bad for one meal, but what exactly are they measuring? Among the most significant set of numbers on the label, and often overlooked, is the *serving size* and *servings per container*. These details put all the other numbers in proper context. Be sure you examine closely the portion size and see how it relates to your real intake of the product.

In the instance of the peanut butter, the listed serving is two tablespoons. Alas, if I were going to splurge on peanut butter, I'd probably not be willing to stop at just two tablespoons of the stuff. Note that peanut butter does not contain cholesterol since it is not derived from an animal product.

Look at the same label with the additional information of the Food and Drug Administration's recommended daily allowance and other sources for each significant element.

Macronutrient	This Product	Recommended Daily Allowance (Male Adult–Female Adult)	Percent of Recommended Daily Allowance in Manufacturer's Suggested Serving
Calories	190	1600 to 2000	12% or 11%
Calories from Fat	140	Less than 20% to 35% of total calories	9% or 7%
Total Fat	16g	Less than 65 to 80g	24% to 20%
Saturated Fat	2g	Less than 20 to 25g	10% to 8%
Trans Fat	0g	Limit your intake	Less is best
Polyunsaturated Fat	5g	160 to 200g	3% to 2%
Monounsaturated Fat	8g	160 to 200g	5% to 4%
Cholesterol	0g	300mg	None
Sodium	100mg	2400g	4%
Total Carbohydrates	7g	300 to 375g	2%
Protein	8g	46 to 56g	17% to 14%

What can we learn from this one example? Good-quality peanut butter is a healthy food, with a few warning flags—five tablespoons would represent 50% of your recommended total fat allowance for the day—and an unadulterated product that does not include trans fat is a great thing.

Here's another nutty example: M&Ms with peanuts are listed at 220 calories, 17% of total fat, and 22% of saturated fat for a serving size of a quarter of a cup. I measured it. That's about 14 pieces of candy. I don't know about you, but my hand would still be heading back for the candy dish after that small amount.

In a nutshell (sorry): Think about the quantity of food you eat and where a particular product fits in that amount. Keep fat below 30% of your total daily caloric intake. And remember that even a fat-free food can still be high in sugar and calories.

Nutrition recommendations change regularly based on new research, and not every person has the same metabolism and other factors. Consult with a doctor or a nutritionist to review your diet from time to time. Many health insurance plans cover some or all of the cost for such advice.

Low sodium/salt. Fewer than 140 mg per serving.

Sugar-free. Less than .5 mg per serving.

Reduced sugar. At least 25% less sugars than a standard formulation.

Light/lite. At least 50% or less of fat, sodium, or sugar found in a standard formulation.

Send an SOS to Food Experts

Help! I left the plastic bag of giblets inside the turkey while it cooked. (Yes, I did that once; hasn't everyone?) Many major food suppliers as well as federal agencies operate help lines for shoppers and cooks. Start by consulting the packaging to see if the company offers assistance. Here are a few I've collected.

Betty Crocker	Betty (and her assistants) are available year-round on weekdays to help with products.	BettyCrocker.com	888-275-2388 or 800-446-1898
Butterball Turkey Talk-Line	Free advice on preparing, cooking, and carving your bird for the holidays, year-round.	Butterball.com	800-288-8372
Empire Kosher	Advice on poultry and packaged products. Year-round weekdays; closed on Jewish and secular holidays.	EmpireKosher.com	800-367-4734
Land O'Lakes Holiday Bakeline	Advice on baking, available during the Thanksgiving to Christmas holidays.	LandOLakes.com	800-782-9606
USDA Meat and Poultry Line	Experts to answer questions about safe food handling and labeling, open weekdays and on Thanksgiving.	FSIS.usda.gov	888-674-6854

Save on a Cuppa Joe

They grow an awful lot of coffee in Brazil (and Africa and other hot climes). And we drink an awful lot of the stuff over here. That's why a bad growing season in the fields can have a fairly significant effect at Starbuck's or your neighborhood supermarket.

Here are some ways to spend less when you feed your coffee jag...

- **Buy in quantity.** Definitely don't buy it by the cup at the local coffee shop every morning. When you see a good price at the local store, stock up. Unopened cans or vacuum-packed plastic or foil bricks of ground coffee should keep for at least two years, while you can store bags of beans in the freezer for as long as six months.
- **Use frugally.** If you don't like to reheat leftover coffee, use a Thermos. You can experiment with reusing coffee grounds by mixing them half and half with fresh grounds.

- **Buy a refillable filter.** If you use a single-cup or other form of coffee machine like a Keurig or Nespresso coffee maker, skip the expensive single pods. Buy a reusable filter and fill it with regular coffee.

Be a Smart Egg

What's the difference between large, extra-large, and jumbo eggs? About 10% in size from one to the other, according to industry grading practice. Therefore, for example, if extra-large eggs are more than 10% higher in price than large eggs, your store is offering you a bad deal.

In New England and some other places in the United States, the local preference is for brown eggs over white. There's nothing wrong with that, although experts say there is no appreciable difference between what's inside. Brown eggs are generally a bit more expensive in New England because the chickens that lay them are larger than those producing white eggs, and hence the eggs are bigger. Now, if you are looking for brown eggs in a place where they are less common, you will probably have to pay a premium because of their relative scarcity—but don't judge an egg by its shell. Oh, and in New England we call water fountains "bubblers" and put "jimmies," not sprinkles, on ice cream cones.

Finally, if you are not sure whether your eggs are still good, gently put one into a bowl of cold water. If it floats, pitch it. If it sinks to the bottom, you should be safe eating it.

CHAPTER 7

Planning for Health and Beauty Care

Your body is most likely the most expensive machine you own. You've got to maintain it for a lifetime. This chapter offers strategies for choosing a doctor, being a savvy prescription drug consumer, and saving money within the bounds of your medical insurance. Then we look at some common accessories for your machine: toothbrushes, eyeglasses, contact lenses, hearing aids, and gym memberships.

- **Handle your health care.**
- **Switch to an electric toothbrush.**
- **See your way to eyewear discounts.**
- **Listen to an independent expert on hearing aids.**
- **Go health clubbing.**

Handle Your Health Care

Health care is one of the largest expenses in the US, about 20% of the Gross Domestic Product. Health care costs include visits to doctors, insurance, prescriptions, medical procedures, corrections (such as eyeglasses and hearing aids), and prevention. The following sections address each of these items in an effort to combine savings with good, sound care. None of this information supersedes a doctor's advice. Keep in mind as well that all forms of medical insurance—private, employer-provided, Medicare, Medicaid, and other programs—face change in coming months and years.

Find Dr. Right

What characteristics do you want your doctor to possess? Here's what I want in a doctor: someone who is well educated...up-to-date on the latest medical tests, procedures, pharmaceuticals, and other treatments...and is willing and able to communicate with and inform me. Assuming you would like the same, how do you find such a doctor? Ask your friends and coworkers for references. If you know a good surgeon, ask for the name of a general practitioner he or she respects.

Other good sources of information: a pharmacist you trust, a school nurse, and even a good insurance agent. You want to talk to someone who talks to lots of other people about health care.

Although I am more than a little skeptical about whether they reveal a true representation, you can check various social media and consumer rating sites for praise or complaints about doctors.

Here are a few to look at…

- **HealthCareReviews.com**
- **HealthGrades.com**
- **RateMDs.com**

The problem with these sites is that they are about as accurate as a TV or radio show's "instant poll" on politics or any other topic. They are *not* scientifically accurate polls. Only someone who chooses to respond is represented in the ratings. Is this someone with an ax to grind, a personal relationship to the doctor, or even someone enlisted by the doctor or hospital in an effort to boost ratings?

In most states, you can request information from a state medical licensing board about a doctor's education, certain professional accomplishments including published research, whether he or she has been sued for malpractice (and sometimes the results), and any state board disciplinary actions. Many of these sites also explain which private medical plans, as well as Medicare and Medicaid, the doctor accepts for payment. You should be able to find some of the same information by visiting your medical insurance provider's website. I checked the Massachusetts board's listing for my personal doctor and reacquainted myself with his professional credentials, history, and academic studies (he's a world-class expert on certain forms of tick-borne illness, which is very appropriate for our very rural area), and I reaffirmed that he has no criminal convictions or health-care facility or state board disciplinary actions. Every state has some form of this sort of report, although some of the specific information categories may vary.

Other websites allow you to check for malpractice suits against doctors. That may or may not provide useful information. Anyone can file a lawsuit. That does not mean the accusation is correct. Nearly all doctors have faced claims or complaints across a lengthy career. Disciplinary action by the state board—for medical, financial, or other violations—is certainly something in need of explanation (or a reason to find a different doctor). Per the website for the Board of Registration in Medicine in Massachusetts, some medical specialties are more likely than others to be the subject of litigation. But they also point out that malpractice claims are not necessarily a predictor of the quality of service.

According to the *New England Journal of Medicine*, about 7% of all physicians face a malpractice claim in any particular year, and over a career, nearly half of all 45-year-old doctors have faced a lawsuit, and as much as 90% of 65-year-old physicians have been in that position. Surgeons and obstetricians/gynecologists have the highest percentage of lawsuits. This does not mean that all lawsuits result in a finding against the doctor. In rough terms, about two out of three lawsuits do not result in payment of an indemnity claim.

Hiring a Doctor

When you are deciding on a doctor, determine the criteria most important to you. You'll want a doctor or medical group that accepts the form of health insurance you have and is within a reasonable distance. It may be valuable to choose a physician who is affiliated with a particular hospital or special care facility. Speaking for myself, I add one more requirement: I want a doctor who is willing and able to spend a reasonable amount of time explaining medical treatments, medicines, and conditions. Put the other way, I do not want a doctor who makes decisions without explanations.

Once you come up with a list of doctors who meet your criteria, try one or both of the following for your top candidates...

- **Call the office and ask for an appointment to meet the doctor.** If you have a particular medical problem or question, that might make it easier to arrange such a session. A doctor who fulfills my criteria would agree to a brief get-to-know-you meeting without involving insurance or private payment. If the office insists on a billable session, that may or may not tell you something. The bottom line: Your goal is to gauge his or her personality and ability to communicate. Does the doctor see you as a person or just a set of symptoms? I know one doctor who resists prescribing medications without a certainty for their need; another doctor of my acquaintance is ready, willing, and able to try (on his patients) just about any medication, anytime. Which is the better physician? Speaking for myself, I go for the one who is willing to explain assessments and answer my questions.
- **Schedule an annual physical, which is ordinarily covered by health plans.** Make sure that your visit will include a meeting with the doctor, not just physician's assistants or nurses.
- **Choosing a specialist is sometimes a more complex task.** Here, I recommend beginning with your personal physician. Don't just ask for a referral to a specialist. Ask your doctor's opinion and recommendation. If you have a good relationship with your primary care physician, you should be able to get a useful recommendation.

And most importantly, do not hesitate to change doctors if you are unhappy with the treatment you receive or the way the office works. The federal Health Insurance Portability and Accountability Act (HIPAA) requires that doctors and health-care facilities allow you to transfer your medical records. Some states allow a reasonable fee for copying or transmitting records, but not every doctor or facility will impose it.

About Medical Practices

In the past, a doctor would hang up a shingle and conduct a medical practice as an individual. These solo practitioners still exist, but they are less common. Today, you are much more likely to find groups of doctors, or those who are employees of hospitals or large health-care facilities. In some ways, this is a good thing for the doctors (since they may be able to concentrate more on quality of care rather than the business management). For consumers, it may or may not be an improvement. A large group may offer more expertise and options, but a solo practitioner may know you, your family, and your history on a personal level.

Here are a few important acronyms...

- **PPO.** A *preferred-provider organization* is usually as defined by an insurance company. A particular policy may offer lower costs or better coverage if you use a doctor or medical facility that is within a PPO. In most cases, you can still see a doctor who is "out of network," but you will most likely receive less reimbursement.
- **HMO.** A *health maintenance organization* is similar to a PPO, except that the doctors and health-care facilities usually organize as a group and then contract with a health insurance company to provide services at negotiated (and discounted) rates. An HMO may offer its own advanced testing equipment like CAT or MRI scanners, and blood analysis.
- **PCP.** If you engage in an HMO contract with an insurance company, you will usually be required to select a PCP (a *primary care physician*) who serves as the gatekeeper or manager of your care. Some HMOs are so large that you have no guarantee of seeing the same doctor each time you come in for care.

And finally, a hospital company may offer its own health insurance plan, offering better rates and coverage to clients who use doctors and facilities within their network.

Doctors and Insurance Plans

Before you sign up for medical insurance, consult online resources or call their help desks. Learn about where you can use your coverage.

Make sure you also understand a particular plan's distinction between in-network and out-of-network doctors and hospitals. If you live in a place with limited resources, or if you travel a great deal, it may be to your advantage to pay for a plan that allows you to use doctors out of your area. Ask about coverage for international travel as well.

There has been an increase in recent years for *boutique* or *concierge* doctors, who charge patients directly for most services, claiming to offer a higher level of care for those who can afford it. They may accept insurance for certain services, or coordinate with specialists who accept insurance coverage for things like procedures and surgery.

Medicare

In general, doctors are not required to participate in any insurance plans, including Medicare (coverage available to all American citizens 65 or older or those with certain specific medical conditions or disabilities) or Medicaid (a federal plan, administered by states in most instances, for low-income citizens or permanent residents). And doctors can choose to accept or not accept insurance coverage from particular private health care plans.

Nearly all hospitals accept Medicare and most accept major insurance plans.

Medicare and Medicaid do not limit you to doctors in your area, but the doctors or medical facility must accept those programs for you to receive full coverage under those plans. In some situations, you can receive care from a medical facility that does not accept those plans and later submit receipts for payments you have made in hopes of being reimbursed. Check with the U.S. Centers for Medicare & Medicaid Services (at CMS.gov or 1-800-633-4227) for advice. Some

Medicare supplemental plans, widely known as Medigap, may bridge holes in coverage; Medigap policies are sold by private insurance companies to work with the federal Medicare plans.

Medicare recipients should seriously consider purchase of a Medigap policy, which is available in several levels of coverage. And, similarly, Medicare Part D plans, which cover much of the expense of prescription medications, are defined by federal law but differ one from another on things like their formulary (the categorization of drugs into differently priced tiers) and on certain additional features that might be offered.

Some plans, including certain levels of Medicare Supplement (Medigap) coverage, offer limited coverage when you are out of the country.

Supplemental insurance plans pay most or all of certain copays and overages. You'll find information about these Medigap plans on the Medicare website as well as websites from the insurance providers themselves. The essential elements of the plans are set by federal regulators, but some plans may offer lower prices than others or additional features.

Similarly, for Medicare Part D plans, you can visit websites or call insurance companies and discuss the specific medications you are currently taking. You can also seek assistance from some pharmacy chains. Some plans will be more suitable for you than others.

Shop for Better Prices

The government (for Medicare and Medicaid), as well as private insurance companies, generally negotiate set prices for most office visits, tests, and procedures. Your medical policy may have a substantial deductible or copay that you have to pay for appointments, many types of surgical procedures or tests. If you have a serious or complex illness or injury, you will go through that amount of patient responsibility pretty quickly. But in certain circumstances it would be to your benefit to try and keep your medical bills as low as possible.

For example, be sure you understand the billing cycles for your insurance. If it is near the end of the year and you have reached your deductible level, it may make sense to schedule procedures, tests, and other billable expenses before your insurance plan resets the counter to $0 when the new year begins. On the other hand—again near the end of the year—if you are facing a large expense it might make sense to schedule the procedure for a few days into the next year to enable you to hit the new year's deductible more quickly and maximize that year's benefits.

The same applies for prescription coverage. Study your plan and consult your insurance company to make sure you understand the timing. It is not an improper question to ask your insurance company about the best time to undergo a non-critical procedure or place an order for medication.

Nothing I said in the previous two paragraphs should ever be a consideration if you are facing a critical illness or condition. In that case, seek the advice of your physician about scheduling.

Don't be afraid to inquire about the charges for medical procedures at various specialists. If you have a good relationship with your primary care physician, ask for advice on keeping costs down. For instance, a capable plastic surgeon may do a fine job in removing a mole on the face and leaving no visible scar, and charge considerably top rates. But if the procedure is in a place less exposed to public view, a general practitioner or dermatologist might be appropriate and less costly.

Some doctors are completely oblivious to the cost of procedures or medications. One dermatologist I visited—quite competent in her work—was shocked when I told her the ointment she had prescribed cost more than $150 even with my insurance plan. To her credit, she did some research and came back with an alternate prescription that was slightly less painful to the wallet.

As far as the cost of procedures and medical equipment, you don't want to put your health at risk by seeking a less-effective cure, but there is no reason not to ask a doctor if there are ways to reduce costs. As an example, general anesthesia is almost always much costlier than local anesthesia. On the other hand—assuming your doctor feels it is not a risk to your health—you might prefer to sleep through it all.

Discuss your options for the procedure that lies ahead of you. If your doctor or surgeon won't spend the time to speak with you, you may have the wrong specialist on your case.

Buy Prescription Drugs Frugally

For many of us, prescription drugs are an essential but painful monthly expense. Nationwide, prescription drugs are a more than $425-billion-per-year industry. The full cost for a course of antibiotics can be shocking, but so too is the annual bill for maintenance drugs for conditions such as high cholesterol, high blood pressure, and arthritis.

Later in this section, I discuss prescription drug coverage available from some medical insurance plans.

If you're paying all or part of the bill for your medications, you can do these important things to reduce the amount of money you spend...

- **Annually audit your medications with your family doctor.** Ask if the medications you take are still appropriate (and if appropriate, at the same dosages). Are there any less-costly therapeutic equivalents? (*Therapeutic equivalents* are not identical to your current prescription, but accomplish the same effect.) While you're talking with your doctor, ask if there are any samples of medication available. Drug companies regularly deliver samples to doctors in hopes they will prescribe them to patients. (*Warning*: Some critics say free sample distribution to doctors leads to patients using more-expensive pharmaceuticals, but it is also a wise way to find out if a new drug works for you or if it causes troublesome side effects.)

- **Ask your pharmacist about ways to reduce costs.** The pharmacist may be aware of generic or therapeutic equivalents your doctor may not know about.

- **Consider ordering by mail or online.** Consult your insurance company or Medicare Part D provider to find out about saving money by ordering long-term maintenance drugs by mail or online. Your insurance company may operate its own online pharmacy, which generally offers the best prices. You will also find that major pharmacy chains will fulfill prescriptions sent them online or by postal mail. Find the full details on using these services and then advise your doctor how you would like your prescriptions fulfilled; most doctors' offices are now equipped to send secure email or fax prescriptions. Certain drugs, including controlled substances like some painkillers and sedatives, require signed paper prescriptions.

I mentioned online pharmacies as good places for maintenance drugs. A *maintenance drug* is one you expect to take regularly, for a long period of time. Prime examples are statin drugs, which reduce certain forms of unhealthy cholesterol, thyroid hormone drugs, and medication to control high blood pressure. If you need an antibiotic to knock out a raging infection, it does not make economic or medical sense to wait a week or so for a pill container to arrive in the mail.

- **Call or visit retail pharmacies and online pharmacies and ask to compare prices.** Some drugstore chains have lower prices, and some offer especially low prices on certain commonly prescribed drugs as an effort to bring customers into the store. As an example, Target and Walmart offer common drugs at deep discount. Prices are usually the same across a chain pharmacy outlet (such as CVS or Walgreen's) but there is no certainty. If the price seems high, take the time to make a few phone calls to check prices. Realize, too, that there is a major consolidation of pharmacy providers. CVS has taken over the pharmacy service at Target stores, and Walgreens—as this book goes to press—is in the process of taking over Rite Aid pharmacy operations.
- **Explore discount prescription cards and programs.** Most of these cards deliver reduced prices based on pre-negotiated rates, and many do not charge membership fees. (Note that in some states, regulations may reduce the value of discount programs.) They make their money from a small transaction fee paid by the pharmacy for bringing the customer to the store. *Here are a few to explore...*
    - GoodRx.com
    - MyRxSaver.com
    - EasyDrugCard.com

Make sure the pharmacy calculates the prescription price two ways—using the discount card as well as your insurance company plan if you have one. Take the lower price. In some instances, you can get significant savings on some medications using these cards, and other times you may save more by using your regular insurance card.

- **Push the boundaries.** My work requires me to travel to some of the far corners of the planet, and with that comes the need for some obscure immunizations and prophylactic medications. When I needed a Yellow Fever immunization recently, I found that Medicare Part D does not pay for that medication. But a little bit of research turned up the fact that a neighboring county's health department—home to a large immigrant community—had a program offering that immunization and a few other strange ones (Japanese Encephalitis, anyone?) at a slightly discounted price. You can find information about things like this through the website of the Center for Disease Control. You can also contact the makers of specialized drugs and ask if they have cost-reduction plans for their products.

In another example, I wanted to get the shingles (herpes zoster) immunization but my rural doctor's office and pharmacies did not stock the medicine. When I contacted the online pharmacy that my insurance company used, they informed me that they had a special program that allowed for shipping the vaccine directly to me by overnight express in a Styrofoam case with ice packs. I received the vaccine and stored it overnight in our refrigerator before delivering it to my doctor for administration. In the end, the cost to me was zero. And my doctor learned how to get this vaccine (and others) for his patients.

Brand-Name, Equivalent, and Generic Drugs

Are you the sort of person who insists on buying Diamond Crystal salt or Domino sugar, or are you perfectly happy buying store-brand salt or sugar in a plain paper bag and carrying the change home in your pocket? Salt is salt, just as acetaminophen is Tylenol and diazepam is Valium. When a new drug is FDA-approved, the company that develops it is given an exclusive right to market it under a brand name for a period of time. When that patent expires, other drug makers—and the original developer—can sell it under a generic name. Generic prescription drugs have the same active ingredients, strength, and dosage form as brand-name counterparts. Therefore, if your prescription is for a new and suddenly popular drug, you can expect to pay a high price (either out-of-pocket or in the form of a higher co-pay from your insurance company) for a brand name.

About half the drugs on the market are available generically. Most insurance companies require doctors to instruct a pharmacy to use a generic when available, unless there is a specific need for a brand name. In some states, pharmacists are similarly required to offer a lower-cost generic if one is available. There are several major international makers of generic pharmaceuticals and over-the-counter drugs. The same company may sell products under its own name as well the name of major drugstores or other retail operations. As this book goes to press, the largest maker of generic drugs is Teva, an Israeli conglomerate now with facilities around the world. In close second place is Sandoz, which is a division of Sweden's Novartis. Both companies make billions of dollars annually.

Nearly all prescription-drug insurance plans use a *formulary,* which classifies drugs into several pricing tiers, and in some instances may disallow certain pharmaceuticals without special permission from the insurance company. There may be a significant difference in price between the lowest and highest tier. If your doctor prescribes a drug from a high tier, ask if there is a therapeutic equivalent that falls into a less-expensive category.

When you shop for over-the-counter drugs like headache relief, cold and allergy treatments, and stomach remedies, you can easily compare the ingredients (and their strength) in a generic or store label to the brand names. Check the expiration dates to make sure that one or the other is not significantly out of date.

Pharmacists must adhere to government regulations regarding expiration dates for drugs they dispense, and drugstores should also be checking the expiration or sell-by date for over-the-counter medications. But be your own advocate and check the dates yourself.

Most medications are still usable well after their stated expiration date, although some may have a reduced potency. If you are taking a medication for treatment of a life-threatening disease or condition, this is *not* the place to cut corners. On the other hand, you are generally not putting yourself at risk by stretching expiration dates a bit.

Ask your doctor or pharmacist for guidance here.

Use an Online or Mail-Order Pharmacy

Online and mail-order pharmacy services promise significant discounts because they can avoid the expense of a brick-and-mortar store. Most of the sites will go to great lengths to assist you on renewals, offering to call your doctor's office on your behalf to obtain renewals of prescriptions you have had filled previously.

Although it is not required, the U.S. Food & Drug Administration and other groups recommend you look for the VIPPS (Verified Internet Pharmacy Practice Sites) seal on the website of online pharmacies. This seal means that the online pharmacy has met state licensure standards as well as other criteria of the National Association of Boards of Pharmacy.

Before you consider ordering from an online or mail-order pharmacy, be sure you know how much you would be charged at your neighborhood drug store. Don't hesitate to ask the pharmacist to give you the best price he or she can, with the promise of a long-term commitment. This is not the time to be shy. Tell the pharmacist you're looking to save money and are considering placing an order with a mail-order or online pharmacy. You might be surprised to find that your local pharmacy may be able to reduce the price or match any offer you receive from another source. This applies to large retail chains, as well. As I said—the smart retailer knows it's better to make a smaller profit than none at all.

Before you call a mail-order pharmacy or visit a website, have this information...

- **If you pay the full cost, shop carefully.** If you don't have an insurance policy that covers prescription drugs, focus on getting the best price wherever you find it. Look into using one of the non-insurance prescription price cards I mentioned earlier. One example is GoodRx (GoodRx.com).

- **Consider the price advantage of an online pharmacy.** If you have prescription coverage from your health insurance company find out if it has an associated online pharmacy, or if it will work with any online pharmacy up to the amount of any co-pay for which you may be responsible. Don't hesitate to contact two or more online pharmacies to compare prices. One online pharmacy may be offering a specially reduced price on a few popular drugs while charging full rates on less common orders. Some prescription insurance plans have a relationship with a preferred online provider. In most instances, you are still free to shop with other providers. Just be sure they take your insurance.

Your Friendly Pharmacist

Every pharmacist and doctor should maintain a record of all the medications you are currently taking, as well as information about any allergies or adverse reactions you had in the past. The goal is to avoid unhealthy interactions between certain medications and to avoid triggering a reaction.

If your pharmacist does not ask you about other medications and allergies, bring up the subject yourself—and consider whether the pharmacy you are dealing with is protecting you properly. If you do use multiple pharmacies to save on individual prescription costs or for convenience when you are away from home, make sure each pharmacy has a complete list of your medications.

TIP

Free 'Script Shipping

Most online pharmacies will ship prescriptions for free, although it may take several days to a week for them to arrive. You usually pay extra for express shipping. Be sure to include that cost in your comparison.

• **Consider when a local pharmacy makes sense.** Immediacy is one advantage of dealing with a neighborhood drugstore. In most cases, you should be able to obtain a prescription within hours of your doctor's orders, and you should also be able to obtain refills on the day you need them. Online services usually require several days or more to process and ship your order. Don't order from them if you need to start using a prescription immediately.

Virtual Doctors and Foreign Sources

Some websites will sell you a prescription drug without requiring you to visit a doctor. Instead, you'll consult with one of their doctors over the phone or via the internet. This is possible because state and federal law permit doctors to prescribe most—but not all—drugs without actually meeting with a patient. Of course, it should be obvious that you're not going to receive a medical examination over the phone line, although you *will* receive a bill for $50 to $100. These services often prescribe medications like Viagra, helping patients who might otherwise be too embarrassed to visit a doctor's office. On the other hand, that drug is one that brings with it some very serious health threats for certain patients. Few, if any, insurance companies will reimburse fees paid to a virtual doctor.

Another nonstandard way to obtain medication at a reduced price is to buy from foreign sources. Travelers to Mexico and some other places around the world are used to seeing drug stores offering a wide range of brand-name and generic drugs without needing a prescription. In general, Mexico and certain other countries allow pharmacists to dispense certain classes of antibiotics, maintenance drugs, and other pharmaceuticals based on their own training. Excluded from these drugs are controlled substances including painkillers. You'll also find online services promising to deliver pharmaceuticals from Canada, India, or elsewhere.

On the one hand, this is not much different from ordering from a domestic online pharmacy. *However, there are some risks...*

• **Overseas pharmacies are not guaranteed.** How do you know that the orange triangular pill marked 6SJ7 is actually the same one you would receive from a neighborhood pharmacy or from a recognized online pharmacy? The pill may not contain the same ingredients. Even if the drugs are legitimate, how do you know if they were properly stored, kept from contamination, and are within their expiration period?

Unless you are willing to have the drugs tested or otherwise analyzed—at your expense—you really don't know if pharmaceuticals you receive from any source, including your neighborhood drugstore, are the real thing. In theory, American federal and state regulators monitor domestic sources. If you buy from an overseas supplier, you'll have to do as much of your own investigating as you can. If this sounds like a lukewarm (at best) recommendation when it comes to buying from foreign suppliers, you're getting the right vibe. I would not buy a drug considered essential to maintaining my health from overseas.

An important point: don't confuse a drug source with its seller. Many drugs are produced at manufacturing plants in distant corners of the world. India, for example, is a major supplier. If you buy that drug at CVS, Rite Aid, or your neighborhood pharmacist, you have a reasonable expectation that the drug is legitimate. If you buy from an overseas source that promises to ship directly to you, hold no such expectation and there is no guarantee.

- **Customs may not allow them.** The U.S. Customs Service may seize prescription drugs you bring into the country for violations of trademark, customs, or FDA regulations. That's one reason to carry your prescription drugs with you in their original bottles, complete with the name of your pharmacy and doctor when you travel out of the country.
- **Insurance coverage does not apply.** Few, if any, insurance plans reimburse for prescriptions purchased this way.

Sample Your Drugs First

If you pay for your drugs yourself, without the assistance of an insurance plan, there are ways to test out a pharmaceutical before you fully commit to it, especially if it is an expensive pharmaceutical or one that represents a new direction in treatment. *Here are a few money-saving tips you can try...*

- **Let your doctor know that you want to try to keep your medication costs under control.** If you pay for most or all of your drug bills, say so.

Oh, Canada

The prices of pharmaceuticals in Canada are often significantly less than in the United States—often 30% to 40% lower. We could get into a political discussion here... but we won't.

Drugs produced in Canada or legally imported to Canada for resale face the same sort of strict regulation that exists in the United States. And the Canadian International Pharmacy Association requires essentially the same standards as those applied by the VIPPS association I mentioned earlier for American online sources.

That said, under US law, it is illegal to import drugs from Canada. However, the FDA has publicly stated it will not prosecute anyone who imports prescription drugs for personal use, which is generally interpreted as a three-month supply of properly packaged and labeled medications. Once again, there is no guarantee here. But if you show up with a reasonable quantity of Lipitor or Retin-A face cream, you are not likely to be stopped at the border. On the other hand, if you are found with an entire suitcase full of packages, problems almost certainly await you.

As far as online purchases of drugs from Canada, you are not likely to run into problems for orders deemed for personal use. Most experts warn against making purchases from a Canadian online pharmacy that does not require a doctor's prescription. Customs agents may have the shipper's name on a list.

Is it worth the hassle? In a word, *maybe.*

- **Ask if your doctor has any samples of the drug to try before you fill the prescription.** Drug companies regularly give doctors sample packets in hopes the drug will become a regularly prescribed tool. You may be able to obtain a full course of treatment for free, or at least enough of the drug to see if it has any effect or any unacceptable adverse side effects before you fill a full prescription.
- **Ask your pharmacist if it is medically acceptable to try the drug before fully committing to it.** Some medications, including antibiotics, should be taken for the full specified period unless there are intervening side effects or other problems. If it is okay to take the new prescription for a short period, ask the pharmacist to partially fill a prescription for a period long enough to see if the drug will work properly for you. Some pharmacists will allow you to come back for the rest of the prescription later. In other cases, you may need to have the doctor's office call in a new order. The cost of buying two smaller quantities of some drugs may be higher per dose than a full order, but balance that against the cost of throwing away a medication that does not do the job.

Go Halfsies

If you're taking pills (not capsules filled with powder, tiny pellets, or liquid), consult with your doctor about ordering them in higher-dosage size and then splitting them in half. Double the dosage usually costs much less than twice the price of the original dosage, and sometimes sell for the same price. In the case of maintenance drugs that you take daily, splitting pills could save hundreds of dollars per year. There are some potential problems if you aren't able to evenly divide pills so that dosages remain the same. Also, some pills require a safety covering to control where in the body the medication will dissolve and enter your system.

- **Do *not* split capsules or pills that have extended-release or protective coatings.**
- **Do *not* try to slice a pill with a knife or sharp razor.** Instead, purchase a pill splitter device. They only cost a few dollars and are usually for sale at the very same pharmacies where you are filling your prescription.
- **Do *not* split pills too far in advance of when you will use them.** You are exposing a portion of the pill. A few days' supply is okay. If you are leaving for a month's vacation, take uncut pills and your pill splitter.
- **Do *not* hesitate to ask your pharmacist for advice as to whether a particular pill is appropriate for splitting.**

Save on Preoperative Hospital Tests

If you are due to enter the hospital for elective, nonemergency surgery, discuss with your doctor or surgeon having necessary tests done at the doctor's office or at the hospital on an outpatient basis before you are admitted to the hospital. Having tests done this way is almost always significantly less expensive than having them done as a hospital patient. Also make sure the facility where you will have the tests performed can transmit or forward results to the hospital as well as to your physician.

After you are admitted, be an active participant in managing your account. Do your best to inform the intake nurse about all recent tests.

Switch to an Electric Toothbrush

Most dentists agree that electric toothbrushes, especially advanced units that get deep into the spaces between your teeth, are superior to manual toothbrushes. Electric toothbrushes have a base that plugs into a wall outlet for charging. Relatively inexpensive battery-operated toothbrushes are better than manual brushes, but not nearly as good as a model with a larger motor and battery that requires charging.

Like the replaceable razor blade (and more modern items like computer printers), many electric toothbrush manufacturers make their money in the refill market. The brushing mechanisms themselves are often relatively inexpensive, but the replacement brushes can be very pricey—sometimes as much as one-third to one-half the price of the original mechanism.

Most advanced electric toothbrush models include a built-in timer that keeps the brush in motion for a certain amount of time. According to dentists, you should brush your teeth for at least two minutes to get the best effect from plaque-dissolving toothpaste. Flip your egg timer instead of spending more for a toothbrush with a timer.

Any of the name-brand electric toothbrushes are almost certain to do a better job at cleaning your teeth than a manual brush, but be wary of purchasing a no-name device. It may be difficult to get replacement brushes for it in the future.

If you travel often, look for an electric toothbrush with a small and easily transportable charging base so that you can take it with you. My wife and I each have our own electric toothbrush (we're very close, but not that close) but we share a charger on the road. The rechargeable batteries typically hold their charge for several days, allowing easy alternation between two or even more devices.

Ask your dentist for advice on toothbrushes, but don't feel pressured to buy a device at his or her office; the prices are almost certain to be higher than at a retail or online store. One exception: Some dental insurance plans may offer discounts or subsidies for the purchase of electric brushes.

Hello Operator? Medical Help Lines

Need some medical advice? Before you make an appointment with your doctor and pay a fee, see if there's a free help line in your area. Some hospitals and other health organizations offer them.

Many health-insurance carriers have this sort of program, connecting you to a registered nurse or other medical professional who can help you decide whether a condition requires a doctor visit or simply treatment with over-the-counter materials. In most instances, this sort of service is provided without charge.

If you have any acute medical difficulty, including difficulty in breathing or severe pain, don't waste time calling a help line. Call 911.

And if you use a cellphone or a voice-over-internet phone, check with your provider to make sure that you are properly registered. That way an emergency operator can find your location. Remember, too, that dialing 911 from your phone when you are away from your address of record may require you to tell the operator exactly where you are as you make the call. Keeping the location service on your smartphone turned on will help some.

Determine the price for replacement heads before you buy a brush system. Consult internet store prices and compare them to retail stores for replacement brushes. Toothbrush makers sometimes offer coupons on their websites.

You may find third-party manufacturers' replacement brushes. Sometimes they are branded for drugstore chains. Be certain they fit your specific device, and consider whether they are of equal or better quality to those sold by the original maker.

See Your Way to Eyewear Discounts

Under the Federal Trade Commission's so-called Prescription Release Rule, eye doctors must give you a copy of your eyeglass prescription after an exam. If yours forgets, just ask.

It can help to understand the differences among three types of eye-care specialists…

- **An ophthalmologist is a medical doctor (MD) or osteopathic physician (DO) who specializes in diagnosing and treating eye diseases.** This doctor can prescribe drugs, perform examinations and eye surgery, and some may also dispense eyeglasses and contact lenses. Your health insurance policy may include annual or semiannual examinations of your eye health, and you may be able to include a vision correction reading in the same visit and for the same fee.
- **An optometrist has earned a doctor of optometry degree (O.D.).** This doctor can examine eyes for vision problems and eye diseases and dispense eyeglasses and contact lenses. In some states, optometrists may diagnose and treat certain eye diseases and conditions and prescribe drugs. Where they are not permitted to provide treatment, optometrists will generally refer patients to an ophthalmologist or a medical doctor.
- **An optician is a specialist who can fill prescriptions for eyewear written by ophthalmologists and optometrists.** In some states they are also permitted to fit and dispense contact lenses. They may not examine eyes or prescribe lenses. About half the states require opticians to be licensed.

The prescription you receive from an optometrist or ophthalmologist should include all the details necessary for eyeglasses or contact lenses.

- **If you need multifocal or progressive lenses,** the prescription should also provide instructions for the location of the change in each lens.
- **If you (like me) require a prism in the lens that corrects for a slight differential in focusing height between each eye,** the prescription should include those details.
- **Some optometrists or ophthalmologists leave out the pupillary distance,** or PD, which is the distance between the pupils of your eyes. This is something an optician can easily measure in the store. You want to leave your purchase options open, so before leaving the office, ask to have the PD included on the prescription.

You can use this prescription to shop for the best price on glasses at a store associated with the optometrist, you can take the information to a competing optician, or you can search for the best price from an internet eyeglass or contact lens seller.

You can do some basic price research at various retailers or online sellers before you have your prescription, but the cost of lenses can vary based on the correction strength and special features (such as prisms). You'll need the full details of your prescription in order to compare prices. The Federal Trade Commission requires doctors to give you a copy of your prescription for eyeglasses or contact lenses at no extra charge. (The examination and prescriptions for eyeglasses and contact lenses are not the same.) The information required in a prescription for glasses is determined by state law.

Here are the typical basic components of an eyeglass prescription…

- The name, address, phone, and fax number of the prescribing doctor.
- **Your name, address, and date of birth.**
- **The date of the exam.** In some states, there will also be an expiration date.
- **The prescription for each eye.** Some states require they be labeled right and left, while others allow doctors to use Latin acronyms: OD (oculus dexter) for the right eye and OS (oculus sinister) for the left eye.
- **The sphere is a measure of the correction strength.** A plus sign or the absence of any operator means a correction of farsightedness. A minus sign means the prescription is for nearsightedness.
- **The cylinder**, or CYL, is a correction for astigmatism if necessary, and also is indicated for far- or near-sightedness.
- **The axis if your eyes require a cylinder correction.** It is represented as a number between 0 and 180, with 90 degrees being straight up from the center of your eye.
- **PRISM is followed by a number and then BU (base up) or BD (base down), if applicable.** This appears on your prescription if you need a pair of prisms to adjust for uneven alignment of your eyes.

Contact lens prescriptions must follow federal guidelines because they are considered medical devices. *Here are basics for what you should see in a contact lens prescription…*

- The prescribing doctor's name, address, phone, and fax number.
- **Your name, address, and date of birth.**
- **The date of the exam.** In some states, there is also an expiration date.
- **The prescription for each eye.** The Latin is the same here as for eyeglasses.
- **The power of the prescribed lens.** As with eyeglasses, a plus before the power (or the absence of an operator) indicates correction for far-sightedness, and a minus is for near-sightedness.
- **The base curve, which is the shape of the cornea.**
- **The lens diameter, which fits the lens in proper position on the eye.**
- **CYL, for cylindrical adjustment, may apply to compensate for astigmatism.** If there is a CYL designation, there is usually an axis adjustment as well.
- **In most cases, a prescribed material for the lens and a particular manufacturer.**
- **If the prescription calls for a private-label lens,** the prescription should also state the manufacturer's name and the equivalent brand name lens, if there is one.

Online Eyesight

A new segment in the eyewear industry is low-price Internet stores that use their own catalog of frames and offer a limited range of lens options, although many have begun broadening their base. This category is led by Warby Parker at WarbyParker.com and Zenni Optical at ZenniOptical.com. Warby Parker will even send you a few frames to try on at home before you make a purchase.

Don't let a local optician convince you that an online eyeglass provider is not as capable as they are at producing a complex lens. Most eyeglass providers use a third party for nonstandard or complex lenses; your local store may be using the very same third party as the online company they seek to disparage.

If you find a frame design you like, and the price is right, I don't see a reason not to experiment with one of these companies—especially if they offer a money-back guarantee.

• **Although federal regulations govern most of the elements of a contact lens prescription,** the expiration date on the prescription is set by individual states. A one-year validity is common.

Both eyeglasses and certain contact lenses can be bifocals or progressive lenses, and these require additional details on the prescription.

Buying Frames and Lenses

The list prices for eyeglass frames are mostly works of fiction. I've seen prices that start as low as $10 or $20 and reach into many hundreds. There is a difference between a cheap plastic frame and a high-tech metal frame made with a shape-memory alloy. But let's start with the fact that some eyeglass shops want to charge an 800% to 1,000% markup. That's why you see so many sales that offer "free" frames with the purchase of lenses or buy-one-get-one-free deals. It seems as if eyeglasses are always on sale, although the particular deal may change from month to month.

And here's another thing: There may be dozens of national eyeglass retail chains, but many of them are owned by the same company. Luxottica Group claims to be the world's largest eyewear manufacturer, designing frames under many different brands and styles. And this maker also has more than 7,000 retail outlets around the world selling frames and lenses. In the United States, Luxottica owns LensCrafters, Pearle Vision, Sears Optical, Target Optical, Sunglass Hut, and other outlets. If one of the retail associates at any of these stores advises you against buying eyeglasses over the internet, you might want to remind him or her that Luxottica also owns Glasses.com, one of the principal online eyeglass sellers. They also own EyeMed, one of the leading vision insurance plans.

If you have a prescription that is at all complex—progressive or multifocal, transition or photochromic (lenses that change from clear to dark to function as sunglasses), a particularly strong prescription that requires a thick lens, built-in prisms, or other special progressions—lenses can easily cost several hundred dollars. (A strong prescription is, by most definitions, +4.00 or –4.00 or greater.)

Though it costs more as well, you might consider adding antiglare protection (which helps when you are driving in bright light or at night under street lights) or an antireflective coating (which reduces the chances of bright lights bouncing back toward a camera or the eyes of people near you). Antireflective lenses are often used by people who work under strong lights, or actors, performers, and public speakers who are often photographed in such conditions. Other options also add to the cost, including special plastic compounds that allow thinner or more durable lenses.

Questions to Ask an Eyeglass Seller

You think your eyesight is fuzzy? If there is one thing that is all but guaranteed to be less clear, it is the pricing methods at opticians. This is especially so at national eyewear chains, home of all sort of hard-to-decipher sales. They promise two-for-one, or free sunglasses, or even list a special price for a certain class of eyewear.

Here are a few things to look for at a retail or internet optician...

• **A well-defined warranty that includes coverage for damage to the frame and lenses for at least a year.** The shop should guarantee to adjust eyeglasses without charge for at least a year (if not forever) and offer a refund if you are not satisfied with the fit within a reasonable period of time.

If you are dissatisfied with the quality of lenses or contacts, don't hesitate to take advantage of the guarantee. I have walked away (with a full refund) from one set of expensive eyeglasses that did not allow good vision, and when I once unsuccessfully experimented with contact lenses, I was repaid all costs. If necessary, you can enlist your credit card company or your state's consumer affairs department to enforce a warranty or refund offer.

• **A pricing scheme that does not require you to pay for something you don't need.** For example, nearly all polycarbonate lenses come with scratch-resistant coating. You shouldn't pay twice. Ask the eyeglass provider for the lens' brand and specification and consult the manufacturer's website. There, you should be able to learn all the lens specifications, including provided features.

• **Additional discount arrangements for students, seniors, former Girl Scouts, or anything else.** Even if your health insurance does not pay for eyeglasses, you may be eligible for a discount at some stores.

Get the Best Specs Price

How do you get the best price? *Here are some tips...*

• **Get a baseline price from one of the major national chains** such as LensCrafters or Visionworks, or franchise operations within stores like Sears or Target (each of which is operated by the parent company of LensCrafters). You should be able to get a price range over the phone, and be sure to ask about any special deals.

• **Visit or call the optical department at a wholesale or discount store** such as Sam's Club, Costco, or BJ's Wholesale, and get a comparative price. Some of these stores have a limited frame selection, but managers may be willing to order a frame you have found elsewhere. In some states, you do *not* need to be a club member to buy from the optical department.

• **Check out the price at one or more online eyeglass stores.** Just search for *eyeglasses*. Many stores offer a wide range of frames and allow you to custom-configure lenses with special features.

TIP

Something for Nothing

Most retail eyeglass stores will adjust your frames for free, even if you did not buy them there. One reason is that so many of the eyeglass sellers are part of the same company. Another reason is that they hope you'll return as a retail customer. Just ask politely if you can have your frames adjusted. I've never been turned down or asked where I bought my eyewear.

The best internet stores include a telephone or chat-based help desk to answer questions. Ask about any arrangements they make for adjusting glasses to fit you. Some online sites are internet outposts of retail stores, which makes it easy to make a purchase and then arrange for a proper fitting.

Your final decision comes down to the best price combined with the best customer service. For what it's worth, the eyeglasses I am wearing as I write these words were purchased over the internet. I knew exactly what type of frame I wanted, and I found an internet store that had the frame in its inventory. I arranged for the completed glasses to be held at the company's retail store and picked them up and had them fitted.

Cut Contact-Lens Bills Down to Size

One hundred dollars for contact lenses! Of course, you'll need your reading glasses to decipher the fine print at the bottom of the ad. Determine whether the price includes exams or fittings, and make sure you know the quality of the service provided.

Here are some important questions to ask when you consider purchasing contact lenses...

- **What is the cost for a contact lens exam?** If you wear contact lenses in some situations and eyeglasses at other times, will I receive prescriptions for both?

Many ophthalmologists and optometrists will write prescriptions for both eyeglasses and contact lenses on the basis of a single exam. Some might charge for a small amount of extra work.

- **What do you charge for contact-lens evaluation, fittings, and follow-up visits?**
- **What do you charge for lenses and a lens-care kit?**
- **What is your refund policy?** Not everyone is able to wear contact lenses, and some designs may not be appropriate for all users. Will I receive a refund of some or all of my money if I cannot wear contact lenses or find a particular brand or style uncomfortable? Some opticians will sell (or give you) a small quantity of contact lenses so you can test them before buying a larger supply. A proper refund policy should cover you for the cost of unopened lens boxes.

Buy Contact Lenses by Mail Order

With your prescription in hand, go to the internet and search for contact lens sellers. You will have to scan your prescription (or take a photo using your smartphone) and send it to an online seller, or provide the name and phone number of the optometrist or ophthalmologist so the service can confirm the numbers.

Among the largest players in this market are 1-800 Contacts, which sells over the phone at its obvious number as well as through its website at 1800contacts.com. Visiondirect.com, another option, is part of the drugstore.com family. You'll also find online sales sites from Walmart, Walgreens, and many other discount retail stores.

Here's my advice on buying from these sites: Establish a relationship with any one of them and then check the websites of several others for the best price. In my experience, you can easily obtain a price match or a price match plus discount by mentioning a better price found elsewhere.

Once you have obtained a prescription and tried out a particular brand and style of contact lenses, there is no reason not to treat future purchases as a commodity. The lenses are going to be the same wherever you buy them, and they do not need to be fitted. You may well find that your local optician will match or come very close to the price of an online service. It doesn't hurt to ask.

Listen to an Independent Expert on Hearing Aids

Never go to a hearing-aid salesperson for advice on whether you need a hearing aid. Their self-interest lies in selling you a device. If a salesperson tries to pressure you into making a purchase, walk away...and call your state's consumer-protection agency.

If you think you have hearing loss, begin with a medical evaluation to determine the nature and extent of the problem. Your doctor may refer you to an audiologist for testing. By some estimates, more than 36 million Americans suffer from some type of significant hearing impairment—about 9% of the population—and many can benefit from hearing aids.

FDA regulations require hearing-aid dispensers to obtain a written statement from a licensed physician, dated within the previous six months, certifying that the patient's ears have been medically evaluated and that the patient is cleared for fitting with a hearing aid. However—and this is a huge loophole—an adult patient age 18 or older can sign a waiver to skip the medical examination. The FDA requires that dispensers not encourage patients to waive the examination and to advise the customer that waiving the examination is not in their best health interest. Why? Because an otolaryngologist (an ear, nose, and throat, or ENT, doctor) might find that hearing problems are caused by middle-ear fluid or wax in the canal. There are other possible causes including infections, chemical imbalance, medication side effects, tumors, and ruptured eardrums.

Once you have a medical diagnosis, consider these steps to help you save money on hearing aids...

- **Check the reliability and service offered by local hearing-aid dispensers.** Ask doctors, friends who use hearing aids, and your state's consumer-protection agency for advice. Some hearing aids are better than others; some require more adjustment and fine-tuning than others; and some hearing aid users are more sensitive to issues of comfort and sound quality.

- **There are no federal laws against internet or even door-to-door sales of hearing aids, although some states have banned this practice.** Buying from a stranger at your door is a bad idea. Buying online is risky because it is hard to get a proper fit and to get service. One exception might be buying a replacement unit for one properly dispensed in the past. Nevertheless, be tested now and obtain a current prescription.

- **According to *Bottom Line Health*, you can save as much as 50% at warehouse clubs like Costco and others.** The equipment may be sold under house brands or name brands. You can also order devices online direct from a manufacturer or a distributor after receiving a hearing test and fitting from an audiologist. And a fast-developing market is in over-the-counter hearing aids. These are usually larger (perhaps fitting over the ear rather than within the ear channel) and perhaps not quite as advanced as the name brands, but the prices are attractive.

- **Seek a trial period.** This is required in some but not all states. The dispenser or manufacturer may give a 30-day or longer period during which you can return the hearing aid without charge (or for a small fee). This is your best chance to obtain the best technology for yourself as well as a comfortable fit.

- **Determine the full details for service, adjustments, and warranties.** Will the dispenser offer you a loaner if your hearing aid needs to be repaired? Is the warranty honored by the manufacturer or by the dispenser? In some cases, the manufacturer may not honor a warranty if the hearing aid is purchased from an unauthorized seller.

- **A relatively small number of private health insurance plans include coverage or subsidies for hearing aids.** Hearing aids can also be paid for via a Flexible Spending Account, offered by some employers and funded with pretax dollars. There is also a Health Savings Account available to individuals and through employers as a supplement to an eligible high-deductible health plan.

- **Medicare and Medigap supplemental plans do not cover hearing aids.** However, some Medicare Advantage plans

What?

The two basic types of hearing loss are conductive and sensorineural. *Conductive* hearing loss involves the outer and middle ear. It can result from a blockage by wax, a punctured eardrum, birth defects, ear infections, or heredity. Conductive hearing loss can usually be corrected medically or surgically. *Sensorineural*, or nerve, hearing loss involves damage to the inner ear. It can be a natural effect of aging or be caused by viral and bacterial infections, heredity, trauma (such as a severe blow to the head), exposure to loud noises, the use of certain drugs, fluid buildup in the inner ear, or a benign tumor in the inner ear. Only in rare cases can sensorineural hearing loss be medically or surgically corrected. It is the type of hearing loss that is most commonly managed with a hearing aid, and often the device can be specifically tuned or adjusted to compensate for particular sound frequencies.

(Medicare Part C), which provides private insurance that merges Medicare Part A (Hospitalization) and Medicare Part B (Medical Coverage)—and sometimes Medicare Part D (prescription plans) also provide coverage for hearing aids.

Go Health Clubbing

Health and fitness clubs can be good for your heart and waistline and damaging to your bank account. The danger comes with the long-term commitment demanded by many of the spas. Check with friends, family, online, and local and state consumer agencies for recommendations or complaints.

Here are some questions to ask yourself and the membership salesperson…

- **What are the contract terms?** Can I take home the contract to read at my leisure? Before you sign the contract, is everything the salesperson promised written in the contract? If a problem arises after you join, the contract will probably govern the dispute.
- **Is there a free trial period during which I can try the club?** Are all classes available with the membership, or do any cost extra?
- **Can I cancel the contract and receive a refund if I change my mind or find the club unacceptable?** Can I quit the deal without penalty if I move from the area? What happens if I get injured or disabled and cannot use the club?
- **How many members belong to the club, and what is its reasonable capacity?** Is there a limit to the number of people who can join? When is the busiest time at the club? Visit during the hours you would go to see if it is overcrowded during that period.
- **What are the staff's qualifications or training?** There's no single good answer here. But if I heard that a club included staffers with appropriate certifications or academic training, I would be pleased. If I heard stunned silence or a fuzzy response, I would not be inclined to enroll.
- **Is childcare available and if so, is it included in membership or does it cost extra?**

Ask for a free pass (or several) to give the club a go. Visit at the times you expect to use the facility. The crowd is going

TIP

Gym Subsidy

Some health insurance plans, and some employers, will offer a subsidy if you join a health club. That's a pretty good advertisement for the benefits that come from regular exercise. Be sure to read all the fine print from your health plan and make sure it matches your expected use of the club.

to be very different at 3 p.m. on a Tuesday versus 10 a.m. on Saturday, and there will probably be fewer staff during quiet times. That might mean less personal attention.

Calculate the actual cost per day of being a member of the club, including sign-up fees, monthly charges, locker-room fees, and any other costs. The final decision is this: Will you commit to getting up from your chair and going to the club enough times to justify the cost? In my opinion, the best arrangement is a club that allows you to pay by the month with no penalty for ending the arrangement. The worst would be a club that forces you to commit for an extended period of time with no way to get out of a contract that proves to be unsatisfactory to you.

CHAPTER 8

Buying for Sports and Hobbies

One person's definition of a boat is a hole in the water into which you pour money. It is also true that ski enthusiasts often try to avoid calculating the per-hour cost of their skis, boots, bindings, winter clothing, and travel. And have you thought about the difference between a box of TaylorMade Project golf balls purchased at a Pebble Beach pro shop, the same box procured at a Walmart store, or the same balls sent by UPS from Amazon? The answer, which almost certainly changes by the hour, was a spread of $15 per dozen from the lowest to the highest price. And you might be surprised which place had the best deal.

In this chapter, I'll unveil some hints to save money on sports and hobbies.

- **Work out a deal on exercise equipment.**
- **Understand tennis-ball ratings.**
- **Be a ski bum.**
- **Boogie to a used snowboard.**
- **Get a hole in one.**
- **Get the best service or prices (or both) on books.**
- **Pay less for magazine subscriptions.**
- **Decide on a camera.**
- **Replace your lost marbles.**
- **Owe, owe, owe your boat.**

Work Out a Deal on Exercise Equipment

If I had a dollar for every exercise machine gathering dust or serving as a clothes rack somewhere, I'd be a very wealthy man (and in no better shape than I am now, alas). Stick with your exercise plan. It'll make your health insurance less expensive!

Here are some tips when buying exercise equipment…

- **Try out equipment at your health club or at hotels, cruise ships, and other public facilities.** Most machines in gyms are heavy-duty commercial models, built to survive nearly constant use. You may be able to purchase commercial models from manufacturers, but they tend to be bigger and heavier.

• **Ask a health club or hotel whether it will sell reconditioned or well-maintained used equipment.** Or, see if they will order new equipment for you from their supplier; allow them a reasonable markup from their cost. Shop around before making such a deal.

• **Think about your personal needs when it comes to design issues.** Recumbent bicycles are easier on the lower back. Upright cycles take up much less floor space. Maybe you want to combine your arm and leg workouts, so choose an elliptical that has moving handles or a rowing machine.

• **Fan resistance on a bicycle has the side benefit of cooling you off with the air it moves.** Electromagnetic bikes run smoother and more quietly.

Exercise equipment has moving parts that can wear out or go out of alignment; electronic controls are also prone to failure. Look for a reasonable warranty and repair parts availability—or increase the chances of avoiding this altogether by choosing a reliable brand with very basic controls.

Also, consider looking for better deals in January (when they're selling a lot of equipment to New Year's resolution keepers) and June (when they're trying to flip inventory).

One more thing: Think twice or maybe thrice before ordering equipment online if it requires you to assemble the device. First of all, you may throw out your back or wreck your knees carrying the equipment. Second, you absolutely have to properly align and adjust the device. This is especially true for items like treadmills, which must be very precisely set up. A possible solution: Purchase online along with a service contract that includes setup.

Understand Tennis-Ball Ratings

Most casual tennis players, including myself when I had a pair of reasonably well-functioning knees, rarely give much thought to that most essential piece of equipment: the ball.

Experts say that once a can of balls is opened, they will be below standards (if not completely useless) in about two weeks. And that's before you even get your racket on them. In a professional match, they open a new can every nine games—sooner if a ball is damaged. (There are six games in a set, and it takes either two or three winning sets to claim the match.) We mortals do not tend to serve the ball at 100 miles per hour or apply a wicked slam that bounces into the bleachers, but the fact remains that tennis balls have a finite life before they are relegated to Fido's collection.

For casual matches, sealed cans are classified as recreational, and most of us will not notice the difference. For leagues and formal matches, championship balls are manufactured with better materials. At Wimbledon or the Olympics, they use professional-grade balls. Using a professional ball will not make anyone mistake you for Novak Djokovic or Serena Williams, but you might get a few extra minutes of play in a match against your buddy. Or not.

There are also a few other distinctions. Extra-duty balls are also called *hard court balls*, meaning they are tough enough to be used on concrete, asphalt, or other hard surfaces. Regular duty are for clay or grass courts. You'll also find high-altitude tennis balls, which, as their name suggests, are for use in locations well above sea level. (Professional federations define high altitude as 4,000 feet or higher.) These balls compensate for the thinner air by having a slightly larger circumference, or less internal pressure, or both.

If you are going to work on your swing or engage in a practice session, you might bring along a set of old balls or buy a bag of them online for a relative pittance. But when the title is on the line, expect to break out a new can early and often. And I can't think of a good reason not to order tennis balls online (big-box stores have discounts), unless your local sporting goods store is willing to meet the price.

Be a Ski Bum

Skiing is a notoriously expensive sport, but you can find ways to do it on the cheap(er).

Buy Skis When the Grass Is Green

Shop for last year's leftovers at the end of the season for the best deals. The second-best time for ski shopping is an early fall preseason sale. The worst possible time to buy is during the Christmas season and in the heart of the ski season.

It is possible to purchase skis online, with or without bindings installed. The problem here is how well the binding will be adjusted to your particular boots and ability. One compromise: Buy the skis online and the bindings from a ski store that is willing to install and adjust the bindings. Do your homework ahead of time and make sure you will have a technician ready to perform the work.

Be aware that many ski shops and technicians will not be willing to install a used binding on a new ski because of possible liability issues. They don't want to be sued if the binding fails to release when it should.

Another strategy is to get a good price on skis from an online source but to hold off on buying. Then visit a ski shop in the off season and see how close they will come to an all-inclusive price for skis, bindings, and installation.

Put Your Boots on Some Used Skis

Ski designs change, skiers progress in their ability, young skiers grow taller and heavier, and older skiers become more demanding of comfort or performance. All of these are good reasons people want to unload otherwise perfectly useable skis each season.

You may be able to save hundreds of dollars at tag sales, swap meets, and used equipment sales. Most ski rental shops want to clear out most or all of their equipment at the end of the season to prepare for the next year. We used to buy equipment at these markets as our athletic young daughter was learning—and growing—every year.

An experienced skier (or ski buyer) can buy the wrong length and design. Be sure you purchase a ski that is the proper length and design for your weight and skiing ability.

And here's a big warning: Do not compromise your safety to save money. More about safety in a moment. *For now, here's how to appraise a used ski…*

• **Inspect the edges.** Modern skis have sharp metal edges that help maintain a grip on ice and hard-packed snow and are essential to turns. The edges should be intact, firmly attached for the entire length of the ski, and not too badly burred. A ski technician can resharpen dulled or slightly damaged edges.

• **Examine the ski's shape for damage to its arc.** Hold the skis vertically, base to base; look for warping or bending to the curve.

• **Inspect the base of each ski.** Minor scratches and gouges are normal, and many can be repaired. What you don't want to see are gouges that go through the base to the ski's interior wood, metal, or plastic core. These can compromise the ski's strength.

• **Check the *camber* (the amount of spring beneath the sole of the feet).** Hold the skis upright, base to base, with the tails on the ground, bases touching. There should be a gap between the skis beneath the bindings. The more camber, or spring, between the skis, the better performance they'll deliver to most skiers.

• **Examine the top of the ski to ensure that it is not *delaminating* (separating from the body of the ski).**

• **Check the binding mechanism.** If the previous owner wore boots that were within a size or two of yours, a technician should be able to adjust its position on the ski and fit them properly to your boots. Regardless of whether you will reuse an existing binding or install a new one, bring the ski to a repair shop to have your boots properly fitted to your binding and adjusted for your weight and skiing ability. If you have any doubt whether the bindings are in working order or appropriate to your weight and ability, replace them with new equipment. Experts say a ski can safely withstand installation of two subsequent bindings in its lifetime without compromising its strength. If you find multiple screw holes from former bindings, do not purchase the ski.

Boogie to a Used Snowboard

Advice similar to buying used skis applies for would-be buyers of used snowboards but with one additional caveat: In general, boarders are much harder on their equipment than skiers.

Again, be sure to purchase the proper length and style to match your height, weight, and style.

• **Examine the base and edges.** The edges should be straight and not coming apart from the board; the top should be well attached.

• **Inspect the top of the board.** Scratches and damage to the artwork on the top of the board are unimportant. Serious cracks or gouges will weaken the board's strength.

• **Look closely at the areas around the bindings.** Check for cracks or stripped screws.

• **Examine the bindings.** Make sure they work properly with your boots and are installed in the style and position you prefer. Two bindings maximum per ski life, please.

Get a Hole in One

If you use the tips in this section for your next rounds, you can focus more on your drive than your fee.

Pay Less for Golf Equipment

A Titleist golf ball is the same whether you pay full list price at the pro shop, pick a pack off the shelf at Walmart, or order a box or two from an internet store. The same goes for golf clothing and accessories: If you know what you want, these are commodities that you can buy based on price.

The one possible exception is a set of clubs. If you don't know much about equipment, it may be worthwhile to buy from a store where you can receive a knowledgeable salesperson's expertise. But if you are looking to buy an additional iron or a new putter for an existing set, consider placing your order through a discount online seller. The possible wrinkle is if you want or need custom grips.

Be sure to investigate the warranty and repair policies no matter your seller; don't assume that the best service is offered by the source with the highest price. Golf clubs are a competitive market and most sellers want to keep customers. They should offer a replacement (either immediately or ordered) if you break a club—whether by accident or in anger.

Another way to save big bucks on equipment, especially for beginners, is to buy used equipment until you are sure you are interested in the sport and know your capabilities. Look for clubs at tag sales or in classified ads. Check with local pro shops and retail stores to see if they have former demo or rental sets available for sale. Some sporting goods and general merchandise shops will buy and sell last year's clubs and most everything else in the way of the sporting goods that clutter our basements and garages. Before buying used golf clubs, make sure there's plenty of groove left on the heads; not too much wear on the grips; that the shafts look straight; and that they handle having the grip and head twisted in opposite directions.

And about those golf balls: Have you ever wondered how many perfectly good balls sit at the bottom of the pond off the twelfth fairway? Check Amazon and other online sellers for bags of a few dozen used balls at sharply reduced prices. A good many of those pond balls, as well as discolored or dirty balls, are harvested, cleaned up, and resold as driving range or practice balls; if they are uncut, go ahead and add them to your bag and spend the difference at the nineteenth hole.

Another way to save on golf balls is to purchase *X-outs*, which are new balls marked (usually) with an X through the brand name to indicate a defect. In theory, an X-out ball is sold at a discount because of cosmetic flaws such as misprinted labels, off colors, or mottled covers. These are fine; what you have to worry about, though, are balls that have been rejected because of imperfect construction. Problems could include an off-center weighting or a damaged cover. The cover damage will be obvious, and you don't want to use any ball like that. Off-center weighting? You'll have to yell "Fore!"

Save Money on Greens Fees

The best way to save money (and time) is to go golfing when the other players are doing something else. Check with courses for off-peak times and off-peak seasons. At many courses, the best prices are offered in the early spring and late fall when the less-than-obsessed golfer is finding other things to do.

My late father-in-law was a seriously casual golfer who took great pleasure in playing on the frozen fairways of upstate New York in the dead of winter to save some money and stay away from crowds. Going the other direction, golf courses in hot places may have reduced prices for duffers who are willing to tee off at noon under the blazing sun.

Check with hotels or visitor bureaus for the schedule of major conventions and sporting events. Otherwise crowded and expensive golf courses may be deserted and bargain-priced at those times.

Get the Best Service or Prices (or Both) on Books

I love a good book, and I appreciate anyone who helps me find a useful or entertaining or thought-provoking or beautiful addition to my collection. And as the author of this particular book, it should also be obvious that I like to buy fine things at reduced prices.

Books carry a list price set by the publisher, but increased competition has made discounting much more common. All things being equal, buying a book for the best price (including any shipping charge) is usually the best way to save money.

But don't overlook the special services offered to their clients by some brick-and-mortar bookstores. The best kind of bookstore is one where the staff knows every title on the shelves and is willing to help you find a perfect match. If you're a regular customer, they may make suggestions based on past purchases; if you're just getting to know each other, the bookseller should be able to make matches based on titles or interests you already enjoy. And good bookstores are social places, with pots of coffee, free WiFi, or readings and signings by authors.

Online sellers like Amazon, Barnes & Noble, and others try to deliver similar experiences (without the coffee). And, at least in theory, their search engines allow you to find a wide array of titles, including some that are not stocked in brick-and-mortar stores (although retailers will order books for you as well).

Pay Less for Magazine Subscriptions

Are you amazed at the variety of magazines in your dentist's waiting room? Don't be too impressed; he or she may be getting them wholesale or for free as a form of advertising.

There are ways you can save a bit on magazine subscriptions.

The first tip is an easy one: Look for the lowest advertised price you can find for subscriptions on *blow-in* cards within an issue, or in direct mail solicitations you've received, or on the magazine's website. Then call the magazine's customer service department (the number may be listed on the ad, but you can also find it in the magazine or online). Ask the subscription department for their lowest price. Then ask for a better price.

Just as with many other businesses, magazine publishers often have many different promotional prices available. Sometimes you need to ask for them. The lower price may come with a longer agreement (say, a two-year deal instead of the usual one year), though sometimes it works in the other direction, with reduced prices on short-term commitments.

You can also check Amazon and other online sellers for special subscription offers. If you are a member of a national association like AAA, AARP, or the like, you may find occasional specials. You could also subscribe to the electronic version of some magazines. These editions, which now often faithfully reproduce every page including ads, can be read on a computer or tablet.

Finally, you could also engage in a form of chicken with your favorite magazines. Ignore the first six or eight letters or emails you receive asking you to renew. Sometimes the price suddenly goes down just before the subscription's actual expiration date; that's also a good time to place a phone call to inquire about what they are willing to do to keep you as a customer.

I've been a loyal subscriber to one particular weekly news and literature magazine for many years, and I know their subscription practices better than most of their agents. I always renew, but I do so at the savviest of prices just before I am due to be taken off their list. (Most magazines make their money via ad revenue, so it's to their advantage to have more subscribers. That's why they can make these lower offers available.)

A Plea for Publishing

When books first began appearing on electronic devices like e-readers and tablets, some shoppers made the argument that the titles should be priced at a tiny fraction of a printed book's cost. Why, they argued, should a book that required no paper or printing or shipping costs cost near the cover price of a book for sale in a store?

Although it is true that an ebook's printing and shipping costs are close to zero, that portion of manufacturing represents a small fraction of the cost. Payment to the author for his or her time, salaries for editors, sales staff, marketing and support, are still part of the equation. Think of it this way: Is the value of a Rembrandt based on the cost of the canvas and paint used by the artist?

One other thing bibliophiles should consider is what I will dub the *self-defeating savings* of used books. If you search, as one example, the pages of Amazon, you will likely see a price for a new book and various prices for used copies. I am all in favor of shoppers getting the most for their money, but consider this: If you buy a used book, the author and the publisher receive not a penny in payment. Why should you care? Because buying used books is a step in the direction of fewer professional authors and publishers.

The one exception I would allow is for the purchase of an antique or out-of-print book. But that's just my opinion. As an author.

Decide on a Camera

Photography has been around for almost two centuries and for nearly all of that time, it was a relatively expensive process requiring multiple steps between the moment of exposure and its availability as a repeatedly reproducible image that could be hung on a wall or printed in a book.

When many of us were a bit younger, the family camera was mostly reserved for two types of occasions: family holidays and vacation trips. And there was one very important bit of economic calculation that most of us were constantly making: Is this picture worth a frame of film that must be developed and then printed?

I took up photography as a hobby as a youngster, and these were precisely the decisions amateurs had to make. Many decades later I can look back at photos I made and—although I value and appreciate the family remembrances and the artistic endeavors some represent—I don't see many alternate versions of the same image. Why? Because at the time I would stop and think about whether a picture was worth taking and the image's optimal settings. Not that there is anything wrong with taking time and being deliberate in one's work. But from a distance of thirty, forty, or more years, I wish I had more versions to examine today.

The Kodak Brownie introduced film photography to the masses beginning in 1900, and prices and capabilities grew markedly the next 70 years. Polaroid brought the concept of "instant" photography to the market in 1948, although that technology reached its peak in the 1960s and 1970s. It was the arrival of the digital camera in the late 1990s that changed the economics and our way of thinking about photography. With a digital camera, film was replaced by reusable memory. Those images could easily be transferred to a personal computer with its own, even larger storage systems, or a compact disk. And using computer software, you could adjust and refine images without a darkroom, and those images could be selectively printed using an online service or sent over the internet to a printer at a local store.

At first some purists scoffed at digital cameras, saying they weren't worthy of professional or artistic pursuits. That argument has mostly fallen by the wayside. By most measures, digital cameras—at amateur or professional levels—are equal to or far ahead of the capabilities of equivalent film cameras. And the most recent migration of photography has been from a device designed solely as a camera to the nearly ubiquitous smartphone.

How do you choose the right digital camera for you?

- **Smartphone-as-camera.** Nearly all smartphones include very sophisticated cameras, offering many of the features of a point-and-shoot device. Where they fall short is in the sensor's physical size and the lens quality. For most casual photographers, though, a smartphone is more than acceptable for basic family and travel photos as long as you don't expect to make poster-sized prints from the images. Consumer Reports lists their best smartphone cameras: ConsumerReports.org/smartphones/best-smartphone-cameras.

- **Point-and-shoot or full control.** As with many other high-tech products, you can go in either of two directions: a fully automatic model that uses hardware and software to make most or all the technical decisions for you, or an advanced model that allows a knowledgeable photographer to make some or all of hundreds of adjustments that affect the captured image. A point-and-shoot camera, some of which are available for under $100, is more than satisfactory for most users. These devices include automatic exposure setting, adjustment for varying colors of light (cool blue mornings, warm orange sunsets, cool indoor fluorescents, warm indoor incandescent bulbs, and other conditions), an automatically focusing lens, a built-in flash, and many other features. Nikon and Canon, two reliable and common brands that offer you full control, offer entry-level cameras starting at over $300 and quickly rising from there.

- **A professional or advanced amateur.** These larger, more expensive devices, sometimes labeled with the awkward term *prosumer,* can find a wide range of high-end cameras with a long list of special features.

Among the most important: high-quality, interchangeable lenses available in a wide range of focal lengths. (The smaller the focal length, the wider the view; a typical wide-angle lens is rated at 20 to 28mm, while a moderate telephoto lens is 135mm.)

These cameras also allow for both manual and automatic control of hundreds of settings: focus points, exposure, color temperature, and much more. You can adjust the sensor, which replaces film, from normal sensitivity to extremes that allow capture of images in near darkness. Nikon and Canon, again, are the most common brands, and their advanced amateur models start at $600 and go up.

Which type is best for you? There is no single answer. I will tell you that I have one of each (actually, more than one of each) that I use in my work and travel. Here is my suggestion: Start with a point-and-shoot camera that lets you make some basic adjustments like a zoom lens and a few exposure modes. Go forth and take hundreds or thousands of pictures—the film is free, remember—and develop your photographer's eye. If you find yourself wanting to go to the next step, consider borrowing or renting a digital SLR or other form of professional or prosumer camera. Enjoy its superior lens and work with the various adjustments and then decide if you want to spend the money for (and deal with the weight and size of) a better camera.

Several online companies rent cameras; I have used them for special situations where I needed an extra piece of equipment for a project. Online sources include Borrow Lenses (BorrowLenses.com) and Lensrentals (LensRentals.com). You may also find that a local camera store (if any are still in business where you live) has rental equipment.

When it comes time to buy, you will find many internet outlets. Some companies are better at answering questions and giving advice to customers, while others are strictly order takers.

A few warnings…

- **If you find an internet seller that is offering a deal that looks too good to be true, it probably is.** Most dealers are pretty close to each other in price. Beware of bait-and-switch deals where you are pushed away from your choice or where you find that the low price only applies with the purchase of other items you do not need or want. Is the product in stock? It does you no good to accept a great price if the dealer cannot deliver the item to you when you need it.

- **Watch out for accessory packages.** Sometimes they offer good deals, but more often they include cheap-quality items better off purchased by themselves or not at all. And watch out for an especially sneaky tactic: Some underhanded dealers remove accessories like batteries, lens caps, and other items that come with cameras and then offer (or require) you to buy them with the camera. Make sure of what you're getting with a purchase before making it, and if you're seeing sneaky tactics, avoid the site.

- **Make sure the warranty for the camera is from the manufacturer and is applicable to where you live.** Some dealers sell cameras that are imported through channels other than the official distributor. These gray-market devices usually do not come equipped with a manufacturer's warranty.

- **Pay attention to details.** If you are purchasing a camera capable of using interchangeable lenses, make sure you know what you are buying. Nikon cameras are officially paired with Nikkor lenses, Canon cameras with Canon lenses, and so on. If you're offered a "famous name"

TIP

Register Your Camera

Register your camera with the manufacturer so that you are aware of any software upgrades or for the occasional factory recall. My current professional camera, which cost me more than I paid for my first car, was recalled by the manufacturer because of a problem. The company ended up taking back my two-year-old camera and replacing it with a brand new, slightly improved model—in the process cementing my relationship with that company.

This is another reason I recommend against buying gray-market products; few, if any, manufacturers will help buyers who obtained their devices in that way.

lens, or not told the brand of the lens at all, you may be getting a package that is less than the highest quality. That said, some third-party lens makers, like Sigma or Tamron, make well-regarded products; make sure you are not surprised when your package arrives.

- **Be sure you understand shipping costs.** Some online stores tack on unconscionably high shipping and handling charges. I'm especially unhappy with shippers that tack on an order processing fee or something like that. This is like your neighborhood grocery store charging you for the time spent by the checkout clerk. I'm also not a fan of extra insurance charges; the risk in sending a package to you is borne by the shipper and the carrier, not the customer. You are not obligated to pay for something that does not arrive in perfect condition or does not arrive at all. In any case, you want to compare the bottom line of one store to another: the item you purchase, shipping, handling, and tax.
- **Know the store's return policy.** Can you return the equipment in a reasonable period of time for a full refund? Does the outlet charge a restocking fee? All things being equal, buy from the store that offers the most generous return policy.
- **Take advantage of the protections against fraud provided by your credit card, as well as the extended warranties that are offered by some card issuers.** Print out a copy of an online receipt, or write down the details—including an order number—for telephone purchases. Chapter 1 talks more about credit card warranties for purchases.
- **Check with local electronics and camera stores, too.** They are fully aware that consumers can buy this sort of equipment online, and in recent years many brick-and-mortar stores have adjusted their prices to match or come very close to online levels.

Replace Your Lost Marbles

Are you missing Colonel Mustard from Clue? Has the cat run off with the top hat from Monopoly? Have you lost all the E tiles from Scrabble?

Don't buy a whole new game if you don't have to. Most of the major American game makers offer replacement parts at reasonable rates; sometimes they'll even rescue your game for free. Go online to the websites for toy makers and search for replacement parts. (Last time I checked, a full set of Monopoly replacement parts, plus a new bank of paper money, sold for $7.99 at the Hasbro site. Hasbro also owns Kenner, Milton Bradley, Parker Brothers, and Selchow and Righter brands, and sells parts for most of those games.

Here are a few to try…

- **Hasbro** at Hasbro.com
- **Mattel** at http://service.mattel.com/us
- **Pressman** at PressmanToy.com
- **Strat-O-Matic** at Strat-O-Matic.com

Don't Play with Toy Safety

If you're buying toys for very young children, you should consider each and every item a potential risk to their health. Are parts (including batteries in compartments) small enough for a child to swallow them and choke? Are there any sharp edges or pointed ends? Are there cords that can tangle around their necks?

We all have borne witness to some tragic incidents in which police or civilians mistook a child's toy gun for the real thing. Some states have passed laws requiring toy guns to be colored bright red or green or that the muzzle end have a brightly colored oversized cap. Better yet, give a kid a basketball or a mitt and ball.

Start by making your own judgment about the safety of toys. An easy at-home test includes seeing if the toy or any of its parts can go through a toilet-paper tube. If it can, it's a choking hazard to children under age 4. Then you can check places like the Consumer Product Safety Commission's Hotline at 800-638-2772. You can visit their website at CPSC.gov or CPSC.gov/en/Safety-Education/Safety-Guides/Toys.

Owe, Owe, Owe Your Boat

The old saying goes like this: The two best days in the life of a boat owner? The day he buys his boat and the day he sells his boat. Hopefully, the former will far outweigh the latter.

The True Cost of Ownership

There are many pleasures to owning a boat, but there also is the possibility of stormy seas. If you are considering buying a used boat, hire a professional marine inspector—one who is not associated with the seller or the marina where the vessel is stored.

A new boat can also be problematic. Just as important as picking out a worthy boat is selecting a trustworthy dealer who will stand behind the sale.

As with the purchase of a car, consider the effects of depreciation. Except for the priciest custom-built yachts and well-maintained classic boats, a boat's value is certain to decline over time. And while you can seek whatever warranty you can possibly obtain from the seller—repairs, transporting your boat to its new location, transporting the boat to a repair shop if required—extended warranties are usually not worth any extra cost.

Now you may or may not want to know the answer to this question: How much is it going to cost you to fulfill your dream? Start with the cost of the boat and then obtain an estimate of its resale value after a year. (You may also want to do the same exercise for a three-year period, which will temper—somewhat—the cost of depreciation.) Subtract the resale value from the cost of the boat to yield the depreciation on your investment. Then fill in the blanks in the following formula.

Sales tax on purchase	____________
Property or excise taxes	____________
Interest on loan for purchase	____________
Loss of income on cash paid	____________
Depreciation	____________
Loss and liability insurance	____________
Dock charges	____________
Winter storage charges	____________
Fuel	____________
Boat and trailer license fees	____________
Estimated maintenance	____________
Total (Add all lines together)	____________

Divide the total by a realistic estimate of the number of days you expect to be out on the water.

Then sit down until the shock wears off. Depending on how often you use the boat, the cost per use can be astronomic. If you live in a warmer climate, you're likely to get a lot more use out of the boat than those who can count on only a few summer months.

If this makes you want to consider renting a boat on a daily or seasonal basis, go right ahead. That may make a lot more sense than owning that hole in the water into which your money flows.

Put an Umbrella Over Your Marine Insurance Policy

Basic marine insurance coverage includes physical damage to your boat, bodily injury and property damage liability, and medical payments. You may also want to consider optional coverage for personal effects, emergency service, and trailers.

Consult your insurance agent for advice on purchasing an umbrella policy to expand your liability coverage. I will make the same suggestion for umbrella insurance coverage for homeowners and car owners.

Umbrella insurance puts a cushion between most sorts of liability and other claims and your possessions and investments. Because it is secondary (kicking in only after other insurance limits have been exhausted) it comes at relatively low cost.

CHAPTER 9

Paying for an Education

Education, once obtained and integrated into your skills and background, is a commodity. And like houses and cars, it deserves proper preparation by the savvy consumer.

For many people, paying for a college or technical education is one of their largest expenses, falling somewhere between a car and a house. This book is for readers of all ages, including young people about to head off to college (and the parents and grandparents of those young people), and for people who are considering school after a long hiatus. The preparation begins, for many, by setting aside money over the years, poring over programs that can reduce cost, researching loans, and adjusting personal earnings and holdings to qualify for scholarships and other assistance.

It is difficult to treat the college acceptance process as a purely economic transaction because in many cases, the demand for certain schools greatly overwhelms the supply. First, ask these questions: Is a college education necessary for everyone and every job? Is a $250,000 education at a top private school twice as valuable as a $125,000 degree from a well-regarded but less prestigious institution, and 10 times better than a degree from a state university? The best answer may come from working backwards from a career goal. Speak to guidance counselors, college advisors, and people already working in the field.

When in the past I hired employees, I was much more interested in their capabilities and proven performance than I was in the name and prestige of the schools they attended.

- **Ease the college bite with advance planning.**
- **Structure your income and assets for maximum financial aid.**
- **Negotiate for a better offer.**
- **Know the pluses and minuses of custodial accounts for children.**
- **Cut the cost of courses before registration.**
- **Reduce the textbook pain.**

Ease the College Bite with Advance Planning

Getting a head start on college financing gives you more time to search for money and may result in a higher scholarship or loan. One of the best gifts a parent or grandparent can give a newborn child is a healthy start to his or her college loan fund. The power of 18 years of earnings, augmented by later contributions, can be astounding. Here are some tips:

- **Apply early for federal student aid.** This probably won't increase the amount of aid you receive, but it might increase the chances of receiving a grant or subsidized loan. The number of students in an incoming class and the amount of available aid are both essentially fixed numbers. File early for college admission and for financial aid. In doing so, you may be taking advantage of a larger pool of money as well as a larger number of admission slots.

In 2016, the federal Department of Education made a meaningful change in the process for the Free Application for Federal Student Aid (FAFSA). The previous opening date for filing the form was January 1, and that presented problems for many applicants who might not have their full financial data from the previous year available until the IRS tax-filing deadline of April 15. The new deadline more closely matches the schedule for the college application process, and also allows students to use tax information from the previous year—at least in the initial filing. For example, a student applying for college admission for the 2018 academic year could file a FAFSA form on October 1, 2017, using tax information from the 2016 tax year.

- **Look for scholarships.** Work with your child to search for scholarships from organizations and corporations early in his or her high school years. Learn the requirements and the qualifications of successful applications well ahead of the deadlines.
- **Beat the bushes looking for lesser-known aid.** Some companies offer assistance for their employees' children. Look at programs offered by national organizations that are involved in the field your child will study (such as Future Farmers of America or Future Teachers of America). In the town where I live, there is a scholarship fund administered by the local government and that residents support by voluntary contribution. Our schools also have a separate program of scholarships—large and small—underwritten by local businesses and individuals. The guidance department at your child's high school should know about these sorts of programs.
- **Search the internet for scholarship programs.** Use search criteria that identify your child—ethnicity, religion, area of study interest, and recreational interests. Avoid any site that charges a fee or asks for personal financial information. You may be getting scammed.

Structure Your Income and Assets for Maximum Financial Aid

The FAFSA guidelines for college financial aid expect parents and students to contribute toward the cost of education when possible. (Contributions from other family members are generally outside of the calculation.) You have to file a new FAFSA form for each year you seek financial aid or loan assistance. The guidelines concentrate on two elements: a percentage of income above a rather low family living allowance and a percentage of the parents' total liquid assets (stock market shares, mutual funds, bonds, savings accounts, and other investments). Your principal home and all of your designated retirement account investments are excluded when tallying your assets.

(Vacation homes and rental properties are generally included in your assets.)

The student is also expected to contribute 50% of any income, after a specified exemption, toward college expenses.

High school guidance counselors and college financial aid offices are good places to learn about the latest adjustments to aid formulas and processes. Once you are up to speed, consider consulting your financial advisor to see if you can do anything to reallocate some of your assets and improve your chances for aid. It might make sense to move more money into retirement accounts, for example. Some workers who receive annual bonuses or commissions might want to look into accelerating or deferring these payments from one tax year to another.

The goal, for many applicants, is to shift income out of the base year for the aid application. The base year is the calendar year before your child begins college. If the income is shifted into the second or later year of your child's education, a college or university could later reduce financial aid, but this doesn't always happen. Most educational institutions allocate funds for the full number of years expected to earn a degree, and the school has a vested interest in keeping your child on its books. In any case, you've already received the benefit of the lower base year.

Consult your accountant to see if there are other ways to restructure your assets and reduce your income during the college years. As this book goes to press, the White House and Congress are considering reductions and changes to a multitude of federal programs. *Here are some examples of strategies to consider…*

- **If you own your own business, you may be able to defer earnings past graduation.**

- **Pay attention to withholding in the year before your base year so that you do not have to contend with a large tax refund.** That counts as income in the year you receive the refund.

- **Hold off on realizing capital gains in investments in base years, or balance gains with losses to avoid boosting your income.** The financial aid formula demands you spend more income than assets.

- **Pay off consumer debt, including credit cards, car loans, and personal loans.** The financial aid formula does not

Save Dough Re Me on Musical Instruments

Before you can send Junior to college, he or she just might have a stint in band. Before running out to buy a Stradivarius violin for your preteen, let him or her scratch away at a much lesser instrument while you see if there is beautiful music to be made.

You can sign up for a rental program through the school, or consider buying a used instrument from another student or at a rental store. Rental stores also are a source for purchase of used musical instruments from the previous class of students. The best time to purchase is at the end of the school year, after units have been returned. Ask for a reasonable warranty on the instrument and make sure there is a good supply of replacement parts for the particular instrument.

As far as rentals, check the internet for deals that might be better than those offered by a local store. The same applies for purchases; search the web for used musical instruments, remembering to seek a reasonable warranty.

take into account your personal debt, but it does weigh your assets against your eligibility for aid. Therefore, it may make sense to use savings to reduce your debt (and your monthly overhead). You are almost certainly paying more for a credit card balance, for example, than you are earning on investments.

- **If you don't have savings available for eliminating consumer debt, consider taking out a home equity loan for the purpose.** The interest rate on this secured loan is very likely to be less than you'll get from other lenders, and some (or all) of the interest is tax deductible. Just be careful not to put your home at risk with a loan beyond your ability to pay it off. And be on the lookout for changes to rules that may come from the White House and Congress.
- **Another source of lower-cost borrowing is the cash value of any whole-life insurance policy you may own.** Be aware that any outstanding loan balance will be deducted from the death benefit.

These strategies—and others—are intended to take advantage of legal exemptions and special programs. In no way am I suggesting you attempt fraud or evasion. That sort of activity is wrong, and likely to get the attention of federal agencies.

If you're comfortable using the Internet, try to qualify (or help your kids qualify) for extra scholarship money online. *Here are some resources…*

U.S. Department of Education	You can get information about the financial aid process, how to apply for college, and other useful tips	Ed.gov
FinAid	This private website explains the financial aid process as well as scholarships and other programs. It is not affiliated with the US Department of Education or other federal agencies.	FinAid.org
Fastweb	The page includes a searchable database of scholarships for different places around the country. Again, this is not a government or official site	Fastweb.com

Negotiate for a Better Offer

Your child wants to go to Beantown and has been accepted at Boston University with an offer of $10,000 per year in guaranteed loans. That's not quite as good as the $7,500 grant and $5,000 loan offered by Syracuse University, though. How should you choose? Before deciding on a college solely on the basis of money, think like a savvy consumer.

First, consider the total cost of a college education after factoring in grants and subsidized loans. A large grant from an expensive school may not be as attractive as a small grant from a college that costs less—that is, if the quality of the education is equivalent.

Call the admissions officer at Boston University and say, "We'd love to accept your offer, but we've received a better deal from Syracuse. Can you match the offer?" Many admissions officers have flexibility to improve on offers if they need to, and relatively few consumers of college education ever ask them to do so.

Your chances of getting more money from a college are greater early in the admissions cycle before all of the available scholarship and loan funds have been committed.

Get Help from Grandparents

Here's a way for Grandma and Grandpa (or other relatives) to help pay for college without incurring a gift-tax liability: Give the money directly to the college to pay the student's tuition and/or room and board. There is no tax on these payments. Consult a tax professional for the latest adjustments to tax codes.

Know the Pluses and Minuses of Custodial Accounts for Children

Many parents set up custodial accounts for their children as a way to save on taxes as they prepare for college bills. These accounts often use the Uniform Gifts to Minors Act or the similar Uniform Transfers to Minors Acts, usually referred to by their unpleasant-sounding abbreviations of UGMA or UTMA, respectively.

The tax code reduces the benefit on the federal level, and various states have different ways of dealing with these assets. Consult your financial advisor or tax preparer. One other thing: When a child reaches the age of 18 (or 21 in some states), he or she is no longer a minor and has legal control of the account. That means he or she could decide to buy a Harley or a ski chalet or take the money to Las Vegas instead of using the funds for a college education.

There also can be an adverse effect on your FAFSA application if you've saved up too much money in an UGMA or UTMA account. Students are expected to pay a higher percent of their savings toward college than are their parents. The decision comes down to deciding whether to pay extra taxes while you save versus receiving more free aid or a low-rate loan once your child is ready for college. Consult your accountant for advice on your particular situation.

Cut the Cost of Courses Before Registration

Every credit your child can earn before enrolling in college is almost certain to cost considerably less than one earned on campus. See if your child's high school offers advanced placement (AP) courses that are eligible to earn college credits. Find out if the college he or she plans to attend will accept the credits and, if so, how many. Colleges generally limit the number of credits that can come from AP courses.

Some colleges offer other ways to earn credits based on tests, community service and awards, and other means. It may also be possible for a high school student to take some courses at community colleges or long-distance education over the internet. Ask high school guidance counselors and college admission officials for advice.

Reduce the Textbook Pain

Some college textbooks come with designer-fashion price tags. That may be because the books are highly specialized and produced in relatively small numbers.

There are several ways to reduce the pain…

- **Buy online.** Shop websites and compare prices to those at the college bookstore.
- **Purchase used textbooks.** They may be available through the college bookstore, or from schoolmates, online from sources including Amazon and other booksellers. Check to make sure you are obtaining the latest edition, not an outdated version.
- **Rent textbooks.** Amazon and other booksellers are experimenting with programs that allow students to rent a textbook for a specific college term. You'll be given a specific due date for the return of the book.
- **Rent or buy a digital version of the textbook.** If you purchase the digital book, it is yours to keep. If you rent it, the title will be scheduled to automatically be disabled at the end of the term.
- **Share textbooks and other materials with classmates.** Make sure everyone involved agrees to make the book available when needed, and also decide how the book will be disposed of at the end of the term. If this arrangement works, it can also bring the added benefit of a study group to help prepare for tests and term papers.

CHAPTER 10

Planning Weddings and Funerals

Face the facts: The United States' divorce rate has been declining, but the death rate is 100%. We can do lots of things to enjoy and extend our lives, include fall in love and commit to spending the rest of it with someone. Life is full of beginnings and endings, but eventually, there is the end.

Here are the two heady topics we'll explore in this chapter…

- **Start your marriage with a discount.**
- **Arrange a funeral.**

Start Your Marriage with a Discount

When our daughter announced she was engaged to be married, it was my introduction to what I came to call the Wedding Industrial Complex, a massive industry that can be more complex than arranging for Space Shuttle liftoff and only slightly less expensive.

I quickly learned that choosing a date and a place for the ceremony were minor and relatively inconsequential details in comparison to the selection and purchase of The Dress.

The Dress

Consider these other hard-won tips:

- **Shop around.** If the bride finds the wedding dress of her dreams in a retail store, it is quite possible the same dress is available elsewhere. Note the designer, model number or name, and any other details such as color, special beading, or accessories. Then call other shops with that information and ask their price.
- **Don't underestimate the value of good customer service.** If one shop is slightly more expensive than another but promises alterations, storage, or free calmative herbal tea for the father of the bride, the mother of the bride, or the bride, factor that in.

• **Don't be afraid to call long distance.** If you could save $500 buying from a store a few hours away, it could be worth one trip for a fitting and another trip to pick it up.

• **Politely let the original store know you are shopping around.** The price may magically melt down to a more reasonable level.

• **Consider buying wholesale or at an outlet.** In the end, our daughter found The Dress at a store in Boston that specializes in wedding gown samples and overstocks from some of the best-known designers. The list price for The Dress was about that of a luxury car, while the sale price was merely that of a week's cruise in Europe.

• **Consider buying a used dress.** The seller may have decided she wants a different one after purchasing, so it may not have even been worn. Some websites specialize in used gowns, and reputable sites, such as Tradesy (Tradesy.com) and Preowned Wedding Dresses (PreownedWeddingDresses.com) offer buyer and seller protection. Just make sure your measurements are correct and recent, and familiarize yourself with the manufacturer's tendency to run true to size (or not).

• **Rent-a-dress.** Just as renting a formal gown for a rare occasion can save you money, so can renting a wedding dress. Rent the Runway (RenttheRunway.com) is a reputable site. However, when you rent a dress, you may not be able to alter it and it may have been worn multiple times, increasing the odds of it having a stain, tear, or ripped seams. Or it may be perfect and priced like a dream.

• **Factor in the cost of extras.** That includes shoes, undergarments, alterations, and accessories like veils and jewelry.

The Deposits

The average total cost of a wedding in the US is about $30,000. Once you establish a budget for a wedding, you will quickly realize the possible value of a special-event insurance policy. This policy covers the value of nonrefundable deposits for the reception, rehearsal hall, caterer, photographer, and (depending on your plans) just about anything else included in the event. You may be required to also include liability insurance to protect the owners of venues.

You can customize special event insurance in case the bride, groom, or their immediate family becomes ill, as well as cancellations or postponement because of weather or other events. You can even purchase *cold feet insurance* in case one side or the other decides to call the whole thing off. That particular coverage is relatively expensive and some would feel that it represents bad karma.

The cost of wedding insurance for my daughter amounted to several hundred dollars. We chose not to buy cold feet insurance, but did cover all contingencies, including weather and health emergencies. Among reputable sellers of these policies are Wedsure.com and Wedsafe.com, as well as several major national general insurance companies. If you buy your homeowners or auto insurance from an agent, you can ask for a recommendation. In any case, be sure to read the policies carefully and be sure you understand exclusions for pre-existing conditions and deductibles. Your goal is to cover everything that could go wrong, and not pay for protection you do not need.

Everything Else

No two weddings, or marriages that follow, are the same. But I know that advance planning can both save money and produce a more memorable ceremony and celebration. *Here are a few tips…*

- **Just see how much a catered dinner will be.** Ask for estimates on floral centerpieces. Check a DJ's prices. Just never say that you're planning a wedding. Items tend to be higher priced when proprietors know it has to do with nuptials.
- **Get married in any month other than May, June, September, or October.** Booking a venue and photographer will be much easier in January, too.
- **Schedule the reception and meal for the afternoon instead of the evening.** Most restaurants and banquet halls charge higher rates for the evening. You can avoid providing alcohol at noon without much negative feedback, as well.
- **Consider a buffet instead of a sit-down meal.** The latter requires lots of waitstaff. Another option is to plan an opulent dessert buffet instead of an elaborate meal.
- **Look for alternate sources for floral arrangements.** You can purchase flowers at some supermarkets or farmer's markets. Hardy daisies, baby's breath, and solidago are less expensive to use, and try green filler with beautiful texture. You may also be able to rent plants from a nursery instead of buying them. You can order cut flowers direct shipped. My daughter arranged for hundreds of beautiful long-stem hydrangeas for her wedding. The order was placed through Costco, a wholesale big-box club, and the flowers were delivered by FedEx, which picked them up at a farm in Colombia.
- **Photography can represent a huge expense.** Consider exactly what you require. You may want to document just the wedding ceremony and not the reception. I helped my daughter and her now-husband negotiate a deal with a well-regarded wedding photographer to shoot the ceremony and the big events of the reception. I did the rest. It is fun to provide each guest or table an inexpensive disposable camera for use during the reception. Collect all the cameras at the end of the party and have the pictures printed to keep for yourself or give to guests as a remembrance. Set up a communal online spot where your guests can upload and share the photos they took with their phones. Dropbox (Dropbox.com) and Shutterfly (Shutterfly.com) are just two examples of such sites.
- **Do you need a band, or will a DJ work?** For that matter, how about bringing a ready-made playlist on Spotify (Spotify.com) or on your phone and using the sound system at the catering hall? You can rent audio equipment if necessary.
- **Encourage your children to elope and then send them a nice check to use as a down payment on a house instead of paying for the wedding and all it entails.** In full disclosure, we gently suggested that to our daughter but she had her own dream. The couple had a very nice beach ceremony, followed by a reception in a spectacular and somewhat untraditional setting—the main gallery of the Whaling Museum on Nantucket Island where we live. And to the credit of our

daughter and son-in-law, they did not spend every last penny they were gifted. The leftover is on deposit as part of their future.

Keep It Local

There are something like 20,000 individual funeral homes in the United States. Many of them are relatively small businesses operated by families or local owners. But by some estimates, more than 15% of these establishments are not locally owned but are parts of national corporations.

America's largest funeral home operator is the coldly named Service Corporation International (SCI), traded on the New York Stock Exchange. SCI operates more than 1,600 funeral homes and 450 cemeteries in 43 states, most of Canada, and in Puerto Rico. Some of its brand names include Dignity Memorial, Dignity Planning, and Advantage, but in most locations the ownership is obscured behind the name of what may once have been an independent local operation. O'Sullivan's and Cohen's Funeral Home, to make up a somewhat plausible name, may have been part of your local community for decades, but the original owners may have sold out to SCI or another national chain a long time ago.

A national chain *may* be able to offer some savings because of its size, but a truly independent locally owned funeral home may be more accommodating of your desire to customize, simplify, and save money on their services. The only way to know is to ask; most funeral homes don't provide prices on their websites (more on that later).

Arrange a Funeral

Why do so many people do so little planning about this most predictable event? Why burden your spouse, significant other, children, or your estate with a considerable expense that is usually planned at a time of great stress?

One of the most troubling parts of the process of dealing with the loss of a loved one is the fact that there are usually many important decisions that need to be made in a relatively short period of time. And to compound the stress, the cost of services and supplies such as caskets are often difficult to assess. I would expect that most funeral arrangements are made without a great deal of thought given to saving money that could be used for other purposes, including caring for surviving family members.

Opting Out

You may decide you don't want the traditional ritual. You can always donate your body to science (which is usually free), be cremated and bypass the traditional burial in a cemetery (though rules vary by state; look up funeral laws in your state to learn more), or be buried immediately (with no embalming or ceremony).

Preplanning or Prepaying

If you've got the heart for it, inquire about prices and request less expensive options. Or ask a trusted friend or other representative to make arrangements on your behalf, instructing him or her about your needs and wants.

You have two basic advanced funeral service options: preplanning and prepaying.

Preplanning

Preplanning means specifying all the services you want, removing those you do not want, and choosing a casket and other supplies. In its simplest form, a funeral home or your representative will have a detailed list of what you chose to implement when needed.

It is not necessary to prepay for funeral arrangements to save on expenses. You, or your loved one, can meet with a funeral home and put all funeral desires on record, including choice of casket and services. This eliminates some of the pain of arranging for a funeral after death and allow for a more dispassionate decision.

You can also consult an attorney or accountant for assistance in setting up a revocable living trust (sometimes called a *Totten Trust*), which can earmark funds to pay for funerals at a later time.

A simpler solution can be to set up a joint savings account with a family member who has *right of survivorship*. That family member can then spend the earmarked money on a funeral. There is no guarantee the funds will be used for the purpose you declare, though. Be sure you have a clear understanding with the account's co-owner, and plan on leaving some extra money in the account to pay for tax on interest earned.

Prepaying

In many cases, this is the best way to combine preplanning with cost savings. You or your representative make all the necessary choices...discuss and negotiate the total price...and then make full or partial payment to lock in the deal. When the time comes, a single phone call should be all that is necessary to get the plan underway. If you prepay for funeral arrangements, be sure you know what you are paying for. *Here are some questions to ask...*

- **Is this the full and final price for the entire process?** Does that include the services of the funeral home, the location for a service (if one is planned), and a burial plot, cremation, or other arrangements? Are there any situations that would add expenses? Make sure the answer to that question is included in the contract you sign. If it isn't, reconsider this funeral home.

- **Am I fully protected against any and all price increases at the funeral home?** The principal reason to prepay for a funeral is to lock in a price. Your costs shouldn't fluctuate down the line after you've paid.

- **How is the prepayment safeguarded?** Some states require that money be placed in trust accounts. In some states you are entitled to receive any earned interest on the deposit. What are your protections against the funeral home going out of business or being sold to another company? In some states, the money is placed in escrow in a bank account to ensure it will be available when needed. Ask the funeral director how the money is safeguarded. Also ask the director to provide for you a copy your state's regulations on such accounts.

Do I or another family member have the right to cancel the contract and receive a deposit or full refund? What if the person covered by the plan moves from the area before death, or if his or her final wishes change? If you are not happy with the answer you receive, take your business elsewhere or open a funeral savings account that can be used anywhere.

If you do enter into a prearrangement for yourself or a loved one, be sure that others in your family are fully aware of the details so that they don't make other arrangements.

Know Your Rights

The Federal Trade Commission's Funeral Rule requires a funeral home to disclose its prices for individual services and items. If you inquire in person, the funeral home must give you a written price list of available goods and services. Ask about service packages as well as individual services. The elements include embalming, cremation, caskets, and use of the home for services. You can also call a funeral home to ask about terms, conditions, or prices—the FTC rule requires the provider to reveal prices over the phone.

In 2016, several consumer groups petitioned the FTC to ask that the agency require every funeral home to post its full price list for products and services on their websites. That petition was pending at the time of this book's publication. Some states, including California, already have this requirement. This lets you get an understanding of the general range of prices and services before you visit or call a funeral home.

Per the Funeral Rule, a funeral provider must disclose, in writing, that embalming is not required by law except in certain special cases, such as when a body must be transported to another state or if a funeral will be delayed for several days. You must also be told of your right to choose direct cremation or immediate burial instead of embalming. The FTC requires funeral homes not to claim that embalming or other processes will preserve a body indefinitely. (On a practical note, embalming is usually recommended or required if the body is going to be viewed, although some religious beliefs do not allow this.) Funeral homes are also required to inform you if they mark up items they may procure for you, such as flowers, clergy, and obituary notices.

If you choose cremation, there is no reason to buy an expensive casket. The container is incinerated with the body. Consider asking for a considerably less expensive container made of cardboard, fabric, or pressed wood. The Funeral Rule requires providers to disclose, in writing, your right to buy an unfinished wood box or an alternative container for a direct cremation, and they must make these available to customers.

In general, the funeral provider must disclose the specific state law that requires you to purchase any particular item on your itemized statement of goods and services selected. The FTC offers information about the Funeral Rule at this site: Blinc.Media/2wWZ5bB. Some states' laws are provided at Nolo (NOLO.com/legal-encyclopedia/burial-cremation-laws), but if yours isn't one of them, search online for *burial laws your state*.

About caskets: The funeral provider cannot refuse to accept or use a casket you bought elsewhere, and they cannot charge a handling fee. (I explain more about obtaining a casket on your own in a moment.)

Most states have a licensing board that regulates the funeral industry. You may contact the licensing board in your state for information or help. (Search *funeral licensing board your state* to get to the right site.) Look on the same sites for information about state-run or state-supervised escrow funds or other ways in which prepayment for funeral costs are protected for consumers. If you want additional information about how to make funeral arrangements and the options available, you may want to contact interested business, professional, and consumer groups like AARP.

Negotiate

Visit the websites of several funeral homes to get a sense of their operations. If they list prices, make a copy and make your own estimate of total cost. Call several funeral homes and ask to speak with a funeral planner. Make it clear that you are seeking to treat this as a purchase, and that you expect to receive the best available price. You will not be the first person to ask for a better deal. If you are not treated properly on the phone, move on to another funeral home.

Have a clear idea of which services you want and which are unnecessary. Not everyone wants a religious service at a second location. It adds expenses for transporting the casket and mourners, and not everyone wants entire jungles stripped for floral arrangements.

Understand the Casket Shell Game

Caskets are often the most expensive single item at a funeral, a pricey piece of furniture that has a very short useful life. And as I've already noted, a casket or coffin may not be necessary at all if the body will be cremated.

The FTC prohibits funeral homes from making claims that caskets are watertight or airtight unless this can be proven. In truth, nearly every casket eventually rusts, warps, or deteriorates. Metal caskets often are described as having gaskets or sealers or other protective devices. The FTC points out that these systems serve only to delay the penetration of water. Wooden caskets are usually not gasketed and do not carry a long warranty period. Many cemeteries (and some state laws) require a burial vault or a grave liner to enclose the casket in a grave; the purpose of this cement device is to prevent the ground from caving in as the casket deteriorates.

A casket is not designed for comfort or longevity. If you pay retail prices, it can work out to be one of the more expensive pieces of furniture you will ever buy. *If you must have a casket, you might be able to save money with these tips...*

- **Choose a less-expensive casket as part of preplanning (or even at the last moment) at the funeral home.**
- **If the family has chosen cremation but the body will be viewed beforehand, ask about renting a casket.** The deceased can be transferred into a lesser container before cremation.

TIP

For Veterans

If you are a US veteran, you may have burial benefits, including headstone or marker and burial in a national cemetery with military honors, at no charge. If the deceased meets certain eligibility requirements, a burial expense allowance is provided. Call the Department of Veterans Affairs at 1-800-827-1000 for more information.

- **Order a casket and supply it to the funeral home.** You can save hundreds or thousands of dollars by shopping for a casket through a website. Search online for caskets. Your local funeral home is required to accept delivery and use the casket you provide without imposing any additional charge.
- **If you've got the nerve and the storage space, you can order a casket now and keep it ready.**
- **You can use very inexpensive containers or vessels in which to hold one's ashes (though cemeteries often have rules about what they will accept).** You are not required to buy from a funeral home's selection of urns; you can buy one from elsewhere and have it delivered there.

CHAPTER 11

Seeking Helping Hands

What do nursing homes, childcare, and lawyers have in common? They are necessary in our modern society. Most people who work in these fields are well-meaning folks who are providing important services. Parents want or need to work outside the home but also need someone to watch their young children. Many of us live longer than our abilities to care for ourselves lasts. And lawyers…well, sometimes you need them and most times you don't want to need them.

- **Find a safe place for those in need.**
- **Choose the best childcare.**
- **Pick a good defense.**

Find a Safe Place for Those in Need

Generations ago, elderly family members may have lived with their children until and unless they needed intensive medical care. Today, the elderly are more likely to receive a progression of care from in-home providers. From there, where? Possibilities include a hospital, hospice for those deemed to be in the final stages of life, a nursing home for people who need a high level of care outside of a hospital, and a rehabilitation center for patients expected to return to their former environs. In the past few decades, two other facility types have become worthy options: assisted living facilities, which help residents with their daily needs and provide a base level of medical supervision, and senior or adult communities, which provide a la carte services from housekeeping to meals and social activities.

Each of these options allows older people to get the most out of their extended lives. The problem is that all of these forms of care cost, and some are extremely expensive. Medicare will pay for a limited number of days in a hospital, nursing home, or rehabilitation center. Medigap insurance, if you have purchased it, will extend the number of days or the amount reimbursed.

Medicaid offers a similar level of coverage for people who have limited means or who have special conditions. Medicaid is available to US citizens and permanent legal residents in certain situations, and is generally administered at the state level.

Invest in Long-Term Care Insurance

If it's not too late, consider buying and maintaining long-term care insurance. This sort of policy pays most or all the cost of in-home care, nursing home, or other assistance. Long-term care is not cheap, and the annual premium becomes higher and higher the longer you wait to purchase it. The issuer sets its price based on your health and life expectancy at the time you apply for coverage.

In general, most experts say the best time to buy this sort of policy is when you are in your early to mid-50s, when you are presumably in good health and financially well established. Prices begin to rise sharply after then—if you can find a company to underwrite a policy. Remember that you must continue paying the premiums every year or you lose all your previous payments.

Consult a financial advisor before considering this form of insurance, and be sure you fully understand the terms and conditions as well as the financial stability of the company issuing the policy. Chapter 35 has more information about long-term health insurance.

It should come as no surprise that coverage eligibility and benefits for Medicaid, and possibly Medicare, are the subject of political debate as of this book's writing and could possibly be reduced.

In general, an individual is expected to pay for a nursing home and most specialized residential care out of personal funds and assets until he or she runs out of money. Many states exclude some holdings, such as the spouse's residence, from assets that you must pay. Children and other family members, besides the spouse, are not generally required to pay for care in most states. The following sections look in more detail at some of the available options other than hospitalization.

In-Home Care

In some instances, you may be able to stay in your own home (or move to a smaller residence) and contract for in-home health services or live-in nursing assistance. The comfort and security of home are the most obvious advantages to this setup. Many health services can be performed in the home, and most insurance plans will pay some or all of the cost. You can also hire assistance for housecleaning and cooking.

In addition, your property's value can continue appreciating. Consider taking advantage of home-equity loans and reverse mortgages to pay expenses during retirement. You will still be responsible for home maintenance, taxes, and other living expenses.

On the downside, some health-care options, such as specialized therapies are more expensive when they are delivered in the home. If you're paying the cost on your own, you can shop around. If you depend on assistance from private or government insurance, investigate to determine the level of coverage.

If you hire a caregiver through a professional agency or institution, it is reasonable to expect that the worker will pay taxes on income and that there is appropriate workers compensation and liability insurance in place; take the time to ask the provider. You can also consult with your insurance agent for advice about your personal liability.

And then there is this: the underground economy. Many providers of services of all sort will ask to be paid in cash, on a casual basis. This may represent a significant cost savings to you. But this may also be a major risk to you: are you protected if the worker is injured in your home? Do they have workers compensation coverage? Does your home or renters insurance provide liability coverage for casual labor? Are they (or you) paying all necessary state and federal taxes?

Nursing Homes

A nursing home can provide full-time medical and nursing care, meals, and a social environment for the aged or ill person unable to care for him or herself. That said, a nursing home can also make a person feel less in control of his or her life, and represents a major change in lifestyle. As I've noted, once private health insurance or Medicare has reached the limit of its coverage, the cost of a nursing home falls to the patient or the family, and is very expensive. Medicaid, which is generally available to people who have low income and have spent most of their personal assets, offers basic coverage of nursing home costs although not every facility chooses to accept Medicaid patients.

Long Term Care insurance generally will pay for some or all of the costs of a nursing home (or, alternatively, assisted living facilities and in-home care) up to the limits of the plan you have purchased. Make sure you understand the policy, including the number of days, months, or years (or the cash value it will provide) for care. Very few policies offer unlimited amounts of coverage.

Do as much research as you can well before the need for a nursing home arises. Consult with advocacy groups for senior citizens and health care organizations. Learn about nursing home facilities in your area (and elsewhere) that might suit you or your loved ones. Consider a consultation with an elder law attorney to learn about your legal rights, and to discuss ways to protect some of your assets.

Shared Living Arrangement

Seniors who are in reasonably good health may be able to find friends, family, or others to share a living arrangement. Some senior citizen organizations—including state agencies for the elderly as well as private groups—offer house-sharing matchmaker services. Ask your local government or a senior center near you for suggestions. Living expenses like these should be significantly less than those for a single-family home, and the residents share in one another's company.

You could also explore accepting a renter into your home, either to provide a source of income or as a form of barter in exchange for certain services such as housekeeping and basic care.

Depending on the housing arrangement, there may not be medical or nursing services available in the home. Also, the retiree may have to pay taxes on profits from the sale of his or her own home and may lose home equity and reverse-mortgage opportunities. Be sure to consult an attorney or financial advisor if you're considering this living situation.

Planned Retirement Community

From luxury condominiums on sun-drenched Florida golf courses to retirement communities in Arizona with their own shopping centers, medical facilities, and entertainment, retirement communities can be attractive if you can afford to live in such places.

Consult a Pro

What if a husband becomes ill and his wife is left home alone? Will medical expenses force her into indigence? Can an individual or a couple make gifts to their children or other family members before funds are taken for health care? The rules vary under different federal programs and from state to state, including protections—in some states—that apply to residences.

It may make sense to put money into a trust or other financial arrange-ment to prevent being forced to spend most of your savings on medical care. This is legal and proper, but not effective in all situations. Before you or a family member face medical expenses that go beyond your current coverage, consult a financial advisor, elder affairs attorney, or other specialist about ways to structure your investments to protect your family. Do this sooner rather than later; in most situations there is a look-back period under which the federal government or state can examine your finances for prior years and look for ways to recoup funds including delaying the start of benefits. In general, as this book went to press, the Medicaid look-back period is five years; bureaucrats will look for transfers or gifts in that time that served to reduce total assets.

Some complexes may offer a private apartment with shared services, including a communal dining hall or delivered meals; home maintenance and some medical and housekeeping services; transportation and entertainment options. On the downside, buying a new home or condominium in a planned community may be costlier than what you made selling your previous home. There is also the possibility that worsening health will force you to move later to a more-inclusive facility, potentially resulting in a loss on your investment.

Some centers offer several levels of assistance in one facility, allowing transition from basic services to assisted living to nursing home care.

There is also the possibility that maintenance charges and other fees will increase over time. You, or an attorney you hire, can also look into the center's financial stability and reputation. Additionally, consult an attorney if any parts of the lease are unclear.

Specialized Care Unit

Housing in these sort of facilities is specifically designed to accommodate the needs of residents, and caregivers are trained to offer appropriate assistance. Persons forced to deal with a specific disease or condition, such as Alzheimer's disease or cancer, may need to move to a facility that includes housing as well as onsite or on-call specialists. On the downside, the arrangement may be unattractive to a spouse or roommate, and in some cases, someone other than the patient is not allowed to stay at the center at all. Other disadvantages include the loss of home equity opportunities related to the sale of a former home, and possible tax consequences if the patient is required to sell investments or accelerate payments from annuities or retirement accounts.

Most long-term care policies will pay for specialized care, up to the time or dollar limits of the plan you have purchased.

Choose the Best Childcare

Time was when nearly every couple with children depended entirely on a single income source. Today, young couples with a newborn or young child are much more likely to both be in the workforce and engage childcare.

Some companies offer childcare facilities at their work sites, a laudable effort to hold on to their valued employees. Federal (and a handful of state) laws have offered tax breaks and other encouragements to employers and employees.

Let's leave aside cost for the moment. I know that's difficult for many people to do, because unless your company offers onsite facilities, the cost of childcare usually comes right off the top of any income that the mother or father will be able to earn. However, the fact is that the most important consideration about childcare should be the quality of the environment and supervision provided.

Traditional childcare options include state-certified commercial operations, informal placements with a relative, or small centers operated in homes. Spend the time to personally visit any place you're considering enrolling your child. Go during the day when the center is in full operation and see for yourself what is going on. Then seek recommendations from current and former clients. Call state or county social-services agencies to ask if there are any outstanding complaints—or compliments—they can share with you.

In addition, here are some alternatives to consider...

- **Childcare cooperative.** Find three or four families willing to alternate watching each other's children on a rotating basis. This situation lends itself well to part-time jobs. Be sure to find out as much as you can about the background of others in the group and visit the homes where the children will stay.

- **Job sharing.** Two parents in the same family or in two different families can share one job, alternating care for the children. Again, look into the background and home situation of any outside partners.

- **Telecommuting.** You can do many jobs at home full time or part time. Your employer may provide a computer and phone facilities, or subsidize your setup. Be realistic about the demands of your job—and of your children—before deciding to attempt to work at home.

- **In-home childcare.** Consider hiring a nanny or an au pair (who will live in your home) to stay with children while parents are off at work. You'll have to weigh the cost of such care against the income you will generate; some parents can even justify a losing financial equation if it allows one or both parents to remain in their job and move up the career ladder. Be sure to consult with an attorney or accountant to fully understand employment taxes, workers compensation requirements, and insurance liability issues. Before you consider an "off-the-books" arrangement, consider the personal testimony of a top executive at Bottom Line Books whose workers compensation policy was called into play when a nanny had an automobile accident with the family car.

Pick a Good Defense

If you're lucky and without flaw, you'll never need a lawyer for defense in a criminal or civil suit. But sometimes things happen, and sometimes you need legal assistance. Besides legal cases, a lawyer is very valuable for real estate, estate planning, and many other significant transactions. Saving money by being your own legal expert could end up being a very expensive mistake.

Pro Bono

Some state bar plans include a free or reduced-rate consultation. Additionally, some states offer programs for senior citizens as well as low-income legal-assistance programs. Check with your state's bar association for information.

Don't expect a full range of services from such free or reduced-cost programs, but they may help you learn precisely what further assistance you need to pay for.

Choose a Good Lawyer

How do you get yourself a good lawyer? I have resisted the urge to let loose with a spate of lawyer jokes (although I've got a ton of them). The serious answer is by conducting a careful search for the most appropriate and affordable candidate.

It doesn't make sense to spend $1,000 to collect a $100 bad debt, and it is equally foolish to pay any money at all to an attorney who has no expertise and experience with your kind of legal issue. Don't hire a real-estate attorney for a criminal defense, or the other way around.

For most personal and business matters, ask for references from people who have had similar situations. Ask friends, business acquaintances, and members of any civic groups to which you belong. A lawyer referral service is another source of information. Many state bar associations offer the service. You can do some of your own basic research by consulting the Martindale-Hubbell Law Directory at Martindale.com. Check the background and specialties of lawyers in your area at this website.

Once you find an attorney (or better, two or three) you think is appropriate, schedule a preliminary consultation. Most lawyers will give you a brief free or low-cost meeting to discuss your case, their experience, and projected charges. Prepare a simple summary of your needs or case and the sort of backup material you have for your position. Ask about fees and whether the attorney himself or herself will do the work or if a clerk or assistant will be involved. Gauge your level of comfort and confidence with the attorney. It's very easy to change lawyers before work begins. It's much more difficult to change lawyers after they have begun working for you.

You can check with bar associations in most states to see if a particular attorney has any negative notations on the record. Beyond that, seek references from people you know and trust.

And though this is not a hard-and-fast rule, don't be swayed by an office that is decorated like a palace. Who paid for that elegance?

Legal Assistance Cost

Most likely, you will pay more than you expect or want to pay. But you can help yourself by understanding how lawyers calculate legal fees and by actively protecting your own interests.

Ask for a full disclosure of fees and expenses before you hire a lawyer. Get it in writing if possible. Ask for a letter spelling out the arrangement. Many lawyers will present you with a contract with the cost details.

A legal fee is usually based on time and labor. The more unusual or difficult the case, the more hours will add up. Most law firms in a particular area and size will charge about the same for similar cases. A small one-person storefront office may have a lower hourly rate than a five-story downtown firm. Also, more complex or specialized cases are usually given to the most experienced or well-connected attorneys, and they generally charge higher hourly rates.

The client is also responsible for most expenses including telephone calls, postage, court fees, and research costs. Some law firms are more insistent in this area than others. A high-tone Boston firm that represented me once charged for every last staple and photocopy. When the lawyer called to update me on the progress, I used to cringe when she'd ask about the weather or my latest travel book. All I could think was "Three dollars a minute—a nickel a second—for the call and her time." She was a good attorney, but I kept social niceties to a minimum.

Here are some ways to save on your legal bills…

- **Do as much documentation organization as you can.** Prepare a folder of correspondence, contracts, and a written timeline of events and conversations. Lay it all out to give your representative as much information up front as possible. (Have a quick conversation with your attorney about how to present your documentation so that they are considered confidential. Otherwise, your documentation could be subpoenaed.)
- **Keep a close eye on bills.** Review them as they arrive and don't be shy about asking for detailed explanations of any items. Where appropriate, request copies of letters and documents prepared on your behalf. (You may be billed for photocopying and postage, but at least you'll have some way to gauge the material work performed on your behalf.)

There are four common types of fee arrangements. Sometimes, you may have a combination of arrangements.

- **Set fee.** For common legal tasks such as drawing up a will, settling a real-estate transaction, or some simple divorce cases, a lawyer may have a set fee. Get a written statement of the charges. You will also be responsible for court costs and expenses related to the case.
- **Hourly rate.** In some ways this is the simplest arrangement. You'll be quoted an hourly rate for all work performed on your behalf. Don't be surprised to find that every 60-second phone call or five-minute consultation with a colleague in the coffee shop will appear on the bill. Be sure you know the hourly rate. Also ask for an estimate of the number of hours the lawyer expects to bill; in most states lawyers are required to provide this. Remember that an estimate is just that: an educated guess. You could ask for a cap on costs, and also to be regularly updated on the balance due. But there is no certainty about the final cost.

You do have the right to question a charge, and state bar associations generally have guidelines on billing practices. And there are attorneys (not very popular with their peers) who will represent you if it appears you have a legitimate reason to challenge a legal bill.

- **Retainer.** This amounts to a down payment toward future fees. Bills are deducted from the retainer's remaining balance. A lawyer can bill jobs against the retainer at an hourly rate or a by-job basis. In some instances, a law firm may bill at a lower hourly rate to clients who put down a retainer with the firm. The retainer may have to be replenished over time as charges are deducted.

- **Contingency fee.** In this case, the attorney collects a fee only if a case is settled or successfully argued in court. The fee comes from a percentage of any award. Contingency arrangements are often used in accident and negligence cases. In general, a lawyer's willingness to take on a case with a contingency fee means he or she believes you have a good chance of winning. It also puts the pressure on the lawyer to do everything reasonably possible to collect a fee. On the other hand, a lawyer in a contingency fee case may be more willing to accept an out-of-court settlement at a lower amount (because that is certain money). You might not have to pay anything if the case is unsuccessful.

CHAPTER 12

Avoiding Fraud

Fraud is the dark underbelly of commerce. There is an entire industry of low-lifes who seek to rob you with a fountain pen instead of a gun (a warning poetically framed by Woody Guthrie). These people can be anywhere: down the block or on the other side of the planet. They might knock on your door, call you by phone, or contact you on the internet. And they are pretty clever at finding ways to trick people into buying their scams—but they're not as clever as a savvy consumer fending them off.

- **Know what to watch for.**
- **Be aware of online scams.**
- **Protect your computer.**
- **Handle a telemarketer.**
- **Deal with merchandise you didn't order.**
- **Fend off pyramid schemes.**
- **Guard against phony charities.**
- **Deal with data fraud.**

Know What to Watch For

Fraud is fraud, whether it is committed face-to-face, phone, web or mail. Most of us would agree that our modern tools like smartphones and the internet are positive things, but very few of us ever imagined the huge growth in fraud they would bring.

Congratulations! You have won the lottery in Nigeria even though you have never been there and never entered the contest. All you need to do is pay a small fee to "expedite" the shipment of your check.

A round of applause! A relative you didn't know you had in a place you've never heard of has named you in a will and there's a large bucket of cash waiting for you. All you need to do is provide us with your checking account number and your Social Security number and wait for the money to arrive.

You are in luck! My client, the former Deputy Assistant to the Assistant Secretary to the Undersecretary of Defense in the Democratic Republic of Unheardofstan has set aside the amount

> **TIP**
>
> **Trust Your Gut**
>
> If an offer sounds too good to be true, it almost certainly is. Also, be wary if someone tries to put a tremendous amount of pressure on you to make a decision right now. If you act in haste, you may end up with a great deal of time to regret in leisure.

of 10 million Kazakhstani tenge and he has selected you as a person he can trust to transfer those funds out of the country. He is willing to pay you a fee of 50% of the money. All you need to do is pay for the courier, which you can do right now by providing your credit card number and your personal identification number.

You wouldn't fall for any of these appeals, would you? Would you? Thousands of people fall for scams like these, and others that are just as blatant. They're obvious when you stop and read the appeal, but not so obvious when someone is pressuring you.

And in recent years, some of the fraud has moved from the hands of relative amateurs to professionals who work from data stolen from banks, merchants, and from social media where some people display all sort of personal information (date of birth, phone numbers, and details that could allow educated guesses about passwords to other sites.) It is essential that you regularly monitor your credit card and bank statements for fraud.

Here are some tip-offs to crooked telemarketers and scam artists…

- **The caller or website asks you for information they should already have.** If someone claims to be calling from your bank or credit card company or internet service provider, they already have your account information on file. If someone calls you claiming to be from a credit card company and asks you for your credit card number, something is wrong. (It's different if you call the number on the back of your credit card or on your statement. In that case, you will need to identify yourself to the company.)

- **They push you to "act now" and "before the offer expires."** While it is not unusual for a special offer to be valid for a particular period of time, it is not standard business practice to pressure a customer to decide right now, right here.

- **They offer a "free" gift or vacation, but demand a handling or shipping charge.** Be especially wary if you cannot obtain details about the prize before having to pay the charge.

- **They congratulate you on winning a prize but then ask you to pay for it** (or ask if you want to buy something to increase your odds of winning a prize).

• **They request for your bank account number or a credit card before you agree to a deal.** Other tip-offs include an offer to send a courier right away to pick up cash or a check.

• **They promise you that their honesty and business practices are of the highest standards.** And then they insist there is no reason to check out the offer with an accountant, the Better Business Bureau, a friend or family member, a lawyer, or the police. To me that is an open invitation to call everyone on that list plus a few others. Or hang up the phone.

Be Aware of Online Scams

I could write an entire book about online scams and it would almost immediately be out of date. That's because, to adapt the caption from a famous *New Yorker* cartoon from early in the age of personal computers, "On the Internet, no one knows you're a dog." What do I mean by that? There are so many ways to deceive online, and so very few reliable tools to detect fraud. How do you know the email you received, which has your bank's logo and slogan, is really from your bank? What about websites that are one letter away from the real thing? The address might read customerservice@anazon.com. Did you catch the n instead of the m? Not everyone would. And how do you protect yourself from someone stealing your personal information, including checking account numbers, credit card numbers, and passwords?

Here are some general guidelines…

• **Have a suspicious mind.** Don't automatically trust that an email offer or request is legitimate.

• **Don't provide financial or personal information unless you are certain that the company asking for it is legitimate.** Look closely at the web address. If you have the slightest doubt, call the company using a phone number you obtain from other sources, like the customer service number found on the back of a credit card or on a mailed statement.

• **Examine your banking and credit card statements regularly and carefully.** Insist on a full explanation of any activity you do not recognize or did not authorize. If you don't recognize a charge, call the financial institution (not the biller) and ask for details.

• **Read statements you receive from companies you deal with.** I was helping a family member and noticed that a cellphone bill showed four phones when they had only three. A bit of investigation found that someone had obtained access to their account a year ago, and they had been paying for this fraud all the time. And then I had to push through to a supervisor to obtain a full refund for all 12 months after the first agent had offered only six months. The easiest way to push in this sort of situation? Ask to cancel your service; it gets their attention.

Email

Examine the sender's electronic return address. (Some email programs automatically display the full address, while others require an extra click or two to display it.) If someone is claiming to be from customer support at Amazon.com but the return address is something like *chipmunk@prankster.com* something is definitely wrong.

If you receive an email that appears to be from your bank, credit card company, or any other financial institution but something appears odd, call the company. Call the phone number on your statements or the back of your credit card or from other official sources. Don't call any phone number listed on the solicitation email.

Protect Your Computer

Use complex and obscure passwords, and change them about every six months (and every time there is a security breach at a company where you are a customer). In your home it is okay to keep a notebook with your passwords, although I suggest a bit of obfuscation. I regularly add a code like L1-4-3-2 alongside passwords indicating that I should reorder the last four characters in that order. I do something similar with the notes I take with me when I travel, a code to scramble or unscramble. And if my list (at home or on the road) ever goes missing I immediately reset all passwords.

Make sure your personal computer is protected by strong and regularly updated antivirus and antispam software. The following programs were voted three of the best by *PC Magazine* in 2017 and include a vulnerability check, which the others didn't. The prices are approximate, of course, and current as of this writing. You can buy the software on these websites or at office-supply stores.

Software	**Website**	**Price***
Avast Pro Antivirus 2017	Avast.com/en-us/pro-antivirus	$50
Bitdefender Antivirus Plus	Bitdefender.com	$50
Kaspersky Anti-Virus	Kaspersky.com/antivirus	$40
McAfee AntiVirus Plus (2017)	Mcafeestore.com/products/anti-virus-plus	$25

*Prices subject to change.

If you use a WiFi system in your home or office, make sure it is protected by a strong level of encryption and that the password to access it is complex and obscure. In general, I recommend you do not use WiFi systems in restaurants and public spaces for anything other than checking your email or browsing the internet. It is relatively easy for a sophisticated hacker to intercept traffic from smartphones, tablets, and computers in public systems. Do not access your banking or credit card accounts or any other site that has your credit card saved in its system. (If you use your smartphone in connection with regular cellular signals, not WiFi, there is less chance of electronic snooping.

At home, make sure your personal WiFi system is protected by a complex password. PASSWORD or 123456789 are not good choices.

Handle a Telemarketer

The good news is that the Federal Trade Commission (FTC) has set some very strict regulations about how a telemarketer can seek your business. The bad news is that the regulations are easy for fraudsters to evade, especially if they are calling from a foreign country, using a false or proxy phone number or location, or they just don't care. Those who seek to commit fraud are criminals, and criminals are not known for following the law. Just the opposite, actually.

That said, here are your rights as a consumer, as defined by FTC regulations and other laws…

- **A telemarketer cannot call you outside the hours of 8 a.m. and 9 p.m.** unless you have given them permission to do so.
- **A company cannot call you again if you have directly asked them to stop calling.** Keep records of any such request, including the date and time, as well as the name and phone number of the caller. If the telemarketer will not give you that information he or she is, by definition, not following legally mandated business practices.
- **If the telemarketer promises a lottery or a prize,** he must not ask for a purchase or payment for you to enter or win.
- **Telemarketers must not misrepresent any information,** including facts about their goods or services, the risk or liquidity of an investment, or the nature of a prize.
- **You must be advised of any restrictions on obtaining goods and services,** and if a sale is final or nonrefundable.
- **It is illegal for a telemarketer to withdraw money from your checking account or make a credit card charge without your express, verifiable authorization.**

As always, there are some exceptions. If you call a marketer, you give up some of your rights. Nonprofit organizations are free to keep calling you, even if you're on the FTC's national Do Not Call Registry (which you can sign up for at DoNotCall.gov). Read more about how to avoid fake charities later in this chapter.

Fake Taxes

The IRS may want your money, but at least it's legal for them to take it. Scams based on taxes and that purport to come from the IRS are very common. Don't fall for them. If someone calls and says you owe back taxes, hang up. Then, either call the IRS at 1-800-829-1040 (if you know or suspect you owe) or 1-800-366-4484 (if you know or suspect you *don't* owe). They will never send unsolicited email or text messages, nor will they conduct business over social media. If you want to read more about common scams or how to deal with them, visit the IRS website at http://bit.ly/1ZvpVNd.

Deal with Merchandise You Didn't Order

If you receive something you did not order, request, or allow to be sent to you on consignment, you can consider it a free gift. This includes packages sent to you or services provided electronically.

You have no legal obligation to do anything, but some experts advise you to write the seller a letter stating that you never ordered the item and, therefore, have a legal right to keep it for free. According to the FTC, such a letter will help you establish that you never ordered the merchandise and may discourage the seller from sending you repeated bills or notices. You may want to send your letter by certified mail and keep the return receipt and a copy of the letter. These scams are almost always committed not by individual people who ordered something for themselves and accidentally sent it to your address, but by a "company" trying to dupe someone into paying for something.

That said, avoid unintentionally giving a marketer permission to send you something. . .along with a bill. Read the fine print carefully when participating in a sweepstakes or when ordering trial or free merchandise. You may be joining a club that consists of regular purchases or that require you to notify them that you are opting out. Another example of this sort of marketing is a *negative option* plan. Book and record clubs like this were once common. (Some still exist, including clubs that send wine, food, and other items.) Under this perfectly legal structure, you are sent merchandise until you instruct the seller to stop.

If you receive bills or dunning notices for unordered merchandise, you can offer to return the merchandise provided the seller pays for postage and handling. Give the seller a specific and reasonable amount of time in which to pick up the merchandise or arrange to return it at their expense. Inform the seller that after the specified time period has passed, you reserve the right to keep the merchandise or to dispose of it as you wish.

Free samples that are clearly marked as such, and merchandise, such as tote bags and pens, mailed by charitable organizations asking for contributions are legal to send to you without your ordering them. In either case, you may keep such shipments as free gifts.

Fend Off Pyramid Schemes

One of the oldest scams, the pyramid scheme, is alive and well—and expanding. It has nearly toppled Eastern European governments, spread onto the internet, and generally recast itself into a thousand variations of the same old song. Also known as *multilevel*, *downline*, *network*, or *matrix marketing*, pyramid schemes typically promise that if you sign up as a distributor, you will receive commissions from your own sale of goods or services as well as from sales by other people you recruit to join the distributors.

Why is pyramiding prohibited or heavily regulated by most states and in many federal regulations? Because plans that pay commissions for recruiting new distributors inevitably collapse once there are dozens or hundreds of layers involved. There comes a point where only the original "investors" receive money and new members are left completely out in the cold.

There are companies that do work with local representatives in door-to-door or "party" sales and that do stay within the bounds of the law. They sell cosmetics and beauty products, or resealable plastic containers and other objects you never knew you needed. If you want to make a purchase, or attend a neighborhood-selling session, do so with care and be prepared for a hard sell. Speaking for myself, when my wife or I are invited to a sales presentation for anything we have not asked for, we politely decline. Remember: the idea is to buy, and not be sold.

Guard Against Phony Charities

Giving to a charity is a noble thing, but less noble is the fact that, by some estimates, as much as 10% of the nearly $400 billion Americans gave to charities in 2015 may have been lost to fraud. Beyond that, tens of billions of dollars were spent not on the causes but instead on simply raising more funds.

When it comes to giving to charities—unless you know the organization and understand how much of your money goes directly to its activities—treat any appeal for a contribution as you would any other consumer or business purchase. To research an organization, visit the Wise Giving Alliance at Give.org. The Better Business Bureau runs this organization. You can search for and get a report for a charity. The listings show those that the BBB has accredited. They investigate and reveal whether the charity meets certain qualifications. They research the charity's governance, finances, and effectiveness, among other criteria. *The FTC advises you avoid any charity or fundraising operation that does any of the following…*

- **Refuses to provide detailed information about its identity,** mission, costs, and how donations are used.
- **Uses high-pressure tactics like trying to get you to donate immediately,** without giving you time to think about it and do your research.
- **Uses a name that closely resembles that of a better-known, reputable nonprofit organization.**
- **Asks for donations in cash or asks you to wire money.**
- **Offers to send a courier or overnight delivery service to collect the donation immediately.**
- **Thanks you for a pledge you don't remember making.**
- **Guarantees sweepstakes winnings in exchange for a contribution.** By law, you never have to give a donation to be eligible to win a sweepstakes.

And there is a difference between tax exempt and tax deductible. Tax exempt means the organization doesn't have to pay taxes, which doesn't necessarily do anything for you. *Tax deductible* means the organization has passed muster with the IRS, and if you contribute, you can deduct it on your federal income-tax return. Buying tickets for your local fundraiser? Those are not something you can deduct from your taxes. Donating to your favorite political party's candidate? You can't deduct that donation from your taxes, either.

If a charity tells you that donations are tax deductible, withhold your gift until they provide proof of that claim. If you plan to declare your contribution on your tax form, ask for a receipt with the amount of contribution and a statement that the donation is tax deductible. If you donate more than $250 per day, the organization will provide a letter clarifying how much you gave, to whom, that you received nothing in return for your donation. In any case, make sure you record your donation, including the dates, amount, and cancelled check number.

If you have questions about details, visit IRS.gov/charities-non-profits/substantiating-charitable-contributions.

Make Sure It's Truly Toll Free

We're all familiar with the concept of the toll-free phone number, but not all area codes beginning with 8 are free.

The set of toll-free area codes in the United States are 800, 833, 844, 855, 866, 877, and 888. Area codes reserved for future expansion include 822, 833, 880 through 887, and 889.

Be careful with other area codes in the 8xx series; some of them are, uh, ringers. 809, 829, and 849 for example, are for calls to the Dominican Republic. There are a few other 8xx area codes for elsewhere in the Caribbean, and some for parts of Canada. And of course, some scammers use these area codes to trap people into calling for fraudulent or otherwise improper purposes.

Watch out for meaningless information such as the fact that an organization has a tax ID number. All organizations, including for-profit businesses, have such a number on file with the IRS. A tax ID number has nothing to do with a group's nonprofit, charitable status.

You can increase the chance that something close to 100% of your donation is actually used for the purposes claimed…

- **Ask if the caller or visitor is a paid fundraiser and what percentage of your donation the fundraising group will keep.** If you don't like or don't trust the answer, donate elsewhere. Or contact the organization itself and ask about making a direct contribution that is not reduced by the fees of a paid fundraiser.
- **Understand that any appeal that includes a "free" gift for your contribution is using your own money to buy something that will be given back to you and spending that much less on its particular cause.** Some charities will report your contribution minus the value of your "free" gift. You can always decline the gift, too.
- **If a solicitor refuses to give specifics (including the name, beneficiaries, or running costs) about the charity he or she claims to represent,** or insists on a cash-only donation, report the call to your state's attorney general and the local police.
- **Don't make a major contribution on the basis of an oral presentation.** Ask for something in writing, including a discussion of the charity's purpose and how your money will be used. Then visit the IRS website at https://apps.irs.gov/app/eos/ to search for exempt organizations. You can also determine if an organization's tax-exempt status has been revoked.
- **Hang up or close the door on any high-pressure appeal.** If your money is good today, it'll be good tomorrow. Never respond to an offer of a courier to pick up your money right away.

And then there are phone numbers that use a 900 area code—also known as pay-per-call numbers. A few decades ago these numbers were relatively common ways for companies to charge consumers for special services ranging from weather forecasts to sex talk.

The use of 900 numbers is heavily regulated, and you have some protection. However, think twice before calling any number that begins with that area code, and be aware that you can dispute charges that might appear on your landline or smartphone bill. Most telephone companies will block the ability to dial 900-area-code numbers at your request. If you dispute a pay-per-call charge on your bill, the phone company cannot shut off your service but can block your future access to those numbers, which is probably a good thing.

All fees and rates must be disclosed at the beginning of the call, before any billing begins, and advertising must make clear the charges that will be assessed. Phone companies are required to list any such charges in a separate section on your bill, including date, time, and type of service provided.

Deal with Data Fraud

I mentioned earlier that a major threat to all of us is data fraud and data theft. Your best defense here is to resist giving out personal information as often as you can. Why does a grocery store need to know your phone number when you sign up for their discount card? If they insist, I make up a number. (If you decide to do this too, write down the number—if you are ever shopping without your membership card, they'll be able to access your account with it.)

Banks and investment companies need to know your Social Security number for tax purposes, but why does any other marketer need that bit of data? Push back and ask to use some other form of identification.

Take advantage of any two-step verification processes offered by stores or agencies. For example, I have my Amazon account set up so that I must enter a password to access my account, and then enter a second numeric code that is sent to my cellphone before any purchase is approved. Fidelity Investments and a few other companies have begun using voice-recognition software to serve instead of passwords for most customer service access; it's a great step in the right direction.

And be on the lookout for news reports and notifications you may receive about data breaches at stores where you have shopped. Immediately change your password and closely monitor your statements for these—and all other merchants. In the event of major hacking of accounts, many companies offer its customers a free period of credit report monitoring so you can watch for any unauthorized use of your personal details to obtain credit or for other purposes.

And take advantage of your right to a free review of your credit report from the major agencies once per year; spread out the reviews so that you consult a different one every few months and then repeat the cycle. In most instances, you are protected against loss due to fraud or theft of information. But it is generally your responsibility to monitor your accounts and notify banks or merchants as soon as the malfeasance is found.

And finally, think twice and thrice and more before you reveal too much about yourself on social media sites. If you list your birthday and your place of birth and your favorite sports team that may be enough of a tipoff for a data thief to guess your passwords for other accounts—if you make the mistake of using simple codes. Similarly, if you list on a social media site all the places you have lived, you are providing valuable tools to a thief who might have to get past certain identity-checking questions on websites that present questions based on your credit report.

PART III

Home Sweet Savings

CHAPTER 13

Maintaining Your Home

Your home is your castle. The savvy consumer is a tight-fisted Chancellor of the Exchequer when it comes to maintenance, repairs, and improvements.

In this chapter, we look at some ways to choose a contractor, how to save money on energy use, air conditioning, and heating. I also help you keep from getting hosed when a water-treatment company tries to sell you equipment or service. If you're interested in reading about home renovations, see Chapter 19. It also addresses the return on investment you may get from them.

- **Set up a neighborhood consortium.**
- **Audit yourself.**
- **Cool off the cost of air conditioners.**
- **Get a warm feeling for your heating bills.**
- **Fill 'er up at the right time.**
- **Fan the flames in your fireplace.**
- **Make yard sense.**
- **Hunt for water leaks.**
- **Paint the town house without going into the red.**
- **Cut a good deal on a chainsaw.**
- **Let water-testing scams roll off your back.**
- **Know the inside story of home water treatment.**
- **Choose a contractor or repair service.**

Set Up a Neighborhood Consortium

You need your lawn mown. So do your neighbors on both sides and up the block.

In winter, someone has to plow the driveway and clear the sidewalk.

And at the neighborhood summer barbecue you learn that two of your neighbors need to have their roofs redone, just like you.

Don't just stand there...form a neighborhood consortium!

Contact a lawnmowing company—even the one that already does work for you but not your neighbors—and ask for a quote to do four or five houses in a row on a regular schedule for your region's climate and rain pattern. There is no reason a smart contractor can't come up with a money-saving deal for a contract that cuts down on travel and setup time. The same would go for snow removal, roof repair, and just about any other job that requires workers to travel to your neighborhood, set up, and later remove their equipment.

You'll need to anoint someone as the financial representative for your consortium, and it probably would make sense to collect money from neighbors in advance—perhaps a month ahead of services rendered. Each participating household could provide a check made out to the mowing, plowing or maintenance company for their share of the deal to avoid any problems with tracking the paid amount.

Audit Yourself

Houses are energy hogs, so read on and see how to get the biggest bang for your bucks and time.

Give Your Home an Energy Checkup

Find out the most fruitful areas for improvement with an energy audit. Contact your local utility to see if they offer free or subsidized home inspections. You can also hire a professional home inspector on your own. Your utility may be able to make recommendations. Average costs vary fairly widely, from $200 to $600.

Weatherizing, heating and hot water systems, thermostats, and major appliances are energy users and losers.

Weatherizing

Weatherizing includes weather stripping, insulation, and windows that keep the outside heat or cold away from tempered indoor air.

The utility that serves the New England island where I live offers free energy audits and rebates on services performed once or twice a year, and we have taken advantage of the service several times. Most recently they determined that the insulation between the attic's floor joists was insufficient to hold heat in our house, and so they arranged for a contractor to come in with a truck fitted out with a blower and flexible pipes to put down six inches of treated cellulose insulation. (This particular insulation type is basically recycled and processed newspaper and cardboard, coated with borates as a fire retardant.) The other job involved improving the weather stripping on doors and along the foundation plate at the base of the house.

Between those two retrofits—which cost us only a few hundred dollars because of a utility company rebate—our heating bill went down at the same time as our large house stayed noticeably warmer without increasing the setting on the thermostat.

Heating and Hot Water Systems

Any heating system can benefit from annual checkups and tuning—especially those that use an open flame. My home is heated by an oil furnace. We pay for an annual cleaning each fall to remove ash from the furnace, change the oil filter, and check other components including the burner itself. Doing so not only allows the system to operate more efficiently but also extends its life. Filter replacements are something you might feel comfortable trying yourself, but leave the cleaning and checkup to the certified, trained HVAC (heating, ventilation, and air conditioning) experts.

Gas furnaces should be inspected and cleaned either annually or biannually according to manufacturer's recommendations, with attention to pilot light and flame sensor mechanisms. Some natural gas or bottled gas suppliers offer free or inexpensive pipe and pilot light checkups.

Heat pumps, which work for both heating and cooling, should be inspected annually as well. Moving parts including the compressor and blowers should be inspected and lubricated as recommended by the manufacturer.

If your heating (or cooling) system works by blowing air through ducts in your house, be sure to inspect and change air filters at least four times a year—when the seasons change, for example—or more often if they become blocked with dust. A clogged filter makes your blower and furnace work much harder. The blower motor should also be inspected, cleaned, and lubricated according to system specifications. Ideally, your HVAC service person inspects the motor during every visit and at least once annually.

If you use electric baseboard heating—in most places not the most efficient way to heat—you can improve efficiency slightly and help reduce the chance of fire by vacuuming the heating fins at the start of each season. Using a thin or brush attachment can work a bit better than your regular hose vacuum attachment.

Most hot water heaters benefit from similar cleaning and tune-up and, depending on their design, from an insulating jacket to help keep water from cooling off too quickly. Check to ensure that the water heater's thermostat setting is not too high. If you've got to severely temper the water coming out of hot water faucets or showers, that's a sign that an adjustment is due.

Thermostats

Replace old manual thermostats with programmable units that you can set to turn down at night or when the house is unoccupied. Program it to turn up the air conditioning when it is needed most. Experts say a change of five to 10 degrees is optimal. Making too large of a differential in program settings makes the furnace or air conditioner work too long and too hard, negating savings.

Major Appliances

Maintain and update major appliances including refrigerators, dryers, washing machines, and other devices.

Vacuuming filters at the refrigerator base and cleaning the dryer's lint trap will go a long way to improving energy efficiency and performance. Keeping the heat exhaust pipe from an electric or gas dryer clear will not only improve efficiency, but also help prevent a relatively common cause of fire in homes.

If your dryer has an old-style rubbed plastic heat exhaust pipe, or a metallic pipe more than about ten feet (or that has any bends or uphill sections), experts recommend upgrading the system to reduce the chances the pipe will collect lint. Even if you have a modern exhaust system, consider an annual pipe cleaning with a high-powered vacuum or a rotating lint brush. It's a job the handiest owners can do by themselves, but you can find specialists who can do it if your attachments don't reach.

Modern refrigerators and clothes washers that meet federal Energy Star qualifications can pay for themselves in energy savings over their lifetime. Ask your utility company or an appliance store in your area about available rebates for installing new equipment. And with that efficient new clothes washer, consider cleaning your clothes with cold or lukewarm water instead of hot. Modern detergents and machines are optimized for this sort of energy-saving choice.

Understanding Energy Ratings for Windows

Windows create the biggest holes in the heat shield surrounding your home. That doesn't mean that you can't select a window design that minimizes heat or air-conditioning escape.

Window manufacturers use a rating called the *U-value* that measures how much heat is conducted through a window or skylight. The lower the U-value, the more energy-efficient the window. You can think of the U-value as the inverse or reciprocal of the R-value of insulation. An official U-rating is accompanied by an NFRC (National Fenestration Rating Council) label. You'll see the ratings posted on window manufacturers' websites and on labels in showrooms.

Again, check with your local utility as well as manufacturers to see if there are any local rebates or federal tax credits for upgrading your windows. It can take years before you earn back your investment, however, as windows don't account for the majority of energy savings.

And then there are old-fashioned fixes that can save considerable amounts of money…

- **Install insulated drapes or other coverings**, especially on north-facing windows and anywhere else subject to wind.
- **Add temporary clear plastic insulating sheets over as many windows as possible in the winter.** In our home in cold New England, we follow the package directions to apply this sort of covering in upstairs bathrooms and a guest room that is infrequently occupied in the winter.
- **Make sure windows are latched closed in the winter.** Perform your rounds every few weeks. Ordinary movement and vibration in the house or wind from outside can sometimes move the latch.

Cool Off the Cost of Air Conditioners

An air conditioner that is too small will run constantly, wasting energy and providing insufficient cooling in the warmest weather. A unit that is too large for the space will cost too much to begin with, and will cool too quickly, not taking enough of the moisture out of the air. (You know the expression, "It's not the heat, it's the humidity?" A good deal of the comfort an air conditioner provides is the result of removing moisture from the air.)

To figure the necessary BTU for an air conditioner, calculate the square footage of the room you want cooled (multiply the length by the width). For a basic room with an 8-foot ceiling, figure 24 BTUs per square foot. A 16 x 22 rec room is 352 square feet and would require an air conditioner of about 8,400 BTU. If the room has a cathedral ceiling or skylights, is a kitchen or other room with heat-producing appliances, or faces south, you'll want to increase the air conditioner's BTU capacity proportionately. A 16-foot ceiling requires twice the cooling that an 8-foot ceiling requires.

Larger systems, including central air conditioners, are measured in tons. This is an old equation based on the cooling effect of melting a ton of ice. In air-conditioning terms, one ton is equivalent to 12,000 BTUs. And so, a four-ton air conditioner is rated as if it were capable of removing 48,000 BTUs of heat per hour from a structure.

But About BTUs

An air conditioner's cooling power is measured in British Thermal Units, or BTUs. For what it's worth, a BTU is the amount of energy needed to heat one pound of water by 1 degree Fahrenheit. In air-conditioning terms, that equation is inverted to represent the amount of energy required to reduce the temperature of a pound of water. Other factors that influence the size of the machine you'll need: the number of windows in the room (especially southern exposure), the amount of insulation in the house and the ambient temperatures common in your area.

Cool Bells and Whistles

When you're shopping for a room air conditioner, look for the federally mandated Energy-Efficiency Rating (EER). Compare units of the same BTU rating to find the one with the highest EER.

It helps to understand a bit about how air conditioners work and where they use electrical energy. An air conditioner is similar in operation to a refrigerator, with the difference being that a refrigerator is intended to cool only the box that contains food while an air conditioner works to cool a bigger box—your living room. Hot air flows over evaporator coils. The refrigerant within absorbs heat as it changes from a liquid to a gas. The compressor within the air conditioner puts the gas under high pressure, with the heat being exhausted to the outside. As the gas cools, it changes back to a liquid and the process continues. A separate fan blows across the cooling coils to push cool air into the room.

Look for some valuable features…

- **An actual temperature setting.** It's better to set a specific temperature rather than use an imprecise rotary dial with settings of 1 to 10 or warm to cool. You may have to keep fiddling with settings on a rotary, which eats up energy. I keep the air conditioner in my office set at 73 degrees, which I find comfortable but not unnecessarily (and expensively) cool.

• **Economy Mode or similar setting.** As an example, on a Frigidaire model this mode allows you to get a bit more out of the cool coils. To begin with, the fan runs for a minute after the compressor shuts off. Every ten minutes the fan turns on and runs for 20 seconds, continuing this cycle until the thermostat determines that the room temperature has risen above the set level. At that point the compressor and fan will both engage for a burst of cooling.

• **Energy Saver or Auto Fan setting.** This setting either manually sets the air conditioner fan to low or, in the case of the auto setting, starts the fan at high speed and gets slower once the room has begun to cool. If the machine senses a spike upward—perhaps because a door to the outside has opened—it returns to high speed until the temperature approaches the setting you chose.

• **A wide range of fan speeds.** Although I prefer to use the Auto setting, it is also valuable to have a range of fan speeds you can manually select. For example, on a very hot day the air conditioner might be running almost continuously and you might find it more comfortable to run its fan at a lower speed.

• **An easily accessible air filter.** The filter helps clean the air in your room. Clean or change the filter several times each cooling season to maintain peak efficiency. A clogged filter can cause your air conditioner to require as much as 5% more energy.

• **A timer.** Except in the most extreme conditions, you'll save money by turning off or turning down air conditioners when your home or office is unoccupied. A timer, especially a programmable device with multiple settings, allows you to adapt the air conditioner to your schedule.

Again, it depends on the temperature range where you live or work. In New England, although it can get warm or hot during the day, it is often comfortably cool at night and we sleep with screened windows open and air conditioning off.

In general, a window unit is not as durable as a central air-conditioning system, and you may need to replace it after 5 or 10 years. However, a window unit is considerably less expensive and also lets you choose exactly which room to cool. It may be the only cost-effective solution for a house that was not designed with air conditioning in mind. Central air systems require a means of distributing cooled air through the house, using duct or flexible pipe systems.

Cool Down Your Air-Conditioning Bills

Once your air conditioner is installed, here are some ways to reduce the load on your air conditioner to extend its life and soften the pain when you pay the electricity bill...

• **Choose an air conditioner with the proper rating.** A unit that puts out insufficient BTUs will have to work longer and harder. A unit that is overpowered for the room will also use more energy than necessary and cost more than a smaller unit in the first place.

• **Reduce the heat gain inside the house.** Turn off lights and television screens when you do not need them. Lower window shades on the sunny side of your house or office. Try to avoid using the oven during the heat of the day. Do baking and broiling in the evening and use microwaves or the stovetop to reheat food the next day.

• **Shade your air conditioner from direct sun with shrubbery or an awning, but be careful not to block the flow of exhausted hot air out the back of the unit.** If you have a choice, install the central air conditioner unit on the shady side of the house or on a window with northern exposure.

- **Don't block air flow with drapes or shades, and try to avoid having large pieces of furniture in the path of the cool air.**
- **Clean or replace filters according to the manufacturer's recommendations.** This also helps reduce pollen and dust. The latest models include filter sensors that will tell you when they need to be cleaned.
- **Adjust the timer so the air conditioner does not run at the highest setting when the house is unoccupied or during the night.** If your air conditioner does not have a built-in electronic timer or clock setting, add a timer at the wall outlet and plug the cooling unit into it. Make sure the timer is capable of handing the amperage. (Consult with the air conditioner maker or a knowledgeable electrical supply or hardware store for advice about proper timing units.) For a central air conditioner, purchase and use a programmable thermostat that allows you to set different temperatures for specific days and hours.
- **To avoid having cold air directly blowing on you, aim air conditioning vents up toward the ceiling.** Cold air is denser than warm air and thus it sinks, cooling the room as its settles. If the air vents are aimed down, you'll need to run the air conditioner longer and harder before it will cool anything more than your feet.
- **If you have a large room, experiment with adding a desk or floor fan a few feet in front of the air conditioner to move the cool air farther along.**
- **Do not put lamps or television sets near the air conditioner.** The heat they generate could affect the thermostat.
- **If it is especially humid, set the air conditioner's fan speed to Low.** It will improve the device's ability to take moisture out of the air.
- **In a large room, you can add an outward-blowing window fan to remove hot air from the room and also help move cool air across.**
- **Similarly, if you are cooling your house's lower level during the day and the upstairs is empty, open windows and skylights on upper floors to allow hot air to escape.** Remember that cool air is heavier than warm air, and most of your cooled air is going to stay on the first level. The warmer air stays upstairs because heat rises. Run a fan upstairs to exhaust hot air.

A ceiling fan can help reduce the perceived temperature and humidity by moving air within the room. Set it to push air downward. On most ceiling fans, that is counterclockwise. If in doubt, consult the ceiling fan manufacturer or the manual you received with that device. (You did save it, right?)

- **Close fireplace dampers so that cool air is not drawn up the chimney.** (In winter, you also want to keep the damper shut except when the fireplace is in use to avoid heat loss.)

Save Money with Low-Tech Air-Conditioning

If you live in a temperate zone or a place where extremely hot days are infrequent, you might want to consider some low-tech, low-price ways to cool your house before buying an energy-hungry

Keep It Warmer

To avoid frozen pipes and other winter damage, most experts recommend not setting your thermostat below 50 degrees. If a storm is approaching that might result in downed power lines or other heating interruptions, consider turning up the heat before the storm. If power goes off for a few hours, the house will be starting from a higher temperature.

In general, the elderly and infirm should not reduce the temperature below 65 degrees at any time and should consult with doctors before making any changes in their environment. Increased falls and blood clots have both been attributed to too-cold temperatures in those who have trouble regulating their body temperature.

The National Council on Aging (NCOA.org) lists several assistance programs for seniors who are struggling to pay their heating bills. The National Energy Assistance Referral project (1-866-674-6327) can also help someone find assistance.

air conditioner. *Most of these tips also reduce the load on an air conditioner as well…*

- **Lower the shades on the southern side of the house to reduce heat gain.** Open windows on upper floors to allow rising heat a place to escape.
- **Make sure your attic is properly ventilated with louvers to permit the exit of the hot air up there.**
- **Use window fans to exhaust hot air and bring in cooler air.** In general, windows on the south side of the house should blow out. Windows on the north side should bring in air.
- **Consider installing a powered attic fan in the highest point of a multistory house.** These large fans can create a cooling breeze throughout the house, exhausting heat to the outside where it belongs and drawing in cooler air from open north-facing windows. A large attic fan can cool for about one tenth the cost of air-conditioning.

Attic fans are rated by the cubic feet per minute (CFM) of air they can move. In most installations, the air goes into an attic and out a vent. To calculate the proper size, figure out your home's square footage and multiply it by the ceiling height. (You can subtract any rooms that will be closed off, such as basements and closets.)

For the best cooling effect, purchase a fan with a CFM equal to your house's cubic feet. Some experts say you can get away with a ventilating fan that gives a changeover of house air every three minutes, in which case you can divide the cubic feet by three to reach an acceptable CFM.

Get a Warm Feeling for Your Heating Bills

For those of us who live in a cold climate, the arrival of heating season sometimes feels like an anti-holiday. It is the day we start to pay for something that is ephemeral. Yesterday's heat does us no good today. Then again, a frozen or burst pipe yesterday is going to cost a whole lot of money tomorrow.

Let's start with two suggestions that should be obvious: Wear layered clothing and a sweater. Try to find a temperature that does not make your teeth chatter or affect your health. *Here are some other tips...*

• **For every degree you turn down the thermostat, you'll reduce your energy consumption by 2% to 3%, depending on how well your home is insulated.** Set the thermostat to 68 degrees or slightly less during the day, and 60 degrees at night or when no one is at home.

• **Install a programmable thermostat that will adjust the setting to match your lifestyle.** It could be set to turn down the heat while you are off to work or otherwise out of the house, bring it back up when you return, and then go down during sleeping hours before restarting the cycle. If you can't spring for a programmable thermostat, set reminders for yourself to adjust it yourself before leaving for work, getting home, and going to bed.

• **Upgrade the insulation in an older house.** Ask your utility company or state energy department for advice about what your home needs and the most efficient use of your money. Many utilities have programs that provide free or subsidized services for clients. (Okay, they're not really free since your bill may include a charge to pay for the program and your taxes may also go into the mix, but why not take advantage?)

• **Use caulk and weather stripping to seal leaks in the gaskets around windows and doors.**

• **Use foam gaskets, available at hardware stores, to block air leaks through electrical outlets and switches on outside walls of the house.**

• **Add a humidifier to a hot air heating system or a standalone unit if you use hot water or electricity to heat your home.** A small amount of humidity in the air will make you a bit more comfortable at cooler temperatures. Regularly clean the unit to avoid breeding mold.

• **Use solar energy to help heat your house.** Open curtains during the day to let the warming rays into the house, and then close them at night and on cloudy days to help insulate against heat loss.

• **Be careful not to overuse kitchen and bathroom fans during the heating season.** Experts say that a fan left running for an hour can exhaust the equivalent of your furnace's output for the same period of time.

• **Vacuum or dust air vents, baseboard heaters, and radiators to keep them clean and to help transfer heat efficiently.** A good old duster on an extension pole can help get ceiling vents. A bottle brush helps get in other tight spots.

• **Keep furniture and draperies away from heater vents or radiators.** They could block heat movement and possibly create a fire hazard.

• **Consider installing a reversible ceiling fan to move air,** bringing heated air down toward the floor in winter and up to the ceiling in summer.

• **Close vents in your house foundation in the winter to insulate pipes and air ducts.** Open the same vents in the summer to help remove moisture. The vents will be visible in your home's foundation.

Want more ways to spend less? *Each of these tips represents a small savings but combined add up to a significant improvement in energy efficiency...*

- **In many older houses, old-style radiators were painted glossy white to make them blend into the wall a bit.** Unfortunately, white is among the worst possible colors. Radiators painted flat black or other dark colors give off as much as an extra 10% of heat. You can also purchase a heat-safe reflective foam or plastic backdrop at most hardware stores to further direct heat into the room.
- **Insulate cold-water pipes for the last few feet before they arrive at the hot water heater.** If the incoming water is slightly warmer, that is less work for the heater. And cold pipes can also wick away some of the heat from water stored inside the tank.
- **Fix dripping faucets, especially those that leak away hot water.** One faulty hot water tap could send a few hundred dollars' worth of water down the drain each year.
- **Be sure the hatch to the filter on an air-blowing furnace is properly sealed to prevent cold air intake to the heated flow.** Use insulation or duct tape. Check with the furnace manufacturer or a heating contractor if you have any questions.
- **Change or clean the filter on your air-blowing furnace once a month during heating season.** A clogged filter reduces your furnace efficiency and also hurts the system's ability to remove dust and pollen from the air flow. You can vacuum some filters to remove dust. Certain designs are also made to be rinsed off. Be sure to follow the manufacturer's instructions.
- **Pull down window shades at night in the winter to help keep heat within the house.** This simple step should save a few dollars per window per season, which can amount to a fair amount in a typical house. Raise the shades on the south side of the house to add some solar heating on sunny but cold days. Heat-reflective and heat-absorbing blinds can work to your advantage, too.
- **Depending on your hot water system, you may be able to save significant money by installing a programmable timer for your water heater.** This device can turn the heater off at times when you don't need hot water—the middle of the night, for example, or during the day on weekends. Make sure your hot water heater is fully insulated to hold on to heated water when the thermostat is turned down, and allow enough time for the tank to come up to the proper temperature for times when you do need hot water.
- **Take showers instead of baths.** With a flow-reduction showerhead (another good investment), a shower uses about three gallons per minute. A typical bathtub requires about thirty gallons to fill.
- **Use cold-water detergent and cold water for most ordinary clothes washing.** Save hot water for diapers, underclothing, grass stains, and other serious soil.

Fill 'er Up at the Right Time

If you don't have an automatic oil delivery service, check with your supplier to find when the prices are at their lowest. In many markets, heating oil is at its cheapest in the summer when demand is low. Take advantage of seasonal fluctuations to completely fill your tank when you need it least. If you're filling a 375-gallon tank, every dime off per gallon is worth $37.50. It should be fine unused for at least a year and a half, provided it doesn't become contaminated. You can buy treatments at hardware or auto parts stores to prevent that from happening.

On the other hand, you should also consider striking a deal with an oil supplier for automatic service. In return for your commitment for a year or a season, the company should offer you a reduced price for fuel or some special services such as a free furnace tune-up.

Don't hesitate to put your business out for bids every year or so. Get a price from a competitor, and then inquire at your current supplier. One way or another, you'll know whether you are getting the best price available.

Fan the Flames in Your Fireplace

There are few more comforting sights on a cold winter's night than a roaring fireplace in the hearth. Unfortunately, a fireplace is not often a very efficient way to heat the house. Here's why: The fire requires a great deal of oxygen, and it also needs a quick and clear exit from the house to the outside. Many fireplaces send heated air from the rest of the house right up the chimney.

At the same time, a roaring fireplace downstairs can cause the rest of the house to get very cold in a hurry. If the thermostat for the house is in the same room as the fireplace, your heating system will shut off hot air or hot water in the places that need it most.

Here are some important tips for fireplace users...

- **Be sure to keep the damper closed anytime the fire is completely out.** As much as 10% of your house's heated air can go up an open chimney.
- **Use glass fireplace doors that limit the amount of air that goes up the chimney.** Heat from the fire will pass through the glass and through vents. Even better: a glass fireplace door with built-in fans that pump heat from the fire chamber into the room.
- **If possible, partially open a window near the fireplace to help the fire draw its oxygen from cold outside air instead of from heated interior air.**
- **Use floor fans or ceiling fans to redistribute fireplace heat to other parts of the house.**
- **Buy your firewood off season to save money.** Don't wait for the first snowfall to place your order. And be sure to get *seasoned* (dried) wood, which will burn better in your furnace.

Make Yard Sense

Natural fertilizer such as fish emulsion can cost two to three times as much as synthetic fertilizer. However, the synthetic product may end up costing the same or less because you have to apply it less frequently (and may be toxic, as well as lead to deadly algae growth in runoff water). Read the application instructions carefully and compare coverage in square footage and frequency instructions.

When it comes to watering the lawn, a heavy soaking once a week is more efficient than lighter regular sprinkling daily. Your grass will develop deeper, healthier roots. And water at night instead of during the day when heat will evaporate much of the water you lay down. Saving roof water run-

TIP

Go Beneath the Surface

If you're going to hire a painter to do the work for you, beyond requesting references from previous clients, ask a few questions. Is the painter insured? Are the painters employees or subcontractors? What painting and training have employees received? What paint and primer brands do you use? Is your company a Better Business Bureau member? At various times, we have hired the low bidder who worked quickly and sloppily, and also paid considerably more for a painter who was obsessive in his attention to detail. Within reason, I suggest paying a bit more for a worker who has superior skills and better testimonials.

off with a rain barrel and using that to water your lawn is even more cost effective, but it requires huge barrels. Replacing even part of your lawn with vegetables or native perennial plants and using rain barrels to water them is even more cost effective, as you won't need to buy gas and mow.

Hunt for Water Leaks

If your water utility company sends you a monthly or bimonthly bill, take the time to study the usage report. Look to see if the amount of water usage has gone up markedly from the previous report, and compare (if you can) the same month or months from a year ago. If there is an upward spike, consider what might have changed. Did you have house guests? Did you install a new dishwasher or clothes washer?

If you pay separate water and sewer bills, the amount of usage should be roughly equivalent unless you are watering your lawn.

Here's a way to check for hidden leaks (a flooded basement is too obvious), assuming your home has a water meter you can read by yourself. Turn off all water-consuming devices, including dishwashers, clothes washers, and icemakers. Go to your water meter and write down its reading. For the next hour or two, stay out of the kitchen and the bathroom. Return to the water meter and check the reading. If it has changed, then something is wrong. It's time to call a plumber.

If you can't read the meter, do what you can to hunt for leaks in the basement, crawlspace, and cabinets in and around sinks and appliances. Walk your property and look for ponding or sinkholes that might indicate an underground leak. Don't hesitate to call the water company for advice.

Paint the Town House Without Going into the Red

What kind of paint should you use inside or outside your house?

Oil paint is old technology and not much used unless you are repainting a surface that already has oil paint in place. Oil paint (typically made with linseed oil) or alkyd paint (based on a synthetic compound) will bond properly with older oil-paint surfaces. Oil-based paint is quite durable, but it takes longer to dry and cleanup requires turpentine or paint thinner, which are themselves a hazard. In some states and localities, oil paint is no longer available or is banned by regulation because of environmental and health concerns.

Otherwise, the trend is clearly in the direction of water-based paint, including latex and acrylic formulations. The many advantages of water-based paints include easier cleanup, the drying speed, and its reduced odor. Latex and acrylic paints are also much more forgiving of the amateur painter, forming a rubberlike coating that hides brush or roller marks. And because they dry so quickly, painters can often put on two coats in one day, saving time and inconvenience.

Paint can contain additives that result in various types of finish, from flat to semi-gloss to high-gloss. The addition of enamel yields a harder and less porous top coat that you can easily clean.

If you are starting work on unfinished walls, the best practice is to apply a coat of primer first. This type of paint adheres well to the surface and in turn provides a good surface for the addition of the final coat. For a few bucks more you can also use paints that are labeled as *self-priming*, an odd neologism that is meant to indicate there is no need for a primer coat. I have used some of these paints with mixed results. In the best case, I paid a premium price for a paint that did not cover the same square footage as a paint intended to go over a primer coat. On the plus side I saved time because I only had to apply a single coat. In the less-than-best case, I found that the self-priming paint—although a thick, high-quality product—nevertheless required a second coat. Either way, you're probably going to need at least three coats.

Finally, keep in mind that paint is one product where you mostly get what you pay for. Better quality paint will adhere better, resist fading or peeling, and generally result in a better result. So don't look for the cheapest paint, but do take advantage of sales on high-quality products. *Consumer Reports* lists certain major brands on its site, though there are varying values within each brand. Evaluator *Better Homes & Gardens* rates different brands at Blinc.Media/2wWKzRs .

Try It On

You don't want to buy paint that you wind up hating once it's on the walls only to have to spend more money buying paint to cover it. How do you choose the right color for your room? The traditional method has been to bring home paint chips and examine them in place. Remember, though, that you are looking at a small sample and an entire wall painted in that color will be much more intense.

Some hardware and paint stores—especially those that will custom mix a color for you—will sell (or even give away) small tins of sample paint that you can apply to the wall. Let the small sample fully dry and see which one pleases you most.

One other thing: Pay attention to the ambient light in the room you plan to paint. A few years ago, we repainted a bedroom with west-facing windows. My wife chose an attractive sea-foam blue hue, which seemed to be very pale and insubstantial as I began work one morning. As I completed painting the walls near the end of the day, the orange-tinted light of the setting sun flooded the room and the color was much warmer and more intense. We like very much the effect the room gets, and learned a lesson not previously considered in choosing a color.

Cut a Good Deal on a Chainsaw

Does your electric carving knife choke when you try to cut up wood for the fireplace? Does your chainsaw make a mess when you use it to carve the family turkey?

Seriously, the most important tip to buying a chainsaw is to match its size to the jobs you'll use it for. An underpowered chainsaw will be frustrating for major jobs like cutting firewood. An overpowered device can be very dangerous for small tasks like trimming back underbrush.

Saws are categorized by horsepower, bar length, chain speed and type, and weight.

The best time to buy a chainsaw is usually the dead of winter when demand is lowest. Prices go up as spring cleaning time arrives, and stay high into the fall in many parts of the country as homeowners stockpile wood for the winter.

Gasoline-powered chainsaws are convenient because they don't require a cord, and often have more horsepower than electric models. On the other hand, they are often heavier, harder to start, require regular engine maintenance, and produce fumes. Electric chainsaws are lightweight and require almost no maintenance other than occasional cleaning and oiling. They have less horsepower, though, and you'll have to keep track of the power cord as you work. An electric unit may be fine for small jobs but is no match for one with a gas engine.

Before you purchase any model, make sure that replacement chains are readily available. If you can't find one before you take the saw out of the store, you cannot assume you'll be able to obtain a replacement when you need it. On the other hand, third-party manufacturers sell chains that work with a wide range of devices.

Make sure that any model you buy has a chain brake, an essential safety device that stops the chain if the saw kicks back or you let go of a safety switch on the handle. Always wear safety glasses, hard-soled shoes, and gloves when handling a saw.

Here are some valuable options for chainsaws…

- **Anti-vibration design.** Better models use shock absorbers and other design elements to reduce vibrations coming to your arms. Not only will this make using the chainsaw more comfortable, but you'll also be able to make neater and more accurate cuts.

- **Low-compression starter.** An easy starting mechanism for gas-powered engines is kinder to your arms and shoulders and easier on the engine itself.

- **Air injection filtration.** A system that cleans much of the dirt and dust before it reaches a gasoline engine's air filter will reduce air filter cleanings.

- **Chain safety features.** Protect yourself with low-kickback chains. Bar tip guards also reduce the chances of kickback by keeping the tip of the chain from touching wood.

Be sure to follow your chainsaw manufacturer's recommendations for proper use of oil for the chain, as well as storage and maintenance. Some makers recommend additives to protect the engine during the winter.

Let Water-Testing Scams Roll Off Your Back

Be wary of a "free" test from a company that sells an item dependent on the results of that test. Some examples: asking an orthodontist whether your kids need braces; asking a transmission-repair shop whether your car needs a new transmission; and asking a company that sells water filters or treatment devices whether your water needs attention. (In each of these cases, and many others, you are much better off paying an independent specialist who draws income from the test or exam and not from the sale of services.)

Do you really know what is in your water? That's a pretty frightening question to most of us and a very powerful sales pitch for some honest and not-so-honest sales organizations. First, instant tests done in your home are not likely to be accurate or informative. Second, the results reported to you may misrepresent safe levels of minerals and other substances. Or, there may be out-and-out fraud about the results, including contamination of the sample or introduction of meaningless but dramatic color changes or instrument readouts.

Ask your local water company for the latest test results of the public water supply. It is supposed to be submitted to all customers by July 1, annually. It may be online. Search for it at Blinc.Media/2wWPz8p and then compare them to state and federal standards available from your state government and the EPA. If you use well water, ask your local or state health department if it offers free water testing.

Under the federal Safe Drinking Water Act, all public water supplies must meet the drinking-water standards set by the EPA. If you draw water from a private well, though, your only protection may lie in state and local law, which may be more or less stringent than federal standards and which may not take into account conditions on or near your property.

To test your water, use a lab certified by your state's health department or environmental agency. You can also obtain a list of state-certified labs from the EPA's Safe Water Drinking Hotline at 800-426-4791. Try the EPA's hotline (EPA.gov/ground-water-and-drinking-water/safe-drinking-water-hotline) or go to the agency's main page at EPA.gov and search for *water guidelines*.

You can also purchase a basic home testing kit for less than $50 that allows you to perform basic searches for bacteria, lead, radon, and pesticide as well as substances that may hitchhike along with your water supply such as iron, hardness, chlorine, copper, nitrate, and nitrite. You can also determine the water's pH level, where it stands on the scale between acidity and alkalinity. You can buy these kits from hardware stores or online sources. A more exhaustive test, performed by a laboratory, might cost hundreds of dollars or more.

Chapter 12 has more information about avoiding scams and fraud.

Know the Inside Story of Home Water Treatment

Home water treatment is a burgeoning industry, and many of the products can improve specific problems. *There are several types of water-treatment units, and no single device can solve all water problems…*

Water Quality

When should you be concerned about the quality of your water? If your home is in a current or former industrial zone. If the source of your drinking water is a river or lake, there is always the possibility of pollution. In theory, this is something monitored by a government agency or sometimes a private company that works under regulations set by an environmental agency. But problems do occur, either as the result of a temporary breach or accident or long-term neglect.

What do you know about the type of pipe that delivers water to your home? How old is the system? For many years federal and state regulations have barred the use of lead pipes or pipes that use lead solder, but not every mile of such conduit has been pulled out and replaced. Older homes may have old plumbing within.

I suggest conducting at least a basic do-it-yourself test. Try it once. If it raises no red flags, perform the test again in six months or a year to see if there is any change.

One other note: Ask your doctor if he or she has any concerns about the water or about your susceptibility to certain minerals or chemicals that may be in it. As an example, the island where I live gets its drinking water from an underground aquifer. We have virtually no sources of pollution that affect the quality. However, because we are surrounded by the Atlantic Ocean, our water is relatively high in sodium. People with certain health conditions, including very high blood pressure, are advised to drink bottled water.

- **Physical filters.** These units use fabric, fiber, ceramic, or other types of screens to remove particles, grit, sediment, dirt, and rust from the water. Some ultra-fine filters can also remove some bacteria, although they should not be used to treat microbiologically unsafe water. Consult your local health department or water department for recommendations here.

- **Activated carbon filters.** This special class of filter can remove some organic chemical contaminants, improving your water's smell, taste, and appearance. Activated carbon filters are available in several forms: granular, powdered, powdered coated paper, and pressed carbon block. This class of filter is not effective against most inorganic chemicals, including salts or metals. Some special carbon filters are appropriate for taking lead out of the water. Activated carbon filters can become saturated with the impurities they remove from the water and must be replaced from time to time—consult the manufacturer or installer for details. Be sure to factor in the cost of replacement filters in your buying decision. Again, check with local health or water departments for recommendations.

- **Bacteriostatic carbon filters.** A certain class of carbon filters contains silver as a pesticide. According to the EPA, though, these claims of bacterial growth control have not been proven. These filters are not recommended for water that is microbiologically unsafe, such as water contaminated with fecal matter.

- **Reverse osmosis (RO) units.** These systems pass water through a membrane to a storage tank. Most designs waste much of the tap water put into them—as much as 75 percent in some units. You must replace membranes from time to time. RO units remove substantial amounts of most inorganic chemicals, such as salts, metals (including lead), asbestos, minerals, nitrates, and some organic chemicals.

- **Distillation units.** These units, which are available in many different shapes and sizes, vaporize water and then condense it. This process removes most dissolved solids, such as salts, metals, minerals, asbestos fibers, particles, and some organic chemicals. Distillation units, however, may not remove all chemical pollutants, and some bacteria may pass through in some instances. Although distillation may be an effective water treatment, the water heating will add to your energy use.

• **Ultraviolet (UV) disinfection.** These units use a light to destroy bacteria and inactivate viruses, without leaving a taste or odor in the water. UV units do not remove most chemical pollutants and may be ineffective against spores. UV systems must be cleaned regularly. Consult the manufacturer's instructions.

For more information about water filtration systems, contact the EPA's Safe Drinking Water Hotline at 1-800-426-4791.

A phone call or a visit to your local health department or water department should provide all the information you require before purchasing a water filter.

Choose a Contractor or Repair Service

First: For major work, especially additions, make sure to visit your local city's website or call to confirm what permits you are required to obtain before starting work. The work may also need to pass inspection from the proper municipal authorities.

Don't be penny-wise and home foolish: Few things end up costing more money than a job done poorly. You are almost always better off hiring a licensed contractor for any structural job or major home system, including carpentry, roofing, plumbing, heating, cooling, and electrical work among them. You should expect a state or municipal license, worker's compensation coverage, and proper insurance for any worker who enters your home. It is acceptable for a contractor to ask for a down payment. It is usually a portion of any supplies they must purchase for the job.

Do not sign any contract that requires full payment before satisfactory completion of the work.

If it is a simple job, such as replacing a faucet or fixing a faulty electrical outlet, you should be able to make a deal based on a fixed price plus parts. Anything more complicated should be based on a written contract that spells out the work to be done and the price for the job.

For major jobs, check out the quality of work by calling former customers. Ask your neighbors *after* they have had work done in their homes about their experience. If you've had good work done by one tradesperson, call and ask for a

TIP

Do Your Own Research

If you venture online in search of service professionals, you will likely come across sites that promise to match you with individuals or companies in your area. Although some of these sites may have the best of intentions, you have a lot of reason to believe their lists are not any better than what you'd find by asking around on your own. Some of the sites have been accused of favoring advertisers or removing bad reviews. Others have faced claims of false positive reviews posted by some of the contractors themselves.

The most prominent of the services is Angie's List, which for most of its history charged a membership fee. It took down that pay wall in mid-2016 with plans to make its money from advertising and other fees. Yelp! is another major player, and it has always been free.

Two others are Google Local and CitySearch. I consider these services and others a way to get some sense of available professionals, but I still perform my own research before contacting any of them for a project.

referral to the specialist you are looking for. For example, call the carpenter who worked on your deck to ask about good plumbers or electricians he or she has worked with. It's hard to avoid conflicts of interest among friends or relatives, but you can at least hope that a tradesperson will not want to jeopardize his or her own reputation by recommending someone not worthy of your trust.

CHAPTER 14

Saving on Home Supplies

Here's a bright idea: Read the small print on lightbulbs to get the most illumination and longest life for the best price. I'll also show you how to buy batteries and how to set your table with discount china and silverware.

- **Find a place to rest your head.**
- **Illuminate the truth about lightbulbs.**
- **Don't pay too much for batteries.**
- **Set your table with discount china.**
- **Replace a missing lemon fork.**
- **Sow your oats online buying seeds and plants.**
- **Smart flower shopping.**

Find a Place to Rest Your Head

Buying a mattress is a dark art. There is a bewildering array of options, models, and stores...and to make things worse, almost no uniformity from one shop to another. Mattress manufacturers—from major brands to small local operations—often produce models for individual stores or make short runs of particular combinations of internal materials and coverings.

When is it time to shop for a new mattress? When your old one feels uncomfortable, sags, has fabric tears, or if your dog prefers to sleep on the floor instead of putting up with the springs poking her in the ribs. In general, most quality mattress sets begin to lose their shape and support after eight to 10 years of use.

What's the difference between a WunderSnore 404 with Ultracoils and a WunderSnore 6SJ7 with Magicsprings? I have no idea, and the salespeople at two competing stores probably don't either. They may be identical but for the name, or they may be completely different. But the fact that mattress makers churn out a staggering number of different (or identical) models of varying names allows both stores to promise you huge discounts from a completely fictitious list or suggested price.

The best advice...

• **Never buy a mattress without trying it out.** You're not buying a brand or a model number; you're buying something that makes you—and anyone who might share the bed—comfortable. Don't hesitate to lie down and try a mattress in the store. Stay a few minutes and try a few positions for comfort. If you're buying a mattress for two, go together and see how well it supports the both of you at the same time.

• **Check the reviews at *Consumer Reports* (ConsumerReports.org) and ConsumerSearch (ConsumerSearch.com), which are independent.** *The New York Times'* The Wirecutter (TheWire Cutter.com) and The Sweethome (TheSweetHome.com) offer reliable product reviews as well. Use these sources' recommendations as a starting point. There still is no substitute for testing out a model yourself, but a review that tells you of consistent complaints about a brand or model can help you weed out some duds.

• **Spend some of your research time determining the seller's trustworthiness.** The internet is a great tool with which to gauge the experience of other customers with a particular store and sometimes a particular mattress.

• **Learn as much as you can about the mattress's construction so you can compare apples to apples (or at least fruit to fruit).**

• **Be aware that some mattresses are thicker than others.** This could mean that your current sets of fitted sheets will not fit. Also, a few extra inches of height off the floor might be uncomfortable for some people. Some extra-thick mattresses may not fit perfectly on an existing bed frame with certain types of headboards.

• **The International Sleep Products Association** (an industry group that is very interested in having you buy mattresses often) says consumers should replace their mattress every seven years. Don't expect your mattress to last forever, but let your body tell you when to buy a new bed.

Here are some things to look for in an innerspring mattress...

• **Sit on the edge of the mattress and gauge its support.** Stand up and see how well it returns its shape.

• **Determine the number of coils within the mattress.** Experts say a full-size mattress should have at least 300 coils, a queen size at least 375, and a king at least 450 coils. The more coils, the better the support. If in doubt about comparing one mattress to another, buy by the pound: a heavier mattress is *usually* better made, although you still have to try it out for comfort.

• **See if you can determine the thickness, or *gauge,* of wire used to make the coils.** Typical gauges run between about 13 and 15½. The *lower* the number, the *thicker* the wire and the *more* support it will offer.

• **Various manufacturers tout their particular construction method.** Most of Serta's products, for example, use coils made from one continuous piece of wire. Simmons places each individual coil in a supportive pocket, while Sealy builds its coils in parallel rows running from one end of the mattress to the other.

The bottom line: They all work. Pay more attention to the total number of coils and how they feel to you.

- **The coils are usually padded with cotton and foam; some newer designs use high-density foam.** If you choose foam, look for a foam density of about 1.8 for the best protection against wayward coils.
- **On top of the coils, mattress makers add padding.** Most makers offer firm, plush, and pillow-top designs. They differ primarily in the thickness and softness of the foam and other materials in the padding. The best tops are firmly sewn and glued in place atop the coils. And be aware that pillow-top mattresses are not intended to be flipped over; they can (and should) be rotated (top to bottom) at least once a year, but you cannot turn them over. In theory, that might mean that pillow-top mattress will have a shorter lifespan, but a premium pillow-top design may be better made than a more basic model.
- **The mattress fabric cover is called ticking.** Cotton materials, including damask or chintz, are generally more durable than synthetics and permit the mattress interior to breathe.
- **In general, it's best to buy a matched set of mattress and foundation.** A quality foundation is designed to match the pressure points of the mattress above it. The exception: if you use a platform bed, it serves as the foundation.
- **If you have a choice of mattress frames, opt for the one with heavier-gauge steel for best support.** For queen and king beds, look for a center beam with supports that reach the floor. Wide rollers are better than smaller ones, making it easier to move the bed for cleaning.
- **Compare specifications, prices, delivery options, and guarantees.** Don't expect to be able to compare identical models at different stores.

So if it is all but impossible to compare identical models at different stores, this should be your strategy: find two or three models you like at two or three stores and compare price and customer service. Then, ask for a better price. Make it clear that you are willing to cross the street to save a few hundred dollars—and do so if the store doesn't find a way to magically melt the price.

Mattress warranties are mostly smoke and mirrors. Their best value is as a protection against a defect in materials or workmanship that becomes obvious within the first few months of ownership. They generally do not protect you from the inevitable decline in support.

Finally, there are foam or latex mattresses that don't use inner springs. Foam mattresses are considerably more expensive than coil mattresses of the same size, but some sleepers have a strong preference for them. In addition, you are encouraged to purchase a water-proof protector for these kinds of mattresses. That way, you can throw the protector into the washer. Note that *some* foam mattresses can be difficult to carry or move from place to place because they lack side rigidity.

Foam mattresses often have a strong chemical smell when they are first removed from their packaging. For that reason, you may want to allow the bed to air out for a day or more before using it.

If you have any special health conditions, ask your doctor or therapist for advice. Otherwise, choose the bed design that feels best to you. Does a particular design of bed feel hot or cold to you? (Foam mattresses do tend to sleep hotter than innerspring mattresses.) Do you feel a pressure point on one design but not another? A few decades ago, waterbeds were the coolest thing but they are less popular now, representing about 5% of sales. Be aware that a waterbed is very heavy once filled, weighing close to a ton. I'm *pretty sure* my home is sturdy enough to handle that weight in our second-floor bedroom, but I don't particularly feel like testing that theory.

There are also beds that allow you to adjust firmness (either the entire mattress or each side, individually). Other beds can tilt upward to accommodate certain health conditions (or for more comfortable reading and television viewing). If these features work for you, and the price is right, they are worth considering. Be aware that some of these relatively expensive beds may have a shorter lifespan because the mattress is being bent regularly, although in theory the manufacturers take that into account during design.

Illuminate the Truth About Lightbulbs

The basic incandescent lightbulb, a globe that tapers to a screw-in connector and contains a filament that glows as electrons pass through it, would be completely recognizable to Thomas Edison, who (as well as a dozen or so other inventors who used the same principle in earlier attempts) patented his device in 1878.

The bulb glows because the filament resists the flow of electricity, creating heat; light is emitted as a side effect. Incandescents have served their purpose well for more than a century, but in our modern era of energy conservation, newer technologies are mostly taking over.

What is the problem with incandescent bulbs? About 90% of the electricity used to produce light is lost as heat. And it gets worse: The heat that these bulbs give off adds to the load for air conditioners or fans, using more electricity. One more point: Standard incandescent bulbs generally have a maximum lifetime of 1,000 hours; higher-wattage bulbs tend to burn out even sooner than that.

Many countries around the world have banned or restricted the sale of incandescent bulbs. In the United States, political obstruction has (as of 2017) blocked a full ban, but it is increasingly difficult to find a wide selection of the old-style bulbs.

How Bulbs Work

Let's start with understanding the old technology and then move to the new. Lightbulbs of all designs have three standardized numbers plus a price—the *voltage* (almost always household standard 110 to 120 volts), the *wattage* (the amount of power the bulb draws), and the often-overlooked light-output rating. *Light output*, measured in *lumens*, indicates the amount of light a bulb produces. Not every 100-watt incandescent bulb gives off the same amount of light.

Shop for bulbs by light output and you will save energy costs. A 60-watt bulb that yields the same lumens as a 75-watt bulb can save you 20% on electricity bills. And low-wattage LED bulbs and other newer designs may draw one-quarter the amount of power—a 15-watt LED bulb producing the same amount of light as a 60-watt incandescent.

A fourth number on lightbulb packages claims to represent bulb life in hours. These numbers are estimates of an incandescent bulb's filament durability and the light-making components of other lighting types. Here is a broad estimate of the expected life for various types of bulbs.

Incandescent	750–2,000 hours
Halogen	2,000–4,000 hours
Compact fluorescent	8,000–10,000 hours
Fluorescent	24,000–36,000 hours
LED	40,000–50,000 hours

What do *bulb life* ratings mean? The industry standard, Average Rated Life, is a reckoning of how long it takes for half the bulbs in a particular test group to fail. If a standard incandescent bulb is stated to last 1,000 hours, that means that in a controlled test half the bulbs will fail by that point; that means that half the bulbs will last longer. However, because bulbs use well-established manufacturing processes, most of the remaining bulbs can be expected to fail not long afterward, perhaps within 10% additional time.

New and Improved Lightbulb Designs

Halogen bulbs are filled with halogen gas, which emits a bright white light. They use less energy and last longer than incandescent bulbs of the same wattage, but can generate a fair amount of heat.

Compact fluorescents, also known as CFLs, use about one-quarter as much energy to produce the same amount of light as an equivalent incandescent bulb. As an example, a 15-watt compact fluorescent gives off about the same amount of light as a 60-watt incandescent bulb. And CFLs can be expected to last about 10,000 hours, 10 times as much as a typical incandescent bulb. The early CFL models had the same sort of bluish-white light produced by fluorescent tubes that have been common in overhead lighting in offices and stores. Current CFL versions use tinted glass and other tricks to warm the color of the light they emit.

And now shelves in hardware and home goods stores are being overtaken by light-emitting diode, or LED, bulbs. These use a technology that produces electroluminescence, which produces very little waste heat. The bulbs work at very low electrical draw and last for extended periods of time—as much as 25,000 to 100,000 hours in ordinary use

TIP

Lightbulb Moment

In general, each time you turn on a bulb—going from cold to hot—you reduce its life. Fluorescent bulbs are especially susceptible, but all types of bulbs are affected.

If a bulb costs twice as much as one of a different design and offers a potential life that is twice as long, you could consider that a break-even proposition. However, the calculations are usually not that simple. Changing a bulb in a desk lamp is usually quite simple and quick; swapping out a lamp that is in a fixture at the top of a cathedral ceiling or buried within the sealed chamber of an outdoor fixture is more of an issue and a heavy-duty bulb might be worth extra cost to postpone time between replacement.

Hot Halogen

Tungsten-halogen filament incandescent bulbs, or halogen bulbs, contain a small capsule filled with halogen gas that emits a bright white light when energized. Halogen bulbs are designed to produce more light, use less energy, and last longer than standard incandescent bulbs of the same wattage, but they cost more than standard incandescent bulbs. They last about 3,000 hours—about three years.

That's the good news. The bad news is that halogen lamps generate a great deal of heat. In recent years, consumer and fire-prevention agencies have issued warnings about widely available halogen torchiere lamps with an open top. Users are advised to take special care, being certain that draperies, pieces of paper, or other objects not come into contact with the bulbs. Turn off any halogen lamp any time you leave a room. I use an upward facing halogen light (called a torchiere) in my high-ceilinged office as the main light. It includes a dimmer to adjust the brightness. It has been at least five years since I last replaced that bulb.

Fluorescents, and especially LEDs, also have the advantage of using considerably less power and generating almost no heat as a by-product. By some estimates, a state-of-the-art LED bulb could save $100 in electricity bills across its lifetime, compared to an equivalent incandescent bulb.

When LEDs first came on the market, some were priced at $10 or more per bulb, which was a hard sell to consumers used to paying less than a dollar for an incandescent. Today, prices for good-quality LEDs have dropped below $2 each and are headed downward; that makes the possible $100 savings on your electric bill even more enticing.

You'll find great prices on packages of bulbs at most big-box stores and online. Also check with your local electricity company to see if it has offers customers discounted—or free—bulbs. Our utility replaced nearly every one of the dozens of bulbs in our home as part of a free annual energy audit.

Don't Pay Too Much for Batteries

The number of battery-operated devices in the typical home has run away like the Energizer bunny—smoke detectors, smart thermostats, television and cable box remote controls, clocks, cameras, and all sorts of toys for men and boys, women and girls.

Who Makes the Best

Will the Energizer Bunny really outrun all of his pursuers? Tests by Consumers Union for its *Consumer Reports* magazine showed that the best performance was delivered by the best-known brands including Energizer, Rayovac, and Duracell. But just a notch below—and often at a significant discount—were batteries sold as the house brands for places like CVS, Costco, Walgreens, and Amazon.

Now think about it: CVS and the others do not have their own factory manufacturing batteries (or anything else). They buy private label products from major makers.

Be wary, though, of no-name brands. They may be poorly constructed and subject to leaking and almost certainly not backed by a warranty you could reasonably expect to make use of. I'm not going to recommend against batteries that come from any particular nation; you can find good quality batteries from China and Mexico and from the United States. But I would not put a cheaply made off-brand battery in an expensive camera or remote control. It's not worth the risk that they might fail when you need them or leak and damage an expensive device.

Types of Batteries

General-purpose batteries, usually made with carbon-zinc or zinc-chloride chemicals, are similar to the batteries we all grew up with. They are acceptable for low-draw devices like remote controls and small clocks. The next step up are alkaline batteries, which have a significantly longer useful life than ordinary or heavy-duty batteries, and are generally a better deal for devices that demand more power. Alkaline batteries are appropriate for most devices—including those you want to depend on (such as smoke detectors) and those you use a great deal (such as portable music players, remote-control units, and flashlights).

Lithium batteries have a higher capacity, and are usually priced higher than alkalines. They are useful in high-tech devices, including digital cameras, electronic flashes, and certain computer accessories like wireless mice. Lithiums generally hold their power without loss for a long period of time; you can recharge them with the right recharger.

Pay attention to expiration dates on packages or on the batteries themselves.

Alkalines have a long storage life; several makers now sell batteries of this type with an expiration date of 10 years beyond manufacture, which means you can stock up on them when you find them on sale. Batteries may still work after their expiration date, but they are more likely to have a shorter usable period and *may* be more likely to leak or otherwise fail when they are past their published shelf life.

Here are some tips to get the most out of your batteries and the devices they power…

- **All batteries have an optimal temperature window.** Most will drop off sharply in temperatures below 60 degrees Fahrenheit and may fail in extreme heat.

- **Store unused batteries in a cool, dry place.** Avoid having the connection points of the batteries in contact with each other or with any other metallic or otherwise conductive material. Doing so drains the power and could generate heat or even cause a fire.

- **Always use a matched set of batteries of the same type, brand, and batch in your devices.** Never replace just one of a pair or larger group of batteries. That could result in rapid discharge of the new batteries and possible leakage.

- **Check the battery compartment of any device for any leakage, damage, dirt, or corrosion.** Many minor problems with the contacts in the compartment can be fixed with a pencil eraser or an emery board (also known as a fingernail file). Finish off your work by gently vacuuming out the enclosure. Consider wearing glasses or goggles and gloves while doing so, and wash your hands afterward.

- **If a battery does leak, carefully remove it from the device.** Be sure to wear protective gloves or use plastic wrap or paper to guard against possible chemical burns or reactions. If the battery has leaked into the internal connectors or other parts of the device, you may need to have it professionally cleaned or restored. If we're talking about a $2 flashlight, dispose of it carefully. If there is leakage to an expensive camera or other electronic device, consult either the store where you purchased it or the manufacturer for advice on proper restoration. See the "Battery Warranty" sidebar for possible assistance from the battery maker.

- **If you are not going to use a particular device for a few months,** remove the batteries and either store them separately from the unit or dispose of them.
- **Avoid exposing batteries to water or other liquids, to extremes of heat, or to damage of any kind.** If the shell of a battery becomes creased, cracked, or otherwise contaminated, remove and dispose of the battery properly.
- **Be sure to understand and follow the instructions of your local recycling or disposal center for all batteries.** Batteries in landfills leak toxins into the soil and ground water. You can search online for recycling locations near you at Call 2recycle.org/locator.
- **Do not attempt to recharge batteries unless they are specifically designed for that purpose.** Batteries marketed as rechargeable are intended to be used with specially designed chargers and devices.

TIP

Battery Warranty

Most major brand-name batteries come with some sort of warranty against damage caused by leakage. In general, the warranty extends only until the printed expiration date on the batteries themselves.

When a battery leaked into a remote control for my stereo system, I received cash from that major battery maker. In theory, their warranty said I had to mail the device to their office so they could determine the cause of the fault. In this case, they just took my word. Check the manufacturer's website for information on submitting a claim.

If you purchased your batteries from a street vendor for pennies and they come in a plain white wrapper from a factory in Transnistria, don't expect warranty coverage.

The Pluses and Minuses of Rechargeable Batteries

Specially manufactured rechargeable batteries may save a bit of money in certain types of devices such as toys, flashlights, and cameras. Never attempt to recharge an ordinary battery, and don't use a rechargeable battery in a device that warns against their use.

These batteries typically cost five to 10 times as much as a disposable battery, but you can recharge them dozens of times. Even when you factor in the cost of a recharging station, they are still a good value. Another plus of rechargeables is that they reduce the number of disposable batteries, with their toxic metals and chemicals reaching landfills. As with all other batteries, you should dispose of rechargeables properly when they reach the end of their useful life.

Rechargeables are not appropriate, though, for long-term uses such as smoke detectors or remote controls. They generally hold their charge for relatively short periods of time between recharges.

Keeping Alive Smartphone Batteries

Most of us use a product that depends upon rechargeable batteries—a smartphone. Nearly all of these devices use a specialized lithium ion cell that is recharged in place.

Manufacturers of these batteries have made tremendous advances in recent years, yielding larger capacity and longer life. But most batteries will begin to lose their ability to recharge or hold a charge over time. With luck they will last at least as long as the phone itself.

You can purchase small external batteries to extend a phone battery's life; they plug into the power connector. Visit an electronics store or online site and search for external smartphone battery or backup unit.

You may also be able to add a phone case that includes a larger-capacity battery or, in certain setups, replace the internal battery with a larger-capacity one. Be cautious doing so, though. It could generate heat or even fire and damage your phone. Consult your phone manufacturer or your cellular provider's technical support department for advice.

Until fairly recently, most smartphones permitted users to open the case to replace batteries as needed. But some of the newest (and most expensive) smartphones have been designed to be as slim as possible and to include varying degrees of protection against water damage. Apple, Samsung, and many other makers have taken away the ability to replace batteries on their latest models.

With a sealed smartphone, unless you are willing to void all warranties and possibly damage the unit, the only way to replace a failing or worn-out battery is to return the device to a repair center.

By the way, it is not uncommon for a lithium ion battery to become warm or even hot while it is in use or is being recharged. If you see smoke or if the phone becomes so hot it poses a risk of fire or injury, unplug the device and turn it off! Then get thee to your local phone dealer.

Recharge Frequency

For most of us, the most logical way to use our smartphones is to plug them in for a good night's recharge when we turn off the lights. That may not be the best way to get the most from their batteries, though.

If you are lucky enough to have a phone with a replaceable battery—a feature that is becoming less common—go ahead and recharge on whatever cycle works for you. And if you are under an agreement with a company that allows you to upgrade your phone every two years (or less), overnight charging probably won't make much of a difference.

However, experts say that every time you recharge the lithium ion battery in your phone you are shortening its life, especially if your high-tech phone uses a technology called *fast charging*, which speeds up the process. It's not that your battery is likely to become overcharged. Nearly all modern phones, including those that conform to the Android standard or are part of Apple's iPhone family, include electronic circuitry that stop the charging when the battery is at its limit. The automatic circuitry is also intended to prevent the batteries from catching fire, which is a real but extremely rare occurrence.

But fast chargers, although they are more convenient, may lead to increased corrosion within the battery and otherwise shorten its life. *There are, instead, a few things you can do to extend the battery's life…*

• **Use your phone until the battery level reaches about 20% of capacity before recharging.** Going much below that level can shorten the battery's life.

• **You don't have to recharge a battery all the way to 100% all the time,** but every few weeks or so try to go through a few cycles where the battery is allowed to reach about 20% and then recharged to 100%.

• **Don't allow the battery to become overheated by the charger or by ambient temperature.** A little bit of heat is going to be produced as you use or recharge a phone, but they should not become so hot that it is uncomfortable to touch. Manufacturers say temperatures about 95 degrees Fahrenheit (35 Celsius) are the upper limit.

• **If your phone battery is draining too rapidly, consult with your cellular service provider for advice on how to manage demand.** In certain circumstances, using a WiFi connection instead of a cellular connection may draw less power (if the WiFi router is closer than the cell tower). Do you need to have Location or GPS turned on all day? Try turning it on only when you travel. Do you have apps constantly running in the background even when you don't use them? Turn them off. If you are using your phone to read a book or play a game and don't need the telephone or data features, switch off the built-in radios by enabling Airplane or Flight Mode. And, perhaps the best way to save power is to adjust the screen brightness to a low level, turning up the light only when necessary.

• **Enable the Low Power setting if yours has one.** Depending on the model, this will dim the display, change color screens to black and white, and slow the processor.

Set Your Table with Discount China

You won't find the most delicate, eggshell-like designs, but you can find some attractive and sturdy china sets at a restaurant-supply store or from online sellers. You'll probably have to buy a case of a dozen (or several dozen) of each piece, but prices can often be amazingly low, and you may find that the dishes will last for many more years than consumer lines. While you're shopping, look for pots, pans, and cooking implements.

Search for *restaurant equipment* listings online or in business directories. You can even ask a neighborhood restaurant where they get their supplies. Most will sell to individuals as well as to restaurants; you'll just have to deal with large quantities. If you come across a company that will only sell to a business, you should be able to work out an arrangement with someone who has a company address you can use for this purpose.

Another possible source is a factory outlet for a china maker. There you may find *seconds* with minor flaws in the glazing or decoration. Just search online for *manufacturer name factory outlet.* Here are a few good internet-based suppliers.

Central Restaurant Products	Industrial-quality appliances and heavy-duty dishware and cutlery	CentralRestaurant.com
Restaurant Source	Professional tools, from toques to towels and gigantic pots and pans. What's a toque? That's the tall white fancied by fancy chefs.	Bargreen.com/restaurant-source
Webstaurant Store	Wide range of equipment including preparation, cooking and cleaning supplies	WebstaurantStore.com

Replace a Missing Lemon Fork

You suspect that Cousin Lenny walked off with the butter server from your prized sterling silver, but your husband blames the family dog. In any case, the silver service hasn't been manufactured in ten years and the store where you purchased the set went out of business after a closeout sale last Christmas. How can you fill out the set?

The answer lies with several companies that specialize in filling holes in silverware sets. If the service is still in production or relatively recent, you can expect discounts from the list price; older sets may be offered at a premium over earlier prices. Prices may also fluctuate with major changes in the price of silver.

Some companies also offer preowned sets and pieces gathered from estate sales and jewelers' stocks. *There is no one store that has all brands and styles, but you may find what you need from one or another of these websites…*

- **Classic Replacements** at ClassicReplacements.com
- **Flatware Finder** at FlatwareFinder.com
- **Replacements.com** at Replacements.com
- **The Silverware Guy** at TheSilverwareGuy.com

Sow Your Oats Online Buying Seeds and Plants

For many years, mail order has been an important way for gardeners to shop for seeds and plants both ordinary and rare. On the internet, the selection is broader than ever, prices more competitive, and the ordering process extremely easy.

As with most other online purchases, I recommend calling the company with a question about your particular climate, soil, gardening skills, or interests; see how accommodating they are before you place an order. Ask, too, about any guarantees they offer. Some offer replacements for plants that do not arrive in good condition. Others extend that guarantee for a full season or more.

We have decorated the exterior of our home with a small botanical garden of hydrangeas (one of the few plants that thrives in our sandy soil and difficult climate). Over the years, we have had a half dozen plants that somehow did not like us or our environs. In each case, the supplier made good with a more cooperative replacement.

The companies have become very adept at carefully packing live plants and make good use of overnight or expedited shipments by UPS and FedEx. Most of these companies will work with you to assure that plants are delivered at the proper time for your particular growing zone. Here are a few of the leaders of the current crop.

Some sellers specialize in flowering plants, others in shrubs and bushes, and still others in fruits and vegetables. A few will sell you just about anything they can ship to your location. Study the websites, make a few phone calls, and speak to customer service for advice on products, including the best planting times.

Amazon	Yes, that Amazon. The company acts as a marketplace for dozens of plant suppliers, and orders are protected by the same guarantees offered for purchases of other products. Search for live plants on the Amazon home page.	Amazon.com
Baker Heirloom Seeds	This site offers flower and herb seeds, but is most famous for its huge selection of heirloom vegetable seeds.	RareSeeds.com
Bluestone Perennials	They offer earth-friendly packing options (plant the pots directly in the ground or send back those peanuts). Sales are common, customer service is exceptional, and you can search for plants by zone, color, water conditions, and other criteria.	BluestonePerennials.com
Burpee	The company dates back to 1876, when founder W. Atlee Burpee borrowed $1,000 of “seed money” to start a mail-order fancy poultry business. The business grew quickly, introducing a number of important strains to America, including iceberg lettuce and the Big Boy tomato. Today you can order seeds as well as fruit, vegetable, and decorative plants.	Burpee.com
Dominion Seed House	An old-line Canadian source for flowering plants and seeds as well as tools. The site offers extensive background on each item, sort of an electronic encyclopedia of gardening. Products can be shipped to the United States as well as domestic addresses in Canada.	Dominion-seed-house.com
Home Depot	You can order live plants and seeds from the big box store's online site, but you have to pick up at the store. They also sell fertilizer, gardening tools, watering implements, and most everything else a depot for the home might offer.	HomeDepot.com

Jackson & Perkins	Many varieties of plants are offered here, with a specialization in roses.	JacksonAndPerkins.com
Seedman	A huge selection backed by a detailed database with descriptions and instructions for tens of thousands of growing things including seeds familiar and quite unfamiliar from around the world.	Seedman.com
Stokes Seed Co	All manner of seed, flowers, and gardening supplies are produced in the company's Ontario location.	StokeSeeds.com
Walmart	You don't have to visit aisle 62 to order plants and seeds.	Walmart.com

Buying fall bulbs any time other than autumn can save you money; just keep the bulbs in a cool, dry place. Visiting nurseries at the end of the growing season, in autumn, can help you save money as well, as they'll be trying to get rid of inventory. And if you want to get really thrifty, arrange a plant exchange with friends. Everyone has something they're trying to get rid of or willing to trade.

Smart Flower Shopping

Way back before the age of the internet, among the first national third-party shopping companies were flower sellers that took orders over the phone. I remember one service that required customers to send payment by wiring money to a store near the intended recipient. Today, online sites in combination with credit cards have made the process extremely simple.

Some of the online services, such as FTD and 1-800-FLOWERS pass along the order to local stores for delivery, while others send expressions of love, thanks, sympathy, or celebration by overnight delivery service.

These online floral sites can be pretty pricey because they apply a premium to the bottom line to pay for their call centers and overhead before arranging for local delivery. Before ordering online, give your (or the intended recipient's) local florist a call and see what they can give you for a decent price. You might also consider buying in bulk—especially if you're trying to buy for an event, such as a wedding. Try Blooms by the Box (BloomsByTheBox.com) and FiftyFlowers (FiftyFlowers.com). Both are geared toward brides-to-be, but they'll sell flowers to you even if you're not getting married soon. The latter even offers free shipping.

My savvy daughter ordered the flowers for her wedding from one of the big-box stores at a deep discount. The boxes of blooms arrived by FedEx from a farm in Colombia in South America, right on schedule and beautifully packed.

CHAPTER 15

Making Your Home More Secure

Chance favors the prepared mind, said the great French scientist Louis Pasteur. What does this have to do with home security and health issues? I operate on the related theory that luck is the residue of planning. A homeowner who spends the time and effort making it difficult for a burglar to enter a home undetected, or who equips a house with smoke, carbon monoxide, and radon detectors is enhancing the chances for his or her own good luck.

This book is about how to save money. One of the best ways for homeowners to save is to spend on preventative maintenance and security. In this case, to paraphrase and update Benjamin Franklin, a dollar spent wisely may be $10 saved.

In this chapter, I'll pass along some tips on home security and peace of mind.

- **Buy something to watch over you.**
- **Detect smoke and carbon monoxide.**
- **Monitor another silent menace.**
- **Invest in other kinds of detectors.**
- **Try a winter plumbing work-around.**
- **Buy the best fire extinguisher.**
- **Take laundry room precaution.**
- **Keep it down out there: dealing with noisy neighbors.**

Buy Something to Watch Over You

The best advice before you set out to burglarproof your home—Think like a burglar.

"Case" your home. Walk around the outside and look for ways to enter. Could a burglar easily force a window or door? Are there places shielded by shrubs or fences where someone could hide out of sight while breaking in?

Your neighbor may not like this, but your goal should be to make your house less appealing a target than the one next door. If your house is better lit, better locked, and just a bit more difficult to get into than another house on the block, most burglars will move on to easier pickings. The following sections reveal some things you can do to make a burglar feel less comfortable.

Lock Windows and Doors

There is no such thing as a completely secure lock, grate, or bar, but anything that slows down a burglar or makes noise will work in your favor.

Deadbolt locks that require a key to open from the inside and the outside are the best way to secure a door, especially if the lock is on a door with a glass panel. Deadbolts that use a thumb knob on the inside are easy for a burglar to reach through a broken window. One downside to deadbolt locks with keys on both sides: You are making it difficult to get out of the house in case of a fire or other emergency. The best compromise is to keep an exit key a few feet away from the door—out of reach from a hand reaching through a broken window—and make sure that everyone in the family knows it is there. Do not use that emergency key on a regular basis.

Additionally, steel doors are more expensive than wood, but because so often it is the wood frame around the door that gives way when burglars break in, *Consumer Reports* recommends installing a metal reinforced box strike, which you can buy for about $10, and installing them with 3-inch screws.

Consider installing a high-tech door lock that requires use of a PIN code or one that opens with a command from your smartphone. (Make sure you also have a PIN code or swipe pattern on your phone to prevent unauthorized users from using it as a key.) Some of the more sophisticated PIN code locks allow you to give cleaning services, technicians, or houseguests a temporary code that you can later erase from the system. Most of these systems have a backup key that can also be used to open the door. Some new models also have video cameras that communicate with the internet by WiFi or cellular signal so that you can "answer" the door even if you are thousands of miles away.

There is not much you can do for sliding glass doors or large windows except to keep them locked. You can add a heavy wooden dowel or metal bar in the channel of a sliding door to make them harder to open. You can also install a bolt into the channel of a window to make it difficult to raise it more than a few inches. There's such a thing as security film that you can install on sliding glass doors or other large windows. It helps prevent glass from shattering. Popular brands include 3M (Blinc.Media/2giL5CT) and ShatterGARD (Shattergard.com/home.html). (Depending on what security film you buy, energy savings may be an additional benefit, since some are tinted to keep rooms cooler.) Most burglars would rather find a small window or entry that they can break relatively quietly.

Use Outdoor Lights

Illuminate hiding places with exterior lights connected to motion-detection sensors. Install them very high up so they're harder to tamper with. Install a system that allows you to adjust the cone of sensitivity for the sensor and allows you to aim the floodlights exactly where you want them to shine. At our house, it took a while to find the proper settings to avoid annoying the neighbors and ourselves during the nightly peregrinations of deer. After all these years, I think we have-unintentionally trained the deer to come to the light so they can find something to snack on after dark. We coexist nonviolently.

Get Buddy-Buddy

Get on good terms with as many of your neighbors as you can. It would be nice if they know when someone is intruding or something is wrong with your house. If your neighbors are close enough to see your house, they are likely to notice when you are away for a while. Ask them to pick up your mail and be on the lookout for anything out of place. If they are really helpful and trustworthy, provide them with your email addresses and phone number so they can reach you in an emergency, as well as the name and phone number of your insurance agent. Bring them a souvenir when you return.

Hold Your Mail

Arrange for packages to be held at depots or the post office when you are away from home for an extended period, or ask a neighbor to collect it for you. Suspend newspaper deliveries while you travel so that your porch or driveway does not fill up with papers, a virtual advertisement that you're not at home. But also ask a neighbor to keep an eye out. Newspapers often still arrive even when you have technically suspended their delivery. Arrange for someone to mow the lawn or clear the snow. Ask a neighbor to park his or her car in the driveway at night when you are away. Even if that is not your ordinary pattern, it is an indication to a possible burglar that someone may be in the house.

Make Your House Seem Occupied

Turn on your TV. Install timers for lights in several parts of the house and set them to go on and off in a realistic pattern.

Hide the Goods

Try to avoid displaying expensive items. For example, don't place paintings or large-screen TVs in plain view of the front windows. After the holidays or your birthday, break down large boxes so passersby can't see that you just received a new game system or 85-inch TV.

If you have jewelry, a coin collection, or other valuables that are easy to carry away and easy to sell, either install a substantial safe (that you can bolt to the floor or install in a wall) or leave them in a bank's safe deposit vault.

Also, if you have a garage with an automatic door opener, it is not a good idea to leave the remote control in your car while it's parked in the driveway. A burglar could spot the control, break into the car, and open the garage door. One way to guard against that possibility is to install a shutoff switch on the garage door opener. An even cheaper option is to take your garage door opener into your house when you go inside and keep it with your car keys,

Safeguard Your Keys

Do not put your home address on your key ring. If you lose your keys and are certain no one can connect them to you, you are better off paying a few dollars to have new keys made than to worry about a criminal making an uninvited visit.

Don't hide house keys under the mat, over the doorway, inside the mailbox, or in any of the other usual places. A clever burglar has a pretty good eye for hiding spots. You might consider leaving an extra key with a neighbor, but be sure your name and address are not attached to those keys either, or a burglar who breaks into that house could end up with a two-for-one deal.

If you have a trusted housekeeper, maintenance person, or neighbor consider leaving that person a key.

We keep a set of keys hidden in a very obscure place on our property. I'm not about to publish the location in this book, but think about things like this: nailed into a brown box on a branch of a tree, or inside a moldy glove under a peg covered by spider webs in an outdoor shed.

Consider a Burglar Alarm

Consult your neighbors and your local police department about their experience with various alarm designs, installers, and monitoring services. There are many options, including professionally installed systems as well as do-it-yourself motion detectors and glass breakage detectors. If you sign up with a company to install a system and monitor calls, try to assure that the equipment belongs to you and that the monitoring service has a reasonable contract period—perhaps one or two years. This will allow you to change to a different monitoring company or renegotiate rates with your existing company from time to time.

Study the alarm company's options. If your home is an open design, you might need only one or two motion detectors rather than half a dozen. Similarly, you may not need detectors on every window and door in your home if the motion detector will notice anyone moving around. Think like a burglar: Where would an intruder go to find something to steal? I know one homeowner whose system consists of just a pair of motion detectors in the stairwell to the second floor of his home. One way or another, an intruder will set it off.

Make sure that the alarm company is acceptable to your homeowner's insurance company. You should be able to receive a discount—often about 10%—on your coverage for theft. You may also be eligible for a credit on insurance if you install a smoke detector that is monitored by a central alarm agency. And a temperature alarm should protect you against water damage if your heating system fails in cold weather.

Detect Smoke and Carbon Monoxide

The most important tip about smoke and carbon monoxide detectors is a very basic one: If you don't have one, get one. If you have one, get a second or third or fourth.

Smoke Alarms

There are few better investments in security than this. Industry experts say that having a detector in your home reduces your chance of dying in a fire by half. And prices of detectors have declined to the point where there should be no hesitation in purchase.

You should have at least one smoke detector on each level of your home or apartment, and some experts say to put them in every bedroom. And you should look to have a mix of photoelectric and ionization models. You can also find units that combine both methods in one plastic box.

- ***Photoelectric*** **models, which work by detecting a reduction in light passing between an emitter and detector, are quickest in detecting smoldering, smoky fires.**
- ***Ionization*** **smoke detectors use a tiny capsule containing a radioactive element that electrically charges a compartment inside the detector.** When smoke enters the device it changes the electrical current and sets off the alarm. Ionization detectors are quickest in detecting a flaming fire with little smoke.

Replace any smoke detector more than 10 years old. If you can't remember the last time you replaced batteries in a detector, replace them now. (Batteries should be swapped at least twice a year, or sooner if a detector's low-power warning goes off. Use fresh alkaline batteries; rechargeable batteries are not meant for detectors because they do not hold a charge for a long period of time.)

If you are constructing a new home or undertaking a major renovation project, consider installing an interconnected AC power system. Many building codes now require these devices. If any of the detectors in an interconnected system detect a fire, all of the alarms work. This is especially valuable if you place detectors in the basement or attic, two remote areas that are common spots for fires to start. A top-of-the-line interconnected system can include a carbon monoxide detector.

If you install an AC power system, add a few battery-operated detectors on each floor as a backup in case of a power failure. Why have both? Because the AC units are usually interconnected and provide the highest level of security, while the battery units are backups if the electrical power goes out.

Follow the instructions of the manufacturer in locating detectors. In general, do not place them near a window or exterior door. Air drafts might direct smoke away from them. Similarly, avoid dead-end corners where air may not circulate properly. Don't place it too far from your stove; the occasional false burnt-toast alarm is better than an out-of-hand cooking fire.

I would recommend buying detectors from a brand name you recognize; don't save a few dollars with a no-name unit. Among the better brands are First Alert and Kidde.

Carbon Monoxide Alarms

Another inexpensive, precious form of protection that should be in homes—a carbon monoxide (CO) detector. Most of these detectors are sold in combination with smoke detectors. Carbon monoxide is a colorless, odorless gas given off as part of the combustion process. Ironically, the risks from CO have gone up in recent years with new construction techniques that better seal homes. If you have an oil, gas, coal, wood, or other fuel-burning furnace, stove, or oven, or a fireplace, you should install at least one of the devices in your home.

Locate carbon monoxide detectors at the entry to each bedroom—especially in rooms that are above or near any device that uses an open flame, such as the furnace, hot water heater, and gas ovens. The very best location is within each sleeping area, on the floor closest to the furnace or appliances. To be even safer, put an additional detector in the basement or furnace room. Some local fire codes require such detectors in various locations; check with your local fire department.

Most carbon monoxide detectors plug into house current, which is acceptable because a power outage will also turn off gas and oil furnaces and hot-water heaters. A battery-backed system, though, is safer if you have a fireplace or a wood-fired heating system. Once again, don't skimp on these devices. Buy from a recognized company like First Alert or Kidde.

Monitor Another Silent Menace

Radon is a colorless, odorless gas that seeps up through the soil; it decays into radioactive particles that can be inhaled and have been linked to as many as 20,000 lung-cancer deaths each year in the US. That's pretty frightening stuff, but the good news is that radon is easily, inexpensively detected. Eliminating radon gas in most cases is similarly simple.

Radon gas, which has been found in every state in almost every type of geology, tends to accumulate in basements and lower floors, entering through holes or cracks in the foundation or through well water. You should be especially vigilant if you have a finished basement. According to the Environmental Protection Agency, about 6% of American homes have radon levels above the danger level. A lifelong exposure to radon in this concentration raises the risk of lung cancer to about 1 in 500 for nonsmokers, and about 15 in 500 for smokers.

You can learn more about radon by visiting the EPA website at EPA.gov/radon and examine a map that shows general levels across the nation.

Radon levels can vary due to temperature, precipitation, and other factors. The best way to test is to perform both a quick short-term test that takes a weeklong snapshot of current conditions and a longer-term test that is more likely to report on varying conditions. The testers consist of a tube of activated charcoal or a specially treated film that is exposed to

Detecting a Warranty

Good-quality smoke and carbon monoxide detectors should come with a warranty against failure within a reasonable period. As I was writing this book, one of the detectors in our home began signaling it had failed. Its label indicated that it was only three years old. When I checked with the manufacturer, I was told the device had a five-year guarantee. Because I had purchased the device online from a web retailer, I was able to obtain proof of purchase. I was offered a replacement, which arrived a week later.

Many years ago, my family's carbon monoxide detector went off. We opened windows and doors and called the fire department, who determined that our chimney—which was also used as exhaust by our natural gas furnace—had become blocked and was pushing CO into the house. Like buying and replacing batteries in detectors, regular chimney cleaning is an expense, but important home maintenance.

Thirty Days Hath September...

Do you remember exactly when you changed batteries in each of the detectors in your house? You could use a felt-tip marker to record the date on the inside of the device as a reminder. Even better, how about picking two dates per year and making them your battery-change days? You can choose January 1 and July 4, or the spring and autumn solstices. Some areas promote changing batteries when clocks are adjusted forward and backward each spring and fall. Add the reminders to the calendar on your phone (or, if you're really traditional, on the good old-fashioned paper calendar hanging in your kitchen). Of course, this won't work for you if your time zone doesn't recognize the time changes.

the air for a specified period of time and then closed up and mailed to a reporting lab.

The tests typically sell for about $20 to $50 and are available at most hardware and home-supply stores as well as from various government or academic institutions. You'll find short-term testers meant to take a snapshot of the current situation as well as long-term testers that are meant to record exposure over a three-month to one-year period. They take into account different patterns associated with seasonal changes including airflow.

If the testers report significant levels of radon, you should contact a person who specializes in removing the gas; the testing company or your local health department should direct you to the proper service. In most cases the repair consists of a power ventilation system that removes basement air to the outside.

Contact your local health department and ask how common radon is in your location. Be sure to follow the guidelines of health and building codes as well as advice from professional radon-testing companies. Detectors need to be serviced, and tests conducted on a regular basis.

It is also possible to have radon in your water supply. If you have a municipal system, your town or city should be monitoring for this and other contaminants. If you have a well, you may need to have a test performed yourself. Once again, consult with your local health department for advice.

Invest in Other Kinds of Detectors

Smoke and carbon monoxide detectors are not the only ways to monitor your home for problems. The following sections explain a few other types of devices you can purchase as a standalone alarm, or as part of an interconnected system.

Temperature Alarm

You can install a device that monitors the temperature inside your home and calls you (or a neighbor or caretaker) if your house drops below a preset level. In our home, a temperature monitor is set at 45 degrees, which is a very definitive indication that the heating system is not working properly. Be sure to place the sensor in the interior core of the house, away from windows or outside doors that might direct a cold blast in its direction. The best of these devices will also tell you if the electrical power to your house has been interrupted. Most furnaces will not operate if they do not have power. Temperature alarms are especially useful in vacation homes and by snow birds who spend winter months away from their primary residence.

You can buy a temperature alarm from online retailers and security stores. We can program our model to call three phone numbers when the temperature has dropped below whatever level we choose, and we can call our house from anywhere in the world and ask the device to tell us the temperature in our house. Advanced models include a battery backup in case of power outage, and can communicate using a cellular connection. Expect to pay about $100 for a good device. You can install them yourself. Pick a location in the interior of your home, away from windows and near a power outlet and phone connection.

Lift Pump or Sump Pump Alarm

If your home has a plumbing system that includes a lift or sump pump, consider installing an alarm that will sound if water or sewage has reached above the level they should not reach. These types of water alarms are best for people who live in areas that are prone to flooding and also for homeowners who have a system that lifts sewage into a municipal system.

The alarm will alert you if the pump fails or if there is a system blockage. A plumber must install the alarm, and you may need an electrician to provide power. The system in our home includes a remote alarm that runs from the basement into a utility closet so that we can hear it. The alarm itself costs about $200. It'll take your plumber an hour or so to install the alarm.

Emergency Medical Summons

If anyone in your household (or family who lives elsewhere) has a medical condition that might require immediate assistance, consider a medical alert system. These can be tied into a cellular phone connection or your home's WiFi system to communicate with other family members or emergency services.

Contact your doctor or local health department for advice about this summons system, or consult an organization like AARP that serves senior citizens. The alert system is relatively inexpensive, but you'll also have to pay a monthly or annual fee for call monitoring.

Try a Winter Plumbing Work-Around

I've made note several times about how we live on an island that is sometimes subject to very severe weather: high winds, sea-driven flooding, and electrical power failure—all of which brings me to a leading concern in the winter: a heating system shutdown.

If a home is adequately insulated, and if you take reasonable care not to make things worse by opening doors too often, a house should hold on to heat for hours. Keep refrigerator and (especially) freezer doors closed as much as possible, and hope for the return of power.

The ultimate concern is a prolonged shutdown that allows the water pipes in your house to freeze. The longest period we have endured was nearly two days, which was probably right up against the limit.

What can you do to reduce the chances of problems from extreme cold temperatures?

- **Disconnect all your outdoor hoses.** The hose can function as a conduit for cold air to the exterior water valve (called a sillcock or a hose bib), and if there is any water left at the end of the pipe it could freeze and burst.
- **Shut off any outside faucet's interior valve.** Most modern plumbing valves have a small brass cap that can be removed to drain water from the dry side of the valve—the section of pipe leading to the outside.
- **Consider a full house winterization.** If you are going to be away for the entire winter, get a price from a licensed plumber for a complete winterization of your home. That involves shutting off incoming water and draining pipes within the house. This process can become complex and expensive if you also have to drain a hot-water heating system and tank. Compare the cost of the winterization plus the cost to restore the system in the spring against the cost of keeping the heat on all through the season.
- **Install a boiler bypass.** This interesting halfway measure is used in some parts of the country and was added to our home by our champion plumber. This is a system that allows you to shut off the water to the interior of the house but continue to feed the furnace and boiler. When the valve is turned off to the house, we run a few faucets and flush a few toilets until there is almost no water in the domestic pipes. Doing this greatly reduces the possibility of damage from frozen water pipes and as homeowner you can easily control it. We keep the thermostats set at about 55 degrees Fahrenheit and head for far-away places with relatively few concerns. Ask your licensed plumber whether such an arrangement makes sense for your particular pipes and heating system.

Take Laundry Room Precaution

In most homes, your washing machine is connected to the hot and cold water supply by a pair of hoses; the flexible hoses are used since copper or rigid plastic pipe could fail because of the machine's vibration and movement.

If the hoses attached to your machine are made of rubber or plastic, replace them every three or four years. If you can't remember the last time they were changed, change them now. An even better option is stainless-steel braided hoses, which should be safe for at least five years. Think of them as inexpensive flood insurance—and change them every five years. Tape a small piece of paper to a place where you can easily access the hoses; on the paper, write the date you installed them.

Buy the Best Fire Extinguisher

You are your own first line of defense against a fire in your home, apartment, or office. There should be at least one fire extinguisher in close reach. Make sure you get the right size. Better yet, get several sizes. Keep one in the kitchen, one in the garage, and one in the laundry room. Make sure each floor in your home has one as well.

The most important lesson to learn is that not all fires are the same. Fires are classified based on the type of material or fuel that is burning.

Fire Type	What Is Burning	How to Extinguish
A	Paper, wood, or cloth	Extinguish with water
B	Flammable liquids including grease fires, gasoline, oil, and paints	Type B extinguisher
C	Electrical devices, wiring, and appliances	Type C extinguisher

Here are the ABCs of fires and their extinguishers…

• **For a home or nonindustrial workplace, you can use a multipurpose A:B:C extinguisher.** These units often use chemicals such as ammonium phosphate. But an A:B:C extinguisher is not very effective against a grease fire. For your kitchen, garage, or workshop, a B:C device is more appropriate. That rating has either potassium or sodium bicarbonate (also known as baking soda).

• **Choose a high number rating.** A number precedes each A and B letter rating (C doesn't have a number rating). The number indicates how good the extinguisher is at putting out those kinds of fires. A 4 means it works better than 2 does, but a higher rating is more expensive. Don't skip on this safety.

• **Consider the extinguisher's weight and size.** Don't buy one that is too heavy or large for all adults to handle. For large, chemical-laden spaces, go for 10 pounds. For smaller spaces, 5 pounds should be sufficient.

• **Read the manual.** Share the instructions for all the extinguishers in your home or office, and conduct informal fire drills. Make it clear who is responsible for pets, how everyone should exit (depending on where they are), and where you should meet after you exit.

• **Regularly check the pressure gauges on extinguishers.** Most consumer-grade units have a shelf life of about 10 years. Throw away any unit that falls below the usable level. Some commercial and residential units can be recharged; check with the manufacturer. Some fire departments will recharge units or give advice. You could also spring for an EN-Gauge (Mija.com/pressure-gauge-applications/fire-protection; contact them for a price quote) sensor, which runs on a 9-volt battery and makes a sound when the extinguisher is no good.

• **Don't buy generic.** Amerex (Amerex-fire.com) and Kidde (Kiddeus.com) are common reliable brands, and prices vary based on rating, type, and size.

• **Buy the best.** Once again, First Alert and Kidde are leading brands. Your local fire department should be willing to offer advice on the best brands of extinguishers, and some even offer inspection of your existing equipment. Some insurance companies offer rebates to policyholders who buy extinguishers, or charge you more if you don't have them installed.

Fire experts advise that in case of a significant fire you do the following in this order…

1. Alert everyone in the home or office and advise them to leave.

2. Call the fire department or local 911 emergency line. If you are using a cellphone, make sure to confirm your precise address with the operator.

3. If it is safe for you to remain in the home or office, attempt to put out the fire with the proper extinguisher. Otherwise, get out and wait for the fire department to arrive.

Again, read the instructions on your extinguishers.

In general, the acronym PASS is a way to help remember what to do: pull the pin, aim at the base of the fire, squeeze the trigger, and sweep back and forth until the extinguisher is empty.

Keep It Down Out There: Dealing with Noisy Neighbors

One man's ceiling is another man's floor, which also applies to walls and doors...and is something that apartment dwellers know all about. What do you do if your neighbor thinks it is perfectly acceptable to crank up her stereo with heavy-metal noise at 3 a.m.? Or how about a homeowner who turns on the floodlights to mow his lawn at 4:30 a.m. on a Sunday? And that dog that barks all night...

You might want to start with a polite but firm request for reasonable quiet. But if that doesn't work, explore your legal rights:

- **If you are a renter, check your lease for a clause called Quiet Enjoyment.** This is a common element of rentals that gives you the right to live in peace and demands that you afford that same right to your neighbors. Your landlord, by making that promise, is supposed to enforce the clause and could evict your neighbor if he or she doesn't deliver you that quiet enjoyment. If your lease provides for that peace and the landlord does not deliver it, you should be able to break the lease and move—or at least threaten to do so. See if you can get a group of neighbors to make the same threat at the same time. There is strength in numbers.

- **Homeowners as well as renters should consult their local government to find the terms of a noise ordinance.** There may be certain times and dates where more noise (such as fireworks) is allowed. A typical law limits certain activities such as lawn mowing, snowblowing, construction work, and outdoor parties to certain hours of the day, and generally do not include the night and early morning. The code may also set decibel noise limits. You can request that police enforce the law. In a worst case you could file a civil suit seeking a court order or even monetary damages.

- **Many governments have ordinances requiring dog owners to keep their animals leashed or fenced and reasonably quiet.** If not, a general anti-noise statute may apply. Consult your mayor, town council, or police department for advice or search online for noise ordinance and the name of your town or city.

CHAPTER 16

Buying Home Electronics

Today, it is nearly impossible to buy a new VCR (especially since they're no longer made). For a while the DVD player replaced it as the way to play recorded movies (if you love your DVD collection, you may want to pick up a spare player while you still can), and today the dominant technology is the DVR (digital video recorder), which itself is on the way to being displaced by video-on-demand and streaming video technologies.

We are living on parallel tracks. Our devices are getting smarter and smarter, but as humans we sometimes wonder if we have reached our limit. But that's why we have kids and grandkids, right? Seriously, though, all is not hopeless. When computers and smartphones and other devices first came out, their capabilities were way ahead of the abilities of users to understand and manual writers to explain. That's why millions of copies of *For Dummies* books were sold. I know, because I wrote more than a dozen of them.

When it comes to buying a product, consider the customer service and warranty offered by the maker before looking at relatively small differences in technical specifications.

Here's a good-news bad-news situation if ever there was one: The longer you wait, the more likely it will be that the next model of whatever device you are considering will arrive with new features you never knew you needed. And in any case, as soon as you take home your new flat-screen HDTV, it is already obsolete.

But if you wait a year, that amounts to 12 months during which you don't get to amaze your friends, family, and yourself.

- **Hang around with a flat-screen HD TV.**
- **Be wary of high-tech extended warranties.**
- **Control your TV cable bill.**
- **Cut the cord completely.**
- **Tune in for a deal on satellite TV.**
- **Chat on the phone.**

Ubiquinet

According to the Consumer Technology Association, a US group representing high-tech products sold to consumers, by 2017 about 71% of Americans will have a smartphone, 73% a digital camera, and 60% a tablet computer. The growth rate and household penetration of laptops and tablets passed that of personal computers around 2014.

And in 2016 just under 90% of Americans (287 million of us) have access to high-speed internet at home, work, or elsewhere. (Just as an aside, and I love to head in that direction, the largest number of internet users is in China, where 721 million people are online. That represents just a bit more than half of their population. The little island nation of Iceland claims 100% penetration for the internet, with all 332,000 residents having access.)

Hang Around with a Flat-Screen HDTV

Flat-screen high-definition (HD) televisions represent a significant improvement over the sets we all grew up with. They are sharper—a higher resolution—brighter, and possessed of a color range well beyond that of older cathode ray tube sets. Flat screens take up no space on the floor, occupying only wall space or a small space atop a piece of furniture.

HDTV Specifics

HDTVs use digital cable, satellite, or broadcast cable signals to produce an image with nearly triple the resolution of a standard TV with a wider, more movie-theater–like screen. And they have proven to be so attractive that they have become a commodity. Although you can pay a lot extra for certain brands and for certain super-duper specifications, the truth is that almost any flat-screen TV is going to produce a great picture and last more than a few years of regular use.

The bottom line, at least when it comes to subjective judgment before purchase, is that you have to use your own eyes and ears to see and hear the difference between various sets. If you can't tell the difference between a $500 set and a $3,000 set, put the savings in your pocket for other things.

The important differences are described in the following sections.

Screen Size

Just as with older sets, the size of a flat-screen TV is measured on the diagonal (the *hypotenuse* for those of you who remember high school geometry). One area in which flat screens have advanced in recent years is in the narrowing of the bezel, or frame, that surrounds the screen. Some of the most impressive sets have a bezel of less than an inch, which makes the frame almost invisible.

Backlighting

Nearly all current flat screens use LCD (liquid crystal diode) technology to essentially open or close the pathway to a tiny red, green, or blue filter. The LCD itself does not produce light, and the TV needs a backlight system to project through the crystal. The original design for LCD flat-screen TVs used a small fluorescent light system. That has been supplanted in many designs by an array of tiny LED (light-emitting diodes). LEDs require a bit less electrical wattage and produce less heat.

Both systems work well, but if you find a non-LED model, make your decision based on the quality of the image and the price.

Another technology, plasma display, used a grid of tiny etched wires to individually illuminate picture elements on the screen. Many users, myself included, found plasma screens to be superior to LCD models. The colors seem more saturated and you can see true black in dark areas. But plasma sets were more expensive, used more power, and generated more heat. They are hard to find now.

The next wave of sets includes OLED (organic light-emitting diode) technology. These sets, which cost more than standard flat screens, may bridge the gap between LED and plasma screens, delivering richer colors and blacker blacks. They're available at a premium price and only from a few manufacturers. Wait until there's competition if you want to get a better price on this particular design.

Viewing Distance and Angle

Exactly how large do you want your screen? Will you be sitting too close or too far to enjoy the experience? And will you be watching at a precise 90-degree angle to the screen, not offset left or right or below or above the precise center of the screen? If you're going to be watching from a fixed position that is close to that perfect center, a rule of thumb is to buy a flat screen whose diagonal screen size is 2.5 times the distance. Assume you'll be watching from 10 feet away. In that case, a 50-inch screen would be about right: 2.5 x 50 = 125 inches (10.4 feet).

Just multiple the size screen you're considering by 2.5. You'll get a total that is in inches. Convert that to feet. Is that how far away you'll be from the screen? Then you're good to go. Or stay and watch. If you will be at an angle from the screen's center, shorten the distance. Various formulas recommend multipliers of the diagonal distance of 2, 1.6, or even less if you want to feel as if you are being sucked into the digital matrix. In this case, you'd multiply the screen size you're considering by 2 (or 1.6, or what have you). Convert the total from inches to feet, and you can see how large the screen should be.

Sound Quality

Digital video signals include high-definition audio information as well. The bad news is that many HD screens come with tiny, underpowered speakers. Take a listen. If the price difference is not huge, choose a set with a better sound system.

The other option is to add an external audio system with an amplifier and a set of speakers. The simplest solution is a soundbar that sits below (or above in certain wall mountings) and includes several speakers and an amplifier, priced between about $100 and $300. A more complex add-on is a surround-sound system with an amplifier with five or more speakers plus a subwoofer that boosts bass sounds to chest-thumping levels, available from about $200 for a basic package to $1,000 or more for a movie-theater-quality system. The system I installed years ago required me to run wires through the wall up into the attic and then down the opposite wall for rear speakers. Today you can make things much simpler by buying a wireless surround system that uses radio signals to fill the room with sound. We love our system—especially for baseball games. We can hear the popcorn vendors moving through the aisles behind our heads.

You'll find audio systems offered by most of the major home electronics makers including Panasonic, Sony, Samsung, Vizio, and others. You can generally expect that the higher the amplifier's wattage, the better the sound quality will be. But the best test is your own ears. Listen to various systems in a showroom before buying. (Even better, see if any friends or acquaintances have a system set up in their home, in an environment close to that you will use.)

Bells and Whistles

Would you like to spend a few thousand dollars more for a 4K set, a curved screen, or wider color gamut? The answer: Only if it matters to you. Those 4K sets are ultra-high–definition screens. If you think the sharpness or resolution of a high-definition flat-screen TV is amazing, take a gander at a 4K set, which can produce an image with about twice the number of individual tiny dots.

The good news is that the image is truly amazing; the less-than-good news is that your friendly (or unfriendly) local cable TV or satellite TV provider may not yet be able to send you a signal with that much information in it. It's kind of a chicken-or-egg situation, with providers saying they are not ready to devote space (known as *bandwidth*) on their cable or satellite signal until there are enough sets out there that can use 4K material. In the short term, there are some internet sources for 4K shows. Stay tuned for more developments.

- **Curved screens.** Are you old enough to remember Cinerama movie screens that promised to immerse viewers in an image projected on a screen curved inward? Makers of curved-screen sets claim the experience is superior; you'll have to be the judge. Some reviewers and buyers think the curve is the greatest thing since, well, TV. Others, including me, think their logic is bent out of shape. Curved screens come at a slight premium over flat screens—as much as a few hundred dollars more for a large display. Only you can decide if the curve is worth the extra cash.

- **Wider gamut.** You may think the HD screen before you has an amazing range of colors (and you would be correct), but what if I said you could get a TV set with a wider gamut of colors, closer to the full range of perhaps ten million colors, which a healthy younger person's retina and brain can perceive? One technology is called *quantum dots or semiconductor nanocrystals*. In one use, they are produced as a filter that sits between the LED backlighting and the LCD picture elements to deliver purer colors. The colors are undeniably superior to a screen without quantum dots, but the extra cost—several thousand dollars more—may not excite you.

Shopping for an HDTV

In my opinion, buying an HDTV should involve at least one visit to an appliance or electronics store to see and hear the devices for yourself. With apologies to the owners of brick-and-mortar retail shops, that does not necessarily mean you have to buy from them unless they are able to give you a great price, superior customer service, or both.

Here are a few sneaky tricks some electronics stores use to encourage buyers to pick a higher-priced model...

• **Different signal strengths.** Make sure all the sets on display have a clean, strong signal. It doesn't usually matter if the image comes from a cable TV feed or from a DVD, but if one set has a snowy or choppy signal, ask a salesperson to make sure it is properly connected. Be especially suspicious if the lower-priced models all seem to have worse signals.

• **Different settings.** Most HDTVs have a wide range of adjustments for brightness, color saturation, and other settings. There's even a setting called Demo or something similar that pumps up the image. The Demo setting may look great in a showroom, but may be much brighter or more saturated than you would want to use in a darkened room at home.

The first thing to determine is if all the sets you are considering are using the Demo setting, or if just some are showing off in this way. It is better to compare colorful apples to colorful apples. After you have examined sets and narrowed down your choice to a manageable three or four, ask the salesperson to change adjustments from Demo to a more reasonable setting.

• **Unrealistic lighting.** Pay attention to the showroom's lighting and sound conditions. Are you trying to judge the quality of flat-screen TVs under a bank of fluorescent lights with a dozen other TVs and stereo systems blaring? Is that the way your living room or bedroom is set up? Some dealers provide good conditions to judge the quality of sets; many big-box and wholesale clubs line up the sets on high shelves and with lighting that is not appropriate for decisionmaking. That's why it might make sense to visit a smaller electronics retailer (if you can find one) and see if they can demonstrate the TVs in a more realistic setting. Then politely tell them the prices you have seen at a big-box store or online and see if they are willing to match or provide some other service such as delivery and setup.

• **Fancy remotes.** There was a time when buyers obsessed over the number of buttons and special features included on the remote control. The fact is that you may rarely use the remote control supplied with the TV if you are controlling a cable or satellite box. Don't get sucked in by lots of buttons.

• **Not enough ports.** See how many inputs the TV has. Most flat-screen TVs receive their signals through HDMI ports in connection to cable or satellite TV boxes. But you may want to also install an internet feed using devices like Google Chromecast or Roku, and these require their own HDMI port. Some flat-screens also have USB ports that you can attach to laptops, tablets, or flash memory sticks as sources of video, photos, or music. The more ports the better, but choose a set with a minimum of two HDMI ports and, if it doesn't blow your budget, a USB port as well.

Researching an HDTV

When you have chosen a flat-screen TV brand or model by visiting a retail store, the next step is to do a bit of research...

• **Find the price for the same model on several websites.** You may find that manufacturers offer slightly different models (or the same model but with a different model number) for sale at big-box or wholesale club stores. You should be able to call the manufacturer or check their website to find an equivalent model.

It's a Super Bowl Time to Buy a TV

A big sale on a big TV can arrive any time of the year, but retailers have in recent years keyed in on a few times of the year for promotion. About 25% of sales occur in the annual lead-up to the NFL Super Bowl in early February. Another 18% buy in and around Black Friday, the unofficial opening of the Christmas sales push that takes place the day after Thanksgiving, with another 7% to 10% buying during Christmas sales.

By the way, some stores have very limited return policies at certain times of the year (for example, in the days leading up to the Super Bowl). Not that you or I would ever do something so crass, but apparently some buyers have bought huge sets for a game or a party and have then returned their purchase.

- **Compare the cost of the TV you found at a retail store to the price online.** Who charges extra for delivery? *And if they do offer delivery, does that include…*
  - Bringing it into your home or apartment?
  - Hauling it upstairs or down?
  - Connecting the set to your cable or satellite box?
  - Hauling away your old set?

If they charge for delivery, add that cost to the TV's price. And don't hesitate to ask a retail store to match a price you find online; they may say yes or they may say no, but there is no harm in asking.

- **What return policy does the online store offer?** Does the retail store promise to take back the TV if you decide it is not to your liking? Is there a restocking or delivery charge from either type of store?

- **How long does the warranty last?** Most modern electronic devices are well made and should last for many years. One way to get a sense of an item's quality is to look at the length of the warranty. In general—not without exception, though—a manufacturer that offers a longer warranty does so because its products tend to hold up well.

And remember the tip from earlier in this book: *Most credit cards will offer an extra year of warranty coverage if you use the card to pay for electronics and other products.* If you have any questions about the extended warranty, call your credit card company and ask. Keep the receipt for the device in the instruction manual, but also remember that a credit card company maintains records of purchases and can back up your claim on its own.

- **Who would perform any necessary service?** Some large retail stores have their own authorized repair departments. Most online stores, including Amazon, will refer you to the manufacturer's repair facilities. Is shipping for repairs free? (And if it is, do you want to ship a 60-inch TV to a repair station?) If repairs are needed, contact the TV manufacturer and obtain information on local repair facilities.

Be Wary of High-Tech Extended Warranties

In general, extended warranties on high-tech items are a bad idea. Here's why: Electronics generally follow a bell curve of reliability, and they usually become obsolete before they fail at the far end of the curve.

About that bell curve...In general, an electronics item that is going to fail before its time will do so very soon after it is first used. (Engineers indelicately refer to this as *infant mortality*.) Whatever you buy should be covered by a warranty for at least the first year, which should cover early failure.

An extended warranty *may* be worthwhile on a few very high-priced and delicate systems, including laptops that will be moved about regularly. These devices are expensive to repair and subject to damage. (Make sure you understand whether the extended warranty covers damage or whether it is limited to parts failure.) You're not going to be able to negotiate the cost of an extended warranty. Do the math yourself.

And once again, remember that most premium credit cards come with an extra year of warranty coverage and some add short-term coverage for damage.

There is no reason to pay $400 to protect a $700 laptop that will be worth $300 in 12 months and $100 after 24 months. As far as I am concerned, most electronics purchases have a two-year life expectancy—the full period covered by the basic warranty plus a credit card's extended coverage. Any use I get beyond two years is electronic gravy.

In the Parlance of Our Times

In this section, I refer to cable television providers, which are the most prevalent source of programming. However, the same details apply to satellite television companies like DirecTV, fiber-optic TV services like Verizon FIOS, and old-school DSL services provided by some telephone companies.

Control Your TV Cable Bill

One of many frustrating elements of dealing with a cable TV company is that you will, in almost every case, be required to subscribe to a package of channels. With all due apology to linksmen and linkswomen, I do not watch and don't want to pay for the Golf Channel. Or, for that matter, to dozens of other channels we find uninteresting, inappropriate, politically offensive, or otherwise unwatchable.

Someday, maybe, cable companies will be forced to unbundle their service so that you can subscribe to channels à la carte. There are various efforts by the US Congress and federal agencies to push cable companies, but change has been slow.

We are nowhere near a full à la carte channel menu, but products like Roku, Google Chrome Stick, Amazon Fire, and other devices that plug into your TV and connect to a suite of channels delivered over the internet are a step in that direction.

Back to cable television providers: The makeup of channel packages is complex and it changes over time. Some channels, including sports and news stations, charge the cable company fees, which are of course passed along to customers. Some other channels pay the cable company to be included, yet somehow customers are still charged for the privilege.

Note, too, that the cable TV provider will often change its offerings and packages. The deal that made sense to you a few years ago may not be the best one for you now. You may be able to save money each month or obtain a better mix of channels. Reconsider your cable TV subscription at least once a year.

Many cable providers allow you to switch among packages from month to month. If you subscribe to a sports channel to watch basketball and with the end of the season you're receiving 24 hours of beach volleyball, look into suspending or canceling your subscription to that one channel until the hoops season begins again.

Another tip that will work in certain circumstances: Don't sign up for two-year deals with your cable company. At or near the end of the year, call customer service and tell them you want to downgrade to the minimum level of service; you might not even have to endure a month of basic TV and slower-than-usual internet before upgrading to a new package at a promotional rate.

If the representative tries to prevent you from doing this, tell him or her you have changed your mind and decided to cancel service completely. In most cases, you will be transferred to the retention department, where people generally have more leeway to negotiate with customers who are ready to cancel. (You don't actually have to cancel if you are given a better deal, or if you decide that there is no better deal to be had.)

Cut the Cord Completely

It is possible, though not yet fully satisfactory, to end your subscription with cable TV and still watch some of your favorite channels.

You have two options: Antenna or internet use.

Use an Antenna

Purchase and install a digital broadcast antenna and pick up signals broadcast in your area. How 1950s! Although relatively few people now receive their local network channels this way, the signals are out there. The change to digital broadcasting that took effect in 2009 was little noticed by most consumers.

Here are the rubs: A digital signal is generally superior to the original analog signal. The signal usually covers an area of about 30 to 70 miles from the broadcast antenna. Some enhanced antennas will pull in signals from 100 miles away.

Basically, if the signal is strong enough to be used it will produce a clear picture; if the signal is too weak, you won't see a picture. Gone are the days of snowy, distorted images. You need to obtain an antenna for your TV—priced between about $25 and $100 and some models can be installed within your house while others have to go up on the roof—and, if you are using a TV manufactured before about 2007, you'll need to purchase an inexpensive digital converter box. Once installed, there are no monthly fees. None.

You can obtain digital TV antennas and converter boxes at electronics stores or from online websites. The converters, priced about $30, are all basically the same. The selection of an antenna depends on how far you live from the broadcaster.

The second problem is that you will only receive broadcast stations. Cable channels like ESPN, C-SPAN, Bravo, and hundreds upon hundreds of others will not be available.

Use the Internet

The other option is to receive your channels over the internet. There are many ways to do this, including packages offered by your cable TV company as well as specialized devices like Google Chromecast, Amazon Fire TV, Roku, and Apple TV.

I use the Amazon Fire device, and find it to be quite satisfactory. It plugs into one of those spare HDMI ports I recommended you look for when you buy a flat-screen TV. You will need a strong WiFi signal in your house, or a coaxial cable from your cable or DSL modem, to connect to any of these internet TV sources. Most Amazon channels are free if you already participate in the Amazon Prime program (which provides free shipping for purchases and other benefits).

Each of these devices brings with it a collection of free channels as well as the ability to subscribe à la carte to certain premium channels like HBO, Cinemax, and STARZ. Amazon, which seems to be gobbling up the world one bite at a time, has branched out into producing its own movie and TV shows and they are included on the Amazon Fire TV device to customers who subscribe to the Amazon Prime service.

A new entrant: internet-based packages from satellite and cable providers. For example, in 2017, AT&T introduced DirecTV Now which delivers many of DirecTV's satellite channels over the internet. And Comcast and several other cable television providers are experimenting with apps that run on streaming devices like Roku to deliver their channels without need for a cable box.

Again, there are two downsides to cutting the cord in this way.

- **You need to obtain a connection to the internet in some form or another.** You could subscribe just to the internet signal offered by your cable TV provider or use a slower DSL signal from other sources. And, of course, cable companies charge a higher rate for internet-only subscribers as opposed to those who bundle the internet along with TV and phone service.

- **The internet TV services do not provide every available channel.** For example, not all the all-news channels are available this way, and there are other gaps, such as certain regional sports channels like NESN in New England. If I can't get the Boston Red Sox from a provider, no deal is going to be made.

Tune In for a Deal on Satellite TV

The other way to get a full selection of TV channels is to install your very own satellite receiver. Service is available nearly everywhere, although some locations may be problematic because of mountains, trees, or tall buildings that stand between your dish and the satellite.

Today there are two major providers of satellite service: DirecTV (which is now owned by AT&T) and Dish Network. Their offerings are similar and include digital video recorders.

The providers of wired cable TV will try to convince you not to buy a satellite service because of potential occasional problems caused by weather conditions. Maybe. But my cable company—the only one we have access to—provides a quality of service I would describe as "fair to good." (Or as the young people might say, "Meh.")

You may find discounts on satellite service from various associations like AAA and AARP, and customers of AT&T and sometimes other telephone and cellphone companies are offered bundles. And both satellite providers seem committed to the same sort of obscure-the-real price advertising strategy, promoting what seems like a very low price but disclosing in the fine print that the second year of a required two-year deal will cost much more. Add the cost of the first year to that of the second and divide by two to calculate the true cost per month.

Here's another big problem: Subscribing to a satellite TV service does not bring you high-speed internet service. You'll need to obtain that from another source, such as (horrors!) from a cable TV provider. Be sure to compare the full cost of satellite plus internet to a cable TV service with internet.

In my rural island location, we can get overpriced cable TV with semi-reliable fast internet or slightly less expensive satellite cable TV and mix-and-match internet service from the phone company or other sources. Neither option is fully satisfactory. I use the cable company for internet and TV, and I'm still paying for hours of golf plus various stations devoted to irrelevant rants and raves. But I would change providers in a heartbeat if I could find one that gave me all I want.

Chat on the Phone

Let me quickly differentiate between a cellphone and a smartphone. A cellphone is a device you can use to make phone calls and receive text messages and perhaps use a few other special apps. A smartphone is essentially a tiny computer in your hand capable of going on to the internet through cellular data or WiFi connection to systems in your home or office. The best of them are amazing in their capabilities. I use a smartphone with a 4.7-inch screen (measured on the diagonal like a TV), a fast processor, expandable memory on a tiny flash memory chip, and a stylus I can use to tap on tiny boxes or to write commands or words that the computer in the phone will recognize.

The two most important decisions are these...

- **Do you want the latest, greatest, and most expensive phone?**
- **Which cellular provider do you want to use?**

Model

Do you want the latest, greatest, and most expensive phone, or would you rather buy or rent a capable (but less flashy device) and upgrade it or replace it once a year or so?

Cellular providers make little or no profit on most of the phones they sell, but they are perfectly happy to let you pay for the phone in monthly installments over 24 months. The idea is to hook customers into paying monthly fees for at least a two-year period without having a formal contract for that length of time.

Another option amounts to a lease or rental program under which you make monthly payments for the phone with the right to return it or upgrade to a newer model after a certain period of time. This sort of program is mostly of value to someone who has the need (or the desire) to change over to the latest and greatest model each time a new one comes out. Be sure you understand the agreement terms if you are offered an upgrade program, and include any extra fees when you assess its value. I use a plan like this for my principal phone, but I have actual need for advanced technologies and other features because I so often travel internationally.

You can also purchase a phone through an online seller or an electronics retailer, sometimes at a discount, and use it with your cellular service. Make sure the phone is fully compatible with the cellular company you will use. Phones you buy from third parties may have different operating system versions. The cellular company will not cover these phones with a warranty. You will have to deal directly with the phone maker in most situations.

You can also purchase a used or factory-refurbished phone. A used phone may work well, but you are bearing the same sort of risk you encounter if you buy a used car. Some used phones are in excellent condition, and some are not. What do you know about the phone's history? Has it ever been dropped or exposed to water? Does it have intermittent electrical faults? Does the seller offer any warranty, and if so, how will it work? Tread carefully here.

Somewhere in the middle are refurbished (sometimes called *recertified*) phones. These may be devices that were returned to a store because the buyer changed his or her mind, or because of a minor fault that was repaired. Or they may be phones that were returned to a cellular provider at the end of a contract or as a trade-in toward a newer model. A refurbished or recertified phone should come with a warranty (usually 90 days, but sometimes a full year) that provides you with the same sort of assurance you would get from a new phone. A refurbished phone is usually somewhere between 50% and 75% off the cost of a new device of the same model. A used phone should be discounted 50% or more.

Cellular Provider

This is a more important decision for many users. Some carriers are a bit less expensive or offer some extra services. Other carriers may have a slightly more expansive area of coverage. In my work, I travel internationally for as many as five or six months of each year. The cellular company that has earned my business for quite some time is one that has a very attractive plan that includes low-cost calls from almost anywhere in the world back to the US and also offers free (slightly slower) data from foreign countries.

Before you agree to a cellular plan, stop and think about how you will use the phone. Do you need a large bucket of data for using the internet? Do you expect to travel internationally?

In general, you get the best deals if you bundle two or more phones in a family plan. In theory, this is supposed to mean family members who live at the same address as the principal account holder. In practice, most cellular companies do not seem to care who the other people on your account are and where they live. (You can also put together a shared business plan, where names and addresses officially do not matter.) Either way, the account holder pays the monthly bill.

Almost all cellular providers now offer so-called "unlimited data" plans, which is generally a good deal for users who surf the internet, check their email, and stream music and video to their phones. Be aware, though, that "unlimited" does not truly mean "unlimited." On most plans like these, when you've used more than a specified amount of data in a particular month, the system slows down the communication rate until the next billing period. So the data is unlimited, I suppose, but the speed—for a small percentage of power users—will eventually be throttled down.

Find out the data limit for an unlimited plan you are considering and see how it fits with your phone use. Although I use my cellphone quite heavily, I have never reached the limiting level, and my cellular provider has actually increased the amount of high-speed "unlimited" data several times in recent years.

Other Considerations

Accoutrements and other extra expenses are worth considering after you make the first two major decisions.

Accessories

Almost every phone user adds a protective case. And then there are accessories like spare chargers and headphones and more. In general, the cellphone provider has the best selection of original manufacturer accessories—and also the highest prices. You will find much better deals by shopping online or at internet cellphone stores. You can also search the electronic aisles of eBay and usually find what you're looking for.

Make sure that any accessory you purchase is specifically for the make and model of phone you have. There is no point in buying a case that does not fit, for example. In addition, go for true protection, not aesthetics, so you can protect your investment. Otterbox (Otterbox.com) is a sturdy brand you can buy for about $30. Incipio (Incipio.com/shop) Reprieve [Sport] boasts good protection for around $20. Prices do vary based on your phone model.

If your phone allows you to change its internal battery, I recommend staying with an original manufacturer's device rather than a third-party manufacturer's battery. It is, in my opinion, simply not worth the risk to put a no-name battery in your phone. It might leak or otherwise damage the phone and your warranty will not cover this.

Escape Clauses

Competition between cellular providers is intense, and it is standard practice for a company to offer to buy you out of your existing contract with another company if you agree to switch to a new contract with them.

Read the terms of the offer very carefully. Be sure you are fully covered for any costs associated with leaving one provider for another. Then study the cost of the new plan you will be entering. There is not much point in switching from one provider to another if you monthly or annual costs will increase, unless the new provider has new services that are of value to you.

And before you make the final decision to switch cellular providers, call your current provider's customer service department and tell them of your plans. They just might magically come up with a way to reduce your costs if you agree to continue being their customer.

Phone Insurance

Cellular providers and retail stores try pretty hard to push you into buying phone insurance (which is often about $10 to $15 per month). In my opinion, this is usually a bad deal.

A new phone usually comes with a 1-year warranty. And if you purchase it using a credit card with an extended warranty plan built in, you have 2 years of coverage. In this case, the monthly fee for phone insurance is redundant.

Your home or renters insurance probably covers your phone for loss or theft. Discuss that with your agent or company to fully understand the level of coverage. And finally, the terms of a phone insurance policy are among the least customer-friendly contracts I know of. Most include a large deductible payment, as well as all sorts of exclusions for problems they will not cover.

If you (or your child or a family member) are the sort who regularly drops phones to the ground or into a swimming pool or otherwise is an accident waiting to happen, consider whether phone insurance might ease the pain.

Don't Forget the Time Difference

How much should you pay for international phone calls? Is free low enough for you?

Several internet phone services offer you the opportunity to place phone calls using cellular data or by WiFi access point. Calls made from cellphone to cellphone have been free for many years; calls made from a cellphone to a traditional wired phone are charged at a few pennies per minute.

These accounts are free to set up. You'll need to deposit a small amount of money to pay for calls to phones, but contacting via computer to the same app account on a computer is free. Be sure to check for any possible changes in the terms of service.

I find Skype (owned by Microsoft) to be the best service for me as a frequent traveler. It can be reached using standard cellphone data connections or over the internet using a WiFi connection. As this book goes to press, Skype-to-Skype calls (when the app is installed on the phone or computer at both ends of the connection) are free, and Skype to landline calls cost just a few pennies per minute from anywhere in the world.

Here are a few of the internet phone services...

- **Oovoo** at Oovoo.com
- **Skype** at Skype.com/en
- **WhatsApp** at WhatsApp.com

Apple iPhone users will find that company's FaceTime preinstalled on their phone.

CHAPTER 17

Buying a Computer and Home Office Equipment

When I first began writing about buying computers, office supplies, and other equipment, I used to distinguish between home and office. Today, that may be a difference without a distinction. Most of us use our computers and other devices to conduct personal business, and many of us bring our work home. Consumers at home can easily shop at stores that cater to businesses, at considerable savings over most other sources of equipment.

Although you can purchase a roll of sticky tape at a supermarket or a package of envelopes at a convenience store, you are all but certain to find better offerings and better prices at big-box stores, office supply specialists, and online. The biggest sellers of office supplies include Amazon and Walmart, as well as warehouse stores like Sam's Club, Costco, and BJ's Wholesale. The two largest US office supply retail stores are Staples and Office Depot.

You can order computers online directly from many manufacturers such as Dell, Lenovo, or Hewlett Packard. You can also see a limited selection of models from the same makers are brick-and-mortar stores like Best Buy or Staples.

Speaking for myself, these days I rarely set foot in an office-supply store. My friendly UPS guy carries the load right to my supply closet door.

In this chapter we explore ways to buy a computer, as well as maintain, protect, and connect it to the internet. I also offer suggestions for outfitting your office. For information about phones, see Chapter 16, which is about home electronics.

- **Get personal with a computer.**
- **Ask questions before buying a personal computer.**
- **Hunt down the best price on computers.**
- **Consider a laptop computer.**
- **Know what to do when your computer won't compute.**
- **Open the door to customer support.**
- **Protect yourself against an unwanted power play.**
- **Post an electronic security guard for your computer.**
- **Don't sit still for a bad chair.**
- **Buy the right desk for your task.**
- **Consider skipping a copier and a scanner.**

Get Personal with a Computer

Personal computers, or PCs, and their smaller siblings the laptop, tablet, and smartphone, are fast and capable, and over the history of computing their capabilities have skyrocketed while their prices have plummeted. The first personal computers cost several thousands of dollars and possessed the computational power of a desktop calculator. Today, you can purchase a tablet computer of almost unimaginable speed and capability for less than $100, or a desktop or laptop computer for about $1,000. And today's models are very reliable.

Whether you are looking at a tablet, a laptop, or a desktop computer, the differences between basic and advanced models is easy to quantify. Understand the difference between memory (which is the working space used by the tablet or computer) and storage (which is where your files, programs, and apps are kept). An advanced computer might have 16GB or 32GB (gigabytes) of memory, and several TB (terabytes) of storage. One terabyte is equal to about 1,024 gigabytes.

In general, more is better, although cost and battery or AC power usage goes up with each step up in memory, storage, or processor speed. Here's a bit of trivia to file away somewhere: the entire contents of the print collection of the US Library of Congress could fit on a 10TB hard drive. My personal machine, which holds my manuscripts, as well as hundreds of thousands of high-resolution digital photos and thousands of music tracks, is all contained in 4TB of storage.

Here's a table that helps you understand the difference between basic and advanced models of computers and tablets.

Element	Details	Basic	Advanced
Processor	Processor speed is expressed in gigahertz (GHz). Generally, the faster the processor, the more it can do per second. But computers also are limited by the internal memory speed, hard disk drive storage, and the physics of moving all that information.	2.8GHz	3.5GHz
Memory	The amount and speed, measured in gigabytes (GB), of random access memory (RAM), which is the internal temporary memory. More memory means demanding programs like games and graphics have plenty of space to operate.	2GB of RAM	8GB, 16GB, or 32GB of RAM
Storage	A byte can represent a letter or character for a document or software. A terabyte (TB) is a trillion bytes. Larger drives mean more space to store photos, music, and documents. Most hard drives spin at 5400 revolutions per minute; faster drives of 7200 rpm allow faster retrieval and storage of data.	1TB	4TB or more

Your Computer History

When personal computers first arrived on the scene in the late 1970s and early 1980s, they were about as complex as the Space Shuttle and priced about the same as a small car when you included disk drives, color graphics, and a monitor. And at the time, there was also a great divide between two types of writers and editors covering personal computers. There were programmers and hardware designers who were trying to write for a non-technical audience, and then there were journalists who were learning to decode things technical for mostly bewildered consumers. I was in that second group.

To use one of those first PCs, you not only had to understand a great deal about the internal configuration and external cables and accessories, but you also had to be willing to take off the covers and plug in chips, expansion cards, and storage drives. But most significantly, the early computers and their accompanying operating system and software had an annoying habit of smoking, choking, and sometimes just plain quitting on you. If you want an example of how things have changed, consider this: If you needed to have service performed on an early model, the most obvious tools on the tool bench were chip-pulling tweezers and a soldering iron.

Apple and Tandy (the parent of Radio Shack) had the first, small triumphs. Then came IBM with its PC in 1981. Within a year there were a dozen or more competitors selling their own version of the PC. Some of them even worked. And so the priority for shoppers then, and through much of the first decade of the PC revolution, was to find a company with good customer service, a good repair shop, and a corporate information technology department at your beck and call.

Element	Details	Basic	Advanced
Expansion options	The number of ports or outlets that allow you to attach external devices, such as hard drives, monitors, and printers. The most common port design today is called USB (universal serial bus). USB ports are available in three types: USB 2.0, the faster USB 3.0, and the developing USB 3.1.		A good desktop computer might have five or six USB ports; a laptop has three or four.

Ask Questions Before Buying a Personal Computer

The very best advice I can give to computer buyers is this: Decide what will be the most important and demanding pieces of software you expect to use, and then buy a computer that is capable of running that software. In other words, choose the hardware that is best for the software, not the other way around.

Products sold by nearly every major computer company are all good quality. The fact is that they may share a great deal of internal parts from the same factories, and the entire desktop, laptop, or tablet may be assembled by a third party. The top manufacturers include Lenovo, Hewlett Packard, Dell, and Apple. The first three are generally intended to work with the Microsoft Windows operating system, while Apple mostly expects users to use its own macOS.

Price is important, of course, but so are where you buy and what manufacturer you choose, as they provide your customer service and warranty.

• **Does the warranty require you to ship a failed computer back to a repair center,** or will the maker send you parts and help you install them (or send a technician to your home or office to fix the system)?

• **Will the manufacturer help with the operating system or software you purchase with the machine if you experience problems?** And for how long after your purchase will they help? (Many computer sellers help with operating system problems for a limited time, and Microsoft will charge a fee or seek an annual contract before offering personal assistance. Luckily, Windows in its most modern version is pretty stable and also includes many tools for troubleshooting and repair.) As this book goes to press, the latest version of Windows is called Windows 10.

• **Does the maker offer an extended service plan for the hardware in its devices, and is the price reasonable?** I ordinarily do not purchase this for desktop machines, but consider it for laptops, especially if it covers damage caused by falls or other accidents.

Most basic warranties cover electronic failure (no spilled coffee or accidental drops) for a year. And remember my advice about using a premium credit card for purchase of many devices of this sort—you'll receive an extra year of warranty coverage for free.

Hunt Down the Best Price on Computers

Now that computers are commodity items, they are almost always on sale or special offer. There are a few exceptions. One is that desktops, laptops, and tablets often go on sale in late summer as students prepare to return to school, and again in the period leading up to the winter holidays. The other exception is that for any computer—desktop, laptop, or tablet—look for special deals any time there is a major introduction of a new operating system or a new technology such as a faster processor, a faster WiFi or Bluetooth wireless system, or fancy new screens. When that new thing is introduced, look for prices on devices one or two steps behind the state-of-the-art. Remember how attractive the machine was yesterday and how enticing the price is today as you buy one step behind the curve. When a new operating system is introduced, machines one step behind usually are capable of being upgraded. Check with the maker for details.

I recommend establishing an account with several of the top online computer sellers, including Dell, Lenovo, Hewlett Packard, and Best Buy. You don't have to immediately buy, but setting up an account often means you will receive special offers.

Be on the lookout, too, for special discounts. Are you a AAA or AARP member? Contact them to find out about discount programs. The same applies to alumni associations. College students (and sometimes their extended families) are able to buy devices at discount. And your employer may offer access to special deals from the computer makers they use in the office.

Check the prices and compare models. Nearly all processors are capable; I concentrate on other things. *Here is how I make decisions...*

• **How much RAM is included?** For modern operating systems and software, 4GB is my recommended minimum and 8GB or more is better.

• **How large is the internal hard drive?** Usually 500MB is okay and 1TB is better. If you are planning on playing back video stored in your machine, a faster rotation speed of 7200 rpm for the drive is better than a slower model of 5400 rpm. Laptops generally have space for only one internal drive. Desktop computers may be able to accommodate two or even three drives. (Laptops and desktops can also work with additional storage on external drives, most of which use USB ports for connection.)

• **For a laptop, how sturdy is it?** If you can examine the device at a store (or look at a friend or coworker's machine), do so. In general, a device with a longer warranty can be expected to last longer because most manufacturers only offer a more generous guarantee if they don't expect to have to honor it.

As a traveler, I depend on my laptop. I need a model with a good keyboard. Although some users look for the smallest, lightest model, I prefer a laptop with a keyboard that I can actually use and a solid construction that stands up to the insults of airport security inspections and makeshift desks on planes, trains, and automobiles. Today, in my opinion, the best laptops are made by Lenovo, followed by Dell and Toshiba.

Consider a Laptop Computer

The idea of replacing a relatively bulky desktop computer and monitor with a compact laptop computer is very appealing. And you can easily take your office or home entertainment system with you on business trips and vacations, or merely from room to room.

Laptops are generally a bit more expensive than their desktop equivalents. And, with the exception of components installed in special compartments (including RAM, batteries, and, in some designs, hard disk drives), you're not meant to open their cases.

Most current laptops feature high-resolution LCD screens, large-capacity hard disk drives, wireless (*WiFi*) capability, as well as Ethernet (wired) internet connections, DVD/CD players for loading programs and playing music and video, stereo speakers, and a video camera for online chats and recording your own videos. They also include USB ports that allow you to attach external devices, such as a printer, additional hard drives, a larger monitor, or your wide-screen television.

There is also a category of super-light laptops that do not include the DVD/CD player and sometimes dispense with the hard disk drive. They instead rely on a wireless WiFi internet connection for program installation and maintenance, and use a form of flash memory to store data. They also include USB ports and Bluetooth wireless communication for certain devices. Be sure you understand the benefits and limits of this sort of device. You are generally trading convenience and perhaps durability for a lighter weight.

Invest in a Computer Printer

Prices for printers, like that for computers, have been spectacular in their decline at the same time as their capabilities and speed have increased. However, printer companies have embraced the same model pioneered by razor makers: Most manufacturers realize they can just about give away the machine and make their money on the ink or toner refills and other parts you will need to buy.

Before you start shopping, think about whether you really need a color printer, which generally is the most expensive to operate. If you only occasionally need color, consider using the services of an office supply store when needed. You can send files over the internet or take them to the store on a flash memory key.

And know this: The least expensive printer is the one with the lowest total cost of use over time, not the lowest initial purchase price. You have to include the cost of consumables in your search.

- **Ink jet printers require cartridges;** most laser printers require new toner cartridges every few reams of paper and replacement drums every few years.
- **Read the specifications to see how many pages you can expect to receive from each cartridge.**
- **Some ink or toner cartridges are considerably more expensive than others.**
- **Consider buying third-party replacement cartridges at lower prices.**

Laser printer toner cartridges are sometimes offered as new or as recycled, refilled products. Most work well. I suggest buying and testing it in your machine before investing in a case of them.

You can refill ink jet cartridges with do-it-yourself kits. In my experience, this is a messy job that is not worth the time, effort, or money. However, you can buy recycled ink jet cartridges that have been refilled at a factory. Again, try a single one before buying many.

And try printing in Draft Mode and in black and white (available in your printer options). You'll use less ink that way.

And did you know that your font choice makes a difference? Large type and boldface use more ink or toner than smaller type and standard fonts. If a font looks heavy and black on the screen, it is certain to require more ink or toner from your printer. Simple fonts like Times New Roman or Century Gothic use much less ink than over-the-top styles like Bodoni Bold or most fonts with the words "black," "bold," or "condensed" in their name.

Know What to Do When Your Computer Won't Compute

One of the worst feelings in our modern world comes when your computer won't start, your printer won't print, or you cannot connect to the internet like usual. All of a sudden, you realize two things: how dependent you have become on these modern contrivances and how utterly clueless you are about how they work and what to do when they won't compute.

Before you do anything else, there are three important steps you can take by yourself…

1. Figure out what has changed since the last time the device worked. Did you install a new piece of hardware or software? Did you vacuum your den or office, and might you have dislodged cables or the power cord? Is the power on?

2. Read the manual. And if the machine and software are working on some level, look for onscreen messages. They just might include advice on fixing the problem or help you explain it to customer service.

3. Check the WiFi router, the cable or other modem, or the internet service itself. Call your internet service provider for assistance. If you can't get online, you should be able to find the phone number on your bill. One of the first things you'll likely be asked to do is unplug the modem, wait a few seconds, and plug back in the modem for internet access; sometimes this sort of device becomes confused and needs to clear its memory with a reset. Internet service providers can also send signals to reset or reconfigure the modem at your end of the cable or wire.

Open the Door to Customer Support

If you're lucky, the device is still under warranty…and the manufacturer actually offers customer service to its customers. That's not a given, but most of the major makers are reasonably good. (You read the warranty information before you bought the computer or printer, right? Even better, you called customer service before you made the purchase. If they won't treat you right when you have a question *before* you buy something, you can't expect them to take care of you *after* they have your money.)

Make the call and be prepared to jump through all sorts of electronic hoops before you speak with a human. Stand your ground, and when you finally do get to speak to customer support, insist on all of the rights in the warranty you have. In a good situation, the manufacturer will walk you through some diagnostic tests or changes to settings. If it is determined that a piece of hardware has failed, some warranties require you to bring or ship the computer to a repair facility; other warranties promise on-site service. Still other companies will send a replacement part and help you make the repair yourself.

In a bad situation, seek assistance from the credit card company you used to make the purchase. Remember them? The one that offers an extra year of warranty coverage, and also in many instances will stand behind its customers when a seller does not fulfill the terms of sale?

Here are some savvy ways to obtain worthwhile support for computer problems…

- **Help diagnose the problem.** If the problem is intermittent, keep a pad by the keyboard and make notes anytime it recurs. Record details on error messages and program behavior. What were you asking the program to do when it misbehaved? What had you done before in the same session? Were there any other pieces of software open or running when the problem occurred?

- **Be prepared to discuss recent system changes.** A good technical-support specialist will focus in on this question right away. What have you done to the computer—new hardware, new software, new settings to programs or the operating system—since the last time it worked.

• **Master the phone system.** Make notes when you use an automated technical-support system. If it requires you to push a complicated combination of buttons to navigate from the opening greeting to the waiting line for a real human being, write down the sequence. The next time you call in, you can push 1-4-1-#-8-3 (or whatever the secret electronic pathway) and save a few moments of wait.

• **Take down names and numbers.** Ask the name of the person who is helping you and ask if there is a way to get back to them directly for follow-up calls. Ask also if there is a case number assigned to your call. Your goal is to avoid having to start at square one with each call you make.

• **Make them take down your contact info, too.** It's valuable to give your name and phone number to the technician in case you get cut off.

• **Take notes.** Keep your own notes on system changes based on suggestions that the technician makes. He or she may say, "Try changing this setting to Auto," and if that doesn't work, move on to something else. You may want to reset your system to its previous state unless you're looking forward to making a bad situation a whole lot worse.

• **Go up the ladder.** If you don't have confidence in the background or ability of the person who is supposed to help you, gently ask if there is someone else at the company who can help. If that doesn't work, ask a bit more firmly for a supervisor. If you're still at a dead end, or if the technician doesn't move you up the line, it's time to raise your sights. Ask to speak with a higher level of support.

• **Make it clear that you are ready to start a social media campaign.** Tell them you're ready to post on Facebook, Twitter, and anything else you can think of. If you purchased an item from Amazon or Best Buy, tell them you will post a bad rating of the device and the company on that website. This actually is something that matters a great deal to some companies, and may result in better service. And you'll feel better yourself.

Protect Yourself Against an Unwanted Power Play

Think of a surge suppressor as a fuel filter for your computer and other expensive electronic devices. It's also very inexpensive insurance against a not-uncommon threat.

We tend to take for granted the electrical power coming from wall outlets in our homes and offices. But in fact, in many localities the voltage regularly rises and falls within a range of 10 to 20 volts due to loads and atmospheric conditions. Nearly every modern computer and electronic device can adjust for power fluctuations within that range. But what happens if lightning strikes a power line, or a transformer in the distribution system fails? In that situation, a momentary power spike or surge of several hundred or several thousand volts can move down the line and into anything plugged into a house or office current. The device does not even have to be turned on, by the way.

I used to live in a rural area of upstate New York, where all the power and telephone lines were mounted on poles. One August afternoon we sat in the relative safety of the rec room watching a violent thunderstorm roll through the valley. Suddenly there was a flash of light a few hundred feet away and an almost immediate clap of thunder and, strangely, a strangled chirp from the telephone. Something drew me to my office in the den, and there I encountered a chilling sight: the blown-apart pieces of my computer modem and a cloud of brown smoke. The electrical spike had traveled down the phone line and into the house, meeting and destroying an unprotected modem and continuing from there into my computer.

I used the first dollars from the insurance settlement to purchase a surge protector that also protects incoming telephone lines.

Buy a Surge Protector

Don't buy this sort of equipment secondhand. You never know what it's been through. Here's how to buy a surge protector:

- **Don't scrimp to save a few dollars.** Look for a solid device with adequate specifications. You might also look for a protector that has a guarantee or insurance policy that promises to pay for losses if the suppressor doesn't protect your equipment properly (though, like insurance payouts, you might have to fight hard to see that money). Expect to spend between $20 (avoid these) and $80. Belkin is one company with a range of solid products, including the Belkin PivotPlug.
- **Be ready for it to die.** They all do, even without a power surge in their lifetimes. Some have a small light that indicates it's time to replace your surge protector, and some stop relaying power when they don't protect from surges. Others just stop working.
- **Prepare to replace or reset post-surge.** If you bought the cheapest one available, you will have to replace it after it sustains a surge; devices that are one step up in terms of quality have a replaceable fuse. The most sophisticated suppressors have resettable circuit breakers.
- **Match the suppressor's amperage capacity to the devices you plug into it.** Don't overload a suppressor or the circuit into which it is plugged. (Laser printers, copiers, refrigerators, and air conditioners or heaters are the biggest power draws in most homes and offices; in most cases they should be plugged into separate circuits.)

Make Sure Your Power Is Uninterrupted

Surge protectors will not prevent you from losing data in your computer's memory if your PC is shut down because of overvoltage or undervoltage. If you are concerned about losing your business plan, the Great American Novel, or other data, consider buying an uninterruptible power supply (UPS), which is an electronic switching device coupled with a large rechargeable battery. A UPS kicks in if power fails or drops below an acceptable level in a brownout.

Buy a UPS with enough power to allow an orderly system shutdown. Basic systems are not intended to allow you to operate your system for an extended period of time. The UPS should have enough power to keep the computer and the monitor running. The Power Saving Back-UPS Pro 1000 (Blinc.Media/2gj1Bmt; yes, that is its real name) by APC gets good reviews, but it doesn't come cheap at around $180. It too has resettable circuit breakers. Advanced models come with software that you can configure to automatically save the contents of any open software to the hard disk and then conduct an orderly system shutdown. Like surge protectors, this is equipment you should buy brand new—even if it hurts your wallet.

Post an Electronic Security Guard for Your Computer

Sadly, some of the best technical minds around the world devote their energies to finding ways to use computers to cause trouble. They have created electronic snippets of code we now call *viruses* that can attach themselves to other pieces of software and travel from over the internet and in emails and install themselves in your computer.

The early forms of viruses were a mere nuisance. Today, most are attempts to outright steal your data, money, or identity. One version installs itself on computers and blocks access to your data until you agree to pay a fee, usually to an overseas location. Not without reason, this is called *ransomware*. If you run into a situation like that, contact your internet service provider or the maker of the antivirus software you have on your machine (or one you should be running) and seek their help in prying the code off your machine.

There are other creeps lurking on the wires who are hoping to steal your login name and password for your banking, credit card, and shopping accounts. You should, of course, regularly check your online statements and email for reports of unauthorized purchases or banking activity; as long as you notify merchants or banks quickly, you should not be liable for fraudulent activity.

Here are some ways to protect yourself against high-tech breaking and entering on your personal computer system...

- **Create complex passwords and change them regularly.** The best procedure is to not write down your passwords (or at the least to not write them down in a location anywhere near your computer). Some users maintain a log of passwords they keep in a locked safe. Don't store them in a file in the computer. If the PC is stolen, so will be your secrets.

- **Consider using a password vault.** It's a special piece of software that stores all of your logins and passwords and can automatically fill them in on websites when needed or be used as a list you can consult. The trick here is that the vault is protected by a single, complex password that you use for nothing else; you can then use nonsensical and difficult passwords for websites (like 6SJ7gH9js02Ju_%) without having to remember them.

TIP

The Password: Swordfish

Always assume that a criminal is capable of guessing the most obvious passwords, and also assume that some of your personal information may be out there on the internet: your middle name, your significant other's name, your cat or dog's name, and your phone number.

When you choose a password, try to use a combination of a few things that are not found elsewhere. Do you have a favorite year that is not your birth year or the year you were married? Who is your favorite author, and can you quickly name one of his or her less-well-known titles? Do you know the phone number of a distant relative (or a former employer or a restaurant)? In this instance, I could say—just as an example, mind you—that a good password might be 1956, Mark Twain, The New Pilgrim's Progress, and 555-1207. *So my password could be*: 56Twain_Pilgrim1207. And in six months, I would change it.

- **Choose your passwords carefully.** Don't be so obvious as to use your name, nickname, telephone number, or other words that a clever thief or saboteur could guess. On my system, I use a word and number combination that means nothing to anyone but me, and I change it every few months. *Example*: the name of an old friend and the middle two digits of your social security number. These are both easy to remember, but unlikely to be guessed.
- **Assign a password to your computer, laptop, tablet, or smartphone.** If someone steals your device and it is properly protected, they are not likely to be able to get to your data within. (They may be able to delete the contents or reformat the drive or flash memory, but your personal information will not be available.)
- **Install a strong virus-protection package.** Keep it updated with new virus descriptions, which are usually available daily or weekly, or sometimes suddenly if a new outbreak appears on the internet. McAfee and Symantec Norton are reliable and cost about $50 for one computer (less for a license for multiple devices). You may also find that your internet service provider offers a free or discounted subscription to an antivirus product.

Don't Sit Still for a Bad Chair

We all know what we want in a chair: a comfortable place to sit and work and that does not cause or aggravate our sore backs, necks, elbows, and tired eyes. Unfortunately, for many of us, that's easier to describe than find.

The basic advice is this: Don't scrimp on quality. An uncomfortable chair will cost you in productivity and number of hours at work, and could even result in health problems.

Here is some advice from the experts on choosing a work chair…

- **Make sure you can adjust the chair so that your feet rest firmly against the ground while your thighs are level on the seat.** The chair should easily adjust in height to accommodate different users.
- **There should be a firm support in the lumbar area in the small of your back.** An adjustable lumbar support is an even better feature.
- **The seat cushion should be rounded at the front to reduce pressure on your knees and hips.** Even better? An adjustment that allows you to set the cushion angle. For most people, the best cushion position is a slight downward slope so that your hips are elevated above your knees.
- **Armrests, if the chair has them, should be padded and should angle forward just a bit.** They should be adjustable so that you can put your arms—at a right angle to the desk—just above the computer keyboard. The armrests should not force you to sit farther back from the desk than is comfortable.
- **Select the casters on the bottom with the floor surface in mind.** Soft rubber casters work better and do less damage on wooden and other hard floors, while hard casters are appropriate for carpeted surfaces. A chair mat protects your floor and costs less than $50 or so. Just make sure to get the right kind; you'll probably need something different for carpet versus hardwood or other

hard flooring because a chair mat made for carpet has nubs that dig in. You can buy them at big-box stores, office-supply stores, or even used office-furniture stores.

- **Make sure the chair has a good warranty of several years.**
- **Give it a spin.** You should not make your decision solely on the basis of a picture on a website or specifications in a brochure.

Visit an office supply store with a wide range of chairs and spend however much time you need sitting down in a few candidates. Adjust each chair so it is comfortable for you, and roll to a nearby desk, and see how each works for typing on a keyboard or writing in a journal or playing computer solitaire.

Once you have made a decision, do one of the following things: Arrange to have the chair delivered to your home or office, or go online and order the same chair.

The chair I am sitting in as I write these words was bought like this: I tried it out in a big-box office supply store. Once I decided on it, I pulled out my smartphone, went to the website for the same store, and ordered and had it shipped. And wouldn't you know it? When I went to the website, I was offered a $20 coupon—which I happily accepted.

You can expect to spend at least $100 on a decent office chair, but make sure you sit in it before you buy it.

Buy the Right Desk for Your Task

The next step in outfitting your office suite is to choose an appropriate working surface and short-term storage module, also known as a desk. Standing desks are becoming more popular; sitting desks that you can convert to standing exist as well; and there's even such a thing as a walking desk, which is basically a treadmill-and-desk combination. None of these options are inexpensive, but back problems might make a standing desk worth it. If you can't afford a true standing desk, try a product that "converts" your desk to one that allows you to stand—more expensive than a stack of phone books, but less stable.

Whatever desk you decide to buy, keep these pointers in mind…

- **Choose the proper height for the task.** A desk that is used for formal purposes and for handwritten work is usually set with a top surface 29 to 30 inches above the floor. (If you're shorter or taller than average, consider getting a chair with pneumatic adjustments so you can fit yourself to your desk.) A drawing table is sometimes a few inches higher, with an adjustable tilt. A desk meant to be used with a computer is usually a few inches lower, or comes with an extendable keyboard drawer that sits a few inches below the desktop. You can also purchase and install a keyboard drawer that slides out from beneath the desk.
- **Make certain that any keyboard drawer is wide and deep enough to accommodate the sort of keyboard you use.** Measure the keyboard and add enough extra space to allow for future enhancements. Pay attention, too, to a comfortable position for the computer mouse. The keyboard shelf should either be wide enough to allow it to sit alongside the keyboard, or there should be an extension tray for the mouse. The worst setup is one that places the mouse above and be-

Far-Flung Faxes

There was a time—probably at a peak in the 1970s and 1980s—when the fax machine was an essential in every office. It was the way to send orders, lists, and sales material. It cost a few hundred dollars. The rolls of paper for the device cost $10 or so each, and you generally needed a dedicated telephone line for it.

Today, fax machines are almost gone. (I could give you a great price on mine, along with a box of fax paper.) They have been mostly replaced by email and cloud storage systems and the occasional overnight mail envelope. Today, among the only institutions still using fax machines are some government agencies, law firms, and health-care companies that feel they need a physical piece of paper to satisfy some law or regulation. Even that small number is declining, as software like Adobe Acrobat allow users to append an electronic "signature" to a document.

If you find you still need to use a fax system to send or receive occasional documents, hold off before buying a machine and a phone line and consider one of several online services that offer to handle both ends of the process in a virtual fashion. You can subscribe on a one-time or monthly basis to some services. Some are even free, supported by an ad that is placed on the front page of transmitted faxes. I have used FaxZero, a free service. Find that company and others on the internet by searching for free fax or fax service.

hind the keyboard on the desk surface. That is a prescription for arm, neck, and shoulder pain.

- **A well-designed computer desk includes provisions for routing the half dozen or so wires that go to and from the computer.** Some desks have holes in the top and back sides for the wires, while others include channels to hold cables.
- **Consider the desk's quality of construction.** Better-quality furniture uses hardwood and is assembled with interlocking wooden surfaces; cheaper furniture uses plywood or particle board and is held together with staples. If it has drawers, check the quality of the sliders and the hardware and see if they move in and out smoothly; if they are balky or misaligned with nothing in them, they will become only worse when they are full.
- **The quality of steel desks is usually related to the thickness, or gauge, of steel used.** Look for solid joints and roper alignments of sides and drawers.
- **Check the warranty.** Desks usually last a long time, which means manufacturers can afford to stand behind them (metaphorically, that is). A very short warranty may be a tipoff of shoddy construction.

Don't overlook used furniture dealers, either; many businesses lease equipment, and some good bargains are available in buying furniture turned back at the end of a lease.

Consider Skipping a Copier and Scanner

The so-called paperless revolution has bypassed most of the business world, and the photocopier has become an essential part of all offices. It is also increasingly used in home offices.

Copiers are mechanical devices, among the more complex machines in most offices. They are prone to jams, wear and tear, and breakdowns caused by the heat they generate as part of the copying process. When I first set up my office, one of the more expensive pieces of equipment was a copying machine. Today, I don't even bother. I can make copies by using a scanner and then printing the image. If you purchase an all-in-one printer it comes with scanner, printer, and fax functions; most have a button you can press that engages the scanner and then sends the electronic image to the printer. On the relatively rare times I need to make a large number of copies, it is easy to send an electronic file to an office supply store and use their expensive, high-quality machines at a price of a few pennies per sheet.

You can purchase a decent desktop scanner for less than $100. Canon and Epson are good brands. You connect them to your computer or laptop using a USB cable, and you can scan photos or text that you can store on the computer, send to a printer, or attach to an email. Higher-priced scanners are capable of scanning entire stacks of papers automatically.

You also can download a scanning app to your smartphone and use it to send documents. Evernote Scannable (Evernote.com/products/scannable) for Apple smartphones and CamScanner (CamScanner.com) for Android smartphones are both reliable options.

Finally, ask yourself if this copy is really necessary. I suggest keeping electronic images of most receipts, contracts, and other important documents. They can occupy a few thousand bytes of space on a hard drive (and on a second and third backup unit somewhere else) instead of space in a file cabinet.

CHAPTER 18

Purchasing Appliances

In most houses the largest energy expenses come from heating, water heaters, and cooling systems. In second place are appliances—electric clothes dryers, refrigerators, clothes washers, dishwashers, ovens, and microwaves.

How do you get the most out of your money? One way is to use any given rebates. How do you get the most from your appliances? Your goal should be Olympian: quicker, faster, cleaner, less expensive.

In this chapter, we'll explore how to use energy ratings for savvy shopping as well as how to get the most out of the devices already in place in our homes.

- **Distinguish EnergyGuide from Energy Star.**
- **Keep your refrigerator cool or consider retiring it.**
- **Get hot tips for oven efficiency.**
- **Fit in with a dishwasher.**
- **Cook up a deal on a microwave oven.**
- **Clean up your washing machine's act.**
- **Pick a clothes dryer.**
- **Guard against vampires.**
- **Fire up a deal on a barbecue grill.**
- **Try do-it-yourself appliance repair.**
- **Get cool news about water heaters.**
- **Get the dirt on vacuum cleaners.**

Distinguish EnergyGuide from Energy Star

If they were to put me in charge of the federal government, I think I would do more than a few things a bit differently. Somewhere on my long list would be dealing with the justifiable confusion between the otherwise valuable EnergyGuide and Energy Star programs. What we have here are two similar programs with guidelines drawn up by three different government agencies, one of them voluntary and the other compulsory with much in common as well as some glaring gaps.

I will place myself at the front of the line for any effort to reduce energy consumption for reasons of both environmental protection and political stability. And, of course, I am dedicated to getting the best price on everything I buy. But the EnergyGuide and Energy Star ratings are just part of the puzzle. I'll explain how to analyze them and decide whether a more expensive model will pay for itself after a few years of use, or conversely, whether a "cheap" model may actually end up costing you more money over its lifetime.

Start with the EnergyGuide Ratings

EnergyGuide is the yellow tag you'll find on many appliances that lists an estimated yearly energy cost and an energy efficiency ratio (EER) for each device. It is run by the US Department of Energy as part of its assignment to help reduce energy consumption or prevent waste established in 1979. Think of them as the home equivalent of the mile-per-gallon ratings posted on new cars.

The EnergyGuide ratings, administered by the Federal Trade Commission, are based on standardized tests to measure efforts by manufacturers to improve insulation, motors, compressors, pumps, and computer controllers. You'll find the tag on refrigerators, freezers, dishwashers, washing machines, window and portable air conditioners, plus a few other devices. You won't find them on clothes dryers or microwave and gas or electric ovens and some other devices because at the time the regulations were drawn up, there was not considered to be much difference in energy use among those devices.

The two numbers on the Energy Guide give you different kinds of *comparative* information; don't think of them as absolutes.

The estimated yearly energy cost may or may not be close to your actual experience because of differences in electricity rates and the manner in which you use the device. But you can look at one air conditioner that reports a $62 estimated cost and another of the same cooling capacity (BTU) that reports an $82 estimated cost and do the math: Over five years, the second unit might cost you about $100 more to operate. Now, I realize that energy costs vary in different parts of the country, but the basic principle applies: if one device is rated as using 25% more power than another, that portion of your electrical bill will rise about that percentage.

Look at the small print at the bottom of the tag to see what cost of electricity was used to calculate the yearly energy cost. It does not matter at all if the stated rate is different from what you pay; it is, though, important that you compare devices calculated against the same electricity rates. If you are comparing a brand new model against a closeout of an older model, check to see if the electricity rates are the same. If not, pull out your calculator (there's one on your smartphone) and adjust the numbers.

Similarly, the EER is a mathematical calculation of how efficient is the conversion of electricity into heat, cold, or clean dishes. There are different EERs for various devices. For example, the EER for an air conditioner divides the stated BTUs by the wattage required to achieve that amount of cooling. The higher the EER, the more efficient the device and the less expensive it is to operate. (In theory, the tests are conducted in a properly sized room with adequate shielding from external sources of heat.)

Now Consider Energy Star Ratings

The other appliance rating program is called Energy Star, and it was created in 1992 by the US Environmental Protection Agency and the Department of Energy. (Why not the FTC? Why make things that simple?) This voluntary program now involves hundreds of companies and tens of thousands of manufacturers, with tie-ins to utility companies. The program's purpose is to award bright blue stars to those appliances that are champions in their category and to encourage consumers to buy the most energy-efficient models. The same criteria have been adopted in the European Union as well as Australia, Canada, Japan, and other countries.

The Energy Star agreement calculates the average energy use of various types of devices and then sets goals for manufacturers that are below those levels. *Here are some of the criteria as they existed in 2017…*

- **Electric dryers.** These devices were added to the Energy Star classifications in 2014 after manufacturers found ways to improve a relatively simple device that consists of a rotating drum and a source of heat. To earn an Energy Star, dryers must use at least 20% less energy than average *without* sacrificing performance. Among advanced features applied here are moisture sensors that detect when clothes are dry and automatically shut off the dryer.

- **Clothes washers.** Energy Star–certified devices use at least 25% less electricity and 40% less water than standard devices. Using less water adds to the savings here. Less water has to be drawn, heated, and disposed of through your sewer system if you have one. Technologies involved here include the use of high-pressure sprays instead of repeated soaking and designs that move clothing around within less water in either front-load or top-load washers.

- **Dishwashers.** Designs that use less water, work with cold water or less hot water, and employ other smart technologies receive high marks here. Energy Star dishwashers generally use about 12% less power and 30% less water.

- **Freezers.** Energy Star devices are at least 10% more efficient than standard models. Advances here include better cooling systems and increased insulation.

The rewards that come from buying and using an Energy Star appliance are good enough on their own: a decrease in your power bill; a reduction in greenhouse gases associated with the generation of electrical power by coal, gas, and oil; and advanced features that should make you whistle while you work. They are a tad more expensive to buy, but you can visit EnergyStar.gov for the best deals. For example, you can go online to Blinc.Media/2vxCIGu and figure out how much you eventually save by replacing an old refrigerator.

But wait, there may be more: Many utilities and governmental agencies have programs that are intended to promote the use of the Energy Star devices. As you prepare to go shopping, check with appliance dealers and your utility company to see if they are offering rebates or other special programs. In recent years I have seen rebates of $50 to $150 for the purchase of Energy Star household appliances, and also programs that included hauling away your old device as part of the deal.

Keep Your Refrigerator Cool or Consider Retiring It

Does your ice cream look like soup, your lettuce like ice cubes, and the floor beneath your refrigerator like a slimy swamp? *Here are some tips to bring a still-functioning refrigerator back to life...*

- **Read the instruction manual—the one you stuck in a drawer five years ago without a glance.** Make sure all the settings are correct for your type of use and environment. If you cannot locate the manual, go onto the internet and search for it on the manufacturer's website. If you cannot find it there, you will find various websites that scan and post manuals of all sorts. Most make their money by posting advertising on the page.
- **Check that air vents inside the refrigerator and freezer sections are not blocked by large items** and not obstructed by chunks of ice.
- **Vacuum the condenser coils at the back or bottom of most units, and do so every six months or so.** It removes dust that interferes with the machine's ability to get rid of heat. Do the job more often if you have pets or live in a particularly dusty area. (Some newer models do not have exterior coils.)
- **If the refrigerator is near a heating vent or a radiator, see if you can turn off or redirect those heat sources without making the room uncomfortable.** Similarly, be sure to use exhaust fans over ovens to take heat out of the kitchen.
- **Remove frost more than a quarter-inch thick in the freezer.**
- **Check the door gaskets for air leaks and make repairs or replacements if necessary.**
- **Call the manufacturer's consumer telephone line and ask for more suggestions.** Make a note of your machine's model and serial number and ask if there have been any product recalls or repair programs.

If you are convinced that your trusty old cold box can no longer be trusted, go ahead and treat yourself to a new refrigerator. The fact is that a good new refrigerator can save $50 to $100 per year in electricity over a typical 10-year-old model of the same size. In other words, it can come close to paying for itself over the course of its average 10- to 12-year life.

Appliance Brands

There are, at the same time, many more brands of appliances than ever before and fewer actual manufacturers.

Whirlpool claims the mantle as the world's largest home appliance maker, and its brands today include Amana, Hotpoint (in Europe), Jenn-Air, KitchenAid, Maytag, Whirlpool, and others.

GE Appliances is no longer part of the General Electric Company, but instead is owned by the Chinese manufacturer Haier with manufacturing in the US and China. Its brands include GE, Hotpoint (in the US), Profile, and others.

Kenmore, a well-known Sears (and Kmart) brand, does not make its own devices. Instead, Kenmore appliances are built by manufacturers such as Bosch, Electrolux, GE, LG, Mabe Mexico, Panasonic, Sanyo, and Whirlpool.

Korean manufacturers Samsung and LG are increasing their presence in the US, with generally well-regarded devices.

Which is the best? Each manufacturer has a range of products that run from budget to luxury, and no one company can fairly be described as the only one to consider.I recommend subscribing to *Consumer Reports* online or in magazine form and relying on their ratings. Look for each manufacturer's overall reliability ratings, and *Consumer Reports'* advice on which bells and whistles are worthwhile and which to avoid.

Ditch the Door

In many states and municipalities, you are required to fully remove the door to any refrigerator or freezer that is taken out of your home for disposal. The intent is to prevent the occasional tragedy of a child trapped in an airless box. Even if there is no law where you live, do the right thing—or insist the trucker hauling away your old device do it for you.

And as with many other major appliances, check with your local utility company and with appliance dealers to see if there are any special rebates or other programs meant to encourage the switch from an old device to an Energy Star model.

Here are some tips on purchasing a new refrigerator…

- **Top-mounted freezer designs are less expensive,** more energy efficient than French doors or bottom freezers, better able to handle large items, have more overall usable space, and are more common.

- **Despite all of their disadvantages,** which include sometimes less efficient use of space and higher energy consumption, side-by-side models have some appeal in very tight kitchens where their narrow doors require less clearance.

- **Bottom-mounted freezers have all the advantages of top-mounted models,** may be even more energy efficient (cold air sinks to the bottom), and place refrigerated food at eye level. You'll have to stoop for ice cream, though.

- **Increasingly popular are French door units,** which have a set of side-by-side doors up top and a pullout freezer at the bottom. These doors tend to have alerts that sound when you fail to close the doors.

- **Measure the available space**—width, depth, and height—for a refrigerator before you go shopping. Pay attention to any nearby furniture that might interfere with the swing of a wide door; check for floor air vents to avoid landing on top of those. This is especially a problem with an L-shaped kitchen where a counter or other appliance may be kitty-corner to the refrigerator. Most top- or bottom-freezer units require about 28 to 30 inches of clearance for their doors; most side-by-side units require less.

  Consider bringing a diagram, with scaled measurements, to the appliance dealer. Your goal is to avoid having to ask the delivery guys to carry your huge new refrigerator back down the stairs and into the truck because it won't fit.

- **Most refrigerator doors can be reversed to open from the right if that is necessary in your kitchen.** I'd recommend having the appliance dealer do the job for you. A slight misalignment in the door can warp the hardware and create air leaks.

- **Choose a refrigerator of the proper capacity.** Buying too large a box will waste electricity.

• **An ice or chilled-water dispenser that you can access from the outside of the refrigerator** is a convenience and can save a small amount of energy because the freezer door may not have to be opened as often. The ice-making equipment will take up a portion of the freezer unit, though.

• **Pay attention to the shelving arrangement.** The unit should be adaptable to your lifestyle, not the other way around.

Get Hot Tips for Oven Efficiency

An oven and a range, especially an electric unit, can be one of the most energy-intensive units in your home. *There are some things you can do to lessen the load on your power bill…*

• **Don't preheat an oven unless the recipe has flour or eggs (per Epicurious).** Otherwise, you're fine to start the oven and stick in your dish.

• **Turn off the oven five or 10 minutes before a recipe is due to be done**—but keep the door closed. The heat in the oven will finish the cooking.

• **Match the diameter of your pot to the size of the stove burner to avoid wasting power.** Pots that are warped or otherwise misshapen on their bottoms will not heat evenly or efficiently on an electric range.

• **If your recipe allows, use a lid on the pot to use less energy and allow cooking at lower temperatures.**

Fit in with a Dishwasher

Looking for an excuse to buy a dishwasher? A modern machine uses considerably less hot water—perhaps six to eight gallons—than does handwashing. Given enough dishes and enough time, a dishwasher can pay for itself. (A lot of dishes, and a lot of time, but you were looking for an excuse to buy a new dishwasher, right?)

To maximize those savings, consider water consumption and energy-saving settings on machines as part of your purchase decision. A dishwasher's life expectancy is perhaps 10 years. If you have an antique model, it almost certainly uses more water than a new machine, and so a new model may actually come close to paying for itself across its lifetime.

Tests by consumer groups show that nearly every dishwasher does a decent job at cleaning basic messes. Heavy-duty messes benefit from extra washing cycles and extra washing wands and sprayers.

• **Examine the loading basket, bearing in mind the type of dishes and pots you expect to use with the machine.** Some features make loading certain items easier, and some are more suited to your particular kitchen than others. If the dishes you use are unusual (larger than normal, say), you may want to take at least two plates with you when shopping for a dishwasher to check their fit.

Before You Run the Dishwasher

If your dishwasher has a pre-rinse or rinse/hold cycle, there's no need to pre-rinse your dishes by hand in the sink. Instead, merely scrape food off dishes directly into a trash can. Avoid putting large pieces of food or a lot of grease and oil down your plumbing system.

Use energy-saving settings on dishwashers to reduce water and heating energy. Turn off your dishwasher's electric (or heated) drying function. Instead, get in the habit of opening the door of the dishwasher when it has finished cleaning. The dishes will dry all by themselves in a few hours.

• **How much are you willing to pay for the sound of silence?** Machines that boast of quietness use extra insulation in their cabinets and may use specially designed mechanical parts. Near silence comes at a price.

• **In a relatively rare example of standardization, almost all dishwashers intended for built-in installation have the same dimensions.** They are intended to fit beneath a 36-inch tall kitchen counter within a space that is 24 inches wide. If you have an unusual kitchen design, including workspaces designed for people in wheelchairs, you'll need to special order units of different dimensions.

My daughter and her husband own an old home with a rather small kitchen; their dishwasher is an 18-inch model available from specialty dealers including outfitters for mobile homes. One other option is a portable dishwasher, which is a unit within a cabinet with casters. It connects to the kitchen sink with an external hose and plugs into a standard electric outlet. Built-in units save space and are often quieter and less expensive to operate than portable machines. However, portable units may be a good idea for renters who can take the dishwasher with them when they move. And it is possible, in some cases, to convert a portable unit to a built-in unit, although the labor involved might argue instead for buying a new unit.

Be sure to read the dishwasher manual and follow its advice about the type of detergent to use. Most modern units work better with liquid dishwasher detergent, but some are designed for old-style powder. The detergent type is more important than any particular brand.

Cook Up a Deal on a Microwave Oven

Microwave ovens, once a novelty, are now an essential in most kitchens. As with most consumer appliances, the trick to buying a microwave oven is to buy one that is the proper size and wattage and comes with the best warranty provisions.

If, like most microwave owners, you will be using the oven mostly to reheat frozen food and for cooking simple prepared dishes, don't pay extra for doodads you won't use. These may include temperature probes and multifunction control panels intended for complex recipes.

Also, think about the largest plate or dish you expect to put into the oven. You might want to bring it with you to the store to try it out. On models with a revolving turntable (a good feature to help ensure even heating), make certain the large dish can turn completely.

The larger the oven, the more watts it should draw for cooking. Even in smaller units, increased wattage will speed cooking. Manufacturers use a six-ounce cup of water as a standard for cooking. A 600-watt oven should take about two minutes and twenty seconds to bring the water to boil, while a 1,000-watt oven will require a full minute less.

Most microwave ovens receiving good marks from organizations like Consumers Union (publisher of *Consumer Reports*) draw 1,000 to 1,200 watts, which usually start at $100. You can find small and very inexpensive countertop units that draw 600 or 700 watts, priced as little as $50 to $100. These units may be adequate for reheating individual plates of food or a cup of soup. In my experience they have a lifetime of a few years and may make sense for some buyers.

Never operate a microwave oven that has any sort of break in its glass or seals around the door. Such flaws should be apparent to your eye. And shut off and then disconnect any oven that is giving off sparks or smoke. If the source of the problem isn't obvious (like a piece of silverware or aluminum foil on a dish, contact the manufacturer and talk about a repair under warranty or at your own expense. Obviously, there is no point in spending $200 to repair a microwave that you could replace for $100.

Clean Up Your Washing Machine's Act

If your present washer is more than 10 years old, you can probably do a lot better. New models use much less heated water and also remove more water before clothing heads to the dryer. By some estimates, an Energy Star washer could save you $180 per year based on average energy prices and usage. That will pay for a new washer pretty quickly. You'll have to decide if you want to get flashy and pay extra for colors (red!) and digital control panels (which are more likely to have glitches than regular old dials).

Make the most of your modern washing machine by using the bells and whistles. Spend the time learning the controls and refresh your memory by reading the instruction manual from time to time.

- **Match water-level settings to the size of the load in the tub.** Unnecessarily high water levels waste the energy needed to heat it and require more power for the washer to work.
- **Follow the manufacturer's recommendations on temperature settings to most efficiently clean your clothes.**
- **When recommended by the maker, be sure to use high-efficiency detergent.** Standard cleaning products may gunk up the interior and cannot be depended upon to produce the level of cleaning you expect.

Front loaders, a new concept for many users, have actually been around for many years. They've been used in laundromats, which should tell you more than enough about their relative durability compared with more conventional top loaders. Most European washers have used the design for some time.

Front loaders dispense with the noisy and sometimes troublesome agitator mechanism, instead tumbling the clothes through recirculating water. They are quieter, use less water (reducing water and heating bills), and are gentler on fabrics. The faster spin removes more of the water from clothing, too, reducing the time they need to spend in the dryer, which is expensive to run.

The advantages of the front loader come at a higher cost because of the heavy-duty suspension and motor systems employed. However, most users will find that over the long run, front loaders are less expensive to use, paying for themselves with reduced energy and repair costs. The first generation of front loaders were notorious for developing mold colonies on rubber gaskets at the door and elsewhere. Newer versions have improved designs that help eliminate the problem; keeping the door ajar between washes and running the occasional hot-water load can help avoid that.

Pick a Clothes Dryer

Gas dryers cost a bit more than electric dryers to purchase and install, but if you've already got gas service in your home, a gas dryer will quickly make up the difference in operating costs over a typical life of 10 to 15 years. Gas dryers require natural gas or propane, plus a source of 110-volt current to operate the motor within. Gas units require a vent for exhaust fumes as well as a way to remove lint, moisture, and heat. Be sure to employ a licensed plumber to install gas lines and exhaust vents.

Electric dryers are easier to install. You'll need a source of 240-volt current, which is a relatively simple project for an electrician. The devices need a vent to remove lint, moisture, and heat.

Consider paying extra for a moisture sensor, which turns off the dryer when the clothes are dry. This saves energy and is gentler on fabrics. To get the most from such a device, try to dry loads of similar fabrics together.

The harder your dryer has to work, the more it's going to cost you in energy dollars and time.

- **Make sure your clothes washer has fully spun out excess water from items before you place them in the dryer.** Even after then, shake clothes to remove a bit more water; don't just dump them from washer to dryer. This prevents some wrinkles and helps them dry a bit faster.

- **Follow the manufacturer's recommendations for temperature and time settings.** Over-drying not only builds up static electricity, but it wears out your clothes faster and costs more.

- **Clean lint filters regularly to maintain the most efficient airflow and help prevent fire hazards at the dryer or in the heat exhaust pipe.**

- **Try dryer balls.** Some are synthetic and some are wool, and may save you a bit of money on dryer sheets and fabric softener if you use those. (The wool and alpaca type also help you avoid using fossil fuels, which are used to make the synthetic type, but all types go without the dryer sheet chemicals that irritate skin and lungs.)

Guard Against Vampires

No, I don't think you have much to fear from Dracula. But techies have repurposed the term *vampire* to refer to many electrical devices in your home or office that draw a little—or a lot—of power even when they are not in use. By some estimates, a well-equipped home may be losing as much as $100 or more per year to devices that are plugged in and not in use.

Tour your home and look for those little power transformers that are used for cellphone battery chargers, wireless telephones, and other devices. Remember, too, that many of your larger devices like televisions and some computers boast of "instant on" features, which means that they are powered on at a low level even when they are off, if you can follow that contradictory description.

You can unplug many of these devices when you are not using them, or add a power strip with a switch that can be used to completely remove electrical power except when needed.

One other device that is usually constantly sipping from your electrical system is a set-top cable TV or DVR box. A few cable companies have begun offering systems that go to sleep after a period of quiet, although even then there is a small amount of power being drawn. You can unplug or use a power strip with a switch to turn off the cable box. If you do, it may take as long as a few hours to reload some of the channel listings and other features. Consult with your cable provider for advice.

Fire Up a Deal on a Barbecue Grill

To own one is to love one—at least until you begin getting tired of cleaning and winterizing it. *Here are a few important savvy tips…*

- **Check with your local fire department about local ordinances.** In some towns you need a permit. I've never heard about a barbecue grill police force, but consider this: If you have a fire that is blamed on your grill, your insurance company could deny payment if you haven't followed all local laws.

- **Some gas grills include outboard warmers and burners,** which may be useful for serious outdoor chefs, but are a pointless expense for most others. To be honest, I never use the external burner on my unit. And pay attention to the specifications for total cooking area for the grill to see if the outboard areas are included in the total. The more important information is the size of the main cooking surface. A basic unit for burgers and steaks can be 300 to 400 square inches. To cook for a large crowd, or for large cuts of meat and whole turkeys, look for a surface of 600 to 800 square inches.

- **Look for a brand name grill backed by a reputable company.** Most outdoor grills will outlast their one- to three-year warranties, which is a good thing. You'll want to be able to replace burners and other parts, so be sure you'll have a source for parts.

- **Clean the grill often.** Depending upon where you live and your lifestyle, consider winterizing the unit with a tight-fitting cover. We used to cook fish, chicken, and even turkey (fabulous and quick on a grill) all year-round, sometimes trudging out through the snow. And then there was the year we didn't use the grill in the winter and spring, and when I opened the cover I was greeted by a mother and half a dozen field mice camped within. One of us shrieked like a child and ran away. The others departed for the fields.

Try Do-It-Yourself Appliance Repair

Note to lawyers of all stripe: The following is intended only for people who are handy with tools, adventurous, and willing to attempt do-it-yourself repairs on certain types of appliances and who also understand that there are some jobs that amateurs should never attempt.

You can perform many simple repair jobs by yourself. For example, replacing an electric dryer's heating coil, an electric oven's bake or broil element, or an electric range's plug-in burner are easy work. Start by disconnecting the device from its source of electricity, please. You can also replace many dishwasher parts, including the heating element, the washing arms, and basket parts. Stay away from the plumbing and controller parts that are hidden underneath or behind the tub.

There are many online sources for parts for most major brands. Some of the companies will even provide a little—or a lot—of advice about how to make most repairs. *Here are a few...*

Appliance Parts Pros	AppliancePartsPros.com
Repair Clinic	RepairClinic.com
Sears Parts Direct (Sears sells its own brand, Kenmore, as well as many other major brands. Sears is today a subsidiary of Kmart)	SearsPartsDirect.com

You can find copious instructions online for replacing a gasket (the seal) on a clothes washer; just search for *replace washing machine gasket*. Beyond that, I do not recommend trying serious repairs on gas appliances of any sort—dryers, ovens, and ranges. Leave that to a licensed plumber or professional technician. Similarly, I do not recommend taking apart your washing machine. They are not all that complex, but they are large and bulky and hard to handle. A small misstep in balancing or aligning a washing machine tub could prove disastrous. Think of a several hundred-pound machine waltzing its way across your laundry room, spraying water in every direction.

Also out of my reasonable recommendations: Repairing high-voltage or specialized devices including microwave ovens, flat-screen TVs, and air conditioners.

In Chapter 17, when I talked about personal computers, I discuss certain parts that you can easily replace on those devices.

Get Cool News about Water Heaters

Many thermostats for hot water heaters are delivered from the factory with a setting of 140 degrees, which is warmer than necessary for most households. Reducing the setting to 120 degrees will reduce energy consumption by about 15% and may also reduce the chances of an accidental scalding. Ask your installer to check the thermostat setting. Also consult the instruction manual or call the manufacturer if you have questions later on.

Consult your water heater manufacturer or your plumber to see if its particular design is appropriate for extra insulation. It's a kind of jacket that wraps around the tank to help keep heated water warm for a bit longer, and foam wrappers that form a buffer around the incoming cold water pipe (to keep it from getting so cold that it makes the heater work harder) and around the exiting hot water pipe to help hold on to heat as it exits the tank.

When your water heater is about 10 or 11 years old, start researching your replacement options. They usually last 12 or so years. Tankless water heaters can help reduce costs, and Energy Star ratings help reduce them even further. You'll probably have to upgrade your natural gas line and venting (which varies based on your existing line and venting setup) but the overall cost savings will earn back that investment.

Get the Dirt on Vacuum Cleaners

You can buy a vacuum cleaner for $50, and you can buy their cousins for more than $1,200. The Miele Dynamic U1 AutoEco upright vacuum ought to make your beds and take the dog for a walk for that price, but alas, its maker merely promises to clean your floors and upholstery.

Buying models a step or two up from the bottom rung usually works well, with the expectation that you will have to replace the vacuum every four or five years. In our home, with mostly hardwood floors, we have switched over to an industrial shop vac for heavy cleaning. These devices are nearly indestructible, although they lack rotating brushes for carpeting.

At heart, they are all the same: A motor spins a fan that pushes air away from the machine, creating a vacuum on the other side of the fan that picks up dirt. Some use a bag to hold the gatherings while bagless models are just that. *Here are some things to look for…*

- **Most vacuum cleaners use an upright design, which is generally more effective with thick or plush carpeting than a canister.** Uprights usually have a rotating agitator brush that helps lift dirt from carpeting, and they are usually easier to move around the room because of their wheeled design.

- **Canisters are well suited for hardwood or other uncarpeted floors** and work well with accessory tools for cleaning furniture, upholstery, draperies, and stairs.

- **Consider the vacuum's weight and construction.** A sturdy one that uses metal may be too heavy to carry up stairs or even from room to room. On the other hand, a very lightweight unit may make too many compromises on component quality.

- **One measure of a vacuum cleaner's power is the number of amps of electrical current it draws.** All things being equal, a twelve-amp motor is more powerful than a five-amp motor. However, some machines are better than others at applying that power-to-vacuum force.

- **You may want to choose a model that is quieter than others with similar power.** There is usually a small premium for this feature.

- **Some buyers will want to look for a vacuum cleaner that includes multilevel filtering of the airstream to remove dust and allergens from the exhaust.**
- **Vacuums with bags are, in some ways, easier when it comes to removing the collected dirt.** And the bag serves as an additional filter against spreading dust and pollen as you clean. But replacing bags on some vacuum cleaners can be difficult, and the bags themselves cost a few dollars apiece.
- **Bagless vacuums let you dump their contents into a trash bin or garbage bag.** If you do not handle them properly, they can make a mess...which you would have to vacuum. And though a bagless vacuum lacks a bag, it adds a filter that you must regularly clean.

CHAPTER 19

Houses: Buying, Selling, and Moving

Buying and selling a house is an example of a task that is simple at its heart, but in practice is often maddeningly complex.

Here's an example: You've put your old house up for sale and have begun shopping for a new and better place to live.

- **What if you sell your old house before you find a new one to move to?**
- **What if you find the house of your dreams before you sell the one that will enable you to pay for it?**
- **What if you can't get someone to offer a fair price for your old home or accept a reasonable offer for a new one?**

There is, alas, no simple answer to any of these knotty problems. There is, however, one piece of savvy advice for all homebuyers or sellers: Don't become emotionally involved in the purchase or sale. What does that mean? Set a reasonable price that will result in a reasonably quick sale, and accept the fact that sometimes local real estate values go down instead of up. Also, carefully consider home renovations based on how much you're likely to get back on your investment.

On the buying side of the equation, guard against falling in love with just one house. You could end up paying too much for it or put yourself in a situation where the loss of a potential deal becomes what seems a catastrophe instead of merely a minor detour in the road toward a real-estate closing.

The process of buying and selling a house involves so many different calculations and steps that it could fill an entire book. (I know, because I've written one.) Here are some basic but savvy tips for selling and buying a home, and moving your stuff once you know your new address.

- **Get a return on home improvements.**
- **Market your home with style.**
- **Negotiate the fee with your broker.**
- **Buy a house at the right time.**
- **Simplify the process with a preapproved mortgage.**
- **Confirm who the agent works for.**
- **Buy or sell on the internet.**

- **Research the neighborhood.**
- **Hire your own home inspector.**
- **Take a timeout on timeshares.**
- **Go smart when you hire a mover.**

Get a Return on Home Improvements

Are you choosing a major home improvement in hopes of recovering the cost when you sell your home? Be cautious. Sellers rarely receive the full amount they spent as part of the sales price. Some home improvements may help attract buyers even if you don't get back the full amount you paid. If you need a repair on the heating, cooling, plumbing, or electrical system or a structural problem, it may be valuable—or required by law—to have the work done before you sell your house.

The value of home improvements varies from place to place, but here are some rough estimates of the return on investment you may receive…

- **Basic kitchen remodel** (new floor, new refrigerator): 75% of cost
- **Major kitchen remodel** (new floor, all new appliances, new cabinets): 60% or less of cost
- **Basic bathroom remodel** (new floor, new toilet): 40% of cost
- **Major bathroom remodel** (new floor, new tub, sink, and toilet): 40% or less of cost
- **Roof replacement:** 65% of cost
- **Windows upgrade:** 75% of cost
- **Siding replacement:** 75% of cost
- **Garage door replacement**: 92% of cost
- **Attic insulation update:** 125% of cost or more

Simpler, less-expensive changes may help make your home more marketable (Bottomlineinc.com/life/home-improvements/wow-this-is-my-house-simple-renovations-that-can-transform-any-home). On the other hand, some renovations don't provide much in return. Save lots of money by not bothering to do them at all. Avoid such renovations by visiting Bottomlineinc.com/life/home-improvements/11-home-renovations-arent-worth-money to read more.

Market Your Home with Style

Yes, your home is lovely. And you are selling it for a fair price. But it is not likely to be the only one of its kind on the market right now. Do your best to make your house stand out from the half-dozen others the real estate agent shows prospective buyers on a single day's visit.

Even if your realtor prepares one, use a computer-based design program to make a one-page brochure about the house, with a floor plan and a description of some of the benefits that come with it. You can insert a photo or two in the brochure, too. Print it out on a high-quality paper. (If you don't have a good printer, prepare the brochure and then send or bring the file to an office supply or printing store like Home Depot or FedEx to have them printed. Each brochure might cost less than 15 cents in color and less in black and white.) Your realtor may or may not create such a brochure to your satisfaction. In any case, he or she will likely use the same program and layout for all of the agency's brochures. Make yours stand out.

When you host an open house or a single prospective buyer, plan on this tried-and-true home seller secret: Fill the house with the smell of baking bread. The scent seems to advertise family values. Even easier? Place a small drop of vanilla extract on a cold lightbulb and then turn on the lamp. As the bulb heats, it will fill the area with another pleasant, homey odor.

A good real estate agent will surely have other suggestions like these...

- **Don't leave it empty.** It is difficult to sell an empty house. You can rent or borrow some spectacular furniture to fill out the common areas of the house. Real estate agents call this *staging* a house.
- **Declutter and depersonalize.** Get rid of anything you don't absolutely need and don't intend to use at your new dwelling, including your favorite knick-knacks. Also, make sure you store or change the part of your house that makes it *your* home. Pack away family photos and religious items. Paint that orange accent wall a safe shade of tan. Think, "hotel décor." Chapter 13 offers tips about hiring painters.
- **Upgrade the things a buyer will touch.** Bright, good-quality doorknobs and hardware are a good place to start.
- **Keep landscaping in top shape.** Increase your curb appeal by keeping the lawn mown and plants tended. However, don't go overboard and pay for a major landscaping remake without careful consideration and advice from your agent. Potential buyers may not like your changes, and it is not at all certain that $5,000 spent on landscaping will add $5,000 or more to the selling price. Instead, if your lawn and garden need sprucing up, consider offering a $5,000 rebate paid to the buyer at closing for that purpose, if your agent agrees.

Negotiate the Fee with Your Broker

Nearly every part of a real-estate transaction is open to negotiation. There is no reason you shouldn't try to get the real-estate agent selling your house to accept a fee below the standard 5% or 6%. (The seller pays the fee out of the proceeds received. It is usually split evenly between the seller's and buyer's agencies. The individual brokers receive a portion of the commission based on their agreement with their employer.)

Here are four situations where you can move the power to your side of the table...

- **If the real-estate market is booming.** Selling your house will be relatively easy and prices are good. The agent is likely to have to spend less time and money. That, in addition to what may be a higher selling price, makes your argument for a reduced commission stronger. (In your contract, you can include a sliding scale for commission that pays more for a quicker sale.)
- **If many real estate agents are competing for your business.** You can tell one or two you will accept the best offer from *them*. Will they reduce the commission or promise special efforts, such as advertising your home as a featured offering?

• **If you're selling your home to trade up to another in the same area.** Tell the agent you will employ him or her as your agent when you buy a new house. This adds back 3% or so to the agent's take on the two deals. The realtor may be willing to reduce the commission on the sale. An agency may respond to you that reducing the commission will make it less likely that a buyer's agent will want to show your current house. (Do you need any more convincing of how the buyer's agent does not always have the best interests of their client?) You can turn around and ask for a split commission (say, 2% to the selling agency and 3% to the buyer's agent).

Buy a House at the Right Time

The best time to buy a home (or a condo or an apartment) is when it makes sense in your personal situation of marriage, cohabitation, or singlehood, and when you can afford the price and handle the entanglements that home ownership brings. If all those difficult stars are aligned, then here's the simple answer to the question.

In general, prices tend to soften a bit in the last three months of the year, after schools have started and the holidays begin in earnest. It's a time of the year when people have other things on their minds and fewer are house hunting. It's also when some sellers begin to straighten out their financial situation before the beginning of the next year.

In a typical year, the market begins to pick up with the start of the new year, with spikes upward in summer approaching the start of the next school year in September. There are other situations in specific places, of course. If you are seeking a vacation home or property in a place where others come to vacation, prices tend to decline after the end of the vacation season and then pick up three to four months before the next high season. For example, summer homes in most places are at peak prices from about April until June or July and drop after Labor Day. Houses in ski country, by contrast, might be relatively less expensive after the lifts stop running in May and pick up again in early fall.

Simplify the Process with a Preapproved Mortgage

One great way to ease the strain of house hunting is to get prequalified—or even better, preapproved—for a mortgage loan. If you do that, you'll know exactly how much money you can borrow and be able to pounce quickly when you find the home of your dreams. The fact that your mortgage is ready to go will make your offer much more attractive to the seller. Some buyers will accept a lower offer from a preapproved buyer rather than from a buyer who has to ask for time to be approved without the certainty that a bank will say yes. Contact a lender to get prequalified or preapproved.

• **Prequalification from a bank or mortgage broker is an indication that a borrower meets the criteria for a loan.** The lender still has to appraise the house you want to buy and agree that your offer is a reasonable one, and you may be subject to interest rate changes between the time you apply and when you lock in the loan. (Interest rates could go down in that time, but they're as likely to go up.) Finally, the bank will want to know that your financial situation has not significantly changed between the time you applied and the closing day.

• **Preapproval is one step closer to a mortgage.** It is a written commitment from a lender to enter into a mortgage agreement with a borrower, providing you have no significant changes in financial status and the home is appraised for a price at or close to the total of the down payment and the amount the lender will provide.

Confirm Who the Agent Works For

Remember this at all times when shopping for a house with the assistance of a traditional real-estate agent: When push comes to shove, a realtor's loyalty lies with the seller, not with the buyer. That's right. Even though you have approached a real-estate agent to help you find the house of your dreams at a price you can afford, in most locales his or her legal responsibility and self-interest lies in helping the seller get as much money from you as possible. For that reason, you should never tell a real-estate agent anything you don't want the seller to know. If you want to offer $600,000 for a house but secretly are willing to go as high as $650,000, keep that second number to yourself. Tell the agent only what you want him or her to present to the seller.

You can listen to the advice your agent may offer, but remember two things in this example…

• **If the agent knows you are willing to go $50,000 higher than your offer,** he may directly or indirectly communicate that information to the seller or the seller's agent.

• **If the deal goes through for $650,000 instead of $600,000, the realtor's commission will be based on a figure $50,000 higher.** That means more commission for the realtor.

There is, however, a developing class of brokers who are more on your side. The word exclusive in the description is supposed to indicate that the agency does not have any homes it is offering on behalf of sellers. *Exclusive buyer brokers* or agents are supposed to be working just for you, although most still

Agent Versus Broker

A real estate agent isn't the same thing as a realtor, and a realtor isn't the same thing as a broker. Why would anything about home buying be simple? An agent has passed a state's minimum requirements to buy and sell homes on a person's behalf. A realtor abides by National Association of Realtors rules and ethics in his or her business. In the next-highest hierarchical rung of real estate titles, a broker has had continuing education and can work independently to buy and sell homes, or work with a larger company (such as Century 21). An agent must work under a broker.

Your commission is negotiable with any of these sellers. A broker working for him- or herself may make more money annually, but that's because the broker isn't splitting the commission with a hiring broker. It isn't because they earn more commission per customer.

receive their income from a commission on the selling price. In theory, they are less likely to work against your interests in a negotiation. However, they still receive more commission from a bigger sale than from a lower one.

> **Going for Brokerage**
>
> You will probably be required to sign an agreement with a real estate broker (or his employing agency) that prohibits you from trying to go around them to buy a home they have shown you. In other words, if a broker shows you a home, you have to buy through that broker—or his or her agency—and cannot make an offer on your own. On one occasion, my wife and I found ourselves quite dissatisfied with the agent who was taking us around town in search of a home. She kept taking us to see homes that did not meet our needs and, not to put too fine a point on it, we simply did not like working with her.
>
> Our agreement with the broker committed us to working with this particular agent for three months. After those months, we went to the broker, asked him to assign us to a different agent, and we quickly found the home we wanted.
>
> Most agreements with agents allow you to opt out of the arrangement for various reasons. If you're not under an agreement with a particular time commitment, you can simply fire the agent. You cannot, though, go back and make an offer at a house you were shown by the first agent without directing a portion of the commission to the original agency.
>
> Ever since our unpleasant experience with the broker I mentioned earlier, I have kept a very short leash on agents. If we don't like the service we are receiving right from the start, we take our business elsewhere.

Buy or Sell on the Internet

The ever-expanding reach of the internet allows you to shop online for a house (or a condo or an apartment), seeing a great deal of information about properties—often more detail than real estate agents used to offer. As an owner, these same sites let you get an estimate of the possible selling price of your home and track the history of homes nearby.

You don't need to have an agreement with a real estate agent to browse these sites. In some cases, you may be able to deal directly with a seller. (At least one of the sites allows owners to post a flag that essentially says, "I'm not planning to move right now, but if you make me an offer I can't refuse, I just might accept it.") Should you use one of these sites? They represent a great opportunity to find your home's estimated sale value and to learn about homes in a place you might consider. Beyond that, you have to decide whether it makes sense to deal directly with a seller or buyer, or use an agent.

Though reports show that it has a limited number of listings, and it doesn't currently have the National Association of Realtors' seal of approval (which Realtor.com does), Zillow (Zillow.com) is a popular site for online house hunters.

Though reports show that it has fewer listings and fewer unique (new) users (as well as lacking the approval of the National Association of Realtors, which Realtor.com does have), Zillow is a popular online site. The information comes from state and local real estate databases, local tax agencies and registries of deeds, and other sources. A house does not need to be listed for sale to be included on the site. A home's verified owners can add or correct details about their property, and set a Make Me Move price for homes not on the market (like I described earlier).

PropertyShark	Concentrates on New York City and surrounding areas, with a great deal of information about specific properties. Basic information is available to everyone. You must register for a free account to delve deeper.	PropertyShark.com
Trulia	Now owned by Zillow, it includes some of the same information as well as listings posted by real estate agencies.	Trulia.com
Redfin	A residential real estate website with information as well as links to real estate companies. Homes listed by sellers and using the site as an agent can save money on the sales fee. Redfin is not available everywhere. Check the site for its list of regions.	Redfin.com

Research the Neighborhood

Before you make an offer on a house, explore the local area. How far is it to the supermarket, and will you be happy shopping there? If you make regular trips to the post office, make a test run there. If your children will be walking to school, park your car and try the route with them.

Investigate the school and school system your child might attend. Visit websites of area schools as well as the state department of education, read online newspaper stories, and ask real estate agents where they send their kids to school. If you dig, you may be able to find a school's records for statewide tests to compare them with the state average and learn about any positive or negative attributes of the school or the neighborhood.

Go back after dark. Is the street properly lit? Are there loud parties on every corner? Does the next-door neighbor have a high-wattage floodlight that shines into the bedroom where you would sleep?

What can you find out about the neighborhood's future, especially one that is being developed or undergoing other changes? If one of the appeals of the area is the undeveloped land all around, don't rely on the broker's or developer's statements about the future of the area. Are there plans for a factory or a Walmart or a prison? Is the local grocery chain closing? Is a plan for dozens of cookie-cutter subdivision homes on the books? Can you gain access to an online website dedicated to the neighborhood? Social media like Facebook hosts private groups that you can request the moderator give you access to. You'll see what kinds of issues pop up in neighbors' discussions and what their concerns are (such as flooding on certain streets or break-ins).

Visit the town or city offices and ask the planning or zoning department about permitted uses.

Visit www3.epa.gov/enviro/myenviro and enter your street address to learn about the neighborhood's (and surrounding areas') environment status, including water and air qualities.

My Story: Bought Four, Sold Five

Over the years, my wife and I have bought four homes and sold five (including two where we assisted family members). Each of the transactions presented a different set of circumstances. *Here are a few details from some of them...*

The first home we purchased was with an agent's assistance. We ended up buying not from an individual but from a bank that had taken ownership of a home on behalf of a corporation that had relocated one of its employees from the region. Although it was not a foreclosure, both the corporation and the bank had a strong incentive to get the property off their books. With that knowledge, we were able to buy the home for below its market value. (The bad news? Mortgage interest rates in the spring of 1981 were about 16% when we signed the deal. They peaked at about 18% in the fall of that year.)

When we sold that first house a few years later, interest rates had declined by four or five points, which allowed us to make a nice profit. We hired a real estate agent and left all the details to her. Because I had been recruited by a large corporation, my new employer offered an interest-free bridge loan. It allowed us to purchase a new place to live while we waited for the sale of our previous home. In certain circumstances, you can obtain a short-term bridge loan on your own from a lender, but remember that you are still on the hook for your former home until it sells. (And although having a bridge loan is an advantage, most lenders want to know all of the details because it still represents debt until your former home is sold.)

The next house we purchased was a nearly completed new home. An agent showed it to us. We were able to negotiate some minor construction changes directly with the builder. When the time came to sell that house, we were going to move a few hundred miles east to a Boston suburb. One evening, we invited a local real estate agent over to make her pitch for us to hire her. *She seemed capable, but she made a huge mistake*: She parked her car, adorned with the name of her agency, in front of our house. Shortly after she left—and before we had signed the agency contract she had left with us—we received a phone call from a neighbor who had spotted the agent's car outside. She asked, "Are you putting your house up for sale?" We told her we were about to do that, and she told us a family member wanted to move near them.

Within a day, we had a private sales agreement at our asking price, which represented a substantial profit over the purchase price. We saved the 6% we would have paid the real estate agent, and invested only a few hundred dollars to hire an attorney to handle the sale details and protect our interests. For the house near Boston, we hired an agent who was willing to put in a fair amount of research ahead of our arrival so that finding a home there took place relatively quickly.

Skipping ahead, we had purchased a beautiful piece of land and later built a summer home on an island off the coast of New England. After a few years, I was ready to strike out on my own as an author. We moved to our summer home and put our house near Boston on the market. *This time we made a mistake*: On the advice of our seller's agent, we priced that house at the top of the market at a time when homes were selling slowly. It took a full year and several large price reductions before we finally unloaded that house. (And we had to make all 12 monthly mortgage payments.)

In later years, we helped relatives dispose of their homes. In one situation, we were approached by a neighbor who wanted to buy the house for his children. It was a great situation, because the house we were selling had some problems with its roof and needed other repairs. The buyer was willing to buy the house as is and pay our asking price. We hired an attorney to handle the details and saved the real estate agency commission. We put the money into a trust to pay our relative's living expenses.

One last story: Another family member needed to sell a home in Florida at a time when the real estate market was in serious decline. The first agent priced the house at top dollar and it sat there like a concrete garden gnome. After four months—the term of the agreement—I thanked the agent for his services and hired a new representative and told her: "Find the bottom of the market, the price at which houses like this are actually selling. And then price this house $5,000 below that point." The house sold almost immediately for the asking price, which in this case was the right price.

Should you hire an agent when you want to buy or sell a home? Yes. No. It depends.

Hire Your Own Home Inspector

Hiring a qualified engineer or inspector to check a house you are proposing to buy is an excellent idea. I wouldn't buy a previously owned home without doing this. For a new home being completed by a contractor, you should have various warranties in the sales contract, but it still wouldn't hurt to have a professional check over the quality of construction, electrical, plumbing, and heating and cooling systems.

Make sure the inspector works for you—not for the seller or the real-estate agent. Although you hope that the house you want to buy is perfect in every way, you do want the unvarnished truth about any problems or shortcomings in construction, maintenance, and mechanical systems. If you go out and find an inspector, there should be no question about where loyalty lies. If you allow the real estate agent to set up the inspection, you are setting up a conflict of interest. The agent wants you to buy the house, and the engineer wants to keep the agent happy and receive future jobs.

Take a Timeout on Timeshares

Few areas of real estate and vacationing garner such black-or-white responses as timesharing. People tend to think it is either the greatest innovation in vacations since the luggage tag or the most egregious rip-off since, well, the luggage tag.

Here's a typical pitch made by timeshare salespeople…

You go on a vacation every year, and you love [fill in the name of the location]. Here's your chance to own your very own vacation home, at a price about the same as renting a luxury hotel room. And that's at today's prices. Hotel rates are always going up, but your timeshare will stay the same. And because you own your timeshare, you can always sell it. And between you and me, there's a price increase coming along in a few weeks that is sure to make timeshares even more valuable in the future.

Here are just a few reasons I don't like this pitch…

- **A timeshare doesn't mean you own a piece of property.** Instead, you own a right to use a portion of a property for a specific part of the year. In some plans, you won't even have rights to a particular suite or room at the resort.
- **You might grow tired of the same vacation place.** What if you change jobs or for some other reason can't take a vacation during your designated week? The timeshare sales staff will likely tell you about vacation clubs that allow you to swap your share. What if there isn't space available when you want to go? And couldn't you just book your own vacation in the location of your choice?

What about prices? Don't accept someone else's estimation of room rates. You know full well how much you are paying for a hotel room, and if you regularly visit an area, you know how much or how little hotel rates have changed over the years. (At the most popular of tourist destinations, including Florida and Las Vegas, room rates have remained stable over the years because of the tremendous level of competition for visitors.)

And then there are little things such as maintenance and repairs. Timeshare owners must contribute to the upkeep of their own units or, if you don't own a specific unit, to the upkeep of the overall structure itself. This can mean ordinary upkeep—painting the walls and shampooing the rugs when the place is newer—to more significant and expensive repairs when the place gets older. What if the heating or air-conditioning system fails? What if the elevator in a high-rise fails? The older the building, the more likely high-maintenance costs will be passed along to time-share holders and by that time the original management company—the one that made all sorts of promises to buyers—is likely to be gone. In its place—a company that makes its profit from maintenance and management fees.

The salesperson's claim that you can always sell your share includes a couple of massive assumptions: first, that there will be a market for your share, and second, that prices will go up. In fact, the history of many timeshares in this country is just the opposite. Resales are difficult and typically involve a significant drop in value.

Check area newspapers, online sites, and real-estate agents to see if there are any resales offered by current owners. Are they offering to sell their unit for below the price you are being offered? That's a bad sign—and contrary to what the salesperson is telling you. If you are still determined to buy a timeshare and find lower prices in the secondary market, why not do so? You can ask the salesperson to beat the price you find from current owners.

Put me down firmly in the camp of the deeply skeptical here.

Go Smart When You Hire a Mover

About one in six Americans will move this year. The vast majority will relocate within the same county. About one in 25 will move to a different state. According to the American Moving & Storage Association, the average bill for a professional state-to-state move is nearly $6,000.

Moving companies take most of the heavy lifting and hassle out of relocating your stuff from one place to another. The bad news is that for many of us, a mover's bill is one of those inscrutable transactions (like auto repair and medical diagnosis). We have to accept more on faith than we want to.

Your bill from most moving companies is based on four major elements—time, weight, distance, and supplies. Usually, the weight charge is the most problematic. Do you really know how much the contents of your house weigh? There is room for misunderstanding, errors, and even fraud in the entire element.

Interstate moves (from one state to another) are generally regulated by both federal and state agencies. Intrastate moves (within a state) generally fall under state laws and agencies.

Here are some ways to keep the costs down and protect your property…

• **Research moving companies.** A brand-name moving company's advertising campaign and reputation are interesting, but the fact is that most movers are local companies who have a franchise or contractual agreement with a national company. Ask for recommendations from neighbors or check with your employer if he or she is paying some or all of the bill. If you're moving to another state, check the Department of Transportation database at www.FMCSA.dot.gov/protect-your-move. Interstate movers have to register with the department and the site reveals their safety ratings and complaints filed.

• **Throw away things not worthy of moving.** That old moth-eaten sofa, your lifetime collection of telephone books, and those unopened boxes of stuff in the basement from your last move should be introduced to the landfill. Get rid of as much as possible *before* you invite the moving company representative to give you an estimate.

- **Put the job out to bid.** Obtain estimates from several companies. Don't be afraid to tell them you are seeking prices from other movers. Be sure to compare apples to apples. Include the same services in all the estimates: packing, unpacking, and extra insurance, for example.

- **Look carefully at the prices quoted for packing and materials.** Put a value on your time for the same job. Get a price for boxes, tape, and packing material you can buy on your own. (The U-Haul rental system and many major office-supply stores sell packing materials. You may also be able to obtain free boxes from supermarkets and liquor stores useable for many items.) If the mover does the packing, go through your possessions beforehand and throw away anything you don't want moved. It's the packer's job to go through the place like a locust, putting everything in a box (including garbage if you leave it on a table or in a drawer.) One advantage of using a professional packer is the stronger position you're in if you have to file a claim for broken items.

- **Understand the nature of the quote.** Most movers will quote either a binding price or a nonbinding estimate. A *binding price* is a firm figure, while a *nonbinding estimate* is a ballpark figure that isn't final until the truck is weighed. Some moving companies guarantee that the nonbinding estimate will not go up more than a certain amount—usually 10% of the estimate. Moving-company estimators are pretty good at their job. The very best option, if it's offered, is this: Commit to a binding price and then when the actual move occurs, have the load weighed. If the shipment works out to be lighter than the binding amount, you'll pay the lower price.If the shipment weighs more than the moving company guessed, they'll nevertheless honor the binding price. If you opt for a nonbinding estimate, tell the company that you want to be present (or will send a representative) when they weigh the load so that you know their reported weight is accurate and true.

- **Consider shipping heavy books by cheap (and slow) book rate at the post office.** Once you have obtained the per-pound cost for moving your stuff, visit the US Postal Service at usps.com and search the website for media mail rate. Pack small quantities of books in small boxes to save your back. For even more back muscle savings (though less money savings), request that the USPS pick up your package (Tools.usps.com/go/ScheduleAPickupAction!input.action). Make sure your postage is already on the packages, though. The media mail rate is often much less than the price per pound quoted by the moving company. The postal service will take its time getting the books to you, which may be a good thing, because you will be arranging the furniture.

- **Choose off-season moving if possible.** If you are flexible on when you have to move, wait for the off season when rates are usually lower. In most parts of the US, summer is the high season for moving.

- **Start early.** In some instances, it pays to begin your move early in the day to avoid overtime labor charges. If you have a binding price, it will probably apply only to transportation costs, not labor costs (or other last-minute add-ons, like asking them to pack boxes when you initially agreed to pack everything yourself).

- **Understand the mover's obligations on a delivery date.** You may be entitled to a payment for expenses or a rebate if your possessions do not show up within a few days of the contracted

Tipping the Scales

Many years ago, I made my first transfer using a moving company. As a business reporter, I thought I knew all the angles. After the truck had loaded all my possessions, I told the driver that I wanted to witness the weighing of the vehicle. He looked at me with a cool, appraising eye and then invited me to follow the truck across town to a commercial scale.

I watched as the driver and his two helpers drove the truck onto the scale and sat there as the operator calculated the weight. I was handed a printout of the numbers—before loading, after loading, and the difference. Quite satisfied with myself for my careful guardianship of my limited funds, I paid the bill when the moving van arrived at my new apartment 540 miles and three states away.

It was a few months later before I fully replayed the scene in my mind and realized that I had most probably paid for the weight of the driver and two helpers—perhaps 600 pounds. Also, federal regulations require that the truck's fuel tank be filled before the preload weighing and the post-load weighing so that the fuel's weight does not factor into the poundage. How do you ensure this? There's no easy answer other than to request to be present at the weigh station and to ask a lot of questions. If you're lucky, the weigh station will be at a truck stop and you can watch the tanks be filled for the preload measurement. (You don't really care if they fill the tanks for the post-load weighing, because if the truck's tanks are low on fuel, that's to your advantage.)

date. The contract should state a reasonable window of time for delivery as well as what the company will do if it misses the date.

- **Be aware of your obligations.** Under most moving contracts, the driver will not unload the truck unless you or your representative meets him with an acceptable form of payment. (Pay by credit card if possible, or by check because you then have proof of making payment. Don't pay in cash!)
- **Document your belongings.** Take digital photos of every item of value, including closeups of model and serial numbers. Keep your receipts and other proof (including the photos) with you—not in the packages that are to be moved.
- **Understand the insurance offered by the mover.** Don't pay for more coverage than you need. Consult your insurance agent to see if your homeowner's or renter's policy covers your possessions in transit from one place to another. Also check the mover's contract to see if the moving company draws any distinction between boxes it packs and those you pack yourself. The company may refuse to offer advanced coverage for boxes it can't inspect or doesn't pack.
    - Basic coverage for interstate moves is *released value liability*, which replaces losses or damages up to 60 cents per pound. This is not a great deal for most items, especially for expensive lightweight items. For example, a 40-pound jumbo flat-screen TV would be covered to the tune of just $24; a handsome suit weighing about a pound would be worth 60 cents.
    - An *added value protection* or *full value* policy is based on the items' actual values. With this coverage, a missing or damaged flat-screen TV would be covered for replacement minus the value it has lost while you owned it, called *depreciation*.
    - *Full-value* or *replacement-value policies* ensure that for that same flat-screen TV, you receive a check equivalent to the price you would pay to purchase a new TV set today.
- **If you do suffer a loss, file your claim—in writing—quickly.** Use your digital photos and copies of receipts to bolster any claims you file. Be sure you read and understand the terms of your agreement with the mover. Hold on to damaged boxes and packing materials until the claim is settled. In general, a mover must acknowledge your written claim within 30 days and must make an offer of settlement or deny the claim within 120 days. You have the right to object to a claim denial or protest the amount offered.

CHAPTER 20

Paying Off a Mortgage

Before you think about getting a mortgage from a bank, divide your decision into two parts: Consider how much of a house you want or need and then decide how much of a mortgage you can obtain and afford. As with most large purchases, there is a difference between a need and a want. I want a huge mansion on a mountaintop overlooking the ocean and a private beach, with a private ski lift and downhill course on the backside of the hill. What I need is a nice, clean, and safe place to sleep and to store our stuff.

It's great when your needs and wants are very close. But the most important thing is to sleep well at night knowing you can afford the monthly mortgage payment plus all the other costs associated with owning a home.

There are many important variables in that sort of decision, of course. You may be able to procure a very nice ranch house in Rochester for $500,000, while that much money might buy a mansion in Memphis and a shack in Santa Monica. The amount of mortgage you qualify for does not vary because of the price of the house. Banks concentrate on your annual income, available cash, and any other debts you have that might affect your ability to repay the mortgage.

- **Understand how mortgages work.**
- **Choose the best available mortgage.**
- **Choose mortgage terms that suit you.**
- **Avoid private mortgage insurance.**
- **Examine the details of an adjustable rate mortgage.**
- **Estimate your own mortgage.**
- **Shorten your mortgage term to save thousands.**
- **Refinance your mortgage when it makes sense.**
- **Carefully consider a mortgage reversal.**

Understand How Mortgages Work

A mortgage is made up of many moving pieces, and alteration to any of them will have a significant effect on closing, monthly, or total payments. The following sections discuss the pieces of a mortgage.

Amount Borrowed

The amount of money you borrow is usually the purchase price of the home reduced by the amount of down payment you have made. In some cases, you might seek a loan that is more than the cost of the real estate because of the need for repairs or improvements.

Points

The lender considers any points you have paid to the lender. Each point is 1% of the loan, and is treated as prepaid interest on the mortgage loan. In effect, you are giving the lender some of its expected profit up front, and for that reason the lender reduces the loan's interest rate. Prepaid points are generally tax deductible (as an interest expense) in the year they are incurred; check with your accountant or financial advisor.

The common wisdom is that if you expect to own the home for a long time, you should consider paying points to reduce the interest due over the long term. On the other hand, if you think you will either sell the home or refinance the loan within a few years, it probably does not make sense to pay points. You would not recover the savings in a short period of time.

Most lenders offer mortgages set up in various packages that include loans that do not require the payment of points or fees (usually the highest rate) as well as offers that require up-front point payment and fees.

Loan Term

The classic mortgage loan is 30 years—360 monthly payments. Most lenders are willing to write loans for shorter terms or, sometimes, longer periods.

As home prices rise, and when interest rates are high, there have been offers of 40-year mortgages. There's no right or wrong answer here, but you need to run the numbers. A 40-year mortgage will mean your monthly payment will be lower, but you will end up paying much more interest over time and you will more slowly accumulate equity (actual ownership). Many lenders will charge a bit more in interest for the privilege because they don't have a clue what interest rates will be that far down the road.

As an example, on a $500,000 loan over 30 years at 3% and a monthly payment of $2,108, after 15 years you will have paid off about $212,000 of the amount borrowed and $167,440 in interest. (Early on in a mortgage loan, more of the monthly payment goes toward interest than reducing the principal. The trend reverses in later years.) If you keep the loan for a full 30 years, you end up paying a total of $758,887.

Now take the same loan—$500,000 over 40 years at 3.25%. After 15 years (paying $1,862 monthly), you will have paid off about $119,000 of the amount you borrowed and $216,000 in interest. You are paying less per month, but also paying down the loan more slowly. The total cost over 40 years is $894,099. Well past the halfway point of any mortgage, more of your payment goes for interest than toward the amount borrowed.

Adjustable Rate Mortgages

There are many variations on this theme, among them a one-year adjustable rate mortgage (ARM). In that plan, the interest rate is reset once a year on a specified date and based on a particular financial index, usually with a maximum amount the rate can rise with each adjustment. If you are certain interest rates are headed down, this might make sense for a house you don't expect to own long. How are you certain? Are you smarter than a banker? Don't answer that question. They don't know with certainty either.

Some borrowers, when interest rates are high, choose an adjustable rate mortgage with the intention of refinancing with a fixed-rate loan when rates go down. That makes sense—if rates go down and if fees and points for the refinanced loan don't wipe out any advantage you gain.

Other variants include 10/1 ARMs, which have a fixed interest rate for the first 10 years and then convert to a loan that adjusts every year for the remainder of the term. This might be a good deal if you don't expect to stay in a home for more than a decade.

You may also see a 5/25 loan, which fixes the interest rate for the first five years and then resets it for the remaining 25 years. Tell me if rates will go up or down and I will tell you if this is a good deal for you.

A balloon mortgage charges a lower interest rate for its relatively short term, and then requires you to fully pay off the remaining principal. You might consider this if you are certain you will be selling the house in a fairly short period of time and are certain the value of the property will increase over time. If the home's value declines, you (or the loan, to be precise) will be upside down or underwater, which both mean you will owe more than the property is worth. That is not a good place to be.

Choose the Best Available Mortgage

For most of us, the single largest expense in our lives—and the largest loan we ever take out—is a home mortgage. It's a frightening procedure, and like most situations where bankers and lawyers are involved, it is unnecessarily complicated.

In general, here's what you are looking for in a mortgage deal…

- **The lowest interest rate for the type of loan you accept.**
- **An acceptable structure for payment calculation**—fixed rate, adjustable rate, two-step, or balloon payment.
- **An acceptable loan adjustment**—prepaid points or an increase in down payment if you choose one or both of those options.
- **The lowest possible closing costs.**

Consult your accountant or financial advisor to discuss any special circumstances.

Here are some ways to save hundreds of dollars each month, and tens of thousands across the term of a mortgage loan…

• **Treat obtaining a mortgage as the most important shopping you do.** Don't sign up with your neighborhood bank because that's where you keep your savings and checking accounts or because you like the free jelly beans on the counter. Be loyal to them if—and only if—they reward you with the best deal. Put your business out to bid by contacting half a dozen banks and mortgage companies in your area.

• **Consult mortgage rates online.** You'll find various individual banks or lending companies online, as well as sites (such as Lending Tree and Quicken Loans) that aggregate offerings from multiple lenders. As a borrower, it's your bottom line that is most important. Most lenders' rates are pretty close. Depending on your situation, it might be more valuable to deal with a lender who promises or claims to respond quickly and set up a closing that suits your needs. (As an example, if you are paying $1,500 per month to rent an apartment and one bank forces you to make two extra rental payments before it will close the deal, their mortgage is in effect costing you $3,000 more than another lender.)

• **Look for alternate sources.** That can include credit unions, clubs, associations, and investment management companies. For example, AAA offers mortgages (or promises special rates at a particular bank) in some states. You may be eligible for a reduced interest rate or other perks if you have an ongoing relationship with a firm.

• **Remember that mortgage loans are negotiable.** When you find the best combination of interest rate, application fee, prepaid points, and other elements, don't hesitate to discuss that deal with other lenders. Tell them: "Here's the best deal I've found. Can you do better?"

Choose Mortgage Terms That Suit You

Understand your own finances and consider your long-term goals. Are you 20 years away from retirement and living in a home you expect to keep after you're no longer working? In that case, you may not want to sign up for a 30-year mortgage. You don't want monthly payments when your income has been reduced post-retirement. Consider a shorter-term mortgage or perhaps a balloon mortgage, which has reduced monthly payments with a much larger final payoff at the end.

Are you just starting out and rather not put all your income into the mortgage? Maybe you want to leave some untouched so you can invest for your children's college, your own retirement, or any other worthy goal. In that case, you might want to consider a 30-year fixed-rate loan.

Although lenders are used to loans with terms of 15, 20, 30, and sometimes 40 years, there is no reason they can't adjust to a number of years that you choose. It's a financial calculation where any and all of the numbers are interrelated.

Do you expect that your monthly income will rise as you climb the corporate or professional ladder? Will your significant other be joining the workforce a few years down the road? Consider a two-step ARM that starts out with a relatively low interest rate and then increases after a specified number of years to a higher fixed rate (or adjusts to a particular level based on a recognized measure of the economy, such as the prime interest rate or a particular banking index).

Consult your financial adviser—not someone at the lending company—and go over your personal situation. Would you be better off paying down the mortgage as quickly as possible, or do you have a better chance of making more money on your investments than you will paying interest on the loan? Your adviser, of course, will factor in things like your tax bracket and the mortgage interest deduction you will receive versus the likely interest, dividend, or capital gain expected from an investment. And then, remember that nothing is guaranteed. Interest rates rise and fall, stock markets do the same, and home values do not always march upward forever. If anyone tells you they know the direction of the global economy with 100% certainty, politely excuse yourself and find someone with a more realistic worldview.

Calculated Move

There are dozens of mortgage-payment and amortization calculators available on the internet. Just do a search for mortgage calculator.

The monthly payments and other details are going to be the same whichever calculator you select. Choose the one that's easiest to use. Be sure to enter the numbers carefully. Some calculators merely ask how much you expect to borrow, while others ask for the home's purchase price and your down payment, which should yield the same loan amount.

If the calculator asks for the amount of property taxes and homeowners insurance, that is only relevant if your lender requires you to put that money into an escrow account for that purpose. If you will pay taxes and insurance directly, don't include the amount in the calculation.

Avoid Private Mortgage Insurance

One of the worst deals around is private mortgage insurance (PMI), which some mortgage lenders or federal programs require you to buy. Others may try to sneak PMI by an unwary consumer. This so-called "insurance" protects the lender, not you. It is intended to encourage some lenders to make loans to less-than-stellar borrowers (in their definition) under certain conditions.

Almost everything is negotiable when it comes to mortgages. Try to remove PMI from any mortgage before you go to closing. But, for example, PMI may be required under some federal programs if your down payment is less than 20% of the purchase price. If you are close to 20% in your down payment, consider putting down more money.

If you do end up with a PMI charge added to your monthly bill, make sure you know the conditions under which it was added. If the requirement for the insurance goes away once you have reached a certain level of equity (per the Homeowners Protection Act of 1998, but there are exemptions), insist on its removal once you reach that amount of equity in your home. Remember: This insurance protects the lender, not you. The lenders determine the rate of equity required before terminating PMI. You can read more about the act and PMI at the Federal Reserve's website at Blinc.Media/2vxrL7H.

Examine the Details of an Adjustable Rate Mortgage

Any mortgage is a gamble. You are betting that you will be able to pay the monthly bill for many years and that the value of your house will increase over time. The bank is betting that you are a worthy risk and that interest rates will not change so drastically as to make their loan a losing proposition. The bank also does not want to see the home's value decline, because if they have to foreclose on a devalued property, both you and the bank are going to be unhappy.

Here are the things you need to understand before you agree to an adjustable rate mortgage...

- **Is the initial rate artificially lower than the market rate to serve as a come-on to customers?** (This common tactic is one that a savvy consumer can make good use of. Some buyers happily refinance their loans every few years to take advantage of initial rates.)
- **How soon after the loan starts will the rates be adjusted?**
- **How often can it be adjusted?** Yearly? Every three years? Every five years? Just once?
- **What index will be used as the basis of the new rate?**
- **How much can the rate go up when it is adjusted?** Is there an annual cap? A lifetime cap? (Do the math to see if you could afford to pay the mortgage if the rate were to go up to its maximum level.)

Racking Up Points

You will find a number of calculators on the internet that help you see the break-even time for prepaid points. Your lender or financial advisor probably has similar calculators you can consult.

When you use such a calculator, enter the amount of money you will borrow, the interest rate, and term. Then you can adjust prepaid points from 0 to the number you want to consider. In general, each point paid on a 30-year loan will reduce the interest rate by somewhere between .125 and .25 (one-eighth or one-quarter of a percent). The discount will vary as interest rates rise or fall.

In a typical situation, the break-even date after paying one point is between five and six years. Paying two points might extend that to seven or eight years, and paying a higher number of points will push the break-even deeper into the loan term.

Over the full course of a 30-year loan, paying a few points can save you tens of thousands of dollars on a loan of several hundred thousand dollars. However, if you resell the house, or refinance the loan, the money paid for points is lost.

Estimate Your Own Mortgage

Try this exercise before you visit a bank or mortgage broker. It's pretty much the same process they will use. Total your gross salary, bonuses, and other income. Divide the amount by 12; then multiply that figure times 0.28 (28%). For most lenders, that is the maximum monthly mortgage payment—principal and interest—they want to permit. For example, if your total income is $150,000 per year, your maximum "permittable" monthly mortgage payment would be $3,500.

Loans backed by the Federal Housing Administration (FHA) are figured on a more inclusive monthly mortgage payment (principal, interest, escrow deposits for taxes or the equivalent if you pay taxes directly, the monthly cost of homeowner's insurance, the monthly cost of mortgage insurance if the lender requires that, and the monthly cost of homeowners' dues). That cost is supposed to be less than 31% of someone's gross income. (Per the previous example with $150,000 income, that would mean a maximum monthly payment of $3,875.)

Certain other guaranteed loans such as Veterans Affairs financing may allow a bit higher monthly payment.

Remember that we're talking about gross *salary*—salary before taxes are held back. Most lenders also look at another number, perhaps 36%, as the maximum amount of your gross income they want to see going to total debt, including mortgage, auto loans, and credit-card debt. If you don't have any other debt, or if your debt is relatively low, you may be able to get the lender to slightly increase your mortgage eligibility.

We're talking here about how much a lender is willing to see you pay each month. As a borrower, you should turn that around and come up with a number you feel comfortable paying each month. What would happen if you or your spouse loses a job? What about health problems or other possible family events that would make it harder to pay the monthly bill? How much of a cushion do you have in savings or investments? Your personal threshold may be lower than the amount a lender is willing to allow.

When you come up with the monthly payment a bank is likely to allow you to make, you can look at other ways to increase the actual loan amount, such as reducing the interest rate (by getting a better deal or by prepaying points) or by adjusting the loan's number of years.

Shorten Your Mortgage Term to Save Thousands

Why are mortgage payments due once a month? There's no particular answer except to say that they have been traditionally set up that way.

- **Make a mortgage payment every two weeks instead of once a month.** Are you paid every two weeks? The net effect is the equivalent of thirteen payments per month and, most importantly, paying biweekly can save you *hundreds of thousands of dollars* over the full course of a loan. You should be able to set up a biweekly schedule when you initiate a loan from a major bank or mortgage company. If you already have a loan in effect, talk to your bank about converting it to a biweekly schedule.

Say you have borrowed $500,000 for 30 years at 3%. The monthly payment would be $2,108. At the end of 30 years you will have paid (are you sitting down?) $258,887 in interest over and above the $500,000 in principal. Now look at the same loan and interest rate converted to biweekly payments. Take the monthly payment and divide it in half. Send that amount to the bank every two weeks. You will pay off your loan four years early and pay $223,190 in interest—a savings of $35,697

• **Add a few hundred dollars to each monthly payment.** Make sure you instruct the bank or lending institution to apply that extra money toward reducing the principal of the loan. Consult your lender to be certain the payments are properly credited.

• **Make an extra, thirteenth payment once a year.** You pay your monthly amount as required and then you make an extra full payment every December (or whatever month you choose). In the loan example just given, with a thirteenth payment, the interest will amount to $225,985 and the loan will be paid in full in 26½ years.

If you do choose to make an extra payment in December, consider the following: If you expect to earn more next year, hold off until January to receive more of a break in a higher tax bracket. If you'll earn more this year or if your income will be about the same in both years, pay in December so you'll receive the tax benefit sooner. The extra payment must be received and credited before the end of business on December 31 to be counted in that year for tax purposes.

This is not sleight of hand. You are making 26 half payments a year or 13 full payments, the equivalent of an extra month's payment. The extra money goes straight to reducing the principal.

Be sure that your bank allows loan prepayment without penalty. Most contemporary mortgages permit this. And then keep a close eye on your monthly or annual statements from the bank to make sure your extra payments are being properly credited against the outstanding principal of the loan.

Refinance Your Mortgage When It Makes Sense

Mortgage rates go up and they go down. In the period after the financial crisis of 2008 and through 2017, rates reached near-historic lows. As this book goes to print, rates are slowly rising from the basement. But say you take out a mortgage when rates were relatively or absolutely high, and then rates decline. If that is your situation, consider refinancing your loan at a lower rate.

Use a mortgage-calculation program and consult your accountant before making a final decision on refinancing a mortgage to obtain a new loan. One of the pitfalls is the hidden cost of application fees, points, and closing costs. As a general rule, experts say that you should consider refinancing your mortgage if the new rate is at least one percentage point lower than your existing mortgage rate and if you plan to keep the new mortgage for several years or more. (Keeping the mortgage for several years allows you to spread out the cost of refinancing against the money you will save at the new rate.)

If your mortgage is insured by the FHA or held by Fannie Mae (Federal National Mortgage Association), Freddie Mac (Federal Home Loan Mortgage Corporation), or some other federally managed program, find out if your loan includes the option for a *streamline refinance*. This is a nearly painless and low-cost refinancing that dispenses with many redundant charges for surveys, title insurance, and other fees.

You can ask your present lender if they will reduce or eliminate some fees for things like surveys, title insurance, and credit checks. After all, you are already their client. There is no harm in asking for a better deal.

Carefully Consider a Mortgage Reversal

If you're retired or are about to be, you may want to consider—*very carefully*—the option of signing for a reverse mortgage as a source of income. A *reverse mortgage* is a form of home-equity loan that pays a lump sum or a monthly payment drawn against the equity in your house. The home owner retains title to the property, albeit with a reduced equity.

I really, really want to emphasize that you should not take out a reverse mortgage on the basis of a recommendation by The Fonz or an actor-turned-US Senator-turned television pitchman. They are paid salespeople, not financial experts. Consult your financial advisor. If you don't have one, pay for time with an independent advisor who does not make his or her income on the basis of commissions for financial products sold. And involve your family in the decision.

These concepts are important to understand…

- **A *standard mortgage*, one taken out to buy a home in the first place, is usually a *falling debt, rising equity loan.***

Here's what that means: Each month (or every two weeks, per "Shorten Your Mortgage Term to Save Thousands" earlier in this chapter) you make a payment to the lender. In the initial years of a standard mortgage, most of the money goes to pay the outstanding interest. Eventually, a higher portion goes to paying down the loan. Near the end of the mortgage term, nearly all of your payment goes toward paying off the loan itself. And so, over time, the debt declines and the portion of the home that you fully own (your equity) rises. If you have chosen wisely and are lucky, the value of your home increases as well. If you completely pay off a standard mortgage, you will ultimately own 100% of the equity in the home.

- **A *reverse mortgage* gives the borrower some or all of the equity in a home as a single cash payment or a set of scheduled payments,** or makes a portion of the home's value available as a line of credit. And so it becomes a ***rising debt, falling equity loan***. Over time, you will owe more money and the equity in your home will decline. If you are lucky, the value of your home will increase. That equity will be to your benefit. But there is no guarantee of that for a reverse or a standard mortgage. A reverse mortgage will become due after the death of one or both of the homeowners, depending on how the loan is structured. Family or the estate can sell the house to pay the amount due or pay from other sources. Since 2014, a spouse who is not listed on the reverse mortgage is not automatically required to pay back a government-insured loan at the time of death of their partner and can remain in the house. In that situation, the lender will expect repayment when the second spouse dies or moves.

A reverse mortgage is a possibly interesting retirement solution for someone who is house-rich and cash-poor, facing extensive medical bills, or for retirees who don't plan to pass along the equity in their home to others when they die. You can use the money for any purpose and, in most cases, do not have to repay the loan, interest, or fees until the house is sold by you or your heirs. You are responsible for maintaining the house, paying taxes, and keeping an insurance policy in effect. If the furnace fails or the roof needs to be replaced, that's still on you. (The same is true for a regular mortgage, where owners are required to take care of the home until the bank no longer has any claim on it.)

There is one important safety net in most reverse-mortgage arrangements: Your legal obligation to pay back the loan is limited by the value of your house at the time the loan is repaid. In other words, you or your heirs should not end up owing more money than the value of the house at the time it is sold. Of course, most lenders will take this into account and limit the amount of money they will lend based on the age of the younger homeowner if there is more than one on the mortgage, life expectancy, and an estimation of your home's future value.

In general, reverse-loan advances are not considered income and are therefore nontaxable and do not affect the amount of Social Security or Medicare benefits you receive. In most states, recipients of Supplemental Security Income or Medicaid benefits are not affected as long as they spend reverse-mortgage payments within the month they are received.

The federally guaranteed program is called the Home Equity Conversion Mortgage (HECM), and it may be the best one. Because it is insured by the FHA, its terms are very tightly controlled. Under HECM, as well as under some other programs that you may be offered, if the outstanding loan balance (the amount of money borrowed plus accrued interest) ever reaches a point where it is equal to or greater than the value of your home, then the debt will be limited by the value of the home if it is sold to repay the loan. In the other situation, if the home is not sold and the loan is repaid from other funds from any source, then the borrower or the borrower's estate is on the hook for the full outstanding loan balance even if that number exceeds the value of the home.

Does all this make your hair hurt? Engage a team of financial experts and think twice, or thrice, or more before going down the reverse mortgage path.

PART IV

Ways to Save on Wheels

CHAPTER 21

Considering a New Car

For most people, buying a new car is one of life's major shopping events, second only to buying a house.

Today's shopper will find a dizzying range of automobiles in dozens of configurations, from major American, Japanese, Korean, and European companies. In 2017, the average price for a new vehicle was about $34,000. If price were the only problem, shopping for a new car just might be tolerable, but most buyers look forward to the process about as much as they would a visit to the dentist for root canal without anesthesia.

Car dealers have expanded their reach into their customers' pockets: car sales, add-ons, leasing, financing, service, and more and they have almost perfected the art of completely confusing customers.

But there is hope for the savvy consumer. Car buyers who know how the game works and who are willing to assert themselves in the car showroom (or on the phone or over the internet) can save thousands of dollars off the list price of vehicles.

The number one tip for car buyers is this: Go to school before you go to the dealership. (And number two: wait before you go to the dealership until very late in the process.)

Your goal should be to know as much or more about the car you want to buy as the salesperson does. Know the car, available options, and the actual cost that the dealer pays the manufacturer. And then remember on which side of the table the power resides: You are the one with the money and the one who knows just how much you are willing to spend.

In this chapter, I will focus on preparing for and then conducting negotiations to purchase a new car. I will hold off for upcoming chapters on talking about selling or trading in your old car and securing a financing or leasing plan.

Here are some of the keys to success in the new-car showroom…

- **Know more than the salesperson.**
- **Pay no attention to the MSRP.**
- **Hold out against the hidden holdback.**
- **Reconsider ordering a car.**
- **Fight back against the annoying, the bad, and the ugly.**
- **Choose new car options wisely.**

- **Start the negotiating process like a pro.**
- **Buy a car without visiting the dealer.**
- **Pick the best day to shop.**
- **Buy a car at the dealership.**
- **Get hip to the games dealers play.**
- **Recognize the beauty of a broken record.**
- **Double-team them.**
- **Drive away from extended service contracts.**
- **Do the math yourself.**
- **Negotiate a better deal at a "no-negotiation" dealership.**
- **Get an insider price.**

Know More Than the Salesperson

The best way to conduct a negotiation for any item, including a car, is to know the product line better than the salesperson. As the buyer, you have one particular advantage: You don't have to buy a particular brand. The quality of vehicles has improved markedly in recent years, and there almost always is an acceptable alternate brand you can consider. And even though all new car dealers pay the manufacturer the same price for the same vehicles, there are differences from one dealer to another and it might be to your benefit to see if one is willing to cut closer to the bone (his or hers, not yours) than the one down the road.

After looking at online content, study the brochures and sales material—especially the pages at the back that list optional and standard equipment. Ask for any supplemental listings of option packages. (Sometimes the option packages are listed only in third-party pricing guides such as Edmund's, which you can investigate at Edmunds.com.)

Spend some time cruising the lots and taking notes on what you find there. I like to make my tours on Sunday mornings, when most car dealerships are closed. I'm looking to get some idea of what types of cars the dealer has in stock, and the option packages ordered. I consider it good news if I find more than a few cars of the type I want to buy, since it increases my bargaining power a bit.

Ask friends and family about their experience with the cars they own. If you find someone in a parking lot getting into or out of a model you are considering, politely inquire of them whether they like the vehicle.

If you care about camber angles and horsepower ratings, read one of the enthusiast magazines such as *Automobile*, *Car and Driver*, or *Road and Track*. Writers here are a lot less concerned about things such as purchase price, resale value, maintenance, and repair. They're more interested in 0-to-60-miles-per-hour speed and high-tech doodads, but there is still information to be learned. Do bear in mind that the publishers of these magazines make their profits based on advertising placed by automobile makers. A "do not buy" recommendation is rare in these publications.

The savvy consumer will want to read the reviews in *Consumer Reports*, the publication of the independent testing organization Consumers Union that accepts no advertising and pulls no punches. Here you'll find independent determinations of miles per gallon, quality of construction, and reliability ratings based on tests and surveys of owners. Car reviews are published in most monthly editions, with an annual automobile roundup in the April issue, which goes on sale in March of each year. You can purchase individual copies of the magazine, subscribe for the year, or buy online access.

Before you set foot in a dealership, go on to the internet and check out prices for the cars you are considering. *I get into this in more detail in a moment, but here is the information you want to collect...*

• **The MSRP (manufacturer's suggested retail price) for the *base price* or *base model* of the model you are considering,** in the *trim level* or *submodel*. For example, a 2017 Stanley Zoomer with auto transmission and 2WD (two-wheel drive, as opposed to 4WD, or four-wheel drive) in LX trim. (The trim indicates the level of engine power, luxury, or bells and whistles. You'll find descriptions of what is included in each trim level on internet sites and in brochures you collect from dealers.)

• **The invoice price for the base model of the exact model you are considering, before any options are added.** The invoice price is allegedly the price the dealer paid the manufacturer for the vehicle. It is almost always a work of fiction, but it is a number you should learn as you begin your negotiation.

• **The *destination or delivery cost* for the vehicle,** a charge imposed by the manufacturer to deliver the car from its factory or from the port of entry where it arrived.

• **The *MSRP* for any options or option package you are willing to pay for.** If you are ordering a car from the factory you should be able to specify exactly which options to add. Buying from a dealer inventory may force you to consider paying for options you don't want. Most dealers can exchange cars with other dealers in the area if you insist on a particular configuration they don't have. If you are buying late in the model year or are considering a leftover from the previous year, the selection of cars is usually quite limited.

• **The invoice price for those same options,** which again is the price the dealer supposedly pays the manufacturer for the enhancements. As with the invoice price for the vehicle itself, the invoice for the options may not include any special discounts, rebates, or special programs offered by the manufacturer to the dealer. However, it is useful information to have as you start negotiations.

You are going to have to pay sales tax if one is levied in the state or territory where you will register the car. That part is nonnegotiable.

And you will also have to pay for registration and license plates, again, nonnegotiable fees (although some states may let you save a small amount of money if you are disposing of a used car and can reuse the old license plates). Most dealers also add a charge for documentation or for handling the registration on your behalf. If the charge is exorbitant, you can object and offer to do it yourself or ask for a fee reduction. Even if the dealer sings a mournful song claiming rightfully or wrongfully about how the documentation fee is required, you can object and record the amount on your side of the ledger of discounts you want.

Where do you find the MSRP and invoice price for cars? Many websites list them. The best websites calculate them as you "build" a vehicle online with the options of your choice. On some

> **TIP**
>
> **Documentation and Fees**
>
> Every state has a different set of laws regarding documentation fees related to car registration. Some do not regulate fees at all. Some set a maximum. And some require dealers to charge every buyer the same amount. But in almost every case, nothing requires you to use the services of the dealer for anything beyond a bill of sale. If you purchase a used car from an individual, you can walk into a registry office and do the paperwork yourself. The same applies for a new car.

of the sites you have to dig to find the invoice price. You rarely find invoice prices listed on the sites of car manufacturers themselves, but some car dealers disclose the invoice price on the internet or post them on the cars. I'm not going to accuse all car dealers of less-than-truthful acts, but I do as much independent research as possible.

Here are some free sites to visit…

- **Edmunds** at Edmunds.com
- **Kelley Blue Book** at KBB.com/new-cars
- **NADA Guides** (from the National Automobile Dealers Association) at NADAguides.com

Consumer Reports has its own Build & Buy Car Buying Service, which promises to get you a price that represents a discount from the MSRP, which is one way to buy a car although not always a way to the lowest price. It does, however, insulate you from most of the unpleasantness that accompanies the buying process. Similarly, Costco and some other membership stores, as well as AAA and AARP, offer similar services for those who want to keep arm's length from the negotiation process.

And other websites offer to stand between you and the dealer at least for the initial negotiations. They will tell you the MSRP and tell you either actual or typical selling prices for the vehicle at dealers near you. I would use this service—as well as Costco or any other you find as the *starting point* for negotiations that are based on a discount from MSRP. One worth considering is TrueCar at TrueCar.com. Some of these sites require a fee or a nonmember fee; many don't.

Amazon has a vehicles section to its website that contains specifications, basic reviews, and a comment section, along with the ability to link cars you own to replacement parts and upgrades for sale. How long before you can order a car from Amazon or connect to a dealer through the site? Stay tuned.

Pay No Attention to the MSRP

How can a car dealer afford a fancy showroom, splashy television ads, and that tray of stale donuts and free coffee and still sell you a car for "$49 over factory invoice"? How about $100

Foreign and Domestic

The big three US carmakers—Ford, General Motors, and Chrysler—are embedded in the American consciousness and indeed manufacture many of their vehicles in the United States, but none of them contain 100% domestic content. In fact, some "foreign" companies contain more American parts than do the domestic makers. (And for the record, Chrysler is now a subsidiary of the Italian carmaker Fiat. To be precise, Fiat Chrysler Automobiles is controlled by its Italian parent company, registered in The Netherlands, with headquarters in London.)

And speaking of foreign carmakers, most major companies have assembly plants in the US. Depending on the company, they may import certain components like engines or transmissions from their own factories abroad or from third-party sources, which often are in Asia. One independent analysis in 2016 said that Toyota's bestselling truck Tacoma and Ford's bestselling truck F-150 each contain about 70% parts made in the US.

Among manufacturers who at the time of this writing assemble some or all of their models in the United States are Toyota, Nissan, Hyundai-Kia, Mercedes Benz-Daimler, Honda, Volkswagen, BMW, and Subaru. Volvo, the Swedish company now owned by a Chinese company, expects to open a US plant in 2018.

And then there is this: Many automakers are building cars or parts in Mexico where labor costs are lower and trade accords do not present a barrier to import into the United States. Over the past decade, the percentage of cars made and sold in the United States has remained steady or declined slightly, while Mexican production has grown by about 40%. Much of Mexico's gain came at the expense of factories in Canada. The politics of trade may, or may not, bring change to this sort of cross-border car manufacturing in years to come.

When you shop for a car, you can see the place of manufacture listed on the federally mandated window sticker as well as on a plate in the doorwell. Our island car, a five-year-old vehicle with about 6,500 total miles on the odometer, is a Ford Fiesta, a design that originated in Ford's European operations but for the North American market is assembled in Cuautitlán Izcalli near Mexico City.

under invoice? The fact is that the dealer cannot afford such deals—at least if the factory invoice price were really the full wholesale price.

Here's the inside skinny: Nearly every car manufacturer regularly offers their dealers discounts from the "official" factory invoice price. Instead of lowering the invoice price, the manufacturers allow dealers to either lower the price to buyers or keep the extra money themselves. And then there are *holdbacks*, which amount to additional profit paid to the dealer after vehicle sale.

Allow me to delve a bit deeper into the definition of three important terms:

- **Manufacturer-to-buyer-rebate.** Here, the car maker offers money back to buyers if they purchase a particular model. The money can be paid directly to you after you take title of the car, or it can be used as part of a down payment against the price of the car. In some situations, the dealer may require customers to sign over their rebate to receive a special price. This seems to be a purposely confusing arrangement. I'd rather negotiate my own deal on my own terms. Note that rebates may or may not be available to customers who lease a car through a dealer.

- **Sales-incentive or dealer rebate.** This is money offered by the manufacturer to spur the sales of a particular model or line of cars. It is usually a prod to clear the lots of vehicles that are not selling well or an attempt to clear a glut of cars ahead of the arrival of a new model or next year's version. The money goes to the dealer and may or may not result in a reduced consumer price, but if you know that the dealer is receiving an incentive or rebate, that allows you to push harder for a better deal.

In mid-2017, according to an industry publication, the average incentive on new cars was about 11%. There, in a nutshell, is how dealers can claim to be selling a car for invoice price or lower and still make a nice profit. Search the internet, especially car-enthusiast blogs, to find out about incentives and dealer rebates. A small number of dealers or salespeople will actually give you an honest answer if you ask them if there are any incentives on particular models.

- **Dealer holdback.** If I weren't trying to be polite here, I might call this a hidden kickback from the manufacturer to the dealer. That's exactly what it is, of course. Manufacturers pay dealers a bonus or credit for every vehicle sold, an amount that is not reflected on the invoice price or advertised to the buyer as a rebate.

Typical holdbacks are 3% on a domestic vehicle and 2% or 3% on imports. This is not insignificant: 3% of a $35,000 MSRP is $1,050, which contributes to the expense of the showroom, TV ads, bad coffee, and the dealership owner's diamond pinky ring.

I explain more about holdbacks in a moment.

If the manufacturer is offering a customer rebate (manufacturer-to-buyer rebate) on a vehicle, think of this as a side deal between you and the maker. You still want to negotiate as sharply as you can with the dealer. Once you have driven down the price to a fair level, you can then subtract the rebate. Don't let the salesperson start out with a magnanimous "gift" of the rebate. Make it clear that you'll use the rebate as part of your down payment but consider it irrelevant to the sales price you are preparing to negotiate.

I've chosen an actual car, its name disguised, outfitted with its standard engine and automatic transmission, with a middle-of-the-range trim level called SE, and front-wheel drive rather than a more expensive four-wheel or all-wheel drive. I've chosen to stay with standard wheels and tires. I don't willingly pay for fancy wheels but sometimes will choose larger wheels and tires for a better ride.

I'm going to construct a hypothetical example of an auto price construction, leaving out of the equation the destination charge and sales tax, which have to be paid one way or another.

2017 American 4dr Sedan SE FWD	
MSRP Base Price	$24,320
MSRP Optional Appearance Equipment Package	$995
Total MSRP	$25,315
Dealer Invoice Base Price	$22,557
Dealer Invoice Optional Appearance Equipment Package	$928
Dealer Net Invoice Cost	$23,485
Dealer Holdback 3% of Total MSRP	– 759
Dealer Net Cost After Holdback	$22,726

If you insist on throwing away your hard-earned cash, you could pay the MSRP, giving the dealer a profit of $2,589, or about 11.5% (plus any incentives from the maker).

Or, you might accept what seems to be a magnanimous offer by the salesperson of $1,000 off the list price. Though the sales manager may make a big show of moaning about how close to the bone he or she is cutting, in truth this still amounts to a profit of $1,589, or about 8%. And that is before any manufacturer-to-dealer rebates or other incentives the dealer gets, and also before factoring in the holdback most manufacturers pay the dealer.

Now let's get serious. It's the end of the model year and the dealer is running one of those specials that seems too good to be true—$1 over invoice! Your price would be $22,727 before destination charge and sales tax. Don't let the salesperson cry about all the money the dealership is losing. The profit in my hypothetical example is $758, before any hidden promotions coming to the dealer from the manufacturer—still a decent profit for a quick deal. (It is also not really your concern about how the dealer divides up the proceeds from a car deal. The salesperson's commission should be between him or her and the owner of the place. Your concern is to keep more money in your pocket.)

Back up and think about the best way to approach negotiations for a new car. Don't think in terms of reducing the MSRP or allow the salesperson to speak in those terms. Instead, ask yourself (and the salesperson) the following question—What is a reasonable profit for the dealer? I think the proper answer is something in the range of 3 to 5%. If that sounds low, consider that the dealer typically holds a car on the lot for only a few weeks—at most a few months. A 5% profit on a vehicle in stock for two months is roughly equivalent to 30% profit on an annual basis.

And you may or may not be aware of any special promotions that the manufacturer offers the dealer. Those rebates tend to pop up near the end of the model year as well as any situation in which the maker has a glut of cars on dealer lots or in a parking lot at the factory or the port of entry. Then add in the fact that most dealers proceed to make money off their customers for years to come through the shop.

And one more thing: As a savvy consumer you have avoided all discussion with the salesperson about a few other sometimes very profitable streams of income for the dealer—a profit on resale of your current car if you trade it in, a fee paid by a bank or the manufacturer if you finance the purchase through the dealership, and the possibility of convincing you to purchase after-market products like an extended warranty (almost always a bad idea), undercoating or special paint treatment (almost always an even worse idea), and a set of radio-controlled fuzzy dice.

Hold Out Against the Hidden Holdback

The existence of a manufacturer's holdback is not a secret, although very few car dealers or salespeople willingly acknowledge its existence. It is part of a wink-and-nod arrangement between the carmaker and the seller in which the dealer invoice is inflated by a few percentage points. When the car is sold, or on a monthly or quarterly or other schedule, the holdback is repaid to the dealer.

Why does a carmaker do this? It is, first of all, part of the game. It allows dealers to seemingly discount the MSRP to near or even right down to the invoice price and still make a profit. Some also point to the fact that most salespeople are paid a commission that comes out of the profit above the invoice, while the dealer gets to hold on to the holdback.

When a Used Car Is New

In certain circumstances, a new-car dealer can sell you a used car and legally call it new. A car crosses the line from new to used once it has been titled at a state registration bureau. Manufacturers and new-car dealers are permitted to operate cars using temporary paperwork and dealer plates. These cars are sometimes used by the manufacturer in testing or by salespeople at the dealership as personal cars. Sometimes the cars just accrue mileage in test drives. The tip-off, of course, is the odometer, which cannot legally be disconnected or rolled back.

If the car you are considering has more than a few dozen miles on it, ask for a full explanation—and a discount off the price you would expect to pay for a new car (perhaps in the range of 50 cents to a dollar per mile).

If you buy a new-used car, you should expect to receive a full new-car warranty. Make sure that is part of the deal you sign. If there is any uncertainty about the warranty, ask for a declaration in writing by the dealer to that effect. If a manufacturer's warranty is not included in the deal, be suspicious about the car's quality. In any case, the seller should reduce several thousand dollars off the new-car price.

Manufacturers can change their holdback at any time, and some calculate them differently from other makers. It can be a percentage of the total MSRP (including options and some fees), or a percentage of just the base MSRP (the vehicle alone). Some makers calculate the holdback from the total invoice or the base price on the invoice.

Here is how holdback was calculated as this book went to press…

Domestic Carmakers	
Buick (GM)	3% of total MSRP
Cadillac (GM)	3% of total MSRP
Chevrolet (GM)	3% of total MSRP
Chrysler (Fiat-Chrysler)	3% of total MSRP
Dodge (Fiat-Chrysler)	3% of total MSRP
Ford	3% of total MSRP
GMC (GM)	3% of total MSRP
Jeep (Fiat-Chrysler)	3% of total MSRP
Lincoln (Ford)	No holdback
RAM (Fiat-Chrysler)	3% of total MSEP

Foreign Carmakers	
Acura (Honda)	2% of base MSRP
Audi (Volkswagen)	No holdback
BMW	No holdback
Fiat (Fiat-Chrysler)	3% of base MSRP
Honda	2% of base MSRP
Hyundai (Hyundai Kia)	3% of total MSRP
Infiniti (Nissan)	1.5% of base MSRP
Jaguar (Tata Motors)	No holdback
Kia (Hyundai Kia)	3% of base invoice
Land Rover (Tata Motors)	No holdback
Lexus (Toyota)	2% of base MSRP
Mazda	1% of base MSRP
Mercedes-Benz (Daimler)	1% of total MSRP
Mini (BMW)	No holdback
Mitsubishi	2% of base MSRP

Nissan	2% of total invoice
Porsche (Volkswagen)	No holdback
Smart (Daimler)	3% of total MSRP
Subaru	2% of base MSRP
Toyota	2% of base MSRP
Volkswagen	2% of base MSRP
Volvo	1% of base MSRP

But Wait, There's More

A manufacturer can do just about anything it wants to help move vehicles, including offer dealers special incentives. Most makers avoid actually reducing a car's MSRP, since they want to be able to sell at or near that price when demand is strong. They also know that most buyers want to believe or know for certain they are getting a discount, even from an artificially inflated price. Other things carmakers can do is give dealers advertising credits, which reduces the dealer's overhead by subsidizing the cost of those annoying advertisements

They can also cut a special deal or rebate some of the cost for *flooring cars* (the interest paid on unsold models). Few, if any, dealers own the new cars on their lot outright. Instead, they make interest payments to the manufacturer for the inventory. Sometimes a maker that needs to clear out its own vehicle backlog will finance cars to the dealer at zero interest, essentially loaning the cars until they are sold.

These and other efforts put extra money in the dealer's account. There are also special programs, often referred to as *spiffs*, that represent immediate bonuses for sales. A manufacturer might inform a dealer that the store will receive a bonus if it can move 60 vehicles by the end of the month, or the owner will be rewarded with a free cruise.

Because of sales incentives with deadlines imposed by the manufacturer, many dealers will turn around and dangle rewards (or threats) in front of their sales force—for example, sell two cars today for an extra cash bonus. That's why it is generally a good idea to go shopping near the end of the month or the end of the year.

Reconsider Ordering a Car

In certain circumstances, it sometimes makes sense to order a car from the factory so that it is equipped exactly as you want it: color, trim level, options, and nothing more. And some dealers will give you a break on the price since they know they will have little or no cost for financing the vehicle, and they will get to hold on to your deposit until the car is delivered.

I'm writing here about vehicles that are assembled in North America—the United States, Mexico, or Canada. It is not always possible to factory-order a foreign-built car for delivery in the United States.

Salespersona Non Grata

Your goal is to get the lowest possible price for the car (and anything else you buy). With all due respect to salespeople, it's your family that is your concern. Don't waste your time listening to a sob story from the other side of the table. A dealer earns money many ways and they need to take care of their sales staff in one way or another. Politely turn the subject back to the price and be prepared to walk out the door. As long as you are reasonable in your negotiations, the matter of compensation for sales personnel is best left to the dealer.

If you are looking for a car with a particular assemblage of options, you may also be able to get a dealer to locate that car on the lot of another dealer and make a wholesale transfer. You shouldn't have to pay extra for this service, and all the other elements of striking a good deal still apply.

But you just might get a better deal, or a few extra options, if you agree to buy a car that has been sitting on the dealer's lot for weeks or months. In almost every case, car dealers don't outright purchase their inventory but instead essentially put everything on credit and must pay interest on the money borrowed (*flooring* or *a floorplan*.) A dealer who is in the hole for a few months of interest on a car is going to be anxious to move said car. The interest payments will stop and the manufacturer will start the process to pass along the holdback.

This is one reason two seemingly identical cars on a car lot sometimes bear different prices. If the salesperson doesn't volunteer a reason, you can draw your own conclusions by looking at the manufacture date stamped on a plate inside the doorwell on the driver's side. If one car is six months older than the other, chances are it has been aging on the lot and costing the dealer money in the process.

Even if there is not a price differential, you can make note of things like the difference in manufacture date and tell the salesperson you'll do the dealer a favor and take the older new car—at an additional discount. As long as both cars are the same model year, it will make no difference in resale value or warranty coverage.

Fight Back Against the Annoying, the Bad, and the Ugly

There are some elements of the car-buying experiences that are somewhere on the spectrum between annoying, bad, and downright ugly. I'm talking about extra charges that appear on the purchase agreement when you finally are ready to formalize the deal. Some of them are nonnegotiable and some of them are set by law, but some of them are attempts to siphon money from your pocket.

The Window Sticker

A car's MSRP as well as other information, including factory-installed options and manufacturer fees, are required to be displayed on any car offered for sale as new. It is printed on a label that has been federal law since the Automobile Information Disclosure Act of 1958. In the trade it is still sometimes called a *Monroney sticker*, named after Oklahoma Senator Mike Monroney who was the bill's sponsor.

The window sticker is printed and glued to the window by the manufacturer, not the dealer. Over the years, various additions, including fuel economy and safety ratings, have been added by law. The sticker is printed by the manufacturer but it must follow the outline set by various federal agencies. The dealer is not supposed to remove the sticker until the car is sold. The dealer can be fined if it is missing or altered. *The sticker must include the following...*

- **MSRP**
- **Details about the engine specifications and transmission type**
- **Standard equipment included in the MSRP,** including wheels, tires, audio equipment, special lighting, and other features
- **Any factory-installed optional equipment,** along with the MSRP for those options
- **Essential details of the manufacturer's warranty for the vehicle**

When you are considering purchasing a specific car on the dealer's lot, look at the window sticker and ensure that it matches the vehicle. You'll find a car's VIN (vehicle identification number) on the sticker, as well as on the top of the dashboard near where the window meets the dash on the driver's side. The VIN is also posted in less obvious places, like the car frame and within the engine compartment, to help prevent certain types of fraud. Make sure the sticker on the window and the dashboard plate in the car match. If they don't, run away from that dealer.

Now look to see what the sticker lists as the standard or installed-option details for wheels or tires. Make sure you are receiving what you are paying for, and not a car where some parts have been swapped out. I'm not saying this happens often, but I experienced a dealer who offered me a car with a lesser grade of tires than was listed on the sticker. He claimed it was an error, but I am pretty certain that the better tires had been moved to another vehicle as part of a deal. And yes, I walked away from the dealership and took my business elsewhere.

Here are some other things you are likely to find on the official manufacturer's window sticker...

- **Destination charges.** The regulations that define the window sticker require the manufacturer to separate the cost of moving the vehicle from the factory or its arrival port to the dealer. This is supposed to be the cost within the United States only. If you are buying an imported car, the cost of delivering the vehicle from a foreign source is supposed to be a part of the MSRP itself.

In any case, destination charges are fixed—in every sense of the word—and not something you can directly negotiate. Figure on a charge in the range of $500 to $1,000 for most cars. I say *fixed* because the destination charge is an average of all shipping costs for the manufacturer. Whether you live across the street from the factory or, as I do, on an island where the dealer must arrange a ferry trip from the mainland, the destination charge will be the same.

• **State and local sales tax.** The sticker will note that the MSRP does not include sales tax, but you will be required to pay the amount to the dealer. Make sure that the sales tax is calculated on the actual price you are paying after negotiation, not the list price. Some states allow you to reduce the purchase price by the value of any trade-in, while others do not permit that adjustment.

If you live in a state that does not levy a state or local sales tax, good for you (although the cost of roads, schools, police, and fire departments and other services have to be paid for in some way). But, in general, if you buy a new car out of the state in which you live, you will have to pay the tax when you register the vehicle in your home state.

• **Advertising charges set by the manufacturer.** Not every carmaker adds this expense to the MSRP sticker, but might place it on the invoice that purports to show what the dealer actually paid for the vehicle. I *always* object to paying this fee, which may add a few hundred dollars to the price. If the dealer won't budge on this particular charge, I make it clear that if there is going to be a sale there has to be an equivalent reduction somewhere else, and that's just the beginning of my negotiation.

• **Documentation fee and licensing fee.** The window sticker will tell you that buyers are responsible for documents and filings with the state's automobile registry. That's just for the office work and perhaps a trip to the dealer's counter at the registry to pick up a license plate and a few rubber stamps.

Some states place a fixed fee or a maximum limit on how much a dealer can charge for documentation. I have seen fees as low as $75 and as much as $600 for what amounts to perhaps an hour's time (sometimes less if the dealer is selling several cars a day or more). If your state does not have a limit, you can and should object to a high charge. I squawk at any charge of more than $100.

And some states don't require you to use the dealer services for obtaining a registration. In that case, you can do it yourself. In one of my more memorable car purchases, my insurance agent offered to take care of all the paperwork of the purchase and licensing as part of his service to me. I happily accepted that offer and struck out the paperwork charge on the sales agreement.

You do have to pay the actual amount charged by the state for processing a new car registration and issuing a license plate, if your car requires a new one. The state sets the registration and license plate fee, based on the type of vehicle.

A Supplemental Sticker

When I see a supplemental sticker on the window, produced by the dealer or a dealer association, I am not a happy man. In the trade, these are sometimes called pack labels, as in a way to pack in some extra profit and hope that the buyer thinks this is part of the MSRP.

What might you find on a supplemental sticker?

• **Additional profit.** My least favorite is a variation of this: *additional dealer markup*, which almost sounds legitimate, or *additional dealer profit,* which lays bare what is being asked. The dealer adds these to the MSRP, which means that the dealer is rejecting the manufacturer's suggested retail price. To my way of thinking, this is a red flag that the dealership is going to be difficult to deal with. Even if they agree to remove the additional markup, this probably means they will stay closer to the MSRP than to the invoice price.

This sort of pricing sometimes appears on vehicles that are in extremely short supply and in very high demand. Although you may have your heart set on a particular vehicle, are you really willing to pay above list price for it? Check to see if other dealers—even ones 50 miles away—are adding to the price in this way. You can either wait a few months for supply and demand to come back to normalcy, or you can consider another vehicle.

- **Dealer-added coatings and services.** You may also find other kinds of perks on a supplemental sticker. Some dealers try to include soundproofing or rustproofing or special paint protection. First of all, these products do not often deliver much benefit to you. Ask the dealer, "Are you saying that without this special product, this new car is going to rust away in five years and the paint will become dull in three?" Listen carefully to what the salesperson says and be prepared to either reject the optional perk or take your business elsewhere.

Years ago, I was in final negotiations over a car purchase and was looking for the last $300 or so that stood between what I was willing to pay and what the dealer was asking. I had identified a particular car and examined it, and now we were talking about the bottom line. The salesman leaned toward me in his best imitation of an "I'm your best friend, you know" stance, and delivered what he thought was the coup de grâce. "Tell you what," he said. "I just spoke to my manager and he said he would allow me to give you a $300 pinstriping job for free. Do we have a deal?" I waited a beat, and then said: "That's worth $300?" "At least that much," the salesman answered too quickly. "Great," I said. "Take that $300 off the price and I'll sign the contract right now." I might or might not have gotten to my price in other ways, but the salesman had made an unforced error by putting a number into play that fit into my formula. I drove that un-pinstriped car for many years.

- **Local advertising costs.** To me, the only thing more annoying than having to endure television and radio and internet ads from dealers with silly jingles or hokey appearances by the owner's family with encomiums about how much fun you'll have is to see a supplemental sticker with a charge for local advertising costs. Think about it: Do restaurants or supermarkets or airlines add a charge for the cost of advertising? They don't. Any smart shopper understands that the cost of doing business is something that is incorporated in the selling price, not added on. You are under no requirement to pay for the dealer's advertising costs as an additional charge. Insist on removal of the fee or take your business elsewhere.

Choose New Car Options Wisely

Let me start by telling you when *not* to make your choice—when you are sitting across the desk from a high-pressure car salesperson who is determined to squeeze the last dollar out of your pocket. As in, "You'll want undercoating and pinstriping, of course." Some options will be of value when it comes time to resell or trade in the car, while some (like undercoating, unusual colors, and fuzzy dice) will mean absolutely nothing. And a few options actually reduce a vehicle's resale price.

You can get a sense of an option's value by checking the resale value from online websites. Check the estimated sales price for a used car with and without the options you are considering to see whether they retain some or all of their value.

Modern cars all come with air bags, with some of the advanced ones offering squadrons of them: front, back, and side impact. Antilock brakes have moved from optional to standard as well.

Here are options that are likely to benefit you when you dispose of the car…

- **Air-conditioning.** In fact, the lack of air-conditioning in most parts of the country may make resale difficult, if not impossible. Many car models now come with air-conditioning as standard. If you have to add AC as an option, expect to pay between $600 and $1,000.

- **Larger or more efficient or technically advanced engines.** A larger engine is not a necessity, but most buyers can count on recovering a large part of the $500 to $2,500 they pay for a larger, more responsive engine on a new car. A larger engine is also valuable if the car will pull a boat or trailer.

- **Automatic transmission.** Although some drivers, myself included, prefer the feel and response of a manual transmission, less than 10% of cars sold in the United States come with a stick. (That probably is reasonably close to the percentage of drivers who know how to use one.) Buying a car with a manual transmission is almost certainly going to reduce the pool of potential buyers when it comes to resale. One exception is for a sports car, where drivers may insist on a manual transmission.

- **Power windows and power door locks.** Once strictly optional, these convenience items are common. Your bottom line on resale may or may not suffer if you don't have them.

- **Cruise control.** This is a nice feature if you make a lot of long-distance trips on superhighways, and often is included in mid- and upper-level trim or special packages but missing on the lowest-price base model. Cruise control can save a bit on fuel and reduce driver fatigue.

- **Theft-deterrent system.** Some systems may reduce your auto insurance premiums and a smart buyer and reseller can make that point.

You may recover some of the cost of these options if you can find the right buyer at resale time…

- **Four-wheel drive or all-wheel drive.** These features add value to a car, especially in snowy places or when a vehicle might be driven off road. This sort of drivetrain sometimes requires extra maintenance, though.

- **Traction control, remote starters, and snow tires.** Drivers in snow country will value these features, which help maintain stability on slippery roads and also allow you to warm up your car from the comfort of your kitchen. If you are reselling the car in Florida, don't expect buyers to be impressed.

- **Lane change warning.** This worthy safety feature uses a set of sensors to locate the road's lane markings and sense approaching vehicles in the lane to your left or right. If you start to move into a lane you should avoid, the car alerts you with a flashing light on the sideview mirror or in other ways.

- **Power seats.** This is a very nice feature if your car is regularly driven by more than one driver. It's also an important safety feature if you need to adjust the seat while you are driving. The best systems adjust forward, backward, up, and down, and can also set the chair angle. A memory feature can automatically adjust to a preset position for a particular driver. This feature may be included at certain trim levels or available as an option.
- **Heated seats and luxury leather upholstery.** Leather seats wear well, and heated seats may be much appreciated in cold climates, but not every buyer will pay extra for them at resale time.
- **Sunroof or moonroof.** This feature improves ventilation (well, the sunroof does) and interior light but mostly makes a drive in the country a bit more pleasant. Some buyers might not care or do not want to pay for the hole in the roof and may wind up waiting to get a car without one.
- **Deluxe sound systems.** An exceptional sound system is very enjoyable during the time you own the car, but a second buyer might not care or might not be willing to pay extra for it. We're talking here about sound systems as delivered from the manufacturer. True audiophiles may want to visit an aftermarket sound system dealer for better equipment, service, and prices. In any case, as mentioned, there is no guarantee your car will be worth more at resale unless you find someone with a particular interest in the sound system.
- **Fancy electronics.** Many cars have options such as GPS and DVD players. If you can do without these items, don't choose them here. You are paying much more for this option to be included with your car than you would if you bought it separately.

Here are some items that almost certainly are not going to be repaid to you at resale time…

- **Appearance packages.** Pinstripes, special decals, paint, trim, and upholstery preservation all add to the dealer's profit but almost never to your car's resale value. In fact, some packages may make it more difficult to resell, just like an unusual color. Personalization is great when it's personalized to your taste.
- **Odd colors.** Some buyers appreciate unusual colors like lime green or tangerine. Other buyers might prefer more traditional colors. It's hard to find buyers for this unusual colors. Make sure it is worth it to you.

Turn Your Head

Backup cameras are de rigeur in new cars. The cameras employ a tiny camera installed somewhere on the back end of the car and a video screen on the instrument panel. The video camera is wonderful at spotting children, pets, and obstacles below the rear window's line of vision. Most project a set of electronic lines on the screen to indicate the direction of your car even if the steering wheel is turned. You should never use the video screen alone—also check the rearview mirror and look over your shoulder.

Start the Negotiating Process Like a Pro

Here's how I bought my most recent car (which was actually me assisting my son, who was ready to buy his first new car). I began by spending a few hours researching cars on the internet, starting with independent appraisals by *Consumer Reports* and moving on to the technical and enthusiast write-ups in the online versions of *Car and Driver* and a few other publications. On behalf of my son—who uses his car in his work and puts many miles on his personal vehicle—I was concentrating on models that were highly rated for reliability and durability. We were much less interested in 0-to-60 miles-per-hour ratings and styling features.

And although both of us wanted a car that would sip economically from its tank of gas, we knew that the difference between a car rated at 24 miles per gallon and one at 30 miles per gallon was probably not all that meaningful. All cars in the same category—in this case, a compact sedan—are going to deliver good performance. Paying several thousand dollars extra for the potential of a few extra miles per gallon is almost certainly not cost effective. You might or might not ever make up the difference in cost over the period of time you own the car.

Once we had narrowed down the selection of cars to three or four models, we examined the available trim levels and option packages. All of that information is available online at the websites of the three manufacturers.

After we had narrowed down an exact model at a particular maker, we moved on—within the same website—to an option to find a matching model in the inventory of local dealers. Entering a zip code yielded a list of three or four dealers within about 40 miles of my son's home, and a list of cars that matched exactly—or closely—the one he had selected. Here we entered into the dealers' websites. On most listings we saw the MSRP and a so-called "special discounted price."

The advantage of doing your initial research in this manner is that you learn what is available on the dealer's lot and you have what amounts to the initial offer by the dealer. That's the price you carve away from, not the MSRP.

When you search for cars in this way, you are asked to enter your name, phone number, and email address. Be prepared to receive phone calls. I often will use a false phone number and a real email address. As soon as I get the first email from the dealer, I send back a reply saying, "Yes, I am in fact soon ready to buy a car but please contact me by email only until I call you."

Buy a Car Without Visiting the Dealer

In my email communications with car dealers, I make it clear that I am really in the market for a car and I specify the particular vehicle, trim level, and options. And I resist responses that are, "Let's schedule a time for you to come in and take a test drive." Instead, I make it clear that my time is valuable and that I want to get as much information as possible before I visit the dealership.

Here's what I have learned in buying more than a few cars in this way: Some dealers get it, and some do not. Many dealers are assigning a salesperson to respond to inquiries that arrive over the internet, and some—but not all—of those salespeople are easy to work with. My goal is to weed out the dealers who give me a problem before I even set foot in their store, and to encourage

Useful Sites for Car Buyers

Here are some websites I recommend for people looking to buy a car.

Magazines:

Automobile at AutomobileMag.com
Car and Driver at CarAndDriver.com
Consumer Reports at Consumer Reports.org/cars
Road and Track at RoadAndTrack.com

Car-Buying Services:

AARP at AARP.org/auto/info-2015/aarp-car-auto-buying-program.html
Consumer Reports at ConsumerReports.org/cro/car-prices-build-buy-service
Costco at Costco.com/auto-program-services.html
Vets Cars at Vetscars.com

Other Resources:

Edmunds at Edmunds.com
Kelley Blue Book at KBB.com/new-cars
NADA Guides (from the National Automobile Dealers Association) at NADAguides.com
TRUECar at TrueCar.com

Here are the top-selling manufacturers of vehicles sold in the United States and Canada. You can find the website for any brand by entering its name in a search engine such as Google or Bing…

- Acura (part of Honda) at Acura.com
- Audi (part of Volkswagen) at AudiUSA.com
- BMW at BMWusa.com
- Chevrolet (part of General Motors) at Chevrolet.com
- Chrysler (part of Fiat Chrysler Automobiles, FCA) at Chrysler.com
- Dodge (part of FCA) at Dodge.com
- Ford Motor Company at Ford.com
- General Motors (including Buick, Cadillac, Chevrolet, and GMC) at GM.com
- Honda at Honda.com
- Hyundai at HyundaiUSA.com
- Infiniti (part of Nissan) at InfinitUSA.com
- Jeep (part of FCA) at Jeep.com
- Kia at Kia.com
- Lexus (part of Toyota) at Lexus.com
- Mazda at MazdaUSA.com
- Mercedes at MBusa.com
- Nissan at NissanUSA.com
- RAM (Part of FCA) at RamTrucks.com
- Subaru at Subaru.com
- Tesla at Tesla.com
- Toyota at Toyota.com
- Volkswagen at VW.com
- Volvo at VolvoCars.com/us

perhaps three dealers to start the process by giving me a price quote on a car that is available right now.

Once I have narrowed down the range of dealers and available cars and have in hand actual price quotes, I contact the salesperson. I specify the exact car he or she has offered—either by VIN or a dealer identification number included in the quote—and I pose the following question by email or over the phone: "Please give me your very best price if I were to come over and buy the car today. I want to know the full bottom line price: the price for the car with all the options you have specified, the cost of documentation, and your calculation of sales tax."

I do this with my three dealer candidates. I am quite determined to cut off communication with any salespeople who do not provide the information exactly as I ask for it. If they respond with, "When can you come in to sit down with me to get the best deal?" I tell them that they will not have a chance at my business if they don't do the deal my way. And when they do respond, I always respond something like this: "Thank you. But that price is still too high. Would you like to try again with a better offer, or should I try one of your competitors?"

I know. It sounds like I am a tough customer. Thank you very much.

The final step: Pick one or perhaps two dealers and call them by phone and push a little (or a lot) more. I have purchased several cars for myself or for family members entirely on the phone. In one case, after the dealer had sent me a copy of the purchase agreement by email, I used a credit card to make a deposit and three days later I made my first and only visit to the dealership to pick up the vehicle.

At worst, you may have to go to the dealership to sign papers and leave a check as a deposit. Make sure the paperwork matches the specific car you are buying and that all the numbers are identical to the deal you have agreed to by email or over the phone. Skip the donuts. They're bad for you.

When do I test drive the car? Sometimes the only time I test drive the car is just before I sign the agreed paperwork just to make sure that there are no obvious defects. The fact is that unless you are a car enthusiast looking for some special, ineffable quality, you can learn all you need to know about a vehicle by reading reviews and examining models you see on

Past the Gatekeeper

If a website insists you provide a telephone number, how do you get a phony phone number that is not going to ring at the home of some innocent neighbor but will get you past an insistent website? In the United States, numbers beginning with 555 and in the range of 0100 to 0199 are reserved for use in movies, television, and books.

You test it out on your own phone: Try dialing an area code and 555-0150, for example.

You can also use an app that you can add to your smartphone that gives you a second phone number. Save that number for a few uses, including a temporary way to communicate with a dealer. I am determined to avoid giving my phone number to someone who will either badger me with calls I do not want, or worse, sell that number to telemarketers.

Some cellular providers offer that second phone number as part of their service. Or, you just search the internet for *second phone line app*.

the street. I also rent cars often as I travel, and I know—for example—that there are very few vehicles I cannot get used to in an hour or so of driving.

Pick the Best Day to Shop

Whether you want to buy a car in person, over the internet or by telephone, you can put the calendar to your advantage. Not every day is the same at a car dealership.

- **The first few weeks and sometimes longer after a hot new model arrives is the worst time to try to get a discount on that vehicle.** If the dealer has more buyers than cars, the price is going to stay at—or sometimes above—the MSRP. It also might mean that the previous year's version of the same car might be available at a good price, or other models may be selling much more slowly.
- **Nearly all salespeople are paid by commission, which means that they have a built-in pressure to sell something all the time.** A smaller commission on a lower price is better than no sale at all. At the same time, carmakers and dealerships are regularly putting salespeople under pressure to sell "right now" by offering extra bonuses or incentives at slow times of the year.

There are two important concepts to keep in mind here: You want to shop on a day when there are more salespeople and cars than customers, and you might as well take advantage of the pressure that car makers and dealers put on their own salespeople. The worst possible time to try to bargain hard is in the middle of a heavily promoted sale when the dealership is packed with customers.

Therefore, among the best days of the year to shop are the day before Thanksgiving, December 24, and December 31—especially if it is snowing. First of all, these are especially quiet days for the sale of big ticket items. A snowstorm or heavy rain (on any day) helps cut down on visitors, too. And those incentives put in place like sales contests and quotas are almost always tied to the end of the week, the end of the month, or the end of the year. Coming in near the end of the day also adds a bit of leverage. The sales force is tired, worn down by a day that may not have been a terrific one, and anxious to go home. You come in fresh, full of energy, and ready to buy a car.

Remember as you walk in the door (or shop over the internet or by phone) that the salesperson needs you and your money. You're doing him or her a favor by not shopping at the other dealer down the block, something you can casually mention. And you can let the salesperson know that you're willing to do another favor by buying a car on this terribly slow day…if he or she is willing to cut you a fine deal on your terms.

Buy a Car at the Dealership

Even if you are going to buy a car by visiting the dealership, I still recommend that you do as much research as possible ahead of time by internet or over the phone. When you arrive at the dealership (late in the month, late in the day, during a snowstorm or heavy rain) do so with a price you have already been offered or see in a print ad. If you see an ad on television or hear one on the radio that includes a price, chances are you are not going to be able to record all the details including incentives, down payments, and the like—but you can try.

Then make it clear to the salesperson that you are a savvy consumer and will make an informed effort not to be taken advantage of.

Studies show a few things that, like them or not, you should be aware of. Please don't blame the stereotypes and prejudices on me.

- **Men are often treated differently than women,** with an assumption that females are less likely to be as fully informed on things vehicular, more likely to react to an emotional pitch, and less likely to push hard for a deal. One study, by researchers at Yale University, said that women are quoted prices an average of $200 higher than men. If you are a woman, fight back. (And consider bringing along a man—even if he is a totally clueless buyer. I'll discuss the advantage of having a mostly silent partner of either sex in a moment.)

There may be a similar treatment given senior citizens and a similar tactic to use: Bring along a younger silent partner who will wait for the proper moment to enter the talks. (While writing this book, my elderly father decided it was time for a new car. He went to a dealer and negotiated a price, and then—with the saleswoman sitting across from him—called me at my desk 200 miles away. Five minutes later—shortly after the saleswoman realized that I knew just a bit about the game and after I allowed her to hear me clicking away randomly at my computer keyboard—the price defrosted by about $1,000.)

- **Some salesmen report a bias favoring white-collar over blue-collar buyers.** Consider dressing up a bit, but avoid the Armani three-piece suit.
- **Take notes.** Not only is this a great way to keep track of the progress from the opening gambit to final price, but it also puts the salesperson on notice that you are not intending to be buried under a windstorm of offhand comments and varying price points.

If you find that the salesman is trying hard to talk you out of buying the car on sale in an ad, or if a saleswoman denigrates the quality of her own product offerings you may be the target of a bait-and-switch.

You, of course, are at the dealership because you have researched the current models and believe that the vehicle on sale is a good deal for your needs and is well reviewed by independent testers. Treat any opinion offered by the salesperson with an appropriate amount of suspicion, because that person's self-interest is obvious. Occasionally, though, a salesperson or a politician accidentally tells the truth. The internet is an excellent way to check for complaints and praise.

That brings me to another point: Take your smartphone or other connected digital device with you. With it, you can quickly check most claims the salesperson makes and even quickly visit the website of a competitor or of an independent car-buying service like that of *Consumer Reports* and a few other organizations, which is a great way to push a salesperson off the dime.

But back to a situation where a salesperson is trying to convince you not to accept the dealer's special deal but instead pay more for something else. If you've done your homework and it's a good deal, go for it—after you've tried to improve on it, of course. If the salesperson tells you it's a bad deal, listen very carefully and make notes. Then be prepared to apply the same argument against any other car that is put forth as a substitute.

Finally, if you believe the dealership was advertising something it does not have available for sale (without disclosing that in the ad), contact your state attorney general or consumer affairs office and lodge a complaint. Or perhaps tell the salesperson you're going to do that and then walk—slowly—toward the exit and see if suddenly something wondrous happens.

Get Hip to the Games Dealers Play

Among the first questions you'll be asked when you meet a car salesperson is this: "Do you want to lease or finance the car?" And also, "Do you have a trade-in?"

Duck! Never begin a car negotiation by telling the salesperson how you plan to pay for the car. If you leave those details for later, you'll have a better chance of keeping the power on your side of the table. The best answer, which is also often close to the truth for a savvy consumer: "I don't know."

And then there is this favorite question that many salespeople are trained to ask the buyer: "How much do you want to pay per month?"

Duck again! What the salesperson is trying to do is get you to focus on something other than the bottom line. With a few clicks on the computer, the salesperson can change a three-year loan into a five-year loan or adjust upwards the down payment, reducing the monthly payment but significantly increasing the real cost to you. Your answer: "I don't know. Depends on whether we can come to a great deal today."

And about a trade-in? Duck once more. You should treat a trade-in or an outright sale of a used car as a totally separate transaction as a way to get the lowest price on purchase and the highest price on the sale. The dealer wants to bundle together the two transactions to try and confuse the buyers. I discuss trade-ins in Chapter 22.

Your single goal is to drive down the purchase price of the vehicle you want to buy. If you later move on to negotiate financing or a lease, you can avoid many tricks of the trade that can inflate the purchase price in less obvious ways.

My recommendation: Come to the table with two prices written on the second page of your notebook—an aggressively low but realistic price you would be happy to pay (let's call it your Happy Price) and a slightly higher price that you would be willing to accept (let's call it your Willing Price).

Do everything you can to get the dealer to make the first move. That can include a price you received in response to an email or phone call, or an advertised price. Or you can tell the salesperson that you know what the MSRP is, but that it is not an acceptable price. Then say, "Give me a better price." Counter with a price that is a few hundred *below* your Happy Price and stick to it for as long as possible. You can explain how you came up with the number, demonstrating your understanding of dealer cost, holdbacks, and rebates. Or you can just say, "This is what I think is a fair price." If the salesperson disputes your logic, answer with a shrug and stick to your price.

You've made your offer, and it's now the salesperson's turn. Make it clear you're waiting to hear a response. If there is no movement on your offer, gather up your papers and prepare to walk out the door. If the price comes down substantially toward your real Happy Price, make a counteroffer.

Most salespeople are trained to keep negotiations underway as long as there is a bit of movement from the buyer. From your side of the table, that does not mean that the salesperson comes down $500 you should go up $500. Be asymmetrical. Go up $100. What's the point of playing a game if you're not going to have some fun? Finally, some salespeople try to push you over the line by declaring that their latest price is a take-it-or-leave-it deal. If the price is not acceptable to you, go ahead and call their bluff: Leave it. Walk toward the door and see if the salesperson or the general manager chases after you. If one or both is hot on your heels, you're in the catbird seat. If they let you stroll, they either don't want your business or your offer was way out of line.

Always remember that there are other dealers and other cars...and other days, for that matter. And you can always come back and take the take-it-or-leave-it price if that turns out to be the best offer in town.

Recognize the Beauty of a Broken Record

The sales force is going to do everything possible to wear you down, through a well-rehearsed sales pitch, double-teaming, and other techniques. Why shouldn't you do the same to them?

Many salespeople are taught to ask: "What do I have to do to get you to buy this car today?" They're trying to get you to simplify your objections to making a purchase and allow them to make you feel as if you are getting your way. If you answer, "I want to pay less," they may drop the price by a few hundred dollars (while still making an undeservedly large profit) and make you feel guilty for asking for more. If you say, "I want to get more for my trade-in," they may boost the money paid for your old clunker and then point to that when you start to talk about the new-car purchase price.

My preferred response is what I call the broken-record method, and it's something any parent with young children immediately understands. Your kids will just keep asking for what they want, in the same way and in the same terms, over and over again. I don't know about you, but I usually end up caving in to my kids just to get them to leave me alone.

So, try it yourself with an auto salesperson...

Salesperson: "What do I have to do to get you to buy this car today?"

You: "Sell it to me for $21,700 in metallic blue with the roof rack, and I'll take your offer of zero percent financing."

Salesperson: "Listen, my boss says he'll let me sell you the car for $23,000 even, which is below our cost. It's the best deal I've ever seen."

You: "That's nice. Here's what I want: Sell me the car for $21,700 in metallic blue with the roof rack, at zero percent financing."

Salesperson: "What if we threw in floor mats, a free steak dinner, and a set of fuzzy dice for the rearview mirror?"

You: "Lovely. I'll take them. $21,700 in metallic blue with the roof rack, the floor mats, and the fuzzy dice. You can keep the steak dinner."

You get the idea.

Double-Team Them

Double-teaming is one time-honored sales tactic at the dealership. If the salesperson you're working with senses both sides have reached a brick wall in the negotiating process, he or she might call in an associate or one of the managers for a bit of a tag team effort.

In the worst situation, the new person at the table may try to begin the negotiation at square one, or may take a much harder line than the original negotiator. The idea here may be to get you to jump at the chance to get back to a deal with the original salesperson. Or, the new negotiator may seem to be such a nice guy that you'll want to strike a deal to avoid having to see your original companion.

Exercise your right to walk out the door if you don't like the way you are being treated. You don't have to talk to a closer or a manager if you don't want to.

Bring Your Own Tag Team

Earlier in this chapter I mention how you might want to bring along a mostly silent partner: He or she can be a friend, a significant other, or anyone else you trust to wait for exactly the right moment to jump into the fray. (Some people call it having a third baseman.) At the very least, your friend can help you stay on your game plan if you start to waver. But you can also collaborate on a game plan, perhaps including a verbal signal.

Let your assistant watch quietly through the first few rounds of bargaining. And then, from your assistant: "This is going nowhere. You've seen better offers elsewhere. Why don't we leave?" Or your assistant can wake up and suggest you make a counteroffer that is all the way back to below your Happy Price even if you have moved a bit away from it. It will drive the salesperson nuts, but that's okay. "You're right," you say. "That was my price, wasn't it?"

It's your very own version of Good Cop/Bad Cop. Have your buddy take a hard line on price while you pull back a bit from the negotiations. The salesperson—and maybe the sales manager—may realize you've got game.

Fight Off a Hostage Situation

There's one more annoying but common tactic among car salesforces: I call it the *us-against-them whine*.

It works like this: After a decent period of haggling, the salesperson suddenly seems to be taking your side, agreeing that your offer is a reasonable one. "Let's write it up and I'll take it in to the general manager to see if she'll accept it," he says. All of a sudden, you're being informed that the salesperson actually doesn't have the authority to strike a deal.

TIP

Take control of the negotiating. Stop letting the salesperson tell you, "You'll have to give me something better to bring to the sales manager." Instead, start saying: "You'll have to do better than that on the price or I'll have to go somewhere else."

When you get tired of hearing the salesperson ask, "What do I have to do to get you to buy a car today?" turn the question around. Ask, "Why won't you let me buy a car today? I'm ready to make a deal on these terms. . . ."

If the salesperson asks you for a little concession on your offer so that he or she can have something new to take to the sales manager, don't do so without asking for a little concession in return. Say something like: "I'll give you $300 more for the car if you include that better set of tires we discussed earlier."

What has truly happened is that you have come close enough to a selling price where the salesperson thinks you can be worn down by the general manager. After a few minutes (probably devoted to a cup of coffee and a donut with the guys in the back room), the salesperson will come out with a hangdog look. "She turned us down," you're told. "I thought we had a good offer, but she says that the car you want is just too hot to let go for that price. In fact, she tells me that there's another customer coming in tonight who wants to buy the car at full price."

It is, of course, all a game intended to get you to cave. The salesperson is not your friend or else he wouldn't be trying to take more out of your pocket than you want to spend. Time to say "No thanks" and then walk slowly toward the exit again. See if the general manager will follow. Be prepared to keep walking if he or she doesn't follow you.

In an odious variation, the salesperson will ask you to give a deposit to show the sincerity of your offer. The effect of this is to make it feel more difficult for you to stand up and walk out the door when your offer is refused. Flat-out refuse a request for a deposit until your offer is accepted by the dealership. You want to keep the power on your side of the table.

Drive Away from Extended Service Contracts

Auto dealers may try to slip this one by you at the last moment, after you have negotiated the price for a new or used car but before you sign on the bottom line. No wonder, either, since these extended-warranty contracts are often a great deal—for the dealer.

Most consumer groups and auto experts recommend against buying such coverage. You'd do better researching the repair and breakdown history of the car you want to buy and checking the reputation of the maker and the dealer. If the dealer tries hard to convince you to purchase an extended warranty, ask the salesperson if that is because the car is unreliable, or because this is a profit area for the dealer. And then still don't buy one.

Here are the danger areas…

- **You don't want to pay twice for coverage you already have.** You can't collect double. How many miles and which systems are covered by the manufacturer? What systems and what time or mileage limitations are in the extended warranty?

- **There may be large deductibles that must be satisfied before you are repaid.** Is the contract valid only at the dealer who sold it to you? What happens if you have a problem on the road? How are reimbursements made? Must you lay out money and then submit a claim, or is the dealer obligated to perform the service and deal with the administrator on your behalf?

- **Verbal agreements mean nothing.** Do not accept any verbal representations about the coverage. If a system is not specifically included in writing, assume that it is not covered by the warranty.

- **The warranty may have exclusions.** If you are purchasing a used car, a demonstrator car that has been used by salesmen but has never been registered, or a fleet lease vehicle, see if the extended warranty has any exclusions. Does its coverage start when you take possession of the car, or is it back dated to when the vehicle was registered by its original owner?

- **The business backing the warranty may not be in business by the time you need it to pay up.** Who is behind the contract: the manufacturer, the dealer, or an independent company? Of the three, the manufacturer is most likely to still be in business at the end of the contract term, followed by the dealer (in most cases). What happens if the provider shuts down? Many service contracts sold by dealers are actually products offered by independent companies called administrators. The administrators act as claims adjusters, authorizing—or denying—claims payment to dealers.

Are you convinced not to pay for an extended warranty?

Do the Math Yourself

You've just spent four hours haggling over every nickel and dime on the purchase price of your new car, perhaps moving on to the trade-in value of your old vehicle, and then dealt with financing. You've wisely passed on unnecessary dealer packs like rustproofing, undercoating, and pinstriping, and you've avoided wasteful extended warranties. Now the salesperson disappears into the business office to prepare the paperwork and comes back with the sales agreement for you to sign.

Stop. Take a breath. Bring out your calculator (there's one on your smartphone). It's time to check the numbers and do the math.

There are dozens of figures to be put in place on the sales agreement and loan or lease application if you are financing the car through the dealer. This means there are dozens of places where an innocent mistake—or a purposeful fraud—can end up costing you hundreds or thousands of dollars.

I'll try to be charitable here. Mistakes happen. But why do they almost always seem to be in the favor of the dealership? *Here are some suggestions…*

• **That notepad I suggested you keep at your side?** It should have all the numbers that should be on the agreement: the purchase price, including the cost of all options, the amount of any deposit, the value of your trade-in if there is one, any manufacturer-to-customer rebates, any dealer-to-customer special offers.

• **After you examine the agreement to assure yourself that the correct numbers are listed, do the math to make sure it is correct.** Rebates and dealer specials should be subtracted from the price, not added.

• **Is the agreed-upon charge for documentation and the official state charge for registration listed properly?**

• **Is the amount of tax calculated based on the bottom line after deductions?**

• **Does the contract list the exact car you agreed to purchase: brand, model, and trim level?** If you are buying a car that is on the lot or one that will be brought from another dealer's lot as a swap, the contract should include the VIN from the actual vehicle. If you are ordering from the factory, make sure all agreed-upon options are listed.

• **Most sales agreements include a New or Used checkbox and a space to list the current odometer reading.** If you are buying a new car, it should say that here. And you should be well aware of the number of miles on the odometer. If the car has more than 300 miles on it from road testing, use that when you negotiate a price. If the box has a much higher number or is left blank, slam on the brakes and walk away: Something may be wrong.

• **If you are financing the car through the dealer (something I explain in Chapter 23), make sure that the loan term (in months or years) is correct and the interest rate is stated properly.** The financing agreement is usually a separate document, and there you will also find the monthly payment, which should match any representations you have been given.

Kelley Blue Book has a loan calculator at KBB.com/car-loans-and-financing. Run the numbers yourself to make sure the payment is correct.

What do you do if you find a whopper of a mistake on the paperwork? If you think it might be the result of an innocent error by the salesperson or the dealership, you can politely but firmly insist that it be corrected. If you believe there has been one last effort to rob you with a fountain pen, walk out the door holding on to a copy of the contract that you can share with your state or local consumer protection agency and the manufacturer who has granted the dealer the right to sell its cars. You don't want to buy from this dealer.

Negotiate a Better Deal at a No-Negotiation Dealership

Over the years, some carmakers (including General Motors' now-defunct Saturn division) and some individual dealerships declared the end to price haggling, instead claiming to reduce prices and sell them as if you were buying boxes of cereal off the shelf of a supermarket. In theory, this idea is likable since it removes a great deal of the unacceptable padding that sits between a dealer's true cost and the selling price. But as you might guess, I am skeptical.

You may come across a dealership that proclaims that its prices are marked down already to save you the trouble of negotiating. As far as I am concerned, that sounds to me like an invitation to engage. You have ways to negotiate a better deal, even if a no-negotiation car store insists on sticking to its price. The trick is to negotiate everything else.

Start by making an offer 3% to 5% below the supposedly nonnegotiable price. What's the worst that could happen? They might accept the offer, counter with a lesser discount, or stick to their shelf price, at which point you can accept it or walk away.

- **If you trade in a vehicle at a no-negotiation car store, ask for a higher price**—above book value—for your old vehicle to give you the equivalent of a discount on the new car.
- **If you are financing the new-car purchase**, ask for a reduced interest rate or a subsidized loan.
- **If you want to add a dealer-installed option or accessory**, ask that it be included free or at a substantial discount.

Remember that the power still resides on your side of the table. Most any dealer or car store would rather make a bit less profit on a deal than no profit at all. Make it clear that you are willing to go down the road to another dealership where they still haggle over the selling price and see if the no-negotiation dealer will really let you walk out the door.

Get an Insider Price

Direct employees of most carmakers and many dealership employees can get insider prices on purchase of new vehicles. The price is usually very close to the invoice price, which is the target area I have been advising in this chapter. Subject to change, here's one way to get a similar deal if you are not an employee but merely "part owner" of a car company.

As just one example, Ford Motor Company offers something called X-Plan prices to people who own at least 100 shares of stock. (You must have held the shares for a certain number of months and you can get only one discount every certain number of months for yourself or an immediate family member. Check with your local Ford dealer or search online for details.) The deal gives you a preset price just above dealer invoice on some but not all Ford vehicles.

This preset price is sometimes—but not always—better than what you could negotiate on your own. And there is nothing that says you cannot use that preset price as your starting point as you make a lower offer.

In addition to employee discounts, you might qualify for other discounts. For example, AARP members can take advantage of an auto-buying program (Blinc.Media/2vxRUmK). Directly ask dealers (and manufacturers) if they offer veteran discounts or go to VetsCars.com to find resources. No matter what organization you are a member of, ask a leading member or search online for *car discount organization*.

CHAPTER 22

Selling or Buying a Used Car

There is one basic reason to buy a used car: In most cases, the moment you drive a new car off the dealer's lot, its resale value drops by thousands of dollars. After then, depreciation slows considerably. If you can find a clean, well-maintained used car that is just a few years old, someone else has paid for that rapid depreciation. Modern cars are pretty well made, and you can expect them to last 100,000 miles or more before they are not worth maintaining and repairing. Of course, there is one basic trick here, too: You've got to guard against buying someone else's problem secondhand. Before you worry too much about buying a used car with a troubled background, remember that even a new car can be a lemon.

Selling or buying a used car is very different from buying a new car. *The biggest difference*: There is no list price. *The second most significant difference*: Although certain basic laws and regulations are meant to guard against misrepresentation or fraud, a used car generally represents a bit of a risk to the buyer. On the other hand, a deal gone well can amount to a much better bargain.

There is also a big difference between selling or buying a used car as an individual, or selling or buying a used car through a used-car dealer. And there is a third situation that can present even more complexities—trading in a used car as part of the purchase of a new car.

In this chapter, I'll explain how to check out used cars, how to consider used-car warranties, and how to negotiate the best price for previously owned vehicles. I'll also offer tips that help you move the power to your side of the table when you negotiate for a used car, and advice for carefully engaging in a trade-in deal at a new car dealership.

- **Know the basics of the used-car market.**
- **Sell a car by yourself.**
- **Get the facts on a used car's history.**
- **Trade in at a new car dealership.**
- **Buy a used car from a dealer.**
- **Check rental car and fleet sales.**
- **Avoid used-car trickery.**
- **Conduct a smell test on a used car.**
- **Call in the Feds for safety.**
- **Learn how to tell a car's model year.**

Know the Basics of the Used Car Market

When you buy a new car, you can reasonably assume that the car has been driven only a few dozen miles in testing and that it has not suffered any accident damage. Beyond that you have a reasonable expectation of support from the dealer under the manufacturer's warranty. Additionally, you can make some assumptions about the car's life expectancy and future resale value based on the history of other vehicles from that manufacturer that were sold as new.

For used cars...well, it's complicated.

When you buy a used car, the number of miles can vary from very low to unreasonably high. Mileage is an important consideration in car buying. If you figure a car has a useful life of about 120,000 miles, buying a car with 60,000 miles on the odometer means you are buying a car with half the expected life of a new vehicle, and that is assuming the car has been properly maintained and driven with care. In addition, the vehicle is most likely no longer under warranty for most components, and repair costs for an older car, especially one with a great many miles on the odometer, is higher than a new one.

Keep in mind these two key tips for buying any used car...

- **Compare the seller's asking price with the average retail price in the *Kelley Blue Book* or another car price guide.** You'll find these online. If you're going to be borrowing money to purchase a used car, your bank or other lending institution may be able to help you determine its value. Most institutions will check the value when you apply anyway. They will not want to loan you more than a car is worth.

Here are some sites to check...

- Edmunds at Edmunds.com
- *Kelley Blue Book* at KBB.com
- NADA at NadaGuides.com

- **Never buy a used car without having a mechanic you trust give the car a full checkup.** An automobile club such as the AAA may offer this service. Ask the mechanic to spend as much as an hour on the job. An investment of perhaps $100 here can end up saving you thousands on a lemon.

There are some things you can check for yourself before paying for a mechanic. *Here are a few...*

- Look for oil or other fluid leaks on the pavement below the car.
- Push down and then release each of the four corners of the vehicle; there should be a reasonable amount of resistance and a quick return to the original place. If it is too easy to push down, or if the car bounces a few times that probably indicates problems with the suspension.
- Check the tires for excessive or uneven wear, which could indicate problems with the suspension and running gear and/or the need for new tires.
- Take the car for a test drive, paying special attention to the brakes, steering, the responsiveness of the engine.

The largest source of used cars is resales by individuals. About 40% of used cars are sold this way, and this is also where you will find the best prices. About one third of previously owned cars are sold off the used-car lots of new-car dealers. The remainder are sold by independent used-car lots and from rental and fleet auctions.

Examine each source.

New-Car Dealers

Here are the advantages of shopping for a used car from a new-car dealer…

- **Dealers may have the largest selection of recent car models, especially those made by the manufacturer they offer in the new-car showroom.** New-car dealers want to showcase the best used cars for the models they sell since it helps bolster their claims about resale value and the quality of their product.

- **Dealers should be well equipped to service used cars made by the manufacturers of the cars they sell new.** This should also increase the value of a used-car warranty offered by the dealer.

- **A well-run dealership understands that its good name in the community is an essential element of its business.** Although they may sell at a higher price than other sources, they are more likely to stand behind a vehicle they sell. They are also governed by federal and state regulations covering elements of the contract as well as fulfilling all laws about safety and emission standards.

- **Under regulations set by the FTC, all used-car dealers must display a Buyer's Guide sticker on the vehicle.** The most important element of this sticker is a written statement of any warranties.

  The Buyer's Guide must include the following information: whether the dealer offers a warranty and, if so, its terms and conditions, including the coverage duration, the percentage of total repair costs the dealer will pay, and which vehicle systems the warranty covers.

  In some states, dealers cannot sell a vehicle as-is. They must offer some sort of warranty.

- **You have a reasonable expectation that cars resold by a dealership have a clean title.** Before signing a purchase contract, however, request to see a copy of the Carfax report or other history of the ownership of the vehicle. I discuss Carfax and similar reports in more detail later in this chapter.

And here are some disadvantages…

- **A new-car dealership is usually the most expensive place to buy a used car.** Dealers have high overheads and also seek to balance profit margins between increasingly expensive new cars and proportionally more valuable used vehicles.

- **You will be dealing with trained, experienced negotiators.** That doesn't mean, however, you can't stand your ground and insist on a fair price.

- **Think twice before buying a used car that is not a specialty of the new-car showroom at the lot.** The dealer's service department may know everything there is to know about Fords, but Volvos are a foreign species in more ways than one. Ask about how they will handle warranty and repair services.

Used Car Lots

Used-car dealers do not have to support the operations of the new-car dealership, and their business model is much simpler: buy at wholesale and sell at retail without any connection to a new-car business. *Here are some advantages to buying from a used car lot...*

• **Prices are often lower at a used-car dealer than at a new-car dealer's used lot because of lower overheads.**

• **Used-car lots usually offer a wider range of manufacturers and may also have some older, less costly vehicles for sale.** A new-car dealer might not want to showcase a vehicle with a dent or faded paint job. A used-car dealer might be willing to make a few hundred dollars in profit on a junker.

And here are the disadvantages...

• **Most used-car dealers do not have service departments, which is inconvenient.**

• **A warranty offered by a used-car lot should be considered suspect unless the dealer can convince you otherwise.** If the lot does not have its own service facility, where are you supposed to go for warranty repairs? If it does have a garage, are the mechanics capable of repairing a 1998 Hyundai, a 2008 Ford, and a 2018 Subaru?

• **Used-car dealers are less likely to have a long list of old customers who have an ongoing relationship with the business, and are often somewhat transitory operations.** They may open and close after a relatively short time in business, they may move to a new piece of land across town, and they may change ownership more often than would a new-car dealership. If all goes well with your car, this is no problem for you. On the other hand, if you have problems within the warranty period or discover misrepresentation in the sale, you may have difficulty reconnecting with the seller.

That doesn't mean every used-car lot is so shaky. Ask around. Check with the Better Business Bureau and with friends and neighbors who may have bought vehicles from them in the past.

About the FTC Buyer's Guide for Used Cars

Used-car dealers must display an FTC-mandated Buyer's Guide sticker on one of the right-side windows of each vehicle. It is required to inform you whether the vehicle is sold with a warranty, with implied warranties, or as is.

Here's what to look for and what questions to ask...

• **Is the original manufacturer's warranty still in effect?** If yes, can it be transferred to you? Is there a fee to do so? What is covered and under what limitations of time, mileage, and systems?

• **If a manufacturer's warranty is unavailable, can I rely on an implied warranty?** Two business terms apply here: Under a *warranty of merchantability*, the buyer has a reason to assume that a product will do what it is supposed to do. A stove should heat water and a car should run (and pass state inspection). If the car does not run, the dealer must fix it or refund the purchase price. The way around this is to sell the car "as is." If you accept that sort of deal, the car is yours to fix, even if it won't move off the car lot. Some states prohibit or place limitations on as-is sales by dealers. A *warranty of fitness for a particular purpose* applies when you buy a vehicle based on a dealer's representation that it is suitable for a particular use—hauling a trailer, for example. You are a lot safer to obtain a dealer's written statement of suitability for a particular use rather than relying on an oral statement.

- **Can you offer a service contract on the used vehicle?** Be sure to study the written terms of that contract, and do not accept any verbal representations about its coverage.

I am *not* a fan of service contracts. They generally have more holes than a block of Swiss cheese. In my opinion, you are better off by starting off with a mechanically sound vehicle and then developing and sustaining relationship with a good mechanic.

Private Car Sales

If you've got the time, and go about it properly, you may find a good deal in buying directly from an owner. Look for ads in the classified sections of your local newspaper, on bulletin boards, and online on sites such as Craigslist.org.

Here are the advantages of buying directly from the former owner…

- **A properly priced used car sold by an individual will come in about midway between the *wholesale price*** (the price a car dealer could expect to receive if it had to dispose of a used car at auction to other dealers) and the *retail price* (the marked-up price a car dealer might ask for resale).

- **In most cases you won't negotiate with a professional salesperson and you can hope for better success in making a deal satisfactory to both parties.**

And the disadvantages…

- **If the vehicle is relatively young, it may still come under the remaining months or years of the manufacturer's warranty; make sure the coverage is properly transferred.** If the car is out of warranty, you're pretty much on your own unless fraud was committed in the sale of the car. Your only recourse may be to sue in the case of outright fraud, such as misrepresenting the model year, an odometer rollback, or other violations. Be sure to obtain any representations about the car, including VIN, mileage, and price, in writing.

- **Closely examine the title to make sure there are no third parties (like a bank) holding a lien on the vehicle.**

- **Take the car to your own mechanic for a checkup.**

- **Some private car sellers are inexperienced at negotiating prices.** They may set their prices unrealistically high and be unwilling to negotiate to a fair level. Some sellers may be emotionally attached to a car or to a price for that car. Remember—and don't hesitate to gently point out—that the resale price for a used car has almost a passing connection to the cost of the car when new. On the other hand, a private seller may be desperate to unload a vehicle to raise money. He or she may be willing to accept less to end the hassle of meeting with tire kickers.

Sell a Car by Yourself

If you are selling a used car to an individual—a "retail" sale—the process is pretty simple. You determine the car's *book value* from easily available listings on the internet or in some publications, adjusting it up or down based on its condition, the number of miles it has been driven, and the presence or absence of certain options. Then you place an ad or list the car on an online site or put a placard in its window and drive around town. When you are approached by a buyer, you can expect a bit of negotiation, but in the end the car should sell for something close to its retail value as adjusted for its condition.

In general, a sale between two individuals is an *as is* transaction, although some states may offer the buyer a small bit of protection. Basically, as long as you do not misrepresent the condition of a vehicle or its history, it is up to the buyer to determine the car's value.

What kind of misrepresentation could get you into trouble?

- **Rolling back the odometer or other tampering that would lead a buyer to make a decision based on false appearance.** It is nice to see a car that has been *detailed* (cleaned up and polished), but be cautious if the engine compartment is clean enough to eat off. A steam-cleaned engine may indicate cleaning to remove traces of oil or other leaks.
- **An imperfect title, such that you do not have full ownership of the vehicle or otherwise cannot sell it.** Clean up the title before you try to sell the vehicle. If you owe money to a lender, in some states they hold onto the title until the loan is repaid.
- **A verbal or written statement that the car is in "perfect" condition (no vehicle meets that criteria).**

Get the Facts on a Used Car's History

More than a few websites will deliver a report on any vehicle. That report will tell you a great deal of information that is gathered from state motor vehicle registries, manufacturers, insurance companies, and other sources. It should tell you about major accidents, airbag deployment, flood damage, multiple owners, inspections, recall information, history of theft or other police incidents, and much more. Some used-car dealers offer to show you exactly this sort of information as part of their sales process. That's not a bad thing, assuming that the report is for the exact car you are considering buying and is recent.

The best-known car history service is Carfax. You can obtain a Carfax report yourself by visiting that company's website (at Carfax.com) and entering the vehicle's VIN, which you can see on every modern car just below the windshield on the driver's side as well as other places including a plate on the driver's door frame and on the firewall at the rear of the engine compartment. Manufacturers also engrave the VIN onto parts of the frame and other body parts as part of law enforcement efforts. You can also search by license plate number. You can purchase a single report for about $40 or get 60 days of unlimited reports for about $55.

Carfax, in my opinion, offers the most complete reports. There are other services that come close, including Autocheck.com.

That's a Wash

Don't fall victim to a washed car—and I'm not talking about one that has been cleaned with a hose and sponge. Cars that have been submerged in water are quite likely to suffer electrical problems, rust, and other issues. I wouldn't buy one and neither should you.

After a hurricane or a major flood, thousands or tens of thousands of vehicles (half a million after Hurricane Katrina in 2005) are declared a total loss by insurance companies. Some of them are crushed and recycled but more than a few end up in the hands of unscrupulous resellers who move them to other parts of the country and put them through a few title changes, washing them of at least part of their history. This practice is illegal, and the flood information should show up on a car history report. But if you see many title changes, especially if you see that a car started its life in a hurricane zone and then showed up months later far away, be suspicious.

Look for signs of water damage inside glove compartments and below seats. Are there stains or missing components? Has the carpeting been changed from the factory-fitted original, for example?

You can also visit the National Motor Vehicle Title Information System at VehicleHistory.gov, a website created by the US Department of Justice in cooperation with state motor vehicle administrators with a concentration on stolen vehicles, cars involved in criminal activities, and other events that would bring a vehicle to the attention of government agencies. This site also offers links to several private services that collect information about a vehicle's history.

Here are some important questions to ask, especially when you want to buy a car for more than a few hundred dollars...

• **Did you buy this car new, or was it used when you purchased it?** If the seller bought it from a new-car dealer, that tells you it was sold under the manufacturer's warranty. If it was purchased used, you're going to have to dig a bit deeper to find out its history because there may have been multiple owners along the way.

• **Has the car ever sustained damage to its body or frame?** Has it ever been in a flood? Again, you should find its history. If the seller says "No," but a Carfax or other history search says otherwise, I suggest taking your business elsewhere.

• **May I see the title?** You want to make sure the seller in fact owns the vehicle, and that there is not a lien on the car by a bank or other lender. You can buy a car from a seller who still owes money on it, but the seller has to pay off the loan to be able to deliver a clean title to you. Check with the motor vehicle bureau in your state for any advice on title transfers. Most states—but not all—include information on the title that would alert you to the fact that a particular car was returned to the road after being salvaged or otherwise repaired from a major accident.

• **Can I take the car for a test drive, and can I take it to a mechanic for a checkup?** The only acceptable answer to both questions here is "Yes." You can learn a lot about a car by driving for 15 to 30 minutes on city streets and also at highway speed. Speaking for myself, it doesn't matter if the seller accompanies me or just hands me the keys. If you are getting close to buying a used car, make arrangements with a mechanic to put the car up on the rack for an inspection that should disclose damages or repairs to the frame...as well as potential problems with the running gear (the drive shaft or transaxle, suspension, and other components)...as well as the condition of the wheels and tires...and the condition of the engine and its components. Cars that come from cold-weather regions where salt or other chemicals are used to clear roads of ice may be prone to corrosion. A good mechanic should be able to spot this too.

Trade In at a New Car Dealership

On the one hand, trading in a used car as part of a new car purchase can be less hassle than selling the old car yourself. The dealership appraises the used car's value, takes it off your hands, and applies the agreed-upon value toward the purchase price of your new car. On the other hand, here's where many car buyers get taken to the cleaners. First of all, the dealer is going to pay you the wholesale price, not the retail price, and then hope to make a few hundred or a few thousand dollars or more by reselling the car. Second, trading in a car gives the dealer many ways to confuse the negotiating process for a new car. How so? A dealer can underpay you for the value of the used car and then give you what seems to be a fantastic deal on the new car.

You will almost always receive the most for your car if you sell it yourself. The next highest price might come if you sell the car directly to a used-car dealer who will pay you the wholesale value but don't tie that sale into your purchase of another car.

If you are shopping for a new car and might want to dispose of your old car as a trade-in at the same dealer, make it your money-saving goal to prevent the dealer from mixing together your trade-in and new-car bargaining. The salesperson at the new car dealership is going to ask you—probably more than once—if you intend to trade in your present vehicle. Try to avoid giving an answer, or say "I don't know" and concentrate on bringing down the new car's price.

Once you are satisfied with the price for the new car, you can change the subject: "I'd like you to give me a good price for my old car." You already have an idea of the wholesale value of the vehicle from your own research, and perhaps have an offer from an independent used-car lot (see sidebar). You, the one with the power, want to have it both ways—the highest possible price for a trade-in and the lowest possible price for a purchase. Therefore, you want to split up the negotiations to your advantage.

Check for a Lowball

A good strategy if you don't want to sell your car yourself: Take the car to a used-car lot that is not connected to the dealership where you intend to buy a new car. Here you can expect to be offered a price close to the wholesale value.

Don't sell the car immediately. Instead, make note of the price you are offered and take that number with you into your negotiations with a new-car dealer. See if they are trying to lowball you on your trade-in.

Remember that you want to negotiate the purchase price of a new car before you even begin to discuss a trade-in of your existing vehicle. Once that is done, if you have brought your car to one or more used car dealers you know its *wholesale* value. For a trade-in, a fair price is somewhere about midway between the wholesale and retail value of the car; in other words, you can hope to receive less than what you could get if you sold it yourself but not less than what the used car lot offers. How much less? Put a value on the time and effort you would have to go through to sell it yourself.

Don't accept a lowball price from the dealer for your trade-in. Many people think that the price they are being given is written in stone. Remember that *everything is negotiable*. The dealer hopes you will not protest a low offer or will try to negotiate only a small increase. If you are offered $5,000 on a car that has a wholesale value of $10,000, demand an explanation.

Be prepared to walk out the door. You can always come back if you are unable to sell the vehicle on your own at a better price, or can't get another dealer to offer you more.

Buy a Used Car from a Dealer

Many of us have a predisposition against used-car dealers, putting them on the trustworthiness scale somewhere down there with politicians. That's not always accurate, but here is one bit of information that is true: There is often more profit to be made in the sale of used cars than new vehicles.

In the previous chapter, I showed how most car dealers work very hard to make a profit of between a few hundred and a few thousand dollars on most sales. Used-car dealers can easily surpass that level of profit if they can buy at wholesale and sell at retail.

When you are buying directly from an individual, you make a bid based on what you are willing to pay and the seller will accept or reject the offer based on what he or she feels is a fair price. The original purchase price is no longer relevant. The owner factors in the value received for the use of the car and then estimates the resale value. If the seller has to drop the price to make a sale, it represents only a paper loss. Things become more complicated if you are buying a used car from a dealer. The dealer may have bought the car at auction or accepted it as a trade-in from another buyer. Either way, the seller knows its cost and will want to make a profit above the price paid.

Either way, the greatest level of uncertainty in a used-car negotiation is the vehicle's condition. Here is where to spend time and money investigating on your own. If you are buying from a dealer, you include in your decision the value of any warranty or money-back guarantee offered.

When new cars are priced high, the used-car market is likely to be strong. An increase in leasing also returns to the market large numbers of relatively new, low-mileage vehicles each year. In some cases, a one- or two-year-old vehicle may be selling at a price pretty close to its cost when new.

The reason: They are being compared to current models that may have risen sharply in price in recent years. Of course you, as the buyer, can—and should—walk away from an inflated price for a used car. There are still good values to be had. There is no reason to pay new-car prices for a used car.

You can look up a used car's value on the lot using the same online tools I mentioned earlier, including Kelley Blue Book and NADA. Input all details, including mileage, model, trim level, options, and condition. Assume that the dealer paid something close to the *wholesale* price. Check that the asking price is close to the *retail* price, and then make an offer closer to the wholesale price and let the negotiations begin.

Check Rental Car and Fleet Sales

Many automobile experts recommend you consider buying a used car from a rental company. Large companies such as Hertz and Enterprise sell former rental cars. Their logic is that these are mostly low-mileage vehicles that have received regular maintenance and inspection. That is all true, and sometimes the price of a car from a rental fleet is quite good. If you choose this route, though, be sure you understand any warranty terms and have the car inspected by a competent independent mechanic before buying it.

Many people are quite happy with this way of buying a used car. I would be leery of such a deal.

Here's why I would stay away from a rental car: Sometimes these vehicles have been well maintained by their former owners, and sometimes they have been worked quite hard. Ask yourself how you treat a rental car when it is in your possession. Drivers are often much harder on rental cars than on their own vehicles, especially during the critical first 3,000 miles during which new cars are supposed to be babied. In addition, though the mileage may be low, the wear may be high—lots of short trips are much tougher on a car than long-distance commutes.

Avoid Used-Car Trickery

Alas, entire books are filled with the various sneaky, dishonest, and downright illegal tricks that some used-car dealers employ.

Your best defense is this: Never buy a car on impulse. If you find a car to your liking at what seems to be a reasonable price, the next step is to take the vehicle to a trusted mechanic of your choice for a complete exam.

As mentioned earlier, the mechanic should concentrate on the running gear (brakes, transmission, and suspension) and test the engine. He or she should also look for undisclosed accident damage and wear and tear.

Beyond that advice, here are a few other important tips...

- **Don't buy a used car seen only at night.** Outdoor lighting or indoor fluorescents can hide scratches and dents, and make a faded or blotchy paint job look near-perfect.
- **Don't buy a used car that you have only examined in the rain.** Same reasons.
- **Start the car yourself after making sure it hasn't been warmed up before you turned the key.** You want to check the battery, starter, and engine in the most challenging condition. The colder the day, the better.
- **If the vehicle is at the seller's home, ask where it has been parked or garaged.** It won't hurt to examine the garage or the parking space in search of splotches of oil or other fluids that dripped on the ground.

Conduct a Smell Test on a Used Car

A *clean* used car usually means one that has never been in a serious accident, caught fire, or otherwise sustained damage to its structure. If a car has been junked or salvaged, that information should appear on its title. If the owner or dealer has conducted repairs, that information may not be easy to get. Ask about the car's history. Also, conduct your own smell test for signs of major repair.

- **All wisecracks aside about the quality of car manufacturing,** you can reasonably expect that the car looks as if it were properly assembled.
- **Pay close attention to the doors.** Do they open and close properly and line up evenly? Test each one. Misaligned doors are an indication of an accident or rough treatment.
- **Examine the finish.** Are there bumps or dimples? These are possible signs of body filling. Is the paint color the same across the entire car? Look under the hood for signs of overspray in a different color or an older age.
- **Does the engine seem newer than the rest of the car?** This is possibly an indication of an engine swap. (That is not necessarily a bad thing, but you should demand a reasonable explanation—in writing—for the change.) Another possibility is that the engine has been steam cleaned, which could be strictly for aesthetic reasons, or as a way to remove evidence of fluid leaks. A properly suspicious mechanic can stress test an engine to see if oil, transmission fluid, power steering fluid, or cooling water spurts out but sometimes those problems are not evident until the vehicle has been driven for a while.
- **Is there evidence of repair to the engine mountings or the firewall?** Both are indications of a possible accident in the vehicle's past. A mechanic should be able to spot this quickly.
- **Does the car seem older than its miles or its age?** Are the seat springs and upholstery shot? Are the accelerator and brake pedals worn smooth? These may be signs that the car has been poorly maintained or driven more miles than the odometer indicates.
- **Examine the carpeting, especially under seats, beneath floor mats, and under the dashboard, for signs of water damage.**

Call in the Feds for Safety

Whom do you trust when it comes to safety—the salesperson or the crash test dummies? And do you expect whoever is selling the used car to inform you about manufacturer recalls? (Recalls apply to the vehicle, and the manufacturer is required to perform them even if the car has been resold many times.)

After you purchase a used car, contact its manufacturer and ask to be listed as the owner of record for the vehicle for recall purposes. You can check for recalls and vehicle safety records on the National Highway Traffic Safety Administration website at NHTSA.dot.gov. You'll also find information on important components such as tires and child seats; about federal laws regarding odometers; and the latest safety information about air bags.

Learn How to Tell a Car's Model Year

Your car carries around with it a unique identifying code that helps buyers, sellers, and state and federal government agencies track its life. It's called a vehicle identification number (VIN), and it is a federal crime to tamper with or remove it. You'll find the VIN on a car in several locations, usually on the dashboard near the lower-left corner of the windshield on most cars, on the firewall under the hood, on the driver's-side door, and on the frame.

The VIN includes a code for the manufacturer and a unique serial number for the vehicle. For this book, the most interesting part of the VIN is the tenth letter of the code, which tells the vehicle's model year. All vehicles made since 1981 have a seventeen-character code.

Here is a fictitious VIN code, along with a key...

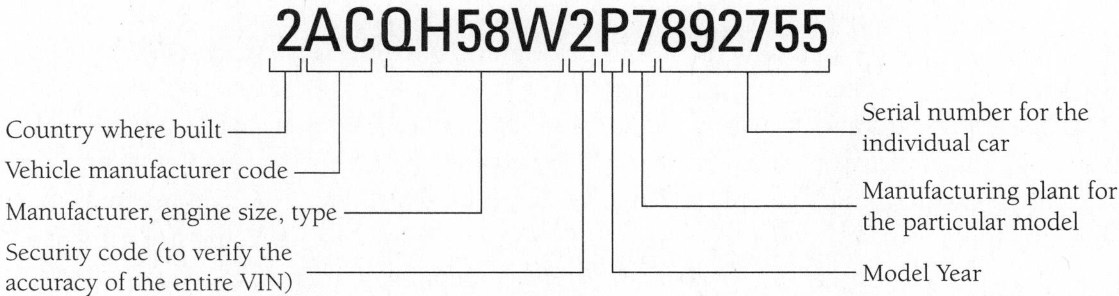

You can easily decode any VIN by entering it into a lookup box on websites. Your insurance company or lending institution can do the same.

Year of the Dragon

Model year character codes began to recycle in the 1980 model year; that's not a problem because the manufacturer can pick up other information from other details in the VIN. *Here's the meaning of that 10th character...*

A: 1980 or 2010	G: 1986 or 2016	N: 1992	W: 1998	4: 2004
B: 1981 or 2011	H: 1987 or 2017	P: 1993	X: 1999	5: 2005
C: 1982 or 2012	J: 1988 or 2018	R: 1994	Y: 2000	6: 2006
D: 1983 or 2013	K: 1989 or 2019	S: 1995	1: 2001	7: 2007
E: 1984 or 2014	L: 1990 or 2020	T: 1996	2: 2002	8: 2008
F: 1985 or 2015	M: 1991	V: 1997	3: 2003	9: 2009

CHAPTER 23

Financing an Auto Purchase or Lease

How will you pay for your new car? The simplest (and often the least expensive) way is to negotiate for the very best price you can get for the purchase of a vehicle and then pay for it with a check drawn from your own savings. If you don't have the scratch, or if you prefer to leave your savings intact, then you have a choice of financing the purchase with a loan or leasing a car.

Car dealers would much rather you not take that simple path. Why? Because there is money to be made in making (or facilitating) a loan or arranging a lease. The financing department is an important income-producer for a dealership. And salespeople are trained to try to get potential buyers not to concentrate on the total cost of a vehicle but instead to think only in terms of the monthly payment. They will push what seem to be very low monthly costs for a lease instead of what sounds like a big number for a purchase. The lease numbers sound attractive, and a lease may in fact make sense for some buyers, but it is important to understand that if you lease a car, you are essentially renting a car for 24 or 36 months (or whatever term you agree to). At the end of the lease, the car goes back to the dealer or leasing company and all you are left with are memories.

You can find ways to move the power to your side of the table when it comes to negotiating financing for a vehicle.

- **Learn how to read a car ad.**
- **Master negotiating the terms of a car loan.**
- **Use a home-equity loan as a source of financing.**
- **Carefully consider the leasing option.**
- **Deal with the repo man.**

Learn How to Read a Car Ad

It's not your eyes or ears. Car dealers really don't want you to read the tiny print at the bottom of the car ads or understand the rapid-fire audio mumble at the end of a radio commercial? Here you'll find some of the most entertaining (and potentially misleading) fiction published today.

Before you sign on the bottom line for automobile financing, make certain you know the loan terms—the terms that are laid out in writing in the loan agreement, not the advertisement or the commercial.

Here are some questions to ask about special offers…

• **Is this an either-or deal—a special interest rate or a rebate from the manufacturer?** If so, compare the rebate value to the amount of money you might save using the special interest rate.

• **Will I have to pay full MSRP or any other form of inflated price for the car in order to receive the reduced-rate loan?** One tip-off that this may be the case is language like this in the ad: "dealer participation required." This means that the dealer is cooperating with the manufacturer to create the special offer. Something has to give, don't you think? Put another way, is the dealer willing to accept a lower price for the car if you pay cash, provide your own financing, or accept a higher interest rate?

• **Does the advertised low price require a larger-than-usual down payment?** One way to artificially reduce the monthly payments is to require that buyers put down a larger portion in advance. That's not necessarily a bad thing, since most experts recommend paying by cash if you can afford to. The point here, though, is to be sure to compare apples with apples as you look at various deals.

• **Is the low price based on a minimum value for a trade-in applied against the purchase of the new car?** Be careful here. Make sure you know the real value of your old car. On the other hand, if you are trading in a junker from the backyard, be sure that the dealer's promised trade-in value does not include exceptions for damage, rust, or high mileage. Don't forget to negotiate the price before you determine the trade-in value.

• **Is the special rate available on all cars, on certain models only, or only on those already in stock at the dealer?** On occasion, some deals that are subsidized by the manufacturer may apply only to cars that are ordered from the factory.

• **Am I required to purchase extra options or services such an extended warranty, or a service contract to qualify for a low interest loan?** This is nothing less than an increase in the price of the car, and you should consider it in that way.

• **Is the loan or lease term unusually short?** Lease terms are 36 months on average. Some dealers have offered unusually low lease rates for arrangements that last only 12 or 24 months because the value of the leased car will still be relatively high at the end of the lease.

Loan terms can be short or long. A short loan period, say 12 months, means that the monthly payment will be much higher than for a longer period, although the total amount of interest paid will be less.

• **Is the loan term longer than I would ordinarily expect?** How long do I expect to keep the car? You can pay off a car loan ahead of schedule; make sure there is no pre-payment penalty. *Consider the following scenarios…*

• $27,000 at 3% for 48 months. You will pay about $598 per month. At the end of the loan in four years, you will have paid $1,686 above the purchase price in interest.

• $27,000 at 3% for 60 months. You will pay about $485 per month. At the end of the loan in five years, you will have paid $2,109 above the purchase price in interest. If you sell the car

TIP

Internet Loan Calculators

You will find auto loan payment and interest calculators on the internet. Just search for *auto loan calculator*. Similarly, you can figure the amount of money that you can expect to earn on savings. Search for *savings interest calculator* or visit the United Services Automobile Association website at Blinc.Media/2vxYJVw.

after four years (which isn't necessarily common), you will still owe the lender about $5,257.

• $27,000 at 3% for 72 months. You will pay about $410 per month. At the end of the loan in six years, you will have paid $2,563 above the purchase price in interest. If you sell the car after four years, you will still owe the lender about $9,158.

Calculators that compare auto loan terms are available at individual bank websites, such as BankofAmerica.com, and at Bankrate.com.

• **What if I put down a larger deposit to reduce the amount financed?** Well, the short answer is that the larger the down payment the lower the monthly payment? But you do need to remember that cash taken from your savings or other investments means you will lose the interest or other income you would have received on that money. Here are two more scenarios in which the car buyer withdraws $10,000 from an investment earning 3% (above the rate offered by savings accounts or CDs, but a not-unreasonable amount for a mutual fund.) *Consider these…*

• $17,000 at 3% for 48 months with a $10,000 down payment. You will pay about $376 per month, and at the end of the loan in four years you will have paid $1,062 above the purchase price in interest. Add to that the loss of about $1,273 you could have earned on the amount you withdrew for the down payment, and that makes the cost of borrowing about $2,335.

• $17,000 at 3% for 60 months with a $10,000 down payment. You will pay about $305 per month, and at the end of the loan in five years you will have paid $1,328 above the purchase price in interest. Add to that the loss of about $1,616 you could have earned on the amount you withdrew for the down payment, and that makes the cost of borrowing about $2,944.

Some people prefer to reduce their monthly payment even if it means withdrawing from their nest egg. Others insist on building up their savings and investments for long-term goals like buying a house or retirement.

Either way, be aware that it costs money to borrow money, and it also costs money to take money out of your savings.

Master Negotiating the Terms of a Car Loan

There is absolutely nothing to prevent you from shopping very hard for the lowest possible interest rate or asking a lender to give you a better deal. If they say no, there's no harm done. But they just might say yes to a reasonable counteroffer, especially if you can point to a better rate from a competitor—either local or on the internet.

For every percent you reduce the interest rate on a 48-month loan, you will save $20.50 per $1,000 borrowed over the loan's full term. That's $410 on a $20,000 loan. This negotiation starts at the car dealership. In the previous chapter, I advised against giving a direct answer when the salesperson asks how you will be paying for the car (and also to hedge on whether you intend to trade in your present vehicle).

Only after you have accepted a good price for the car should you move on to financing.

Actually, let's move back a few steps. Before you set foot in a car dealership, do the following...

- **Contact a few area banks to find their best auto-financing rates.** You are looking for the annual percentage rate (APR), which is a federally defined cost of borrowing that you can compare from one lender to another. The APR may vary slightly based on the term (the number of months for the loan), and some lenders require a certain percentage down payment.

- **Check with credit unions and other financing sources, including auto clubs, for their rates.** Your auto insurance company may also offer a loan program.

- **Search online for internet banks, lenders, and companies that serve as portals for groups of lenders.** Try Lending Tree (LendingTree.com), for example. Enter the term car loan and see what comes up.

Some lenders will preapprove you for a loan up to a certain amount, ready to wire or courier a check to the auto dealership once you reach an agreement.

But wait: When the paperwork is complete at most dealerships, they usher you into the finance manager's office. He or she will study the paperwork, probably tell you what a great deal you've gotten, and sometimes embellish a little to say that it's such a great deal that the boss is going to chew out the sales manager about it. Don't let it all pile up too deeply around you. Make it clear you have spent enough time at the dealership.

The finance manager will then say something like, "We can finance this for you at 3.2% for 60 months" and start pecking away at the computer or calculator. If that is a better deal than you've found on your own, or if this was a promotional rate that was part of your negotiation, you are all set. But if you can do better elsewhere, say so. "I can get a loan for 2.88% from AAA," you can respond, "and I've only just started shopping around for a loan." The finance guy is almost certainly well aware of what rates you can obtain elsewhere. Ask the dealership to beat those rates. If they can't or won't, get the loan from your best source.

If the dealership matches or beats the rate from a bank or other lender with the same terms, you may find it easier to do all of your business in one place. If the dealership wants to charge more, I would suggest taking the best offer.

Remember that the dealer is always looking for ways to bring in a few hundred dollars more in profit, and one of the possible sources is a finder's fee paid the dealer by a bank or another lender. Just as in the negotiations over the car's purchase price, the dealer is going to start with as high a loan rate as possible. You want as low a rate as possible.

Oh, and at many dealerships the finance guy is going to try and sell you more things, sometimes even trying to add back some of the profit items the salesperson tried to get you to buy: paint protection, rustproofing, window security etching, fuzzy dice. Just say no. You've already made your deal and if you want to add things to your car it is almost always less expensive to do so yourself or at an aftermarket automotive store.

While they've got you seated there, they might try to sell you *gap insurance*, which is intended to cover the difference between what your auto insurance company would pay you if the car was a total loss and the outstanding balance on your auto loan. This is almost always a bad deal, and especially at the car dealership. Discuss this sort of coverage with your auto insurance agent or company and see if you can improve your primary coverage at a lower cost.

And no, you don't want to buy anything else, including life insurance or a vacation timeshare plan or carpet cleaning from the dealer. Really.

Etch-a-VIN

What is window etching? Your car comes with a VIN plate visible through the front windshield on the driver's side. That same kind of plate is installed in other places on your car in less obvious spots. Despite that, some very dedicated thieves might try to change one or more of the VINs plates and resell the car. To make that a bit less easy, you can have the VIN etched in small print on all the windows using a laser or chemical process.

Check with your insurance company to see if they offer a discount from your comprehensive coverage for etching. If they do, you can have your windows etched at some auto clubs or purchase a do-it-yourself kit for about $20, while dealers will try to charge you at least $100. It can't hurt to ask the dealer to throw it in for free.

Use a Home-Equity Loan as a Source of Financing

Homeowners can usually obtain a relatively lower-cost loan by tapping into some of the equity they have built up in their home. And interest you pay on a home-equity loan may be tax deductible, reducing the cost by your tax bracket. Consult your accountant or financial advisor.

On the down side, there may be loan origination or closing costs on some home-equity loans. And, most important, you do not want to take out a home-equity loan if you are at all uncertain about your ability to repay it. In a worst-case scenario, defaulting on a home-equity loan could result in losing the roof over your head rather than merely losing the flashy new car in the driveway.

If you already have a home equity line of credit, you can simply pay for your car with a check and have the amount added to the outstanding loan balance in that account.

Carefully Consider the Leasing Option

Before I get into the details of capitalized cost reduction, origination fees, and disposition fees, remember this about leasing: When you pay off an auto loan, you own the car. At the end of a lease, you have to turn over the keys.

A properly cared-for car at the end of three years can be worth 25% to 50% of its original purchase price, which is almost certain to be much more than the total difference between loan and lease payments. It is also true that a loan agreement is much less restrictive than a lease. You are free to sell the car at any point and can close out the loan without penalty. You can make major alterations, from installing a moon roof to a new paint job. And you are not limited to a specific number of miles over the period of the loan.

All that said, on a per-month basis, leases are almost always considerably less costly. And some people like the fact that under a lease arrangement they can always be driving a new or nearly new vehicle, and don't have to worry about disposing of a vehicle in the sometimes-treacherous waters of the used-car market.

So here's how the salesperson or the finance manager is going to bring up the subject: "Wait, wait. The boss is letting me give you a spectacular deal if you sign right now. How about a 2017 Subaru Legacy for $199 per month!...*mumble, mumble* $2,000 down payment...*mumble, mumble*...for a 36-month lease and no more than 1,000 miles per month of use. Or, for the very same price of $199 per month, a luxurious 2017 Acura ILX. Wow, will your friends be impressed...*mumble, mumble*...$4,199 down payment...*mumble, mumble*...36-month lease and 1,000 miles per month...*mumble, mumble*...and $700 disposition fee after three years just because we can." Those are real offers, and so are the mumbles.

Leasing, once almost used only by big business, has become a common option for consumers, especially when new-car prices rise. Leases now account for about one quarter of all new-car deliveries.

When you lease a car, the financing company buys the car from the dealer or the dealer pays off its invoice to the manufacturer. Whoever is doing the leasing figures out its interest costs for the lease term and carefully calculates an estimate of the resale, or *residual*, value at the end of the lease term. Your cost is the amount of money the leasing company has to pay in interest to borrow the money for the car plus the estimated amount of depreciation during the lease term, a bit of profit, and as much additional profit as the lessor can work into the fine print with things like origination and disposition fees. If the lessor expects to receive a high percentage of the purchase price when it disposes of the car at the end of the lease, then it can make its monthly charges lower. That's why leases for very expensive cars can sometimes be a good deal. They hold their resale value.

If the bottom falls out of the market for the car you have leased and the car is worth less than the residual value, that's not your problem. The lessor has to bear that loss. On the other hand, if your leased car is in much greater demand than expected at the end of the lease, you can buy the car at its undervalued residual price.

Leasing from Dealers Versus Third Parties

Leases are usually arranged by the dealer, and often in a direct program from the manufacturer. However, you can also arrange for a lease through a third party. The only advantage to using a leasing company is that you can strike as sharp a deal with the car store as possible, and then use that price as a basis for negotiating with the leasing company.

A possible disadvantage is that leasing companies don't necessarily have much involvement with their customers and, at the end of the lease, you may be delivering the vehicle to a wholesale lot that just wants to get the transaction over with. If you lease from a car dealer, that company and the manufacturer have a vested interest in trying to get you to buy or lease another vehicle. They may treat you better.

If you exercise that option to buy the car at an undervalued residual price, you can then proceed to sell it to an individual or the dealer and keep the difference. (Some lease agreements charge the customer to exercise a purchase option.)

One more thing: A leasing company or dealership can drive down the apparent lease cost by requiring you to come to the finance office with several thousand dollars down. This is not a deposit, and it is not money you will ever retrieve. It is sometimes called a *capitalized cost reduction* (or *cap cost*). It reduces the amount of money the leasing company has to borrow but it increases the overall cost to you for the lease.

Be sure to study the lease terms. If there is, for example, a $3,600 cap cost on a 36-month lease, that is the equivalent of an additional $100 per month you would be paying to borrow that car for three years.

Since leases are calculated on the basis of the car's expected resale value, the terms will stipulate the maximum number of miles you can put on the odometer. A typical deal will limit mileage to 12,000 miles per year. If you go over that limit, you have to pay a specified per-mile fee at the end of the contract. (And if you end up putting substantially fewer miles on the car, you are giving a gift to the leasing company and costing yourself money on the deal.)

The most important thing about leasing is this: Do not concentrate solely on the monthly payment. That is, of course, exactly what the car dealers and leasing companies flash in front of you. If you do that, you are ignoring a much more important number—the total cost of ownership and all of the terms. And finally, at the end of the lease you have to return the car in very good condition. If there is damage to the bodywork or paint, or stains on the seats, or anything else the lessor can point to, you will have to pay for the extra loss in value.

We leased a car many years ago and, following the exact language of the agreement, returned the vehicle to a wholesaler at the end of the term. The car was in very good shape. A few weeks later, we received notification from the leasing company that we were on the hook for a new battery because the one in the car we had returned was faulty. It was a complete fabrication by the wholesaler, but there was nothing I could do about it. The car was long gone, and so was the evidence. I learned a lesson. If I ever lease again, I will insist on a receipt from the person who receives the car attesting to its condition inside and out.

Decode a Lease Offer

Ask these questions about a potential lease…

- **How many months does the lease term run?**
- **What is the vehicle purchase price for the car?** And no, thank you, I do not intend to pay full MSRP for a vehicle. The price of a car for leasing can be negotiated just as if you were buying it for cash. Work on getting a great price for the purchase of the car, and then say, "Let's figure out the lease price for that car, based on the purchase price we just agreed to."
- **What is the APR and the lease rate on the loan?** This is often hidden by the use of other terms, like money factor or lease factor. Then you can expect to see some strange number like 0.00125. Here's what you want to do with that: multiply it by 2,400. It doesn't matter how long the lease term is. The product of 2400 x .00125 is 3.0, which is the APR or annual interest rate. The APR should be about the same as, or less than, the best interest rate you could get if you were buying the car with a loan. If the money factor converts to a high APR, the deal is not a good one.
- **How much of a capital cost reduction is expected for the lease?** Remember, this money down at the start of a lease is cash you will never see again. It artificially reduces the monthly payment. Divide that up-front amount by the number of months you'll be leasing, then add that number to the monthly lease payment.
- **What is the residual value of the vehicle at the end of the lease term?** What are my options for purchasing the vehicle at the end of the lease? What will be the total cost to me to purchase the car at the end of the lease, if I choose to do so?
- **Is there an origination fee at the start of the lease or a disposition fee at the end?** These fees are nothing less than profit padding, above and beyond the money that is made from interest on the loan and potential resale profit. Remember that there is nothing to prevent you from attempting to negotiate any and every element of a lease agreement. Start with making an offer that removes the origination and disposition fees from the deal or cuts them down to size.

TIP

Repeat Customer

If you are returning one leased car and taking out a new contract through the same dealership or leasing company, you may be able to receive a waiver of any security deposit on your new car and avoid some other fees that apply to new customers.

Here is where it makes sense to have a second quote from a leasing company. See which of the two, the dealer or the leasing company, is willing to give you a better deal.

- **Am I required to pay a deposit that will be held until the car is returned at the end of the term of the lease?** Again, you can try to reduce or eliminate the deposit. And you should be able to compare deposits between the car dealership and an independent leasing company.
- **How many miles am I allowed under the lease term?** What is the excess mileage fee? If you know you will be driving fewer miles than the lease term, ask for a new deal with a lower allowance. This increases the residual value, and there should be a corresponding reduction in the monthly lease payment. On the other hand, if you fully expect to drive a few thousand miles more than the allowance, negotiate a rate based on that. The new rate should be less than the cost of the excess mileage fee.
- **Who will receive the car at the end of the lease?** If it is the dealership, you may have some protection against unsavory business practices because they will want you to sign up for another deal. If it is a wholesaler or other third party, there may or may not be an incentive to take care of you properly.

Negotiate a Lease

Just because a leasing company or a dealership quotes you a price doesn't mean you shouldn't try to work out a better deal. Of all of the numbers on a lease agreement, the residual value is usually not negotiable. But, start your negotiation by bargaining down the capitalized cost, which is based on the car's purchase price. Bargain down the price just as you would if you were buying the car.

The money factor, the lease equivalent of the interest rate, is also open to bargaining.

Don't concentrate on the bottom line for your monthly lease payments. Insist on seeing an itemized list. The dealer is required to give you one, but only if you ask. Check the arithmetic. Add all the costs on a calculator. Double-check sales tax rates and computations.

Things can become complicated here. In many states, sales tax is only due on the amount the car will depreciate during the lease term. In that scenario, you are only paying tax on the portion of the vehicle's value you will be using during the lease. This is yet another reason to obtain a second quotation on an automobile lease from a company unassociated with the car dealership. You can compare the calculations and ask pointed questions about each line of the contract. If the answers are not the same at both places, one of them is wrong and you need to investigate further, perhaps with the assistance of your accountant, financial advisor, or a banker.

You can find your state tax rate by searching on the Internet or by visiting TaxRates.com/calculator. Be aware that in some locales, there is both a state and a local component to sales taxes.

Finding the Best Deals on a Lease

A car's type and model can influence the money factor and interest rate. Finance companies owned by the major car companies sometimes offer the best rates on vehicles that the manufacturer is trying to unload. You can figure out which models are in this category by looking for advertisements of large rebates for customers seeking to *buy* the car.

The fact that a manufacturer is pushing a particular model does not mean there is anything particularly wrong with that car. More likely they misjudged how many vehicles to make or consumer behavior changed.

On the other hand, if a car is particularly popular, you may find a better lease price by going to an independent leasing company. They'll also be happier to do business with you on a popular car since the vehicle is likely to have a higher residual value at the end of the lease.

Deal with the Repo Man

This is information I hope you never have to use. If you are in default on an automobile loan, most states permit the lender to repossess your car at any hour without prior notice. Read your loan agreement carefully to understand your rights and obligations.

In general, once your car has been repossessed, the lender can keep or resell the car to recoup its value. Your contract, and state law, may allow you to buy back a repossessed vehicle by paying the full amount owed on it, plus reasonable expenses connected with its repossession.

Any personal property found inside the vehicle cannot be kept by the creditor and must be returned to you.

A "repo" company can generally take hold of your car anytime it is in a place where they have free access—a public street or a parking lot, for example. In general, most state laws prohibit entry into a locked garage or any threats of force or violence.

If you come to an arrangement with the creditor to extend or change your loan agreement because of a default, obtain a written statement of the new terms and be aware that this may constitute a new contract, voiding the terms of the original deal.

Once-in-a-Lifetime Error

My accountant, who is *almost* as good as I am at squeezing sellers to within an inch of their profit margin, once negotiated a lease on a nice car on terms he found acceptable. And then when he received the paperwork, he found that someone had made two mistakes: The capitalized cost reduction was lower and the annual mileage was higher than he had agreed. He quickly signed the contract, took possession of the car, and never told the leasing company of their error.

He told me about the deal at the time it happened, and so I believe him when he said that if the mistakes had been in the favor of the dealer or the leasing company, he would have refused to sign the contract until the deal had been corrected.

CHAPTER 24

Attending to Car Maintenance

Every move you make, every trip you take...parts of your car are wearing out. Start with the obvious things like tires, which have a finite life based on miles driven and proper care along the way. Then consider things like the battery, which has a predicted life span of months but can be affected by your driving and your vehicle's charging system.

Before getting into things such as oil filters, though, I help you find out if there are any unofficial or unpublished warranties on new and used cars. And finally, I lay out the benefits of pumping your own gas and the potential cost of speeding.

- **Maintain your car properly.**
- **Use official parts at an unofficial garage.**
- **Operate your car in cold weather.**
- **Take advantage of secret warranties and advisories.**
- **Buy tires without being taken for a ride.**
- **Take charge of a battery purchase.**
- **Get the most mileage from the gas you buy.**
- **Be wary of "miracle" fuel additives.**
- **Fill it up yourself.**
- **Understand the real cost of speeding.**
- **Be a savvy driver in the parking lot.**

Maintain Your Car Properly

You can save money by waiting longer between oil changes and other maintenance. In fact, your car will likely keep on moving for years...until it comes to a grinding and much more expensive halt. It makes sense to spend a bit more on car maintenance than necessary. Rather than scrimp, a much savvier strategy is to perform minor maintenance tasks early and often—meeting or exceeding manufacturer's recommendations. A typical recommendation from a new carmaker these days, for example, calls for an oil change every 7,500 miles or 12 months and an oil filter replacement every 15,000 miles. Some car owners step up the pace, changing the oil and filter every 3,000 miles.

Be especially vigilant about shortening the interval between oil changes if you do a lot of stop-and-go travel, take short trips, tow a boat or trailer, or operate your vehicle in extremes like very hot or cold weather or very dirty or sandy environments. My car, which lives outdoors near the beach on an island where the farthest I can drive is about ten miles, qualifies for extra TLC on all accounts.

The best deals on ordinary maintenance tasks including oil and filter changes, air filters, lubrication, and checks of transmission fluid, transfer-case oil, coolant, and many other tasks are found at high-volume service operations such as Jiffy Lube and other companies of its type. Among their advantages are speed (a team of four or five members descend on your vehicle), price, and the fact that you can witness the work being performed. Visit the website of the company for discount coupons.

I do not, however, recommend that you use a jiffy or minute shop for major maintenance tasks such as engine tune-ups and suspension adjustments. For those you want to go to a specialist or to the dealer. You'll pay more for the work, but the complexity of modern cars demands the attention of a mechanic trained on a specific line of vehicles.

Use Official Parts at an Unofficial Garage

Do you prefer using factory-authorized replacement parts even if a garage that is not an official manufacturer franchise does the work? Or does your warranty agreement require you to use brand name parts? No problem. Find out from your mechanic what parts you need, buy them from the parts department of your car dealer, and then take them to your preferred garage. Make sure that you keep your receipts and that you are not double billed by the garage for parts you provide. You're almost certain to save money on labor at an independent garage.

Operate Your Car in Cold Weather

Those of you who live in southern California, Florida, and other points along the Sun Belt are excused. Everyone else should know it's worth spending a few minutes each fall preparing a car for the coming winter. Not only will the following suggestions help you drive safely in snow and ice, but they may save you big dollars on towing and repairs.

- **Pack a winter survival kit in your trunk.** Include a foldaway shovel, temporary chains or portable tracks to give your wheels traction, and several safety flares. If you have a car with rear-wheel drive, consider leaving a large bag of cat litter in the trunk. The weight helps with traction, and in an emergency you can spread the litter on snow or ice to help you pull out of a slippery spot.
- **Install winter wiper blades.** This type of blade adds a rubber or plastic covering over the wiper's linkage, keeping them flexible and reducing the chances that the blades will freeze in place. Winter blades cost between $15 and $20 per pair, depending on your car. If you buy them from

your local auto-parts store, they will probably install them for you. You can easily find winter wiper blades online at big-box stores, which may cost less, but could be a tad more hassle on your end. (If you're having trouble, search for *installing wiper blades* on YouTube for a how-to video. The manufacturer may also offer an online video.) Bosch, AERO Premium, and Valeo brands offer reliable products in this category.

- **Fill your windshield washer tank with winter-grade solvent.** The antifreeze in good quality washer liquid will keep it from freezing except in the most extreme conditions, and helps keep the windshield clear of dirt and ice. You can add 16 ounces of isopropyl rubbing alcohol to a gallon of regular wiper fluid, too. A frozen washer tank can damage the pumping system, necessitating an expensive repair. If you'd rather buy something premade and don't mind spending more, Rain-X De-Icer wiper fluid boasts reliability to -25 degrees.

- **De-ice your locks.** A few times each winter, squirt de-icer into your car's exterior locks to keep them from freezing. Be sure to keep the de-icer in a readily accessible place outside of the car. It won't do you any good frozen within the car. You can buy de-icer at your local big-box or auto-parts store for very little money, but you can go super cheap and make your own with rubbing alcohol or hand sanitizer (which is alcohol-based).

Keep On Tracking

Super-cold and very snowy conditions require extra care.

Portable tracks are basically machines that go on your tires, giving you extra traction—sort of like a tank. Some vehicles can use them, and some can't. Before you buy them (and they aren't inexpensive), make sure your vehicle meets the specifications for the brand you're ordering. If you decide to buy them online, search for *portable tracks tires* or *snow tracks cars* (or something similar, to clarify that you're searching for a vehicle). Track N Go (TruckTracks.com/en) is a very popular brand. Oh, and don't forget to buy more than one; they're sometimes sold separately.

And how about the engine? In theory, gasoline-ethanol blends and modern sealed gas storage systems mean you should not worry much about water building up and freezing in your gas tank. But if you live in the deep, deep freezer, consider adding fuel line antifreeze every few fill-ups. This chemical prevents moisture in your fuel tank from freezing and blocking the flow of fuel. Your local auto parts store will have what you need.

Take Advantage of Secret Warranties and Advisories

Has your new car run roughly from the day you drove it off the lot? Is the paint peeling over the hood? Has the dealer replaced the battery twice? These problems are not supposed to happen to a new car or to a properly maintained older car. Though the new car warranty may pay for some or all of the cost, sooner or later it may run out—and you've still got the problem.

Ask the dealer if the manufacturer has issued a service advisory or technical service bulletin about the problem. There may be a more permanent fix that the manufacturer pays for. It's to the dealer's advantage to get you out of their hair, especially if the manufacturer will pay the bill and make both of you happy.

Your car dealer should be helpful, but if they're not, or if you want to check for yourself, consult the National Highway Safety Administration website at NHTSA.gov/cars/problems, where you will find recalls, technical service bulletins, and defect investigations. The site is easiest to use if you enter your car's VIN.

If you experience a recurring problem with a new car, start by asking the dealership for help contacting the manufacturer in seeking a remedy. If that does not work, contact the manufacturer yourself and ask to be put in touch with the national or regional customer care or customer service department. They may be able to instruct the dealer to make a repair that is outside of ordinary warranty coverage.

Several states have "lemon" laws intended to protect buyers in this situation. In some of these laws, the manufacturer is required to repurchase a car from a buyer if the vehicle has experienced significant problems that the maker or dealer has not been able to fix within a reasonable period of time. Contact your state's consumer protection bureau or its Secretary of State's office to see if you are protected this way.

Be sure to keep records of the problems and the dates they occurred, as well as all receipts for repairs, whether they are within the warranty period or not.

Buy Tires Without Being Taken for a Ride

How complicated can buying tires be? After all, we're talking about a black rubber donut, right? Wrong. The savvy shopper selects the proper size, classification, performance, speed rating, and load rating, and then moves to price and warranty.

Start with tire type. If you could magically do all of your driving in one kind of condition, the choice would be easy. Instead, choose the type that most closely matches your driving.

Tire Type	Tread Life	Traction and Ride	Price
All season	Long	Smooth, quieter ride with ordinary traction and handling. On a front-wheel or four-wheel-drive, all-season tires should provide adequate traction in snow, but not the same traction as a snow tire provides.	Relatively reasonable
Touring all season	Long	Better performance and handling, but greater noise and moderately harsh ride.	Mid-range
Performance	Shorter	Wider tread and a lower profile, performance tires are for high-speed precision driving (the sort of which normal citizens like you and I don't do). On the downside, they are unpredictable in rain and worse in snow. Harsh and somewhat noisy ride.	High
Performance all season	n/a	Better rain and snow for high-speed driving.	Mid-range to hign

Tire Type	Tread Life	Traction and Ride	Price
Snow, winter	Shorter	Special tread stays pliable at extremely cold temperatures. Good on snow-covered pavement; noisy and mushy on dry roads; unlikely to be fuel efficient. Installed on the driving wheels (the front on a front-wheel drive, or the rear on a conventional rear-wheel car). Most drivers use them only in harsh, snowy winter months.	Mid-range
Studded snow tire	n/a	Snow tire variant adds metal or hard rubber studs that help on snow and ice. Many states have banned studs because they damage roads. Can be less safe on wet roads. Find studded tire regulations at DrivingLaws.aaa.com/tag/studded-tires. These aren't an ideal option.	Mid-range to high
Rain	n/a	A channel moves water away from the tread, allowing good traction on wet roads. If you live in an area that is notorious for wet conditions, consider these.	Mid-range to high
Sand, off-road, high-flotation	n/a	Balloon-like and wide. Not generally recommended for high-speed use on highways. Squishy on paved roads; poor traction on snow and ice. Basically for use on four-wheel-drive and sport-utility vehicles.	High
Drive flat, run flat	Shorter	These tires have reinforced sidewalls and sometimes other designs that allow you to continue driving even after air has escaped due to a puncture or relatively minor damage. This sort of design is safer in case of blowout. Most tires allow about 100 miles, at a reduced speed of no more than 50 miles per hour, which should be enough time to get to a service station. For drivers who frequently pass through areas where they would rather not stop to change a tire or wait around for help. Stiff sidewalls can translate into a harsher ride even when fully inflated. And some carmakers do not provide a spare tire if the car is equipped with run-flat tires, which may prove a problem if the tire is seriously damaged.	High

Tire Type	Tread Life	Traction and Ride	Price
Self-sealing	Shorter	Include a flexible inner lining that is capable of sealing around an object like a nail that punctures the outer tread. For minor damage, the tire may be able to continue in service; more significant damage will require repair or, more likely, replacement. Less expensive than run-flat tires, but like those, they offer a bit more security in case of damage (because you needn't get out to change a flat).	High

You can learn a great deal about various tire designs and ratings on the websites of tire dealers and manufacturers. For independent reviews, consult *Consumer Reports* and similar magazines and websites.

Tire Size and Rating

There is a dizzying array of tire sizes and ratings. You'll find information on your current tires molded into the sidewall. The car manufacturer's recommended range of sizes is in the owner's manual and on a sticker on the driver's door jamb.

Modern tires are sized by their width (measured in millimeters), their aspect ratio (the relationship of the sidewall height to the tire width, also called the profile), a letter code for speed rating on some tires, a construction type indication, and the diameter of the wheel on which the tire is mounted. Some tires add a load rating and other specifications. *Here are two examples…*

- **P215/60SR15.** This is a passenger-strength tire with a width of 215mm, a profile of 60%, an S speed rating (which I explain a bit later in this chapter), an R for radial construction (which is sturdier and simultaneously more flexible, meaning you get more wear out of them), and designed to mount on a 15-inch wheel. Passenger tires are constructed for cards, minivans, and most SUVs. Heavy-duty trucks (like those the utility company uses) need heavier-strength tires.

- **P245/70R16 105S M+S.** This passenger tire has a width of 245mm, a profile of 70%, and is meant for a 16-inch wheel. Not all tires bear a speed rating. You'll find that information on the sticker that is attached to the tire when it is new. The 105S label gives the load rating (explained later in this chapter) and an S speed rating. This tire bears an M+S label, which indicates it is appropriate for mud- and snow-covered roads.

Speed ratings indicate performance at high speed. You're not likely to drive any car at the speeds the tire makers use for their ratings, but the higher the rating, the more stable the tire is on the freeway (and often the harsher the ride at slower speeds). The codes follow.

Again, those of us who don't get a paycheck to drive in a circle can rely on a low to mid-range rating. If your face could ever possibly be emblazoned on a trophy, consider something else.

Load ratings are presented on a sliding scale. The ratings refer to each tire. Here are some of the numbers and their meaning.

An 105S rating, for example, means the tires can carry 8,156 pounds (including the vehicle's weight) at 112 mph, which is faster and heavier than I ever expect to travel. I appreciate the safety margin, though. If you have a normal passenger car, the lowest rating will work. If you haul or otherwise carry heavy-duty loads, ask your tire dealer what rating you need. The lowest rating won't cut it.

Buy the Right Tire

Buy as good a set of tires that makes sense for your style of driving, type of car, and how long you expect your vehicle to last. If your car has 90,000 miles on it and you expect to deliver it to the junkyard within the next 10,000 miles, there is no point to buying top-of-the-line tires. In that instance, you might want to look into buying good used tires from a tire recycler or a junkyard. If you can't find decent tires there, buy the least-expensive brand is at your local tire dealer. On the other hand, if you are replacing tires on a fairly youthful vehicle, use the information about tire type and ratings to choose the appropriate type.

Look for a tire from a major manufacturer, backed by a reasonable guarantee. Read the fine print carefully to understand how the warranty works. In most cases, you will receive a prorated credit for the tire if it fails within the specified period.

There are more tire makers than I have space to list here. *Here are some manufacturers that are rated highly by independent testers like Consumer Reports…*

- **Bridgestone** is a Japanese company that purchased the American tire maker Firestone in 1988.
- **Continental** is a German tire maker with global operations, it also owns General Tire.
- **Cooper** is an American tire maker that also sells under other names for some discount tire stores.
- **Goodyear** is an American company.
- **Hankook** is a major South Korean manufacturer.
- **Kumho** is another major South Korean manufacturer.
- **Michelin** is a French company that owns the BF Goodrich and Uniroyal brands.
- **Pirelli** is based in Italy.
- **Toyo** is a Japanese tire maker that also sells tires under the Silverstone label.
- **Yokohama** is another major Japanese manufacturer.

You will generally find the best prices at discount stores and at tire dealers rather than at service stations. The last place to shop is the car dealer, unless they are offering a special deal.

You can also find mail-order sources for tires. Unless you are buying tires mounted on new wheels, you'll have to arrange for the tires to be mounted at a service station or tire dealer when they arrive. Be sure to compare the total cost of the tires, shipping, and installation to the price at a store.

If you use snow tires, you can save a bit of money and wear and tear on the *bead* of the tires (the part that forms an air seal at the wheel's metal lip) by installing the snow tires on wheels and changing the installed units seasonally. You can recycle the wheels when the snow tires reach the end of their useful life.

Taking Care of Your Tires

Some experts recommend tires be rotated every time you change your car's oil. It'll help balance the wear and make them last longer. Consult the seller of your tires or the manufacturer for their recommendation on time, and on the pattern to be used. Some makers suggest moving tires from front to back on the same side of the car, while others prefer swapping in an X-pattern.

If you run over something nasty (like a nail, not an animal), take your tire for repair at the local garage. If the gash is small enough they can repair it, you can continue using your tire. If it's something big enough that a patch won't do it, you'll have to buy a new tire.

TIP

Battery Check

How long has that battery been sitting on the shelf at the store or dealership? Even a new, unused battery will lose some of its ability to hold a charge even if it is idle. Ask to see the manufacturing or shipping date on the battery and try to avoid one that is more than six months old. Some companies list the date in easily recognizable form. Others use codes for the month and year. That information should be available at the seller.

Take Charge of a Battery Purchase

Begin by checking the specifications in your car's manual. Don't buy less than what is called for. If you live in a very hot climate, seek a battery that is designed to withstand the stress of high heat. Residents who live in very cold locations (and visitors driving to these areas) should buy a battery that is built to work when the thermometer drops. (If you're driving for a cold visit, you could conceivably rent a car at your destination, as it will be ready with the right kind of battery and other cold-weather accoutrements. However, that rental price won't outweigh the price of a single new battery for your own car.)

Hybrid and electric car batteries are another beast altogether.

Traditional Car Batteries

Here is a guide to some of the numbers you'll find at the auto parts store…

- **CCA**, or *cold cranking amps*, is a measure of the battery's ability to start an engine in cold weather. CCA is calculated at 0 degrees. Experts recommend buying a battery no lower than the specified rating of your car's manufacturer and *no higher* than 200 points above the recommended level.

TIP

That Ubiquitous Sticker

In some states, AAA clubs offer a mobile battery installation service for members. When you call to report a dead battery, a truck will arrive to offer a jump start (if that will help) or a replacement battery.

Taking this route, though, does not guarantee you a good price on a battery or even necessarily the best battery for your vehicle. I would recommend instead a jump start or a tow to the nearest discount auto parts store than can offer you a range of batteries and installation.

- **CA,** or *cranking amps*, is a measure of starting power at 32 degrees, which makes this a less-significant number than the CCA rating in extremes.
- **Reserve capacity** is an estimate of how many minutes your car's engine could run if the alternator fails or the belt breaks, which would mean the battery was not being recharged. A good reserve capacity allows you to drive an hour or more—enough time to make it to a garage for a repair and avoid a tow. Good batteries have a capacity of 90 to 120 minutes.
- **Group size** indicates the box dimensions and where the terminals are placed. In most instances, you should stay with the group size recommended by your car's maker. Today's vehicles don't generally adapt to a change in battery size or shape. Buy for your car's specifications.

Warranties cover one of two periods.

- **A free replacement period,** which tells you the length of time the manufacturer promises to replace a failed battery without charge. It is typically one to two years, but sometimes less.
- **A prorated total warranty period,** which indicates the period when the maker will give you a credit toward a new battery purchase. The longer you've used the battery, the less it is worth as a trade-in. It's more likely to fail as time goes on.

That second period of time often works like this: In the fourth year of a five-year guarantee, you might receive 25% off the suggested list price of a replacement battery from the same maker. You might receive 10% off in the fifth year.

Go for as long a free warranty period as is reasonable. While it never hurts to ask for more time or coverage, most warranties are standard depending on the brand and where you purchased it.

And if your battery seems to have quit working, first check for corrosion on the connectors; that is sometimes the culprit. This is quite common. If you feel confident, try following Napa's online instructions for cleaning the corrosion, always making sure to wear the appropriate hand and eye protection: http://napaau.to/2s91Yni.

Along the same lines, you can buy the right battery at your local car-parts or big-box store (dealers will be more expensive), and if you're lucky, they'll install it for you. Of course, the car-parts store employees are much more likely to install a battery than is the big-box store employee. You also can install the battery yourself, taking proper precautions to protect your hands and eyes.

Hybrid and Electric Car Batteries

Because this market is evolving so quickly, things are likely to change very rapidly over time. Hybrid and All-Electric cars are designed to work with a specific type and size of battery, not something that can be easily comparison-shopped. These vehicles use large banks of nickel metal hydride (NiMH) or Lithium Ion (Li-Ion) batteries.

Manufacturers generally provide a robust warranty for the batteries of these types of car. In fact, that should be a primary consideration of yours if you are shopping for a hybrid or electric vehicle.

You may never have to replace the batteries during the life of the car. A typical warranty runs for 80,000 to 100,000 miles. If you are still driving the vehicle outside of the warranty, replacement of the battery pack for that vehicle could cost as much as $3,500. And replacement is a job for professionals, almost always at a dealership of the original manufacturer.

We can expect battery prices to decline (and performance to improve) as more and more electric vehicles are sold. The next generation of batteries may use other chemical designs such as manganese and sodium-ion.

All-electric vehicles like the Nissan Leaf and the various Tesla models use Lithium Ion batteries with life expectancies of 10 years or more. Nissan offers an 8-year warranty and also offers a monthly payment plan that offers replacement of the battery pack with a newer design when warranted; Tesla believes its version of batteries will last even longer, offering an 8-year unlimited mileage warranty.

Get the Most Mileage from the Gas You Buy

Don't waste money on fuel that is too rich for your car. Gasoline makers offer several mixtures of fuel with different octane ratings, a measurement of the amount of antiknock ingredients in the fuel. There is no advantage to using a higher rating than your engine requires. Higher-octane fuel does not deliver substantial increases in miles per gallon or horsepower in a properly maintained engine.

Most modern automobiles are designed and tuned for regular gasoline, which is usually 87 octane. Perhaps only 5% of vehicles need premium fuels. Check your car's manual to find out its minimum rating.

There are other things you can do to spend less gas money…

- **Go by the book.** Follow manufacturer's recommendations for tune-ups and oil changes.
- **Keep your tires properly inflated.** An underinflated tire causes more friction and uses more gas; an overinflated tire is more easily pierced and makes for a rougher ride. (And both conditions affect tire performance and life expectancy.)
- **Fill 'er up—but not too much.** Be careful not to overfill your tank if you are going to park it in the sun. You'll lose some gas through evaporation.

Be Wary of "Miracle" Fuel Additives

It sounds so wondrous—even miraculous: a chemical that supercharges your gasoline to increase mileage. But in truth, according to the Environmental Protection Agency and the Federal Trade Commission, most products with this sort of claim are, at best, a waste of money. At worst, they may hurt your engine.

Think of it this way: Even if an additive did deliver on claims of, say, a 10% boost in mileage, that might save a gallon or so from a full tank of gas. If the additive costs the same as or more than a gallon of gas, you're saving nothing.

Fill It Up Yourself

How about paying yourself every time you visit the gas pump? It is an option available in most states and localities. Saving a dime per gallon by filling your own tank at the gas station may sound like small change, but a typical driver putting 15,000 miles on the odometer at 20 miles per gallon can save $75 per year here. That'll pay for the deluxe set of fuzzy dice you always wanted...or an evening out at a fine restaurant.

You can find further discounts on gasoline purchases through stores such as BJ's Wholesale, Costco, or Sam's Club. Some convenience stores offer clubs that knock down the price of gasoline if you agree to use a special debit card that pays for your gas from your checking account. You also can rack up points by doing your grocery shopping at certain chains and then applying those points to fuel discounts at specific gas stations. Finally, some credit cards do the same sort of points-earning reward for fuel.

Understand the Real Cost of Speeding

According to the US Department of Energy and car makers, your vehicle's miles per gallon decreases markedly as you go past 55 miles per hour. Driving 65 miles per hour increases fuel consumption by about 15%. Pushing the speedometer to 75 mph (which is above the speed limit on most highways in the US) increases fuel consumption by about 25%. Time is money, of course, so figuring out how much time spent driving versus how much fuel you're using may mean you're okay with going faster.

If your car delivers 30 miles per gallon on the highway, here are your approximate per-hour gasoline costs, based on a gasoline price of $3 per gallon...

55 mph	$5.50 per hour
65 mph	$7.65 per hour
75 mph	$10.00 per hour

And, of course, if you find yourself the lucky winner of a $150 speeding ticket, the cost of a few miles per hour are even greater. Your insurance premium will probably increase for a few years as well.

Be a Savvy Driver in the Parking Lot

Nobody wants to pay to have his or her car repaired, even if it's a little fender bender. For most of us, the most dangerous place for our automobiles is not the superhighway—it's the supermarket parking lot. The parking lot is a place with a lot of coming and going, runaway shopping carts, and some generally unusual traffic lanes. Another high-risk area is at the airport, where people are always in a rush to come and go. Parking lots are also common places for petty theft.

You can do a few things to improve your chances in parking lots...

- **Back into your space.** Or pull through back-to-back spaces so you're still fronting out. When you are ready to leave, you have a better view of obstacles and oncoming traffic.

And a bonus: You're more likely to notice if you left your headlights on if you walk away from the front of the vehicle. You don't want to unnecessarily drain that battery if your headlights don't shut off automatically on their own.

- **Park defensively.** Find a spot next to a wall or a support column to defend at least one side of the car from dings. If the lot is not crowded (and security is not an issue and you don't mind the extra exercise), park in the distant reaches where you may end up without company. Park next to an expensive car in good condition. Owners of banged-up old heaps obviously care very little about their own wheels, so why should they watch out for yours when they open their car doors or pull out?

- **Protect against theft.** The safest strategy is to never leave anything of value in the car. If that's not possible, do whatever you can to hide something worth a smash-and-grab. Keep items in the trunk, for instance. If you have a hatchback or minivan with an open storage area, consider purchasing a tonneau cover that sits above the packages in the rear. In a pinch, throw a tarp or blanket over your items. If you must rearrange items before you leave the car, consider doing so somewhere away from the parking lot or garage so that anyone casing the place doesn't see you do so.

PART V

Banking and Finance Tips

CHAPTER 25

Shopping for a Loan

Don't imagine for a moment that a bank is doing you a favor by making you a loan. Actually, it's the other way around.

Banks exist to make loans. It's the primary way many of them make their money. They are constantly looking for new ways to give their money to customers and then collect interest. That's why your mailbox fills up with offers for credit cards and equity loans. (Chapter 20 discusses home mortgages.)

With this in mind, remember one of the key messages of this book: almost everything in commerce is negotiable. Apply for a loan at several banks and institutions, compare the offers for the best rate and terms, and tell a few loan officers that you're giving them a chance to improve on their deal. Reveal the best rate you've been offered and ask them to do better.

- **Know what bankers want.**
- **Decipher a consumer credit report.**
- **Don't waste your credit line.**
- **Don't cosign a loan unless you're willing to pay it off.**
- **Dip into home equity loans and lines of credit**

Know What Bankers Want

Banks aren't doing you a favor. They're in this for the money. Their goal is to make as much money as possible on the loans they make and lose as little as possible on bad risks. It is therefore not unreasonable for banks to ask potential borrowers to jump through all sorts of hoops and reveal a great deal of personal and financial information aimed at making the lender feel comfortable with the prospect that you will repay the loan.

Personal loans are usually based on collateral—a car, a boat, or a portion of the equity you have put into your house purchase. A banker will want to see that you have sufficient income to repay the loan, but he or she will also be comforted by the fact that the bank will hold on to the title of your car or boat or file a *lien* against your house in case you can't make the payments. What does that mean? If you fall too far behind in paying back a loan of this sort, the lender has the right to seize (also known as *repossess*) the car or boat or put in a claim against your house—or almost any asset.

If a lender puts a claim—also called a *lien*—against your home or other property, it could lead to a repossession or cloud the title, making it all but impossible to sell the possession until the lien is cleared.

Business loans are more complex, since they are usually based on an assumption that an investment will eventually yield a profit. This book is about consumer finance, so we'll stick to the personal side.

This book's purpose is to provide ways for you to buy more while paying less, and that includes loans. If a bank's reason for being is to earn money by making loans, a successful institution will look for ways to attract and hold on to good customers. You can—and should expect—to be given preferential status for loans and credit accounts from banks with which you already do business. And don't hesitate to ask for a better deal—a lower interest rate, a lower down payment, or other services.

Start by knowing the market. If the bank down the street is offering an auto loan at a quarter-point lower rate than your bank, it is perfectly reasonable to ask your current bank to meet or beat that offer. And if they won't, take your business elsewhere.

Sometimes you get the best service by working with a small, local bank where managers may have more flexibility. At the same time, the major national banks have become adept at offering premium services to customers with whom they have longstanding relationships or large amounts of money on deposit or on loan (or both). It is valuable to be able to call a specific bank executive for assistance, or when he or she occasionally calls or texts me with a special offer.

Whether you are a premium customer or not, treat your bank as you would any other business. Ask for a better deal. You just might get one, or you might need to find another institution that wants your business more.

Decipher a Consumer Credit Report

They're out there, and they're watching you: the keepers of information at consumer credit-report agencies. With the spread of the internet and online commerce, the amount of data and how fast it's collected have increased exponentially.

If you apply for a credit card online, you'll begin by entering some information about yourself: your address, your Social Security number, your sources of income, and much more. That goes into a database. And when the bank, credit company, or retailer wants to verify what you've told them, it reaches into the files of consumer credit report companies. Just the fact you have applied for more credit—and the lender's decision—also goes into the file. Once you establish the line of credit, the lender regularly reports to the credit agency how much money is available to you, the average balance due each month, and any bits of bad news such as late payments and defaults.

The US has three major credit report companies: Equifax, Experian, and Transunion. Equifax and Transunion also operate in Canada.

What will you (or someone investigating you) find in these records?

• **Identifying information.** Your name, former name, nicknames, current and previous addresses, Social Security number, year of birth, and current and previous employers. In most instances, your spouse's name and his or her financial information are not on your report. This information is mostly drawn from your responses on credit applications.

• **Trade lines.** Your credit history, including specific information about each account (credit card, auto loan, mortgage, and other borrowing)—date opened, credit limit or loan amount, balance, monthly payment, and payment pattern during the past several years. The report also indicates if there is a cosigner, such as your spouse, who is also responsible for the loan. The source for this information generally comes from companies and lenders that do business with you.

• **Public records.** Bankruptcy records, state and county court records, tax liens, wage garnishments, monetary judgments, and filings by collection agencies. In some states, overdue child support is also reported. Data here are drawn from public records and lenders who have filed legal actions.

• **Credit inquiries.** The names of any companies, agencies, or others who have obtained a copy of your credit report for any reason, including lending companies and employers. When you apply for a loan or agree to a background check for a new job, the fine print almost always gives permission to the would-be lender to check your report. This is considered a *voluntary inquiry*. When credit card companies and other lenders are looking for new business, they may check your report beforehand to preauthorize an offer. These *involuntary inquiries* are kept on record for two years. Note that lenders may check only one or perhaps two credit-reporting agencies. A single report may be incomplete. And, like it or not, inquiries by law-enforcement agencies are not listed on the version of your record you are allowed to check.

Positive information—your successful use of credit—remains on your report indefinitely.

Here's what's* not *supposed to be in your credit report: your race, religious or political preferences, personal lifestyle, medical history, friends, criminal record, or any other information unrelated to credit.

However, some indicators may reveal this information: loans from credit unions or associations connected to religious or ethnic group societies, loan arrangements made with hospitals or doctors, or almost anything other than dealings with major national lending institutions.

And your past mistakes are not supposed to hang over your head forever. Federal law requires that most negative information be erased after seven years. Forgettable occurrences include late payments, accounts turned over to collection agencies, and judgments filed against you in court. A Chapter 7, 11, or 12 bankruptcy remains on your credit report for as long as 10 years. Most credit-reporting agencies will remove a reference to a Chapter 13 bankruptcy—which sets a court-approved repayment plan for debt—after seven years and some remove all bankruptcy reports after that period of time.

By federal law, all credit agencies must have procedures under which consumers can see their report for free at least once a year. In addition, if a lender turns down your application for credit because of information found on your report, you have the right to ask to see the disqualifying data. Additionally, once you have seen your report, you have the right to challenge information you say is incorrect and the agency must investigate and make the change if they can corroborate your claim. I check my reports regularly and sometimes find undamaging errors like incorrect information about former addresses.

In one instance it took me more than a year to remove an address for an apartment that one of my children had rented. He had listed the home where he grew up as a former residence, which is reasonable enough, but somehow that ended up linking my credit report with all of his later personal addresses as he went through college and on to his own career.

Go on the internet and search for any of the three major credit report companies: Equifax, Experian, or Transunion. You'll find procedures to request a viewing of your report at their website. Do not agree to pay for any extra services such as credit monitoring or FICO scores (a calculated score that gives a quick reading of your worthiness as a borrower. Credit monitoring is not generally necessary unless you have a reason to believe your identity has been assumed by someone else. FICO scores are now available for free from many credit card companies and on some bank statements, and you can also ask for the score from many lenders. Fuzzy dice should come free, too.

Equifax.com 866-349-5191
Experian.com 888-397-3742 or 714-830-7000
TransUnion.com 877-322-8228

And though it is possible to ask for all three of your reports from the trio of top agencies, that might not make the most fiscal sense. Instead, check a different one every four months and then start the cycle over—for free—the next year. Only if you see something seriously wrong should you contact multiple agencies at the same time—and if there is an error by the agency, that resets the clock anyway.

It is possible to block or freeze your credit report by contacting each of the companies. Each has a process allowing you to prevent third parties from accessing your report without your specific permission. You can do this over the internet or by letter. Either way, be precise when listing your full name and other required details. They must match *exactly* the record they are keeping.

A block does not prevent existing creditors from posting updated information to your report. Plus, you have to lift the block, or notify the agencies of a particular lender you want to allow to read the report when you decide to apply for a mortgage, loan, or credit card.

Don't Waste Your Credit Line

Credit card companies want you to use the credit they extend to you. Once you prove yourself a trustworthy customer, they're almost certain to increase the credit line without even asking if you'd like more, please. You are also almost certain to receive dozens of offers for new credit cards, many of them free of an annual charge (at least for the first year) and offering all sorts of giveaways like points or miles that you can redeem for cash or airline tickets.

It is true that no one will force you to use a card. It is also true that having an unnecessarily large credit line or too many credit cards could end up costing you money when it comes time to apply for a mortgage or personal loan.

It works like this: When you apply for a loan, the bank or institution uses a formula that relates your income to your debts. Your credit history will indicate all open lines of credit—credit cards, equity lines of credit, automobile loans, and personal loans—as part of your total possible indebtedness. You could end up in a situation where a lender could decide against making a loan or rank you as a higher risk (and charge a higher rate) because of the debt you could amass using lines of credit.

Cancel any cards or lines of credit you don't intend to use. Check your credit history at least once a year in search of errors and look for open lines of credit you don't intend to use. If you cancel a line, be sure to ask the lender to notify credit-reporting agencies.

You can also ask a credit card company to lower a card's credit line or you can refuse an increase they bestow upon you. Doing this could add a few points to your credit score if your total available credit is out of line with your income or ability to repay money borrowed.

Don't Cosign a Loan Unless You're Willing to Pay It Off

Think twice—and maybe three or four times—before you cosign someone else's loan. Think about it this way: If you are being asked to cosign, you're being asked to take a risk that a professional lender won't take. If the borrower met the criteria, the lender wouldn't be asking for a cosigner.

That said, it is fairly common for parents to cosign apartment leases, car loans, and other borrowing to help their young adult children establish themselves in life. But if your child is 55 with a bad credit record and wants the Bank of Mom and Dad to back him up on a car loan, perhaps you might want to say no and help him or her find a different way. If you still want to be helpful and have the money to do so, make a *private* agreement with your child that will not end up on either of your credit reports. Still dangerous, but it's not threatening to your own record.

Under a standard loan agreement, the cosigner may be required to pay up to the full amount of the debt if the borrower does not meet obligations. You may also have to pay late fees or collection costs. *But wait, it gets worse*: In some states, the creditor can collect an overdue debt from the cosigner without first trying to collect from the borrower!

The creditor can use the same collection methods against you that can be used against the borrower, such as suing you or garnishing your wages. And the fact that the debt went into default may become a part of your credit record. Even if you're not asked to repay the debt, your liability for the loan may keep you from getting other credit; creditors will consider the cosigned loan one of your obligations.

If you choose to cosign, you may be able to negotiate the specific terms of your obligation. For example, you may be able to have the lender modify the language to limit your liability to the principal on the loan, and not include late charges, court costs, or attorneys' fees. Ask the lender to agree, in writing, to notify you if the borrower misses a payment. That will give you time to deal with the problem or make back payments yourself without having to repay the entire amount immediately. Finally, make sure you get copies of all important papers, such as the loan contract, the truth-in-lending disclosure statement, and warranties. You may need these documents if there's a dispute between the borrower and the seller.

Dip into Home Equity Loans and Lines of Credit

Borrowing against the equity you have built up on your home is one loan that is relatively easy to obtain and at a lower cost. What is *equity*? It is the value of your home above and beyond any mortgage and other borrowing against it. For example, if your home is worth $500,000 and the remaining mortgage balance is $100,000, you have $400,000 in equity.

A bank or other lender can look at that situation and see a very low risk in making a loan. They are not likely to loan you the full amount of your equity because real estate values do not always rise, and they have to be convinced of your ability to repay, just as with any other type of loan.

A home equity loan (as a lump sum payment to the borrower) or a home equity line of credit (an amount that can be drawn against by transfers to a bank account or by using a debit card linked to the loan) is a *second mortgage*, meaning it is subservient to the principal mortgage. That's the reason it is based on the home's equity rather than its full value. But if you are unable to pay back an equity loan (or a first mortgage), the lender can force the sale of the home to get back the money it has loaned. Any money left over after the sale, plus fees and expenses related to the sale, go to the borrower, who is now homeless.

Equity loans usually have lower rates than consumer loans, and in certain circumstances may have a lower rate than your primary mortgage. (I ran into that situation myself when my personal banker called to tell me his bank had instructed him to contact his best customers and offer home equity loans at a great rate, without closing costs or other fees. The rate he quoted was several points below the mortgage we had from the same bank. I asked him if we could use the equity loan to pay off the mortgage. There were a few moments of silence before he answered, "Yes. But I would move quickly." I did. When I spoke to the banker a few days later, he told me the offer had been revised shortly after I had pounced on it. I saved thousands of dollars per year by taking the deal, thank you very much.)

The interest you pay on a home equity loan may be tax deductible. Consult your accountant to learn the limits on the amount of eligible interest. You can use the proceeds of an equity loan for any purpose, but many people consider it a good way to pay for home improvements and upgrades since that (in theory, at least) raises the home's value. Chapter 19 reveals the upgrades that offer the biggest return on investment.

Now one important concept: A home is usually an *appreciating asset*. That means in most situations, its value appreciates, or increases, over time. That is what makes it a good investment for many people. If you use the equity loan to buy a new car, you are acquiring something that is usually a *depreciating asset*. It begins losing value the moment you drive the car out of the dealership, and will continue doing so over time. If you use the equity loan to pay for an extravagant vacation, you may have a wonderful time, but you have not acquired an asset at all.

For these reasons, tread carefully before using an equity loan. If your goal is to own your home free and clear, this might not be the best bet for you. On the other hand, if you spend carefully and can lay out a plan for your finances that allows repaying all loans on a schedule that is comfortable for you and your family, equity loans can be a very useful element of your credit plan.

CHAPTER 26

Using a Credit Card to Your Best Advantage

Charge! I am no longer amazed about where I can use plastic. Actually, it feels strange to open my wallet for cash. You should be able to use your card at doctors and dentists, the US Postal Service, supermarkets, and automobile parking attendants. I have made the down payment on a new car using a credit card, which not only earned me points but also gave me a bit of comfort knowing that the card issuer would stand behind me if there were a problem.

Used properly, credit cards are among the greatest conveniences available to the savvy consumer. *Here are three good reasons why…*

• **They're safer than cash.** If a credit card is lost or stolen and you notify the issuer quickly, your liability is minimal or none at all. Lose your wallet? You're not getting that cash back.

• **Online records are handy.** Credit card statements (and online records) help you keep track of where you spend your money, establish proof of purchase for warranties, and provide records for tax purposes.

• **You get perks.** The best credit cards offer benefits including cash rebates, frequent flyer mileage, free rental car or airline insurance, and/or extended warranties.

Notice what is missing? The credit side of the credit card is its least appealing feature. It is going to be a tax-free day in Washington, D.C., before I willingly pay 18% interest, or more, on a meal I ate six weeks ago, a play I went to a month ago, or a pair of shoes I haven't taken out of the box yet. Credit cards are among the worst loan deals, right up there with pawnbrokers. Their worst feature is the revolving-loan provision, which states that if you owe $100 one month and charge another $300 in the next month, you owe interest on $400, not just on the amount that is outstanding from the first due date.

In this section I explore some strategies to help you be a savvy consumer of credit card service.

- **Choose the best card for your needs.**
- **Keep your personal details to yourself.**
- **Set up autopay from your checking account.**
- **Understand your credit card company's fine print.**
- **Close an account officially.**
- **Get out from under a revolving balance.**

Cash Versus Credit

I have expressed my opinion that credit cards offer some tremendous advantages.

I do want to make note of an academic study, by Priya Raghubir (at New York University) and Joydeep Srivastava (at the University of Maryland), that concluded that people who pay cash tend to keep to a tighter budget than those who use plastic. Forking over a wad of dollar bills makes a purchase very real. Credit cards defer the pain.

- **Pay off your highest-cost loans first.**
- **Be aware of credit card blocking.**

Choose the Best Card for Your Needs

I use a credit card as a convenience to aggregate most of my spending into a single bill. Depending upon when in the month I buy something, I can have as many as seven weeks before I have to pay. (Find out when your monthly statement closes and buy just after then. It will be about a month before the next statement is reckoned, and you should have 21 days to pay the bill.) Other people use them other ways.

• **Some people use credit to finance purchases.** If you expect to pay interest on outstanding balances, your first priority in deciding on a credit card should be the annual percentage rate. Be aware that credit card companies can change their interest rates. Always be ready to take your business elsewhere—but first make a phone call to customer service and ask for a lower rate. You might receive a reduction if the company realizes they might lose you as a customer. (You're much less likely to get a reduced rate if you were late on any payments.)

If the credit card issuer is trying to entice you with a low interest rate, be sure to read the fine print. Some employ a legal form of bait and switch. The rates are low at first and then climb to the upper reaches. Other cards are tied to the prime rate or to another index. Read the details to learn how the rate is calculated, when it can change, and how high it can go.

• **Some people use credit for convenience and for special features.** If that is you, those features, not annual percentage rate, should be your top priority. If you never have an outstanding balance, the interest rate is of only passing interest to you. Read carefully the fine print about rewards. It is common that you will be required to charge a minimum amount within a two- or three-month period in order to receive the bonus.

Years ago, we updated the heating system in our home from electric baseboard (something that caused real pain each month between November and May when the bills arrived) to an oil furnace. The contract with the oil company called for payments of $3,000 on agreement, another $3,000 when the system was installed, and a final payment of $3,000 one month after it was up and running. The oil company took credit cards for fuel delivery. I told them I would use plastic for the furnace payments. The net result: I spread out the payments for almost four months, paid the bills when due so that I didn't owe any interest, and earned 9,000 miles on my frequent-flyer account.

There are hundreds, probably thousands, of cards available, from the big three—American Express, which is a financial institution of its own, as well as Visa and MasterCard, which work in conjunction with other banks and businesses to process charges—to those like Diner's Club and Discover. Then there are store cards, specific to a particular retailer or gas station. You'll also find co-branded cards, issued under the name of an airline, hotel chain, or retail store that use the services of one of the major card issuers.

If you are interested in using a credit card to purchase an extended warranty, theft protection, rental car insurance, and a few other special services, see Chapter 1.

If you're like most consumers, your mailbox and your email inbox are daily stuffed with offers for credit cards. The ones I study are those that offer me money back (cash is always in fashion) on purchases, followed closely by cards that accrue rewards points that I can use as if they were money (for purchases at airlines, hotels, or certain retailers). In third place, for me, are cards that deliver bonus airline miles (because frequent flyer plans are sometimes difficult to use).

Don't waste your time and effort on a card for an airline that you rarely fly. One advantage associated with some of the airline cards is that they may waive the fee for one or more checked bags when you use that particular airline, and sometimes give you priority boarding or certain other little perks.

Up Your Short-Term Spending

Here's what I do when I choose to accept the gift of 50,000 reward points or airline miles with a requirement of a certain level of short-term spending—I switch over automatic payments I already make for things like cable television and internet, cellphone service, and the like. If I need an extra $500 in spending to reach the needed level, I can prepay a month or two on one of these services that I know I will owe anyway.

Keep Your Personal Details to Yourself

It is almost impossible to maintain complete control over your personal information anymore. There are just too many people and services who are collecting bits and pieces about you for various reasons. In fact, a credit card issuer is going to ask

About Those Chip Cards

In 2015, the United States began to grudgingly catch up with Europe and many other places around the world with the issuance of chip-embedded credit cards. The small encoded chip is meant to replace the magnetic stripe on the back of cards as a means of communicating with the card issuer. The theory is that it is much easier for a thief who obtains the information on the stripe using a hijacked card reader to create a phony card of the same design than it is to produce a phone card with the chip.

The chips are still not in use on every card, and as of this book's publication, not every merchant had readers that used the chip. That is not really a problem for you, the consumer. Merchants that do not have a chip reader, though, are liable for fraud from phony cards. You, as the consumer, are not liable for fraudulent charges as long as you report them to your credit card company within 60 days after you receive your bill with the fraudulent charge.

for your Social Security number and other details in order to assure itself that you are a worthy credit risk.

At a retail store, it is not unreasonable for a seller to ask to see some identification to prove you are who you claim to be, but you have the right to block them from recording information from that proof of identification. If you purchase something online using your credit card, you will most likely be asked to provide your billing address as well as the shipping address. This is a way for the seller to confirm your identity. You'll also be asked to provide the security code that is printed on your card—on the front for American Express and on the back near the signature box for most other cards.

But once you have the card in your possession, there is no need for you to give a seller your Social Security number or date of birth. If they ask, push back. Your credit card company has this information on file as part of your application. And while we're on the subject, never disclose your credit card number or Social Security number in response to a phone call, email, or postal mailing you receive. If you receive a phone call from someone purporting to be from your credit card company, they already have your name and account number on file. Treat anything else as potential fraud.

Two recent wrinkles in credit card security may make sense for you, adding a layer of protection against fraud.

- **One-time codes are an arrangement between you and the card issuer** where you contact them from your cellphone or computer and receive either a one-time credit card number or a one-time card verification number for a purchase you are about to make.

- **Two-step verification works like this: You make a purchase online or at a store that is fully wired.** Before the transaction goes through, a special code is sent to your smartphone as a text message. The purchase goes through when you enter that code onscreen or into a terminal at a retailer.

If you add either of these features to your account, your card should be of no use to anyone who obtains its number unless they also have access to your smartphone, which itself should be protected by a sign-on code, fingerprint reader, or swipe pattern.

Set Up Autopay from Your Checking Account

Nearly every credit card issuer allows you to set up automatic payments, with a link to a checking account in your name. Instead of getting a paper or online bill, the money toward credit card payment comes directly out of your checking account. This is a way to avoid overdue payment and interest charges. Be sure the balance in your checking account is enough to pay your credit card bills; that also helps you avoid minimum balance fees from your bank. You also receive all the benefits provided by the card issuer.

You can instruct the card company to take payment for any of the following amounts from your checking account:

- **Total new balance is the full amount due under the current statement.** Charges made after the close of the previous statement are not due until a new statement is calculated.
- **Minimum amount due is the amount the credit card company requires you pay to avoid a fee for missing a payment.** You'll also have to pay interest on the remaining balance. Paying the minimum isn't a good idea because you wind up paying more in interest over the long haul.
- **Fixed amount may be enough to pay off the balance, or it may trigger interest charges on any unpaid balance.**

Watch Out for Typos

My wife paid off a credit card account that was not set up for autopay. She arranged for the payment, but she entered an amount that was twenty cents less than the balance due. The next month, we received a bill with an interest charge of $80, representing the charge for that pair of dimes as well as all the charges made after that. I called customer service immediately. An agent recognized that we were justifiably outraged savvy consumers and quickly removed the charges.

Understand Your Credit Card Company's Fine Print

Understand how your credit card works. Under most agreements, you have no grace period for any purchases added to an account with an outstanding balance. In other words, if you owe $2,000 on a card and make a $500 purchase, you will immediately owe interest on $2,500.

The best defense, of course, is to avoid owing money on a relatively high-interest credit card account. Second-best defense may be to use more than one credit card, paying off in full as many accounts as possible each month and not adding new charges to a card that is already accruing interest.

I Cardly Knew You

Canceling credit cards doesn't help increase your credit score. In fact, canceling a card can negatively affect your credit score, according to *U.S. News & World Report.* Before you cancel a card, consider how long you've had that card. The longer you've had it, the more positive the effect it has on your score, assuming you have relatively young credit. Also, most scores consider how many accounts you have. Having no credit cards can negatively affect your score, and so can opening lots of accounts around the same time,

Accounts that you've closed will appear on your credit reports for at least 7 years, but be marked as closed.

Before you use a new credit card, read the important bits of small print on the agreement about the following aspects: annual fee, annual percentage rate, late charges, and grace period.

Annual Fee

Typical charges range from free (usually accompanied by a higher-than-typical interest rate and sometimes fewer special benefits) to about $95 for a basic premium card that delivers some special benefits. Some super-premium cards (platinum, titanium, and whatever unusual color or construction marketing folk can imagine) can cost $650 or more per year, although they may offer benefits that make sense to certain users, such as free access to airport lounges, credits for certain travel expenses like baggage checks, or trusted traveler programs at American airport security or immigration lines.

Many credit cards that charge an annual fee will try to entice you by offering the first year free. I pay the annual fee on two cards that offer specific perks that are of value to me, and I regularly cancel new cards after eleven months and twenty-nine days. I mark the anniversary on my calendar.

Since I have both personal and business credit cards, one strategy is to change from one type of account to the other every year, picking up bonus points or miles each time. "Why, yes," I tell the credit card company, "I would be happy to accept 50,000 free points on a new business credit card. And while we're on the phone, would you please cancel my personal card? But be sure to transfer all of my accrued points to the new account." And yes, it works just like that.

It does not matter to the Internal Revenue Service (or the banks) if you make business charges on a personal card, or the other way around. It only matters that you properly categorize expenses when you fill out your tax forms.

Annual Percentage Rate

Lower is better than higher, of course, if you expect to ever run a balance. Pay attention to the small print on adjustable-rate schemes, where you want to know how often and by how much the rate can rise.

Late Charges

Most cards apply a fixed late charge as well as starting the interest meter any time you fail to make a minimum payment. To add insult to injury, many credit card issuers reserve the right—it's there somewhere in the tiny print—to increase the annual percentage rate if you miss a payment. If the company does this, get on the phone immediately and ask customer service to reverse the action. If they don't, pay off the amount due and move on to another card.

And don't be shy about calling your credit card company every once in a while to ask for a lower interest rate or some other special deal. Tell customer service you have a better offer from another company. Have the details in front of you so you can be specific. Sometimes you'll be rejected, but sometimes you'll be rewarded with a better deal. And you can always take your business elsewhere. Why might this work? First, credit card companies want your business—the average account brings in hundreds of dollars per year in interest payments, plus the money earned from fees charged to merchants for your purchases. Second, credit card companies know that it costs them money to acquire new clients.

Grace Period

The grace period is the time between the date the bill is drawn up and the date the account must be paid. A typical period is about 15 to 21 days. The longer the grace period, the more advantage the card gives you.

Today nearly every credit card company encourages you to receive your monthly statement on the internet, offering a range of notification and warning emails or phone text messages to help you keep on top of your account. This can appeal to you if you travel. It also allows you to search for transactions online instead of rummaging through overstuffed file cabinets.

If you're simply not comfortable paying your bills online, stick with paper. If you have the capability and can handle a bit of a learning curve, switch your statements to be online only.

Close an Account Officially

I'm not afraid to take advantage of the latest and greatest offer of any sort, including credit cards, if it helps me hold on to my money longer or otherwise benefits my bottom line. I'll gladly accept 50,000 free points or miles for a new card and then move on to the next great offer before the introductory period expires.

If a credit card has no annual fee, you can simply keep the account open. But certain cards charge annual fees, usually starting at about $50 and running as high as $650 per year for super-duper premium plastic. If you receive more value (free baggage on airlines, car rental upgrades, or other benefits) than the cost of a card, consider renewing the card.

Now comes a counterintuitive element of credit card economics. Up to a point, it is to your benefit to have as large an available line of credit as possible. This is because your FICO and other credit score metrics look at the ratio of your outstanding balance to available credit. If you have a total available credit line of $20,000 spread across four or five cards, as well as an average monthly balance of $5,000, your ratio would be 25%. That is not at all shocking to a lender. Let's say, though, that you cancel two cards that you rarely use. Your available credit line might drop to $10,000. With the same average monthly balance of $5,000 that makes your balance-to-credit ratio 50%, which will likely hurt your FICO score.

Your goal should be to have as large a credit line as possible, and to watch expenditures and monthly payments to keep your outstanding balance as low as you can. I know, it's counterintuitive. But if you want to cancel a card that is no longer your favorite, consider applying for a different one to boost your overall credit line.

As long as you pay your bills on time, it is not unreasonable to have multiple credit cards. I have more than I need, but each of them offers a benefit of some sort. And my FICO score is quite healthy; thank you for asking.

Get Out from Under a Revolving Balance

Do whatever you can to avoid large, long-term outstanding balances. You are better off taking money out of your savings to pay bills in full or carefully using other lower-cost money sources, including home equity loans.

If you end up paying interest when you don't intend to carry a balance, you'll need to do a few things to shut off the meter…

1. **Call the credit card company's customer-service department and find out your current balance, including interest charges.**

2. **Don't make any more charges on that card until you pay off your balance to zero.**

3. **If you can afford to, arrange to immediately transfer, from your checking account, enough money to pay off the balance as it stands at that very moment.** It's not a bad idea to include extra money to cover any charges you may have put on the account since the last payment. Ask customer service for advice on how much you should pay to absolutely, positively erase the outstanding balance.

4. **If you cannot afford to pay off your outstanding credit card balance from your checking account or savings, you are not handling your finances well.** Credit card interest rates, in the range of 16% to 20% on an annualized basis, are the next-worst thing to a loan shark. Find a way to spend less, earn more, and pay as little interest as possible.

Pay Off Your Highest-Interest Loans First

If you've got to choose among various outstanding bills, pay the one that has the highest interest rate—almost always a credit card or personal bank loan. For the same reason, financial experts advise against reducing the size of your mortgage with extra payments when you have outstanding credit card loans. Mortgage rates are usually lower than credit card rates, and interest on home mortgages, including home equity loans, is tax deductible.

And again, within reason, you are better off paying your credit card bills even if you have to dip into your savings. Compare the money you earn on your savings to the money you lose on the interest to see why. If you're worried about impoverishing yourself by spending your savings, you're asking the wrong question. Instead, ask yourself why you are going into debt if you are unable to pay off your loan without spending your savings.

Be Aware of Credit Card Blocking

When you rent a car, rent a pair of skis, or check into a hotel, you may be putting down a deposit without realizing it. It's called credit card *blocking*, and it is a term for a temporary hold on your credit line. For example, a hotel may block an amount equal to the expected bottom line on your stay, and in some cases may add expected charges including meals, drinks, and incidentals. The block is removed when you pay your actual bill. Merchants want to use the blocks to be certain that your credit line will actually be available to them when you check out. A rental car company may put a substantial block on your account as a protection (for them) in case of any problems with the contract.

Why does this matter? If you are close to the credit limit on your card, you could end up in an embarrassing situation (like having your card rejected while trying to make a purchase) without realizing it. You should also be vigilant when your credit card bill arrives. Make sure that you are not double billed for a hotel stay or car rental. Always check your credit card statements to make sure you have been properly billed. Credit holds are usually not shown as charges but instead show up in a "pending charge" category.

CHAPTER 27

Banking and Investing

You can't talk about money without talking about banks and investments. The topics are practically inseparable unless you're stashing your hard-earned salary in a mattress—and there are better ways to protect what you have (and maybe earn a little more while you're at it).

- **Bank thriftily.**
- **Invest wisely.**

Bank Thriftily

Though they often don't act as if they know this, banks need you more than you need them. They need you to make deposits. They need you to take out mortgages...open credit card accounts... buy mutual funds and insurance...and more. That's right. Consumer-oriented banks are selling products, and they want you to be the buyer. Be a savvy one!

Buy the Best Checking Account

A checking account is, in essence, a savings account that is meant to hold short-term deposits and issue payments to others. Because most people do not keep the bulk of their money in a checking account, and because the bank incurs expenses when managing payments issued from it, checking accounts generally pay little or no interest on deposits. And most banks charge a monthly fee or require a minimum account balance.

When you want to open a new checking account, find the type of account that results in the lowest monthly or annual fees. Be sure you understand any minimum balance requirements and charges for bank services. A half hour of research online, on the phone, or across the desk from a bank representative could save you $100 or more per year.

Here are some more ideas to maintain your edge...

• **Once you have an account, review it at least once a year**—and also after any notification of policy changes. It may make sense to switch to a new plan if your operations—or the bank's—has changed.

• Keep an eye on what your bank's competitors are offering. Ask your bank to match any special offers. They often will. If they won't, be willing to change banks to save on fees. Why should you be loyal to a bank if it is not loyal to you?

• Make use of direct deposit of paychecks, Social Security, and other such payments. Your bank might reward you with a break on fees and, in any case, you will have quicker access to your money and avoid the possibility of lost incoming checks.

Take It Online: Direct Deposit, Online Bill Pay, and Automatic Payments

The banking industry (and the US Postal Service) has changed tremendously in the past decade or so partly because of online banking—being able to see account balances online, transfer funds from one account to another, pay bills from your computer or smartphone. Various industry surveys now say that more than half of adult consumers do much or all of their banking online, rarely venturing into a branch office.

Consumers used to receive stacks of individual bills from merchants and utilities as well as a monthly statement from each credit card company. (And there was also a fat monthly envelope from the bank containing a statement and the original paper checks we had sent out as payment in the previous cycle.) And then we would have to write out checks for bills, place them in envelopes, put a postage stamp on the front, and mail them out. If an incoming bill was delayed in the mail, or your outgoing payment held up for some reason, it was quite easy to accrue late fees or interest charges.

Today, almost all of that has changed, and almost entirely for the better. I can go months without having to write out a check or visit a bank to make a deposit. I handle almost all my transactions automatically or by visiting my bank's website and the websites of the billing companies. Those relatively few checks that arrive in my mailbox are deposited to my bank account using an app on my smartphone.

I'll briefly go over the services available to most banking customers. Call your bank or visit its website for more details. *Here's how most banking is done today...*

• Direct deposit. Most employers prefer to automatically deposit your paycheck into your checking account. It saves

Bonus Cash

As I was preparing this chapter, I received a piece of mail from an online bank that was opening its first physical branches in our region. They offered a $400 bonus for new accounts, with the proviso that at least two direct deposits be made within 60 days. That was an offer much too good to turn down, and I didn't even have to close my primary account at another bank. A few months down the line, after I've received the bonus, I'll decide which financial institution is worthy of my continued business.

The bank is gambling that the relatively small hassle involved in changing direct deposit checks from one institution to another will tend to make you stay with them. Maybe. I figure it took me all of 10 minutes to fill out the online form to move a direct deposit from one bank to another. That's not a bad deal to earn $400.

Direct deposit checks can come from employers, from Social Security, and from certain types of investments such as retirement fund distributions and some annuities.

them money on printing and mailing. You'll need to provide your account number and the routing number, which functions as the electronic mailing address for the payment. You can find both numbers at the online site for your checking account and on a paper check if you have them. The federal government and most state governments also offer direct deposit for things like Social Security and disability payments and tax refunds.

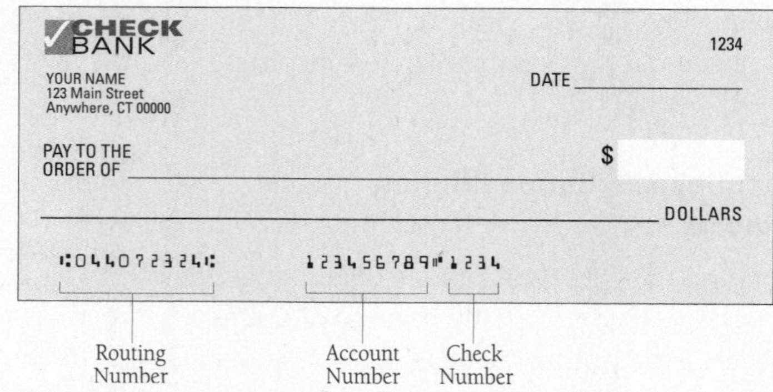

- **Smartphone deposit.** Most banks now offer apps that you install on a smartphone and allow you to conduct most financial transactions this way. (Make sure you have a complex password in place for the app, and a different strong password or other form of protection for accessing your phone.) Also, do your smartphone banking at home. Public WiFi is a favorite place for thieves to steal information.

With this system, you can use the built-in digital camera found on most smartphones to take a picture of the front and back of a check (signed and marked for deposit.) Follow the instructions displayed on the phone, including selecting which account you want the money to go to. When the system has all the information it needs, the funds generally will arrive in your account within one business day, following the same availability schedule you would find if you went to the trouble of visiting the bank. (Hold on to the original check until the funds show up in your account.) Some banks have a daily or monthly limit on the amount of money you can deposit this way. Consumer and business accounts have slightly different rules about the amount of time a bank can put a hold on deposits before you can withdraw or spend the funds. Again, the same rules apply to online banking that apply at a teller's window.

- **Electronic transfer.** A company or individual can arrange for a quick transfer from one account to another, again using the checking account number and the routing number (or sometimes a special wire transfer number). Some banks may charge a fee for an expedited wire transfer.

From your own checking account, you can arrange to electronically transfer funds to or from various accounts you have at the bank, including savings, checking, home equity, line of credit, and charge cards. You can make these transfers, usually free, immediately or schedule them to occur later. You can also set up recurring transfers. For example, you can instruct the system to withdraw $250 per month and place it in an investment account. A dwindling number of banks may charge you to transfer money to an account at another institution. You may be able to get around that fee by authorizing your investment company to reach into your account and withdraw money for your account with them.

- **Electronic bill payment.** You can permit companies to automatically withdraw balances from your account when they are due. Many people pay their utility and phone bills this way, and you can authorize almost any other business to initiate a transfer.

I'm not aware of any particular security risk with authorizing electronic withdrawals from bank accounts. Just keep an eye on your accounts every few weeks, and don't hesitate to call and question any debit you don't recognize.

Another option is to set up automatic payments for recurring charges to a credit card. That way you can earn points or cash rebates, and then set up your credit card account so that it is automatically paid off each month from your bank account. Yes, it's a circle within a circle, but once you set it up, it will do the work all by itself every month.

- **Online check payment.** Here you can instruct the bank to pay any bill on your behalf. You provide the name and address of the payee, your account number with them, and the amount to be paid. Most online bank systems will maintain an address book for you so you can just click on a name and enter an amount to be paid. You can have the bank send out the check immediately or you can schedule payment for a particular day—and you don't have to pay for a stamp.

Some large companies arrange with major banks for your check request to be converted to an electronic transfer. Otherwise, the bank's computers will produce a neatly printed check and put it in the mail. Plan your check payments to meet due dates on your accounts.

Watch Out for the Demise of the Float

Some smart investors—and sloppy bookkeepers—used to keep their checking accounts afloat by *playing the float*. It was a process that involved moving money around from account to account to pay bills and earn interest, taking advantage of the fact that it used to take anywhere from several days to a week for checks drawn on nonlocal banks to clear. Today, technology has all but eliminated most of this float. Most checks clear on the same day they are deposited or the next day.

The only exception here is the online check payment feature at banks. When you order a check to be sent from your account, your bank gets to take the money out of your account and hold on to it until the check is cashed by the recipient. Even if it is only a matter of a few days, a few pennies earned times millions of transactions add up and help pay for the service.

In any case, as a consumer it makes sense to maintain overdraft protection at your bank. This amounts to a short-term line of credit that will protect you from bouncing a check and from the sometimes-outrageous fees banks and stores may charge for a returned check. Be sure you understand the terms of the overdraft account, including the interest rate charged. And when you are notified by the bank that a check has been paid by the overdraft account, pay off the full amount immediately to avoid paying interest for an extended period. Call the bank and make sure the slate is wiped clear.

Save Money on Check Printing

Your friendly neighborhood bank, or its online equivalent, will be happy to order a full set of checks and deposit slips for your new account and provide you with new materials when you run out. Some banks provide free checks for established clients.

On the other hand, if the bank starts talking about printing, service charges, and shipping fees, don't think you have to accept that deal. You can do a whole lot better on your own, saving a lot of money. Individuals and businesses can order checks from several national firms. The checks you receive will be accepted just as readily and you may also be able to choose from a much larger selection.

Just search online for *checks*. The leaders follow.

- **Carousel** at CarouselChecks.com
- **Checks in the Mail** at ChecksInTheMail.com
- **Vistaprint** at Vistaprint.com

Walmart and Costco have their own connection to check printers.

Be aware that many online companies will try their hardest to sell you all sorts of things you don't want, like gold-plated check boxes, mailing labels, rubber stamps, and the like. And many offer free or discounted shipping, but then post dire warnings about how you really should upgrade to priority printing and express mail. Read the offers carefully. I don't write all that many physical checks anymore and I am perfectly willing to wait three weeks for my order (and save enough money for a nice lunch).

There is no particular reason *not* to use a third-party check company rather than the bank's printer. The information you submit online for your checks is no different from what will appear on the checks, which any recipient can see. Again, just keep an eye on your bank statement. The obligation lies with your bank to protect you against fraud committed against your account.

Save Money with a Credit Union

Banks are the very underpinning of our capitalist society. That's not meant as a knock. It's just a reminder that bankers are in it for the money. Even George Bailey of the classic film *It's a Wonderful Life* had to come up with the scratch somehow. Most major banks are owned by corporations and, in the end, they are responsible to their shareholders first and account holders second. There are some financial institutions that—in some ways—operate differently.

- **A mutual bank is one that is owned by its members**—those who deposit money there. Mutual banks may have lower fees and be easier to deal with, although their small size may limit their offerings. They tend to be more conservative in lending policies, and are probably not the place to finance your megayacht.

- **Credit unions are nonprofit organizations that offer many of the same services as banks.** You may be able to save hundreds of dollars on checking and credit card accounts, as well as on personal loans. Credit unions used to be only available to members of an association or employees at a particular institution, but in more recent years most have opened their doors to any comer.

Some may require you to join an association or make a small donation (as little as $5 for some institutions) to a local charity to qualify you as a member.

Compare mutual banks and credit unions to those of the big banks, and choose the one that offers you the best range of services at the lowest fees. In some places, credit unions offer auto and home loans at a lower interest rate. Over time, even an eighth of a percent can amount to a nice pile of savings.

You can search for a credit union near you at CreditUnions Online.com.

> **TIP**
>
> **An Unlikely Shortchange**
>
> I cannot cite any particular instance where an ATM has dispensed an amount of money different from what was asked for, or what the receipt showed. If somehow this happens, I suggest immediately calling the phone number on the back of your ATM or debit card. Modern ATMs are very sophisticated, and nearly all of them are under watch by video cameras.

Use Your ATM Card Smartly

My wife sometimes claims that if I were to open the cash section of my wallet, moths would fly out. Maybe. But that's not because I never buy anything. I can go months without touching cash or fumbling with coins. I use credit cards, debit cards, automatic toll transponders, and payment systems on my smartphone. I can go cashless in taxis and vending machines, and I fully expect the next time I run into a neighbor's daughter selling Girl Scout Cookies, she will accept electronic payment.

However, you do want to carry a bit of cash with you just in case. And the easiest way to get some folding money is use a debit card at an ATM kiosk. Automated teller machines began to arrive in large numbers in the 1970s, and now are almost everywhere. They can dispense cash, accept checks for deposit, and perform a number of other banking tasks. (All of those functions, other than doling out cash, can now be accomplished on a smartphone or computer.)

Here's more advice, some obvious and some not…

- **Be sure you understand your bank's charges for ATM use.** Some banks allow unlimited free use of their local machines for ordinary deposits and withdrawals, while others apply fees. That doesn't mean it isn't worth a $1 charge to make an emergency cash withdrawal on a Sunday, but if your bank levies a fee, you might want to think twice about using the machine in the lobby of the bank when the teller's cage is open inside.

Nearly all banks apply charges—sometimes rather steep—on the use of their cards at ATMs other than their own. This can be the competing bank next door or one halfway around the world. Be sure you understand the current fee schedule before you use the machine. And don't assume that there is only one price list, either. Ask your banker about better deals for customers with multiple accounts or a minimum balance.

- **Keep your personal identification number (PIN) secret.** Never disclose your code to a merchant or to a telephone caller. If you are asked for the code by an officer of your bank for a good reason, change the code immediately. As with all our computer tasks, it is very important to protect your ATM card with a strong PIN or password. Don't write the PIN on the back of the card or store it on a slip of paper in one of the pockets of your wallet. Don't use the last four digits of your phone number. Most banks won't let you set a PIN of 1111, 9999, or 1234 and few other obvious codes.

- **Always take your ATM receipt.** It contains information about your account. Most current machines offer you the option to print an image of a check you may have deposited. That's a good way to keep a copy until the deposit has cleared.

- **Check your receipts**—deposits and withdrawals—against your online and monthly statement and immediately inform your bank of any transactions you did not authorize or do not recognize.

- **Report a lost or stolen card to your bank at once.** You can call customer service to have the card immediately frozen so it cannot be used.

- **Take a look at the slot where you insert your card.** If it looks tampered with in any way, don't use the ATM. If there are two ATMs together, check the slot on both and if one looks different from the other, don't use either machine. Criminals install card readers in the slots. It captures your information as you insert your card and then they come back later, collect the card reader, and use your information to purchase things or to sell to someone else.

- **Be aware that ATM terminals have become a favorite site for robberies.** It's always a good idea to have a family member or friend watch your back as you work the machine. Always look around before approaching an ATM. If you are arriving by car, park close to the terminal but don't block the view of the machine with your vehicle. As you enter your PIN, block the keypad so someone nearby cannot see your code. Similarly,

Waive ATM Fees Goodbye

Be on the lookout for perks offered by some banks and financial institutions that promise to waive any ATM fee imposed by a bank outside of their network.

At the investment company Charles Schwab, I established a checking account that is linked to a debit card. I use that card and account for one purpose only—I can go to any ATM, anywhere in the world, to obtain cash. They not only reimburse me for any fee, they also convert foreign currency to dollar equivalent at the current exchange rate without imposing an additional charge. It's enough of a lure that I have, over the years, expanded some of my investments to that company. I want to keep them happy with me.

do not make a big show of checking the amount of money received. It is better to do so away from the machine in your car or elsewhere.

- **If an ATM is hidden from view or poorly lit, go elsewhere.** If you regularly use ATMs, find the ones that seem safe, such as those inside businesses like supermarkets and malls. If you see anything suspicious, cancel your transaction and leave immediately. If someone follows you from an ATM, head for a busy, well-lighted place and call the police.

Don't Pay Twice for Safe-Deposit Box Insurance

If you maintain a safe-deposit box at a bank, read the fine print. Also check your annual bill. Some banks automatically charge you for insurance on the box's contents, which you may not need if you have a properly drawn homeowner's or renter's policy. Typical fees are about $25 for $5,000 worth of coverage.

Check with your insurance agent. If you are already covered for loss, inform your bank that you will decline the insurance and pay only the rental fee and any tax. There is no point to double coverage. You cannot collect twice for the same loss.

Invest Wisely

This book is mostly about savvy ways to spend your money, but I didn't want to miss the chance to pass along a few of my favorite conservative ways to build up more cash to spend. You can find dozens of weighty tomes with detailed suggestions on ways to earn more on your investment. Some of them even make sense.

Hire a Financial Manager

I long ago decided that I was better at earning money than I was at finding and managing investments, so my basic modus operandi is to leave that to the experts. I also make sure that my interests are foremost in the equation. The purest way to do this is to hire a financial advisor who charges by the hour or for a set fee, and does not receive commissions on buys and sales in your account. This sort of advisor can help set you up with a major financial company (like Fidelity or Charles Schwab, for two examples) that put into effect a plan established by you and your advisor. You can arrange to review your portfolio annually or even more often, but through it all your advisor knows that bad advice will likely not be rewarded with future visits.

The other way is to engage a broker or an advisor who will develop a plan with you, make recommendations, and (with your approval) buy and sell mutual funds, bonds, and individual equities. Remember that a broker makes a commission on both purchases and sales, and will still make money from you regardless of whether they give bad (or incorrect) advice. If you go this route, go with someone who comes highly recommended and then keep a close eye on your portfolio. If your commission-based advisor is providing poor advice or consistently underperforming the market, consider changing advisors. Your holdings can be moved from one advisory company to another.

And whichever route you take, be sure to add another professional to your team: a capable accountant who can help you handle the tax side of your personal affairs.

Ask friends, family, and business acquaintances for recommendations for a financial advisor. Then ask the advisor to audition for your business.

Here's a link to an article from BottomLineInc that includes some pointed questions to ask a financial advisor: BottomLineInc.com/wp-content/uploads/2017/06/QtoA_ChoosingFinancialAdvisor.pdf.

In 2017, the White House proposed loosening or eliminating some of the fiduciary requirements for investment companies. Those rules require advisors to put their clients' interests above their own profit motives. Why? I have no answer. But with or without the requirement, you should always ask yourself whether a recommendation to invest or sell or restructure your holdings is the best move for you. If you can't see the logic, insist on an explanation and be ready to take your business elsewhere if you are not satisfied with the answer.

Build Your Nest Egg Through Market Highs and Lows

There is only one sure way to make money in the stock market: Buy low and sell high. But if you're a conservative investor willing to take a small amount of risk, there is an investment scheme that almost always benefits the long-term investor, and it is a scheme that works even when the market is skidding downward.

Dollar-cost averaging works like this: You determine a specific amount you intend to invest on a regular schedule and then apply it to the price of a stock or mutual fund each time. Start by picking a stock for a company that has some substance—a utility, a major manufacturer, an established airline or cruise line. These types of companies have an established source of income as well as an inherent value (called a *breakup value*) based on the assets they own. In other words, their share prices are not likely to ever descend to zero.

For example, say you intend to invest $1,000 per month in a stock or in a mutual fund. When you start, the shares are selling for $10 each and you buy 100. A month later, the market has gone through a spectacular rise and the shares are selling for $20 each. You buy 50. A few months down the road, the market has come back to earth and shares sell for $5 each. You buy 200. By buying more shares when prices are low and fewer when they are high, you are establishing a moving average price. So long as you end up selling your shares at a price above that average, you're going to make some money on your investment. The fact is that, over time, nearly every stock and mutual fund increases its value even if you have to ride out a market downturn and wait for a recovery.

Dollar-cost averaging has these advantages…

- **Some investment experts say it is a particularly good strategy if you are buying a highly volatile stock**—one that goes up and down a great deal over time—or even a volatile commodity such as gold.

- **It fits in well with human nature and society.** Although a lump-sum investment in a quality stock almost always yields a substantial profit over time, most investors (starting with me) receive much more pain from losses than they do pleasure from gains. You want to reduce risk as much as you can, and that is one of the beauties of dollar-cost averaging.

• **It sets up a pattern of regular investing,** just as you are in the habit of making monthly payments on a car loan or a mortgage. You don't have to make an investment decision each month. In fact, you might want to set up an automatic money transfer from your bank account or your paycheck to a brokerage or mutual fund account for the purpose. And an automatic plan forces you to keep investing in a falling market, which goes against the natural instinct to pull out. Since our economy generally operates on the assumption that the stock market will go through cycles, toughing it out through a fall and then holding on until shares recover their value is a good way to build a nice portfolio.

TIP

Transfer In Kind

If you switch from one investment manager to another, or from one investment company to another, try to avoid unnecessary tax costs for shares of securities you want to hold onto. Ask about transferring the shares *in kind* rather than as cash. This is only possible if the securities are available at the new company.

Be sure to involve your tax advisor or accountant in any decision related to taxes.

Watch Out for Mutual-Fund Gotchas

I'm a big fan of mutual funds because you are buying the expertise of people who spend all day worrying the numbers. Their self-interest lies in finding a way to make money for their shareholders. My basic strategy is to find a good, diversified group of mutual funds and add to them over time.

There are also those who prefer *exchange-traded funds* (ETFs). These are securities that track an index (like the S&P 500 or the Nasdaq 100) or a particular basket of bonds or commodities. Unlike mutual funds, an ETF trades like a common stock, with the price changing through the day like a common stock. ETFs generally have lower fees than mutual funds (in part because the sellers do not have to maintain squads of analysts to pick stocks to buy or sell).

I am not a financial advisor. As you have already seen, I recommend you hire one. *Here are some important mutual fund gotchas you should be aware of…*

• **When you own stock in a particular company, you are liable for the payment of capital gains taxes on the shares when you sell them.** If you hold on to shares for 10 years, the tax is calculated on the difference between the price you paid when you bought the shares and the price you received when you sold them. You should be able to rely on the brokerage company to track your shares' cost bases, but it also pays to hold on to the paperwork as you make purchases. Capital gains taxes are low, generally lower than tax on earned income, so don't obsess about them. Having a gain is always better than having a loss.

- **When you own a mutual fund that invests in stock shares,** which most do, the managers of that fund may be buying and selling shares daily, resulting in capital gains or losses. If the gains outweigh the losses, the fund must distribute those gains to investors, and the holders of the mutual fund end up with a tax liability.
- **If you buy into a mutual fund late in the year,** you can end up owning a piece of that capital gain even though you did not profit. This doesn't mean you shouldn't buy into a good mutual fund, but if you're investing near the end of the calendar year, find out when distributions are made and buy in after that date.
- **It is tempting to try to time the market by switching from one mutual fund to another to catch the latest and greatest wave.** You may make more money—on paper—in this way, but you are also building up a series of capital gains even though you have stayed fully invested. Each transfer, including those within a family of funds offered by one mutual fund company, is considered a sale for tax purposes.

PART VI

Smart Travel

CHAPTER 28

Renting a Car

When it comes to holiday travel, Americans take to the road. According to the US Department of Transportation, about 91% of all long-distance travel—over the river and through the wood—is done by car. If you're driving your own vehicle, you can make the trip a bit more secure by following the car maintenance advice in Chapter 24.

Or perhaps you're renting a car for your adventure. Or you're on a business trip. In 2016, the automobile rental industry in the US was a $28 billion industry with more than 2 million cars available.

When you think about it, renting a $30,000 car for $40 or $50 per day is a pretty good deal. The trick is to keep it a good deal.

- **Understand auto rental companies.**
- **Save money at the auto-rental counter.**
- **Drop the cost of one-way rentals.**
- **Obey the second driver rules.**
- **Save time when you rent a car.**
- **Watch out for rental gotchas.**
- **Avoid damage claims.**
- **Know the facts about rental car insurance.**

Understand Auto Rental Companies

Running a car rental company is a complex business. You might imagine that Avis or Hertz or Joe's Rentals purchases a vehicle from the same dealership as you and then comes up with a rental rate that pays off the cost until it eventually reaches the point where it can make a profit. That's not at all how it works. (After all, a $30,000 vehicle rented for $50 per day would require 600 rental days to break even, and that does *not* take into account the cost of maintenance, licensing, advertising, offices, and employees.) Instead, rental car companies are essentially the flip side of the auto leasing industry. Most rental companies purchase cars at deeply discounted prices directly from manufacturers or other sources. Then they keep a close eye on the resale value of their cars, prepared to sell off vehicles at the best possible moment.

As an example, a rental company might obtain a $30,000 vehicle for $25,000 and sell it as a relatively low-mileage used car for $15,000. In this example, the cost of ownership would be about $10,000. Now renting that car for $50 per day would require only about 200 days for you to break even. That fits with a typical business plan that calls for resale of these vehicles within two years of purchase.

Auto rental prices typically rise and fall markedly. In slow economic times, vehicle owners tend to hold on to their cars for longer periods of time, which may serve to increase the value of younger used cars like those from rental car fleets, which allows for lower rental car rates. On the other hand, if more people are leasing cars for personal use or buying new cars more often, that can result in a glut of used cars on the market. Rental car companies may then need to boost rates in order to make a profit.

Rental rates in many places are also sensitive to seasonal variations. For example, cars offered for rent in Florida in the winter are usually priced much higher than they are in the summer. Places with this sort of seasonal variation may offer great deals to customers who want to travel out of the area in the direction of greater demand. I'll explain more about that later in this chapter.

Save Money at the Auto-Rental Counter

Here are some tips on how to pay less for a set of rental wheels...

• **Compare the rates of several rental car companies.** Look for the same class or size of vehicle, and read the fine print to learn if you are being offered an unlimited mileage price or one that adds a per-mile charge beyond a certain level. Figure out the number of miles you expect to drive during your rental period, and see which deal is best for you.

You can compare the rates of multiple rental car companies by using one of the many travel websites like Orbitz, Priceline, and Travelocity. And then there is AutoSlash, which not only compares rental car companies for your trip, but also applies discount coupons. The company can reduce your rental cost after you've made your reservation but before you've picked up the car if its computers find lower rates and make the change on your behalf. *Here are some helpful car rental websites...*

• **AutoSlash** at AutoSlash.com

• **Orbitz** at Orbitz.com

• **Priceline** at Priceline.com

• **Travelocity** at Travelocity.com

• **Check several locations in your area.** Sometimes it is less expensive to rent from a facility located away from an airport (where the company often has to pay extra in order to operate.)

In some locations, though, the opposite is true: A high level of competition at the airport might result in lower prices there than at other locations.

- **Consider pick-up perks.** Some rental car companies offer pick-up and drop-off services for clients. Enterprise generally offers this from its neighborhood (not airport) locations. Call the local number for any rental agency and ask for this sort of assistance (or look on the website for local stations).

- **Travel on weekends.** Most rental car companies make the bulk of their income from business travelers, who typically rent during the workweek and have limited travel flexibility. You will usually find lower rates for leisure travel on the weekend, and many companies define the weekend as running from Friday morning through Monday morning.

- **Take it for a week.** Weekly rental rates are usually priced at about the same level as five daily charges. If it fits your schedule, you might as well hold on to the rental car for the two "free" days.

You won't save money by renting for a week and returning it two days early. And if you reserve a car for five days and later hold on to it for even one day more, you may end paying a penalty. Why? Because the company may have already accepted a reservation for the vehicle on days you originally said you did not need it.

- **Consider what size and type of car you need.** A family of four with suitcases will probably not be comfortable in a subcompact, while a couple out for a drive in the country has no need for a seven-passenger van. In general, small cars cost less to rent. In some situations, though, a rental agency may have too many large cars and will offer better deals for them.

- **Consider reserving the lowest-priced special-offer car.** These vehicles tend to be in limited supply. In the worst case, you get exactly what you asked for. In times of high demand, you could be upgraded to a higher class at no extra charge if the one you have reserved is not at hand.

- **Ask for an eleventh-hour upgrade.** If you find that the agency actually does have the car you requested but you don't really want that model, ask about the charge to upgrade to a better one. Some agencies have lower rates at the counter for last-minute changes of this sort.

- **Check in with your credit card holder.** Some credit card companies have negotiated lower rates if you use their card for making and paying for a reservation. You may also find similar deals through auto clubs and other associations.

- **Join a rental-car company's loyalty program.** Do so even if you don't rent cars very often. Members regularly receive special discount offers, and some of the major car rental companies award points for each completed rental that can be eventually used for free rental days.

- **Read the airline in-flight magazine as you fly to your destination.** This is a prime place for advertisements from rental companies. If you see a better rate at another company, stop by their counter when you arrive.

- **Rent a fantasy car.** Want a Ford Mustang convertible for a trip down the Pacific Coast Highway? Some rental companies allow you to reserve a specific car (usually at a higher rate) if you have a fantasy you want to indulge. Maybe you want to rent a very expensive sports car to impress classmates at a class reunion? Be aware, though, that your personal auto insurance or the supplemental insurance that comes with many credit cards may not cover exotic and very expensive cars. Call your insurance company and the credit card company for advice beforehand.

Pay to Point

Many car rental companies offer you the opportunity to earn airline frequent flier points or miles for rentals. That's generally a good thing, but read the rental agreement's fine print carefully to see if there is a fee associated with the points.

You don't want to pay more in fees than the points are worth. Speaking broadly, airline miles are usually worth about a penny a point: One hundred points or miles are worth about $1 when used to buy a flight. If the car rental company fee is $3 (or $1) for one hundred points, that is not a good deal and you should not request the points—and check to see that the rental agreement does not include the fee.

• **Rent before you buy.** If you are on the cusp of buying a new car, check with local car rental agencies—or with the dealer—to see if they have that model available for a one-day or weekend rental and take it for a real test drive. I've even seen some (though not many) car dealerships promote this, even to the point of offering to refund rental charges if you end up buying a car from them.

Drop the Cost of One-Way Rentals

In general, rental companies charge more for vehicles that are picked up in one place and dropped off in another. They do this because the car's movement may create an imbalance of supply and demand. For example, in the summer resort region where I live, one-way rental charges during high season can add $100 to $200 *per day* to the rental cost. That is especially galling if I plan to keep the car for several days once I arrive at my destination.

You may or may not be able to avoid these high charges, but there are some things you can do. For example, look into the cost of renting a car at one-way rates for the long leg of travel, and then turning it in and renting a car at local rates for the remainder of the time. You can rent a car from Boston to New York for one day at a one-way rate of perhaps $200. Once you arrive in Boston, return the car to the rental agency and rent a car for a few days of local use at prevailing rates, which might be about $50.

Here's another situation: If you rent a car at a location that has widely varying seasonal demands, you may be able to obtain extraordinarily low prices if you are taking the car to (or near) a place the rental car agency would like it to be. For example, renting a car in Florida at the end of the high season (typically about May 1) and bringing it north to Washington or New York can be inexpensive.

The reverse process also applies: Lower rates bringing a car to Florida (or another seasonal destination) at the start of the season usually works to your advantage.

Obey the Second Driver Rules

Be honest with the rental company about additional drivers who may drive the car. If you have an accident, the rental company may claim you violated their contract and refuse to pay any coverage you purchased. Even if you decline the rental company's insurance because you are already covered, your own insurance company may give you trouble if the rental car company declares you in violation of the rental agreement.

Most rental companies will allow your spouse or certain coworkers to share driving. Be sure you understand the rules and get a written copy. Additional driver coverage usually adds anywhere from $3 to $10 per day. Ask about flat-rate coverage for a multi-day rental.

Some credit card companies and certain special offers from rental car companies may expand the number of allowable drivers or lower the cost of adding them. Call your credit card company and the rental car company for full details.

Save Time When You Rent a Car

Joining a rental-car company's priority club can shave a fair amount of time off your wait at the airport. All of your important information—name, address, driver's license, and credit card numbers—will already be on file, along with your rental preferences. For that reason, make sure you use—and change often—a complex password that strangers cannot easily guess. That applies, of course, to all accounts that involve personal or financial information.

Even better, club members can usually go to a special check-in counter at the airport or skip the check-in completely, go directly to the car lot, and look for a sign with their name and the car's parking space. You'll just show your driver's license to the guard at the exit and away you'll go.

Watch Out for Rental Gotchas

How does a $24.99 rate become a $62.37 bill? It's simple—you didn't read the fine print. Car companies can raise the bottom line on your rental dozens of ways. It's up to the savvy consumer to seek and find ways to remove them from the bill one by one. Here are some of the gotchas that could get you if all you do is look at the top line of the rental agreement rather than the bottom line:

- **Read the fine print carefully to learn about *blackout dates,*** which is when an advertised price may be unavailable.

- **Watch out for a fee for airline or hotel points.** Like I mentioned earlier, you should only accept the points if they make economic sense to you.

- **In some airports, renters are assessed a fee if they use a rental car agency that has a car lot on the airport grounds.**

- **Be sure you understand the rental agency's fuel policy.** *At most companies you have four options…*

Your Past Haunts You

Some rental car companies will check your driving record before handing you the keys to a car. Some places do this to all renters, and some do it on a random basis. If your record of citations and accidents is clean or only lightly dinged, you should have no problem. If you have a questionable record—and you know who you are—it might be worth the effort to ask for assurance you will be allowed to pick up the car. I know this is like waving a red flag in front of a bull, but you don't want to take the chance that you'll be turned away at the counter.

- Pick up the car with a full tank of gas and return it with whatever fuel is left. When you do this, the rental company will happily fill the tank for you, usually at a rate considerably higher than you'd pay at a nearby station.
- Pay for a tank of gas ahead of time. You have no responsibility to refill the tank when you return the car under this plan, but you'll receive no credit for any fuel left in the tank, either.
- Pick up the car with a full tank of gas and stop off to fill the tank at a service station on your way to the airport when you return. This is almost always the most economical way to rent a car.
- Some rental companies will simply indicate on the agreement the gas tank level (usually demarked in eighths of a tank). If the car goes out five-eighths full, it should be at that level when you return it. The problem with this scheme is that it is sometimes difficult to precisely match the fuel level when you refill, and you could end up putting too much in the tank or being assessed with a fee for arriving with too little fuel.

Avoid Damage Claims

Do not move your rental car until you have walked around it once or twice to check for damage, including dents, scratches, and broken glass. If you find any problems, ask for another car or demand that the agent attach a signed report on the condition of the car to the rental agreement. Look for stains on the upholstery or carpeting, too. Some car companies ban smoking in their cars, and some will assess significant fees if you bring along a dog who leaves behind fur.

Many rental car agencies accompany you to your car to conduct the walkaround, but there are many stations where you will be handed the rental agreement and the keys and pointed in the direction of the car. Don't move the vehicle without doing the walkaround. If you notice a potential problem, walk back to the counter and insist it be noted on the agreement.

The same applies to fuel levels. I can't begin to count the number of times I have sat down in the driver's seat, turned the key, and noticed that the tank was less than full. If the rental agreement includes a notation that the vehicle was delivered with 7/8ths of a tank, that's what you should aim to return it with. But it is not always easy to precisely fill a tank to a particular level; any extra gas you put in the tank amounts to a gift to the rental car company.

I once rented a car that was festooned with stickers warning against smoking, but my walk-around inspection focused entirely on the exterior. After I had signed the agreement, I sat down in the driver's seat and promptly stood back up to insist on a different car—one that did not smell like the interior of an ashtray.

Know the Facts About Rental Car Insurance

Do not pay for insurance coverage you don't need. (Chapter 32 explains vehicle insurance.) In addition, do whatever you can to avoid having to pay collision damage waivers (CDW) at the rental counter. The daily rate for such coverage is one of the worst deals in insurance. CDW coverage can add $10 to $20 per day to your rental costs. At $10 per day, this is equivalent to an annual policy costing $3,650!

The coverage is not required, and in some states it is not permitted. CDW is not technically insurance, but instead it is a promise that the rental company will pay for damages to the car. If you decline the waiver, you accept responsibility for any damages up to the car's full value. Under CDW, however, the company will not pay for bodily injuries or damages to your personal property. The fine print may also revoke your coverage if the rental company believes you drove negligently, on unpaved roads, or out of the state in which you rented the vehicle. Some companies void their CDW coverage if a driver drinks alcohol or if an unauthorized driver operates the car.

If you are traveling on business, check with your employer to see if your company has a policy to cover you. If you own a car, call your insurance agent and find out how well you are covered under your present policy for any rentals. Check with your credit card company to find out about coverage. They may provide for rental cars charged to your account (usually

Rental Coverage in Foreign Countries

If you are traveling outside the US, double-check with your insurance agent and credit card issuer to be sure what coverage you have. It may not apply to luxury or exotic cars in foreign countries. And don't rely entirely upon the extended rental car coverage that comes with certain credit cards. Not every country is included, and some countries (including Italy as this book goes to press) require you to purchase at least a basic level of "cover."

If your personal automobile coverage and your credit card coverage do not protect you adequately in a foreign country, ask your insurance agent about a special rider for international driving. Or, if you plan to be abroad for a few weeks, you may want to contact an insurance agency in the foreign country or obtain a foreign coverage rider. Check with your insurance agent or search the internet for vacation policies. Obviously, you should compare the costs of the policies to the rental company's rates.

with the exception of luxury and off-road vehicles). Consider upgrading to gold or platinum levels to increase your auto coverage if necessary.

The rental company may also offer *personal accident insurance* (PAI) to pay some or all medical costs related to an accident. Again, this may be unnecessary duplication. Your personal or employer-provided medical plan should take care of injuries suffered while on the road. Medicare, or Medicare in combination with Medigap, should also provide sufficient coverage.

Personal effects coverage (PEC) or *personal effects protection* (PEP) is intended to protect your luggage and possessions from theft or damage. Your homeowner's or renter's policy may provide coverage for thefts from a rental vehicle. Again, check with your insurance agent.

CHAPTER 29

Navigating Air Travel

In some ways, air travel is an example of our modern technological society at its best. You can get from just about anywhere on earth to almost anywhere else in a day or less. Sometimes the longest part of a journey is the trip from your home to the airport and through the security checkpoint.

In other ways, air travel is free enterprise at its worst, a confusing bazaar with prices changing by the hour. That's why two people seated next to each other on the same plane can pay fares hundreds of dollars apart, and may both have to suffer through the culinary delight called airline food.

The savvy consumer, of course, is the one who pays the lowest possible price for an airline ticket and spends as little time at the airport. The information in this chapter will help you do those things, as well as to protect you from problems that can happen along the way.

- **Buy your ticket.**
- **Navigate the airport.**
- **Handle your landing.**

Buy Your Ticket

Shopping for an airline ticket is much different than it used to be. There is no person sitting in an office waiting to orchestrate your travel to distant lands (or to your family's house). Now you're shopping yourself. The following sections offer considerations that you might not know about, and that will, hopefully, help you save money.

Make a Bid for Airline Tickets

If you're willing to take a chance on airline tickets, there are a few ways to enter into something close to a reverse auction. Here's how it works: you enter the route you want and the date you want to fly (one way or roundtrip) and the number of tickets. Then you enter a bid and hope that the schedule works for you. Priceline.com claims to have introduced this form of bidding for airline flights. That site also allows you to bid for hotel rooms and rental cars the same way.

Before You Book

Sure, you want to hit the beach in July and the slopes in January. But reconsider your timing if you want to save money.

- **Don't expect great deals for Europe in July and August.** You might get lucky in May or October. The Caribbean between Christmas and the end of April is very busy, but not so much in the summer.

Here's an example of the fine print for a domestic journey on Priceline: "Your trip will start between 6am and 10pm on your travel date. Your exact flights and times will be shown to you once your purchase is complete. Although we always look for nonstop flights first, Priceline flights may make up to one connection." And then I checked an international flight: "The airlines will choose your flight times. Your trip may start anytime from 5am on your travel dates to as late as 2am the next day, and may arrive anytime on the day after departure."

On domestic flights, if you don't get a nonstop flight, Priceline explains that the connection time is supposed to be no more than three hours. On international flights, it's a little squishy: "75% of international connections are three hours or less," which means that 25% could be longer. That connection policy brings with it the possibility of an unusually long flight because of a connection. You could end up (just to make up an example) with a flight from Boston to Paris that requires you to change planes in New York or Washington in the wrong direction for your itinerary.

The good news is that, depending on where you want to fly and how busy that particular day is, you may be able to save between 15% and 30% off advertised fares once you include Priceline's ticket fee. The not-so-good news is that you are giving up the chance to pick a preferred departure or arrival time. You might end up with a great flight, or you might end up with one that cuts into your vacation or business schedule.

As I wrote this section, I checked on flights from New York to Rome and found nonstop scheduled flights, with full information about the airline and the departure and arrival times, priced at about $800 with a duration of about 9 hours in each direction. And I also found special deals priced at about $500 with a layover in Kiev, Ukraine and a total travel time of more than 30 hours each way.

I have successfully used Priceline and other auction sites for hotel rooms. I have chosen not to buy airline tickets blindly for two reasons: first, I do not want to take the chances of losing one or two days of my time on a roundtrip, and second, although nearly all airlines are acceptable there are a few carriers that I choose not to use because of concerns about reliability, safety, or comfort.

Note that all carriers that fly into or out of the United States must meet certification requirements of the Federal Aviation

Administration. That doesn't mean that all carriers have the same record of reliability for on-time takeoff and landing, or that every airline has a great record when it comes to delivering checked baggage along with passengers. And if you are buying flights between Ulaanbaatar, Mongolia and Beijing, China you just might end up on MIAT Mongolian Airlines, which may or may not meet your definition of flying the friendly skies. But I can get you a great price.

I know of no guaranteed way to get the best price for a flight (or a hotel room) other than to check several sites and pick the best deal you see. You also can never know whether the price you receive today will be higher or lower than the price they will offer tomorrow. In general, though, prices for travel tend to rise within the week before the date of a flight (or a hotel) stay.

Helpful: Once you find what you believe is the best price for a flight or a hotel on a general travel site, visit the airline's or hotel's website. You may find even better prices or special offers there.

Consider Joining an Airline Club

If you are a modern road warrior who knows the concourses of major airports better than your own backyard, consider joining an airline club. The clubs, which typically cost about $400 to $500 per year plus a one-time sign-up fee, return some of the civility that is missing from air travel and especially airports. You'll find quiet rooms with comfortable chairs, desks with telephones and laptop chargers, television and game rooms, and complimentary or low-price snacks and beverages. Just as important, most airline clubs offer special service desks for making and changing reservations, obtaining boarding passes, and other airline functions. Other features may include conference rooms available for free (or a minimal charge), baggage storage rooms, and exercise and shower rooms.

Should you join a club? The best way to answer is to look closely at your travel schedule. Take the annual fee—say it's $500—and divide it by the number of visits you are likely to make. If you figure you'll pass through a club 25 times in a year, the cost of membership works out to $20 per visit, which is very reasonable for the service provided. If you're likely to

Pack a Snack

Most international flights still offer meal service. Most domestic airlines, however, have eliminated meal service in economy class on short flights (usually those less than three hours). If you're lucky, you'll be tossed a bag of pretzels, cookies or chips.

Some credit cards associated with an airline will give you a discount on the overpriced food that is offered for sale on certain flights, but there is nothing to prevent you from bringing food on board that you purchased in the airport (from restaurants *after* the security checkpoint). And you can still pack your own lunch from home, providing you stay within the often-changing rules of the Transportation Security Administration. The TSA will generally prevent you from bringing anything wet or in paste form, but a wrapped or packaged cheese sandwich (as this book goes to press) should make it through the X-ray machine just fine.

You can visit the TSA website to see a list of prohibited (or allowable) items (subject to change, of course) at TSA.gov/travel/security-screening/whatcanibring.

use the club only half a dozen times in a year, the cost rises to about $85, which may be a bit high for a few free drinks and a comfortable chair.

The biggest problem is that most airline clubs are specific to a single airline. A few extend privileges to flyers on other airlines, and a few clubs are independent of airlines but exist only in a few airports. For about $75, you can also purchase a day pass to use some airline clubs. That privilege may be extended only to holders of the airline's credit card, or members of their frequent flyer club. The cost of a few day passes a year may be a better deal, especially if you don't always fly on the same airline.

You should also look into the airline club benefits that are associated with some of the ultra-premium credit cards. They may include access to certain clubs in specific airports. For example, as this book goes to press, American Express's Platinum Card includes access to the Centurion Lounge Network, Airspace Lounges, certain Priority Pass Select lounges, and (if you are flying on Delta Airlines) to Delta Sky Clubs. Similar programs are offered by high-level Visa cards and others. If the selection matches your travels, these are good deals. If the airlines or airports you use are not included, the benefit is of no use.

Club members do not receive special treatment when it comes to upgrades, but there is often a special desk within the clubs that may help them rebook in the event of cancellation. The lines are sure to be shorter, and you do have a drink while you wait.

Consider these questions…

- **How many clubs does the airline operate and in which airports?**
- **Do you have the right to visit another airline's club?**
- **Are you permitted to bring a guest?** How many per visit?
- **If you are traveling with your family, can your children accompany you?**

Talk to an Airline

Again, not many of us still call an airline to book a flight, and even fewer of us use a travel agency. Airlines want you to use websites because not staffing their phone lines saves them money. They have also mostly eliminated the commission they used to pay to travel agencies and so today, few agencies sell tickets except as part of larger packages that include hotels, rental cars, cruises, or other big ticket items.

And many airlines now tack a service charge onto airline fares if you book a ticket via phone instead of online. Regardless, you may want to call an airline, especially if you have a frequent flyer account or an affinity credit card or otherwise stand out from the crowd. If I have a legitimate reason, like an especially complex reservation involving multiple credit cards for those in my travel party, or a nonstandard routing, the agent will usually waive the fee. (If she won't, ask calmly to speak to the supervisor. That alone may spur the agent to waive the fee. If neither the agent nor the supervisor will waive the fee, you can still book online.)

Be very specific when you speak with an airline reservationist and explain why you are unable to book online. An ad or promotion may promise the "lowest available fare"—but that does not guarantee that you'll be paying as little as possible. That fare may be sold out for the flight or date you are asking about, or there may be some special promotion you need to ask for by name.

Here are questions to ask of the airline, or to search for on your own at an airline website or a travel website like Expedia, Orbitz, Travelocity, and the like…

- **What is the lowest possible fare between these two cities?** The rate will almost certainly include the most restrictions, including advance purchase deadlines, limitations on travel times and days, and severe cancellation penalties.
- **Should I consider different starting and ending points?** Some nearby airports cost less because of increased competition or more availability. Residents of the New York metropolitan area, for example, should compare flights to and from LaGuardia, Kennedy, and Newark airports. From New England, prices might vary from Boston, Providence, Hartford, or Albany. In Florida, major airports within reach of large parts of the state include Miami, Fort Lauderdale, Tampa, and Orlando. If you can save hundreds of dollars on a set of tickets, that should more than pay for the cost of transportation to a slightly farther airport. Ask about fares from your small local airport, too. Calculations can be complex. You might find a slightly more expensive fare at an airport that will cost you less to get to by car or public transportation.
- **Is there a better day or time to fly to get a better deal?** This assumes, of course, that you have some flexibility in your travel dates.
- **If I change my dates or times or accept a connection instead of fly nonstop, can you book me at the lowest possible fare?** Sometimes nonstops are less expensive than those with a connection, and sometimes the opposite is true. It's all about supply and demand.
- **Are there any special promotions or sales in effect that I might not know about?** Again, the deal you learned about might not be the one you were quoted.
- **Are there any sales beginning soon?** Some agents, and some airlines, are kind enough to tip you off to upcoming sales. And for flights booked in the US (to both domestic and foreign destinations), federal regulations require airlines to allow consumers to cancel reservations without penalty within the first 24 hours after they have made them. The only exception: reservations made within 24 hours of the scheduled departure time.
- **Why is the fare you are quoting me higher than the lowest possible fare?** Then let him or her explain.

TIP

Dig a Little Deeper

You may have to dig down a few layers on the website, but most major online travel booking sites have a customer service phone number where you just may be able to find a real, live human being who may be able to help guide you to a better fare or itinerary. Chapter 1 has more information about finding hidden customer service numbers.

Choose the Best Day to Travel

Supply and demand. *That's the basic underpinning behind the price of most things for sale, including seats on an airplane…*

For domestic flights—with the exception of holiday periods and special events—airplanes are usually *less* full on Tuesdays, Wednesdays, and Saturdays and airfare is usually lower on those days. (Looking the other way, seats are generally fuller, and prices higher, on Mondays, Fridays, and Sundays.) Thursdays usually fall somewhere in between. If you have the flexibility, fly outbound and return on one of the less-traveled days. If that's not possible, you still are likely to save some money if one of your travel days is on a quieter day.

For international flights, the *lower* airfares are usually Monday through Thursday. Higher demand and higher prices are usually found Friday through Sunday.

Pick the Right Time to Buy

In general, experts say that you'll get the best price on airline tickets if you buy in advance—but not too much in advance. Airlines generally post their schedules about a year in advance. (On July 4, you'll be able to buy tickets for flights as far away as July 3 of the following year.) But you can think of the initial price as the list price before any sales or special offers are applied.

Travel experts say the best time to buy a domestic ticket is three months before your date of departure. For international travel, four or five months ahead of departure may be best. Tickets that you buy within 30 days of the departure date are likely to be priciest.

If an airline has many unsold seats on a flight, it might drop the price on remaining tickets in the days leading up to departure or as late as the day before. There is no guarantee this will happen, though, and if you absolutely must travel, you might find that the prices have gone up instead of down.

Now, avoid turbulence.

- **Check prices on at least one travel booking site.** The majors include Expedia, Orbitz, Priceline, and Travelocity. Prices are usually the same or close at all of these sites. Find the best flight for you and note the airline and flight number. Then price the same flight on the airline's website. Sometimes the airlines undercut the fares shown on travel sites (or, looking at it a different way, the travel sites sometimes tack on service charges you might otherwise not notice).

- **Check prices on travel sites that are part of your credit card company's offerings.** For example, American Express has its own department that sells flights, hotels, and car rentals. Sometimes they have special discounts or other enticements, such as extra award points in their own programs.

- **Avoid flying around holidays and event.** Flights during holiday periods and in advance of special events (like sports championships or major conventions) are going to be priced as high as possible. If you see a good price for travel during these times, grab it.

- **Start shopping Monday for a pop-up sale.** They can occur at almost any time (except for holiday periods). Travel experts say that the most common moment is Monday afternoon. The reduced prices usually pop up on the airline's own website then, and also on travel booking sites like

Travelocity and Expedia and others. Later that day or on Tuesday morning, other airlines usually react to adjust their prices for the same routes. Move quickly when one is offered.

- **Get in the loop.** Join the major airlines' frequent flyer programs and consider obtaining an affinity credit card, which is tied to airlines. You are then more likely to be notified about special sales.

- **Start with one ticket.** Airlines allot a specific number of seats on flights for each class of ticket they sell. Say you are looking to buy six tickets for a family trip. If you ask for a price for six seats and there are only three seats available at the lowest price, you are going to be quoted a higher rate for all of your family. The best way to shop is to begin by shopping for just one ticket. Find the lowest price. Then adjust your online query to see if the price rises. In this example, you might find three tickets available at the lower rate and three at a higher rate. Make two separate bookings and pocket the difference in cost.

Here is a perfect example of a good time to place a phone call to an airline and ask them to help you get seats next to each other.

- **Be sure you understand the airline's baggage policies before you buy a ticket.** Nearly every airline charges people who bought the cheapest tickets extra for checked bags. As this book goes to press, Southwest Airlines allows two bags without charge; JetBlue added a $15 fee for the first bag in 2017. Other airlines charge $50 or more. So, if Southwest fares are slightly higher than, say, Delta, be sure to factor in the cost of checked baggage if you will be asking the airline to carry the weight for you.

Try Tuesday

There are airline analysts who say the best time to search for a great deal is Tuesday afternoon, after 3 p.m. Eastern time. It's a complicated route to that recommendation, but here goes: the most common time for an airline to announce an airfare sale is Monday, with tickets available on Tuesday. Other airlines flying the same route monitor their competitors' prices, and there often is a bit of downward adjustment on Tuesday, with prices settling into place by the afternoon. Of course, there is nothing to prevent an airline from busting a move Thursday at midnight.

Navigate the Airport

Getting through the airport is sometimes as challenging as navigating, on foot, with a hand-drawn map, sans compass. Follow the tips I introduce in the following sections and you'll be in and out of the airport and at your destination in no time.

Arrive at the Airport at the Right Time

When should you arrive at the airport for your flight? There have been times when I have dropped off my bags, dashed across the terminal, through the security checkpoint, and arrived breathless at the gate to hear the agent declaring the final boarding call for my flight. "Thanks for waiting for me," I tell the flight attendants as I move to my seat. Of course, that same dramatic arrival could have just as easily ended up with the following greeting: "I'm sorry, Mr. Sandler, but because you are late we have given your seat to a standby customer. We'll see if we can book you on another flight sometime this month. And let's hope we can find your luggage."

In fact, quick jogs to the door of your airplane are probably gone forever. Although sometimes you can get lucky with no lines at the check-in counter (or computer kiosk), the baggage drop-off, and the security checkpoint, and your airplane has been assigned to the nearest gate. The much more common experience: half an hour to get to the check-in counter, half an hour to an hour to get through security, and then learning that your plane is parked at a gate in the next county.

Most airlines recommend arriving two hours before the scheduled departure time for your flight, and sometimes as many as three hours ahead of time for international travel or flights on the busiest days of the year. If you're flying from a foreign destination to the US, check with your airline. You may need those three hours before departure because of extra security screening and, at some airports, baggage and carry-on inspection.

If you want to get a heads-up before you head to the airport, look at the airline's website for the flight you are about to take to check on available seats, although that display may not be accurate if the airline does not allow all passengers to choose seats ahead of check-in. You'll have an idea of what you're going to face at the gate, and you might be able to change to a seat you prefer.

Most airlines now allow you to check in online, usually starting 24 hours before scheduled takeoff time. That may also coincide with the release of seats they held back in hopes of selling a particular spot on the plane at a premium.

Consider the Joys and Pains of Curbside Check-in

One way to shave some time off your airport check-in is to give your bags to the curbside check-in counter. If you have your boarding pass, you should be able to proceed directly to security and, from there, to the departure gate.

However, follow these important safeguards before walking away from your bags…

- **Make sure your flight has not been canceled and is on schedule.** If there is a problem with your flight, hold on to your bags and join the throngs at the check-in counter (or, even better, whip out your smartphone and call the airline).

- **Check carefully that your bags are marked with proper tags for your destination.** Make certain that copies of the tags are attached to your boarding passes. Pay special attention to the tags if your trip includes a plane change. If there is any part of the tag you don't understand, ask the porter to explain it to you before the bags disappear down the chute into the bowels of the airport.

Save Time in the Terminal

You can shave off a bit of time here and there.

- **Be weight conscious.** Most airlines set a weight limit of 50 pounds for passengers in economy class, often allowing about 70 pounds for those with business and first class tickets. If your bag exceeds those limits, you'll have to pay an additional fee—often $50 to $100. Or, you can step aside at the check-in counter and try to rearrange the contents of your various checked and carry-on bags to bring them all below the limits. You will find the weight (and size limits, see below) on the website for your airline.

- **Know the correct size.** Airlines also set the size for a standard bag, usually calculated as a linear measurement. A typical measure is 62 inches as the maximum sum of the length, width, and depth of your bag. Oversize bags are also subject to additional fees.

- **Pack your bags with care.** Know what's in your bags and keep any objects likely to attract the attention of the security screeners in an easily opened location. If your hair dryer is suspiciously shaped and regularly sets off alarms at the security checkpoint, you might want to keep it at the top of a carry-on bag. That way you're less likely to have to unpack an entire suitcase.

- **Tag your bags in several places with your name and address.** After you've done that, stick a few of your business cards or a piece of paper with your name and address inside the bag's outside pockets. Limit the information listed on them to your cell phone number and email address or your business address. You might not want to advertise the fact that your home is unoccupied, especially when you are departing from an airport nearby.

- **Mark your bags.** Do something to make your black fabric roller bag stand out in some way. Tie a bright ribbon to the handle, place colorful tape on the top, or attach some unusual stickers to the top and side.

- **Make a little list.** Before you head out on a trip, make a detailed list of your bags and their contents, and photograph them. Then put the information in your wallet and send a copy to yourself by email. You'll need the information if you must file a report with the lost luggage department.

- **Travel light.** Use a suitcase that will fit into an overhead rack or under the seat in front of you. This will speed up your check-in process. You may be able to use a computer kiosk to get your boarding pass and head directly to security and your boarding gate. When you arrive, you can skip the luggage claim and walk out the door with your bag in hand.

- **Get your boarding pass before you go to the airport.** Most airlines let you check in for your flight using a smartphone or computer, usually within 24 hours of departure. If you use a computer, you can print out a pass with a bar code. If you use a smartphone, you receive an email or text message that includes your bar code. Security and boarding gate agents scan it.

- **Understand the latest security rules.** Subject to change, the TSA limits liquids or gels in carry-on bags to amounts of 3.4 ounces or less, and the containers must be carried in a clear, resealable single-quart plastic bag. You also cannot bring weapons or anything that could possibly be used as a weapon. Read the rules, which are available online. Put liquids and other allowed-but-restricted-items like baby formula and medicines, in your checked bags, not in carry-on luggage. If you're unsure what you can bring on a plane in your carryon, check the TSA website at TSA.gov/travel/security-screening/whatcanibring or send a tweet to the TSA to confirm: @AskTSA.

- **Be prepared to empty your pockets of all items.** Scanners will find wallets, coins, pens, smartphones, and anything else. At some airports, you have to remove belts with metal buckles. One way to speed up your passage through the scanner is to put all of these items into your carry-on bag before screening, or put them in zippered pockets of a jacket you are wearing and then put the jacket through the scanner.

- **If you are a frequent flyer, consider enrolling in TSA PreCheck.** You'll need to show up at a designated office (usually at an airport) for an in-person interview, submit to a background check and a fingerprinting. In return, you'll receive a relatively quick passage through security without the need to remove shoes, belts, and laptops. The rules are subject to change, as is the fee, which was $85 per person as this book went to press.

Pack Your Pockets

One way to temporarily reduce the weight of your carry-on bag is to put as many of your personal items as possible in pockets of a jacket. (Keep the scissors at home, though. They're among the TSA's most commonly confiscated items.) In winter, I travel with a ski jacket that has six large zippered pockets. In summer, I use a slightly less capacious golf jacket. I have never had my jacket weighed by an airline.

Some jacket manufacturers even offer travel apparel with an amazing capacity for items like phones, tablets, and corned beef sandwiches. SCOTTeVEST is one such company. You can find them at SCOTTeVest.com.

Don't Check Your Bags if Possible

Dante did not know about baggage claims at crowded airports. If he did, they might have been one of the regions of hell. As I noted, the best way to avoid the hassles of baggage claim, of course, is not to check any bags. Sometimes that isn't possible, though. Here's what to do in that case.

You can find the allowable dimensions for carry-on bags from your airline's website. If you will fly on several different airlines, plan on traveling with a bag that meets the smallest allowable luggage, not the largest. Sizes are set so that bags will fit in overhead racks, which are not the same on all airplanes. Some airlines will list actual measurements as a limit, like 22 x 14 x 9 inches, while others will post a number that adds those measurements and says your bag cannot exceed (for example) 45 linear inches.

Airlines also list a maximum weight for carry-on bags, some as much as 40 pounds and others as little as 20 pounds. That said, as this book goes to press, I can say that rarely have I had my carry-on bag placed on a scale. That's a good thing, because my bag would fail the weight test most of the time. But to be safe, try to come as close as possible to the posted limits.

Some airlines, at some times, are very strict about limiting the number and size of carry-on bags. Most airlines allow one piece of carry-on luggage per passenger plus a personal item, which is usually defined as a purse or a laptop case. You may be required one or both items under your seat rather than in overhead racks. Some planes have larger overhead racks than others, while some jumbo jets with as many as nine or 10 seats in a row may simply not have enough space. Gate agents are stricter about the rule when the plane is full.

As this book goes to press, United Airlines is the first major domestic airlines to assess a fee (of $25) for carry-on bags for passengers who purchase their lowest-price ticket, called Basic Economy. Other airlines including Frontier and Allegiant also charge for bags placed in the overhead bins.

Here are some ways to maximize your carry-on capacity and be more comfortable while on board…

- **If possible, choose flights that are less crowded.** Fly off-peak hours and midweek, for example.
- **Pick flights on larger planes, which have more storage space.**
- **Choose the appropriate seat.** If you can, snare an aisle or window seat next to an empty middle seat and stuff your belongings under one or both seats. Avoid the bulkhead row and some exit rows, which do not have under-seat storage in front of them.
- **Don't use up your limited allowance on small bags.** If you travel with a laptop, get a bag large enough to take the computer as well as chargers, your tablet, and any business papers.
- **Board early to take possession of whatever space is available.** (That is one good reason to join an airline mileage program or enroll in an airline's credit card if either grants you early boarding privileges.)

Handle Bad News About Lost Luggage

Your suitcase may contain $20,000 in jewelry (it shouldn't!) but the law says that the most an airline is obligated to pay for lost baggage on a domestic flight is $3,500—and that amount is based on your possessions' depreciated value, not on their replacement value. Plus, you will need to provide receipts or other proof of value for most items. On international flights to most destinations, bags are valued at approximately $1,586 per bag, again with proof of value required for expensive items. For travel in some parts of the world, the limit is even less. If your trip includes both a domestic and an international leg, the lesser international liability applies. That figures, huh?

Don't pack a $4,000 brooch or a $5,000 camera in your checked bag. If you must travel with these items, put them in your carry-on bag and keep them close at hand at all times. You can purchase excess liability coverage from most airlines, or buy a separate travel insurance policy.

If you have flown on more than one airline on the segment of your trip, tracking your misplaced bag is the responsibility of the last airline on your trip.

Better Your Chances of Arriving on Time

In good weather, in the absence of work stoppages, and with a bit of luck, most airline flights arrive more or less on time. Beyond that, you can improve your chances. It starts with doing some savvy things to enhance the likelihood of taking off on time.

- **Select the first flight out in the morning.** There is a good chance the airplane will be sitting at the gate after having come in late at night. Airlines rarely schedule departures between 1 A.M. and 6 A.M., allowing for some time in the schedule to make up for delays of the day before. Delays

Hedging Their Bets

One reason most planes arrive on time is that most airlines publish schedules that include a bit of padding—sometimes as much as an hour for international flights and nearly as much for domestic connections. That way, even if the plane is delayed on takeoff or landing, the airline can usually still ask for a round of applause.

almost always cascade throughout the schedule. If a midday flight is an hour late, all of its later arrivals and departures are at least that much late. Problems with gates and air-traffic control can multiply the delays.

- **Choose a nonstop flight.** The more takeoffs and landings, the more chances for delays. If you can't get a nonstop, try for a direct flight, which in most cases is a plane that goes from your departure city to your destination but makes one or more stops. With a direct flight, at least you will have possession of a seat on a plane with the best of intentions of delivering you to your destination. (Pay close attention to the schedule, though. Some airlines have what they call direct flights with a single flight number but a change of planes is required at one of the stopover points.)
- **If you must have connections, consider where they are.** Try to go through a less-congested airport or one less likely to have weather delays. For example, a flight with a connection through Chicago may be more prone to delays than one through Cincinnati. A flight with a change of planes in Denver in the winter may not be as reliable as one that uses Dallas as a hub.

Learn How to Handle a Canceled Flight

Most of us have been there: first the plane is late, and then the takeoff is delayed, and finally there's an announcement saying, "We're sorry to inform you that flight 189 has been canceled. If you will line up at the check-in desk we will rebook you on another flight." A full planeload of unhappy passengers dashes across the lounge to queue up in front of agents at the desk.

The savvy consumer heads in another direction. *Here are some better options…*

- **Call the airline's toll-free reservations number.** You'll save time and you may be able to snare one of a dwindling few remaining seats on the next flight without having to stand in line. If you are a member of an airline's frequent flyer club, call the number dedicated to those in most favor with the company.
- **Find a customer-service desk for the airline.** If you can't find one of those, find a helpful agent at another airport gate who is not otherwise engaged in loading another flight.
- **Hit the club.** If you are a member of the airline's airport club, go there for priority service.

Get a Bump

Airlines love to fly their planes with every seat occupied by a paying customer. In fact, most companies count on flying sardine cans for the largest portion of their profit. It is also true that a certain percentage of travelers who hold airline reservations fail to show up at the gate. And so airline companies have put their computers to work to come up with formulas that say something like: Flight 131 on Monday mornings usually has a 3% no-show rate, which can translate to 12 seats on a 400-seat jumbo jet. The computer records might show higher absence rates on early-morning flights.

Some accountant somewhere came up with this strange solution: If a particular flight has a historical no-show rate of 3%, then the airline should sell 103% of tickets for that plane. It's called *overselling*. If everything works properly, the no-shows won't show and the people who bought a ticket for a seat that didn't exist will walk onto the plane without ever knowing they were in danger of being bumped. If things don't follow the computer projection, the airline is put in the position of having to refuse a seat to some of its paying customers.

In April 2017, United Airlines secured millions of dollars in bad publicity when it called in airport security personnel to drag a passenger off one of its flights, giving new meaning to the term "involuntary bumping." United has since promised to never do that again, and says it will offer as much as $10,000 in compensation to a customer who voluntarily gives up a seat when they need it. They'll start lower, and probably never reach their sky-high offer.

Here's the way it usually works: the airline will offer an incentive to volunteers who are willing to give up their seats and take a later flight. They might offer a few hundred dollars in vouchers that you can exchange for future air travel. The more overbooked the flight, the more desperate the gate agent becomes. The next offer is a free roundtrip ticket. If you accept that, you are at least doubling the value of your current ticket. (My best deal was $1,000 in travel vouchers for each of four tickets—which cost me $400 each—plus a suite in a four-star hotel, dinner, and breakfast for the family. We flew home the next day knowing that I had in my pocket the tickets for our next vacation.)

Think of the process as a reverse auction. Put a value on your time and inconvenience and judge how desperate the airline is for your seat and how much competition you can expect from other travelers. If the power is on your side of the table—more oversold seats than volunteers—you can push for a better deal. If you want to increase your odds of getting bumped, travel on a Friday afternoon when businesspeople are anxious to get home, or at the start or end of a holiday period such as the days around Memorial Day, Labor Day, Thanksgiving, or Christmas.

You will be even more attractive to an agent—for purposes of bumping, at least—if you are able to turn over two or more seats, which was the case when I sold four tickets in one deal.

A few other tips to improve your chances of being bumped and receiving an above-average payout, if you so desire…

- **Consider the cost to you of being bumped.** Is it merely a matter of being a few hours late when you have some spare time? Will you miss a day of work? Will you have to pay for a hotel at the destination because it will be too late to drive home or take public transportation? Come up with a price you are willing to accept.

• **If the boarding lounge is very crowded,** let the agent know you *might* be willing to give up your seat for the right compensation and sit or stand near the counter.

• **If the initial offer is below your price, turn it down but let the agent know you will accept a higher offer.** Even better, let the agent know you will accept whatever the final offer is to the second-to-last person to give up a seat.

• **If the agents start to get desperate for someone to bump, ask for your price plus more—** an upgrade on the next flight, a pass to the airline's lounge, dinner while you wait.

If your flight is delayed or canceled because of weather or mechanical problems, the airline is not obligated to do anything more than give you its best wishes and an offer to take you to your destination at its next convenience. However, if you were bumped from an oversold flight against your will, the airlines must compensate you for the inconvenience. Note that you are not considered to have been bumped if you arrive late at the gate or otherwise fail to check in on time.

If the airline books you on another flight that gets you to your destination within an hour of your original appointed time, they owe you nothing, although an airline will rarely stiff its customers that way. According to federal rules, if you are delivered one to two hours late for a domestic flight or one to four hours internationally, the airline must pay you an amount equal to double your one-way fare, up to $650. If you are more than two hours late domestically or four hours on an international flight, the maximum goes up to $1,300.

Pick the Best Airline Seat

You've got to sit somewhere, so why not go for the best? Several websites, including SeatGuru.com, allow you to compare one seat against another on the specific type of plane you'll be on.

In a crowded travel market, there's not always a lot of choice available, especially within a few weeks of departure. Most major airlines now designate parts of their economy section as premium seats, charging extra for the right to select one of them; if the seats are not sold, when you arrive at the check-in counter you may end up placed in a premium seat without extra charge.

Here's a guide to some of the pros and cons of various seats in the plane...

• **Safety.** The wing area is the strongest part of the plane and, on most planes, there is a wing exit. As a bonus, the exit seats usually offer a bit more leg room. You must be willing to accept the assignment as part of the safety crew and be able to open the heavy door per the flight attendants' instructions. Children under the age of 15 and disabled travelers cannot use these seats. Another relative safe spot, according to accident investigators, is near the plane's tail.

• **Comfort.** Some flyers insist on an aisle seat because they can more easily get up and walk around on the plane. If you're not in an exit row, the aisle seat is a bit safer than a window or middle because you're in a better position to sprint to the emergency exit. And in any case, you're the first to get up into the aisle when the plane lands safely. On the down side, in an aisle seat you're more likely to be bumped by the food cart and passengers walking the aisles, and you may be disturbed by others in your row when they want to get up.

Other flyers, myself included, prefer the window seat. First, although I have flown millions of miles, I still enjoy the view; the light through the window helps me work with my papers or laptop computer; I can lean up against the wall to sleep; no one will disturb me when they get up for a walk. The window seat's shortcomings include there being a bit less leg room, and narrower under-seat storage. There are no good reasons to recommend the middle seat in a three-across row.

- **Quiet.** The noisiest part of the plane is alongside and behind the engines. Most modern planes have their engines mounted on their wings, and so the entire back half of the plane will hear more noise than the front. Older planes that have engines mounted at the back of the plane and on the tail, include MD-80 (and cousins MD-82 and MD-83, MD-88, and MD-90) and Boeing 727 models. You also may want to sit away from the galleys and the bathrooms. You can find the plane type and cabin layout for your flight by visiting the airline website, or Seat Guru at SeatGuru.com
- **Ride.** Some travelers are immune to turbulence while others swear they can tell the difference between a seat at the back (supposedly the most prone to bouncing) and one over the wing (perhaps a bit more stable).

Practice Airline Safety

Airplanes crash. That's a fact. It's also true that it is significantly more dangerous to drive to the airport than it is to take off and fly halfway around the world. The likelihood of surviving a major plane crash is not good, although some people do. There is often not a great deal of logic about who makes it and who doesn't. (If it makes you feel better, though, consider the fact that the people up front in first class and the pilots usually arrive at the scene of the accident first.)

Anyway, here are some things you can do to try to improve your safety on a flight.

- **Choose your airline wisely.** Although the Federal Aviation Administration says it won't allow an unsafe airline to take to the skies, you can still pay attention to news reports and industry sources. US airlines are closely monitored—much more so than those of many other nations. If you are flying overseas, you can enhance your safety by sticking to US carriers, followed by major national carriers of foreign nations.

  You can search the internet for news and reports on individual airlines. One non-government site that rates major airlines can be found at AirlineRatings.com/airlines-ratings.php.
- **Choose the best seat.** The window seat in the exit row over the wing is generally considered the safest place to sit. Second to that are aisle seats in rows near an exit row.
- **Listen to the preflight safety patter.** Though you've heard it all before, listen to find out if there are any unusual features to the plane you are on. Locate the nearest exits in front and behind you and count the rows to them so that you'll know where to go in a smoky, dark emergency.
- **Dress sensibly.** Wear comfortable tie shoes or sneakers. Leave high heels, flip flops, and slip-ons in your luggage. Wear natural fiber fabrics, which are less likely to catch fire or melt in flames.

Learn the Tricks to Avoid a Seatmate

Let's face it—sometimes you just want to be alone. You want to stretch out and sleep on a long return trip; you want to do some work on your laptop computer; you want to read the potboiler you bought at the airport newsstand.

You know what you don't want: a nervous neurotic who wants to discuss his life story with you...the life-insurance saleswoman who thinks it is appropriate to investigate the details of your life and financial situation...or the unpleasant dropout from the school of good manners and good grooming.

Consider these tips to improve your chances of sitting next to nobody.

- **Select a flight that is not fully booked.** A basic rule of logic says that if there are no empty seats on the airplane, your chances of sitting solo are slim. Choose a flight that leaves at an off-peak time (midmorning or early afternoon on a midweek, nonholiday-period flight, or some but not all overnight flights). You can check online when you shop for a ticket to see how many seats are available, but that does not guarantee against a last-minute rush of late bookings.
- **If you are traveling with someone else, book the aisle and window seats in a three-seat row.** The middle seats are the last ones assigned, and if you end up with someone in the middle, you should have good success in convincing that unlucky soul to trade for one of your seats to reunite your party.
- **When you arrive at the gate, ask the agent if the seat next to yours is vacant.** If it is not, politely ask if he or she can move you. You may have to wait for the last moment to board, but a friendly gate agent may be able to hold open a row for you.

Make Yourself Comfortable in Midair

An airplane cabin is not to be confused with a health spa. The air is extremely dry and often not well refreshed. Just about anything in the air—from odors to germs—is moved efficiently through the cabin.

Here are some things you can do to maintain your health onboard an airplane.

- **Stay lubricated.** Sharply increase your intake of water and juices to combat dehydration. Water may also help combat jet lag and altitude sickness when you arrive. Avoid alcohol and caffeine (coffee, tea, and cola drinks), which work the other way.
- **Do some housekeeping.** The seatback tray table upon which you will place your food or reading material is, by some appraisals, about as unhealthy an environment as a cat's litter box. Do yourself a favor and wipe down the tray with a packaged moist towelette, or ask the flight attendant to stop by with a cleaner.
- **Keep your pipes clear.** Ascent and (especially) descent can be painful to your ears. It's caused by an imbalance in your sinuses, a condition that can be cleared up by opening the Eustachian tubes, which run from each middle ear to the nasal passages. I am old enough to remember how flight attendants (stewardesses as they were called) used to walk the aisles offering chewing gum as a plane was about to come in for a landing. That's still a good idea, especially for children. Another way to open the tube is to pinch your nose, close your mouth, and attempt to breathe out through your nose. If you do it right, you'll feel a relieving pop in your ears.
- **Consult your doctor about taking an over-the-counter or prescription decongestant.** This is especially true if you have a cold. The downside to decongestants is that they may make you drowsy, which could be problematic if you need to drive or make a business presentation when you get to your destination.

- **Keep your blood flowing.** It's not a good practice to be completely sedentary for long periods of time, especially if you have any type of circulatory problems. If you suffer from any significant medical conditions, consult your doctor before taking a long flight. Try to get up and walk around several times on the flight. It is also a good idea to dress in loose-fitting clothing. Some passengers wear compression socks to help blood circulation.
- **Sleep if you can.** Some of us can fall asleep in most any position. I usually can catch a few hours of uncomfortable shuteye on a night flight. Others, like my wife, are either constitutionally or willfully unable to sleep on a plane. You may find that a lightweight neck pillow will help you get comfortable. Consult with your doctor about whether a low-strength sleeping pill might help you. However, you don't want to fall so deeply asleep that you cannot protect yourself in the event of an emergency or be unable to handle a normal disembarkation on arrival.

Handle Your Landing

You've made it this far—booking your flight, packing, getting to the airport, boarding the plane, and landing at your destination. Now what? Immigration and customs at a foreign airport, baggage claim if you are lucky, the lost luggage office if you're not. Finally, you can hope to get out of there: rental car stations, parking lots, or taxis. What fun!

Fight Against Jet Lag

The human body was designed long before a time when you could walk into an airport in New York at breakfast time and step off in London for dinner (or depart London at dinner and arrive in New Zealand for breakfast). We pay for this wondrous ability with something called *jet lag*, which is our body's reaction to zooming across time zones with abandon. For most of us, it feels like something between a hangover and mild case of the flu: exhaustion, dizziness, headaches, and a general failure to compute.

There's not a whole lot you can do to choose flight schedules for transcontinental journeys. Most trips from the US to Europe depart at night, arriving in the early morning. Heading the other direction, they generally leave by midday, landing on the US East coast in late afternoon. There are just a few flights that buck that trend. I know quite well the British Airways and Virgin Atlantic flights that leave New York in the early morning and arrive in London in time for a later dinner. There is no equivalent daylight flight to Paris, Rome, or Athens.

Flyers from the West coast to Europe have it even worse, leaving in the morning or early afternoon of one day to make a connection in order to arrive across the Atlantic the next morning.

Here are some tips to get the edge on jet lag.

- **Several days to a week before your flight, make gradual adjustments to your ordinary schedule to bring yourself closer to the time zone you are going to.** For example, before heading east to Europe, by the time you depart, you could get to sleep earlier and wake up earlier than usual.
- **Skip the alcohol and coffee on your flight.** Substitute an extra ration of water and juices.

• **If you arrive in daylight, reset your body clock with a walk in bright sunlight.** If local time calls for going to sleep, head for a bed.

• **Try to get onto local time as quickly as possible,** even if it means fighting off sleep for hours. Switch your meals to the local schedule, too, but eat a light dinner before bed to help you fall asleep. For most people, carbohydrates (sugars and starches) help promote sleep, while protein (a slab of steak) can keep you up.

• **Ask your doctor about taking melatonin,** a food supplement sold at many health food stores. Make sure there are no adverse interactions with any prescription drugs you take or any medical conditions you have. Melatonin is a chemical that your body naturally produces at bedtime, and some studies indicate you can set your internal clock by taking a dose at the appropriate time for bed. (You can get a head start by starting melatonin a few days before your trip and gently adjusting your bedtime and morning alarm in the direction of your new time zone.)

Avoid Duty-Free Duress

The idea of duty-free shopping on international flights is appealing to some. Here's your chance to purchase foreign and some domestic products without paying state and local sales taxes, excise taxes, duty, and other surcharges. Duty-free shops in airports operate in a legal netherworld that allows them to act as if the items they have for sale have never entered the country. Their warehouses are bonded by customs authorities, and all sales are limited to people who will not be immediately reentering the country. At some shops, your order is delivered to you as you board your airplane. Some airlines operate duty-free shops with flight attendants hawking wares on board the plane.

Here's the problem: in a highly competitive marketplace, the duty-free shops do not always deliver the lowest prices. (One reason may be the high cost of operating a store within an airport.) Discount shops outside the airport may have lower prices, even with taxes and duty. Know the prices of items you may buy, including perfume, liquor, cameras, and jewelry. Nonresidents may be able to get a refund of value-added taxes for purchases they made within a foreign country. That may bring the price in line with those at duty-free shops.

Plus, you are in a high-security environment. Buying items like wine, liquor, and perfume at duty-free shops is one way to bring liquids aboard an airplane in carry-on luggage. (You cannot bring large bottles or containers of liquid through the security checkpoint, but duty-free shops exist on the so-called secure side. You can place purchased items in your carry-on bags.)

And be aware that if you are flying internationally and you must change planes along the way, you might be required to go through another security checkpoint and lose your liquids. Once you enter the European Union, as an example, flights to other member nations of the EU are essentially domestic flights, but things could be different if you fly into the EU and then fly to a non-member country. Your airline may be able to inform you of security requirements, but details are sometimes hard to find.

Understand Value-Added Tax Rebates

Many countries, including most European nations and Canada, have a somewhat hidden sales tax on purchases, called a value-added tax (VAT) or a Goods and Services tax (GST). As a nonresident visitor, you are usually entitled to a refund of some or all VAT or GST when you take your purchases out of the country.

Obtain information on tax refunds at tourist bureaus or major shops. Some countries permit retailers to send you the refund directly, while in others you must apply to the government for your money back. And in some countries, some agencies are allowed to immediately pay your refund minus a service charge. If you have any questions about the legitimacy of such an offer, contact an area tourist bureau or government agency.

Understand Customs Duties

Visit the website of your destination's customs bureau and your return country before heading out on a trip. Learn about taxes (also called *duties*) and other limitations. As this book goes to press, US citizens and legal residents are permitted to bring back into the country $800 worth of goods per person. The amount can be combined for a family filing a single customs form, so a family of five could bring in $4,000 worth of goods without having to pay duty. Always ask for and carry with you the receipts for purchases that you make abroad and are bringing with you into the country. That way you can accurately list items on custom forms.

US citizens may be able to save money on duties for expensive jewelry and art that they purchase in foreign countries by buying products in an unfinished form. Check with the US Customs and Border Protection (CBP) Department for details before traveling.

If you purchase something outside the country and arrange to ship it home, you are responsible for any duties assessed on the product. You don't need to declare these items when you arrive in the US. Customs agents at the border are only concerned with items you are bringing with you. Check with CBP for details.

If you plan to leave the US with valuable jewelry, cameras, or other items, carry proof of purchase or register the items with CBP before leaving home. That way there is no question about you bringing them back into the country as personal items.

The excitement of flying to a foreign nation, or of returning home from a visit abroad, can quickly turn to annoyance when you find yourself in a line of hundreds of tired travelers waiting to go through passport control.

Other than joining the diplomatic corps, you can do a few things to speed your way through the process…

- **Fly a national carrier to and from its home country.** For example, take Air France to France or British Air to the United Kingdom. Citizens of a country often prefer to fly on an airline from home, and as an American you have a good chance of finding fewer foreigners like yourself waiting to go through the passport booths reserved for visitors. Similarly, when you return, you may find fewer people waiting to go through the booths for US citizens.

- **Fill out your entry cards carefully and fully on the plane.** Head directly for the passport lines. Answer questions simply.

- **Be solemn and polite.** Don't make small talk or try out your jokes on the immigration official. They are looking for people who seem nervous or are trying to distract them. Answer the questions you are asked and don't give the officer a reason to pull you out of the crowd.

An App, Skip, and a Jump

The US Customs and Border Protection Service offer a smartphone app that may help reduce your wait time when you return home. Called the Mobile Passport App, it requires you to enter your passport information into the program and pose for a photo using your smartphone camera.

When you land after an international flight, you turn on the app, enter your travel information, answer the familiar arrival questions, and transmit it. If all goes well, you receive a bar code on your phone so you can skip the lines at immigration and head for a special counter where the code is read. You'll have to show it a second time after you pick up your baggage and pass through customs inspection.

I have the app, and it actually works—although you may need help from an agent to scan the code, and you are all but certain to get some dirty looks from the hundreds of tired passengers queued up for a standard inspection. As this book goes to press, the mobile app is said to work at 24 major airports in the US.

You can get the app at MobilePassport.us or via your cell-phone's app store.

Know What to Do When Your Luggage Is Lost

If you are the last person waiting at the carousel, your bags may have gone on a trip by themselves. Head immediately for the airline's baggage office, which is usually near the baggage room. Similarly, if you find your bags damaged, your best bet is to file a report before you leave the airport. You may be at home or at hotel before you discover something is missing from your bags. Most airlines require you to notify them within twenty-four hours of your arrival. On international flights, you ordinarily have seven days to make notification.

Fill out the forms immediately, describing as specifically as you can the bags as well as their contents. Remember that the airline will use your form as the initial basis for searching for missing items as well as paying a claim if they cannot be recovered. Don't surrender your ticket receipt and baggage claim tag. The airline will have the originals in their system. Hopefully you've got photos of your bag and belongings (as I advised earlier in this chapter) that you can use to substantiate your claim. (I recently filed a claim against American Airlines when they tore the front pocket off a piece of luggage. They asked me to send them a picture of the damaged suitcase, which I did. They accepted that—and my "before" photo—as proof and sent me a check.)

If you are in the middle of a trip, make sure the airline knows how to reach you while you are on the road as well as when you return home. In certain circumstances, an airline will provide a toiletries kit or offer a voucher so you can buy essential items.

The good news is that most misplaced baggage is eventually found, and airlines do a good job of reuniting passengers with their bags. You can increase the odds in your favor by paying close attention when your bags are checked and by clearly marking your bags with your name and address. Help yourself out by packing prescription drugs and other important personal items in your carry-on bag.

Zip Through Airport Parking Lots

If you will drive to the airport and leave a car in a parking lot, check online or call ahead to find out how crowded the lots and garages are. If space is tight, you might want to use a different lot at the airport or off-site.

Here are some more savvy tips on airport lots.

• **Many airports have two or more types of parking,** including long-term lots (which are far from the terminals) and more expensive daily lots (which may be just across the road from the check-in counters). Some airports also have valet parking services. If you are flying first class or business class, check with your airline to see if they have any special arrangements for their full-fare customers.

• **If you're looking forward to making a hasty exit from the airport when you return from your trip,** park close to the exit instead of close to the terminal. You may have to lug your bags a bit further, but you may also be able to avoid an annoying traffic jam on the garage's upper level.

• **Hide your parking receipt in your car so that you won't lose it.** (Yes, I know someone out there is going to say that leaving the receipt in the car is an aid to a thief. But if you're hiding the receipt out of sight, your car is no more likely to be broken into than any other. And a thief could very easily obtain a parking ticket from the entry machine or work in cahoots with the garage.)

• **Make a note of your parking space number or take a picture of the parking space with your smartphone.** Your phone might even have an app that can direct you to your car when you return.

Get a Taxi at the Airport

Few things are less fun than arriving at the airport after a 10-hour red-eye to find several plane loads of other travelers already in line at the taxi stand. You don't want to get ripped off if you're from out of town and don't know your way around.

These tips may keep you from being ripped off when you take a taxi…

• **Know where you are going.** Consult a map (there are some fine smartphone apps you can use that will tell you the distance and the best route) before jumping into a cab. Ask the driver how he will take you to your destination and don't be afraid to follow along on your smartphone app.

• **Know the approximate mileage to your destination or the standard flat rate.** If you are getting into a cab at the airport, ask the dispatcher there for the price range for your trip. If the taxi charges a flat rate, determine the price beforehand

TIP

Pack This App

Several airlines, including American and Delta, have smartphone apps or links on their websites that allow you to track your bags as you travel. You enter the code from the bag tag and learn where your bags are. I have used the app while waiting to board a plane as one level of assurance that my bags were going to fly with me—and indeed, they did.

To download American's app, visit AA.com/i18n/travel-info/travel-tools/american-airlines-app.jsp. For Delta's app, visit Delta.com/content/www/en_US/mobile.html. To see if your airline has such an app, search the airline name along with *baggage tracking app.*

Bypass a Taxi

Uber, Lyft, and a few other online car-hailing services like Gett have disrupted (in a mostly good way) the taxi industry in the US and many locations around the world. Once you set up an account with a service like these, you can call for a car from nearly anywhere. The app shows you an approximate or exact price for various types of cars. Once you accept an offer, you can track the car's approach and arrival.

If you are using Uber, you will know the driver's name and his or her car and license plate. Once in the car, you can track your location as you proceed to your destination and even share your pickup and destination details with someone else as a safety measure.

At some airports, Uber and other non-taxi services are not allowed to use the regular waiting lots and instead are positioned off the airport grounds. In my experience, they rarely require more than about 10 minutes to arrive, sometimes with candy.

I have used Uber domestically and in Europe without any problems. This is not meant as an endorsement of that particular company. I would hope that its example of using technology for convenience and lower prices will be adopted by more traditional taxi companies as well.

and check the quoted rate against a list that should be posted inside the cab.

- **Watch out for scams.** Make sure the meter is at zero before you get into the cab and read the posted notices in the cab for information about additional charges such as airport, nighttime, or luggage surcharges.

- **Be sure you understand—ahead of time—policies on ride sharing.** Except in certain circumstances such as rush-hour crunches, most such programs do not require each passenger to pay the full fare indicated on the meter.

- **Get a signed receipt, with the driver's name clearly indicated.** The receipt should be the same as the name on the license that is displayed in the cab, if there is one. The receipt should indicate pick-up point, destination, and the total fare. The receipt can be your evidence if you want to file a complaint with the local regulatory board for taxis.

Even less fun than getting a taxi and getting the runaround? No taxis in sight. *Here are some strategies to get out of the airport quickly...*

- **Ask the taxi dispatcher if there is a better place to wait for a cab.** It may make sense to walk or take the airport bus to another terminal.

- **See if there is a ride-share program at the airport.** The dispatcher will bring together groups of passengers heading to destinations near each other. Even if there is no official program, there is nothing to prevent you from asking people at the front of the line if they are going near your destination. Offer to split the fare—or even offer to pay the entire fare—and you will probably be able to move forward quickly.

- **Consider booking a car service or limousine before you leave.** Rates for car services are usually close to those of taxis, while airport limos are surprisingly affordable most times of the day. You can share the cost with others in your party, and you can skip the taxi line completely.

- **If you didn't book a car service before you left, call for a vehicle when you land at the airport.** The dispatcher may have a car en route to the terminal with a passenger.

CHAPTER 30

Considering a Cruise

Traveling by cruise ship is one of the best ways to sample a region of the world. traveling by ship is a great way to see much of Europe, South America, Central America, the Caribbean, as well as coastal wonders of Alaska, Scandinavia, and large parts of the US and Canada. And you can sail to ports like Lima or Sydney and use them as your entry point to the interior.

You pay a single price and receive all of the following: a place to sleep; breakfast, lunch, and dinner that is anywhere from good to excellent; entertainment of nearly every sort, from nightly stage shows to lounge acts to lectures and special appearances by artists and other entertainers; and transportation from place to place.

Department of full disclosure: When I am not writing books like this one, I travel the world as a destination and enrichment lecturer for Silversea Cruises, an Italian company that most experts—not just me—consider to be one of the most luxurious small-ship cruise lines. That relationship had no effect on my comments in this chapter, and the company has no involvement with the publisher of this book.

- **Compare cruise lines.**
- **Compare ships.**
- **Shop like a cruise pro.**
- **Know your package deals.**
- **Save money on shore excursions.**

Compare Cruise Lines

In 2016, about 24 million people went to sea by cruise ship, an increase of nearly 70% across the past decade. But just like many other industries, there has been a consolidation of many brands under a relatively few corporate umbrellas, which reduce competition. Cruise lines are in some ways similar to airlines and hotels: If a ship sails with an unfilled cabin, that is income the cruise company will never recover.

And so, although some cruise lines or individual ships consistently sell out at a premium price, there are also many great deals available. Keep in mind that a ship's size and quality might be different from your expectations. In general, you get what you pay for. Some of the most luxurious ships are small vessels with 200 to 400 guests, a very high number of crew per passenger, and a large amount of space per person. If that doesn't float your boat, there are megaships with 5,000 or more passengers, a dozen restaurants, water slide, ice skating rink, and an outdoor movie theater.

First, let's look at the industry. You can find a treasure trove of reviews and comparisons on the internet. Many websites publish commentary and ratings by travelers. Unfortunately, in my opinion, none of them is beyond the reach of bias because the same sites also either sell cruises or link to partners for the same purpose. If you read the reviews carefully, you can get a sense of the service quality and accommodations offered by the various lines. You'll also find quite a few unreasonable expectations and silly objections to minor perceived slights.

The cruise industry is one of the last areas of travel where a good travel agent may be worthwhile. Cruise lines still pay commissions to agents, which cuts both ways: an agent can afford to spend time advising you because he or she will be paid for that time, but that same agent has a financial interest in what you book. If Cruise Line X is offering undisclosed bonuses to agents this week, the advice they offer may be swayed. Ask friends and acquaintances for recommendations on travel agents who have steered them straight in the past.

Here is my ranking of the major cruise companies based on years of cruise experience. You can consider the size ship you want to take and investigate further at the provided websites. For our purposes, a small ship is one with fewer than 1,000 passengers. A mid-sized ship holds between 1,000 and 3,000 guests, and a large ship holds from 3,000 to 6,000.

Crystal Cruises	Top tier	Owned by Genting Hong Kong; has midsized luxury ships	CrystalCruises.com
Seabourn	Top tier	Part of Carnival Corporation; operates small and midsize luxury ships	Seabourn.com
Silversea Cruises	Top tier	A privately owned Italian company that operates five small luxury cruise ships plus four small expedition ships	Silversea.com
Azamara Club Cruises	Above midrange	A small fleet of midsized ships, part of the Royal Caribbean family	AzamaraClubCruises.com
Cunard	Above mid-range	A small fleet of large luxury ships absorbed into Carnival Corporation	Cunard.com
Regent Seven Seas Cruises	Above midrange	About half a dozen midsized to large ships; a subsidiary of Norwegian Cruise Lines Holdings	RSSC.com
Oceania Cruises	Above midrange	About half a dozen midsized-to-large ships; a subsidiary of Norwegian Cruise Lines Holdings	OceaniaCruises.com
Viking Ocean Cruises	Above midrange	The oceangoing branch of Viking River Cruises; has a fleet of half a dozen midsized vessels	VikingCruises.com

AIDA Cruises	In the vast middle	Large ships catering to the German market; part of Carnival Corporation	AIDA.de
Carnival Cruise Line	In the vast middle	The Carnival Corporation, with 10 cruise lines in its portfolio, has about half the total cruise market worldwide; Carnival Cruise Line has more than two dozen midsized to large ships in its fleet	Carnival.com
Celebrity	In the vast middle	About a dozen large to very large ships; is part of the Royal Caribbean group	CelebrityCruises.com
Costa Cruises	In the vast middle	Eleven large to very large ships; part of the Carnival Corporation	CostaCruise.com
Holland America Line	In the vast middle	Mostly large ships; part of the Carnival Corporation	HollandAmerica.com
MSC Cruises	In the vast middle	Part of the second-largest container ship company in the world; more than a dozen ships, with very large newer vessels	MSCcruisesusa.com
Norwegian Cruise Line	In the vast middle	About fifteen ships; owned by a group of venture capital companies	NCL.com
P&O Cruises (UK)	In the vast middle	Large to very large ships catering to the UK market; part of Carnival Corporation	POcruises.com
P&O Cruises (Australia)	In the vast middle	Large ships; part of Carnival Corporation	POcruises.com.au
Princess Cruises	In the vast middle	Part of Carnival Corporation; large to very large ships	Princess.com
Pullmantur	In the vast middle	A small fleet of large fleets; caters to the Spanish and Latin American market; partly owned by Royal Caribbean	Pullmantur.es/en/
Royal Caribbean International	In the vast middle	The second-largest conglomerate of cruise lines; has about 25 large to very large ships, including the three largest cruise ships at sea, each with space for 6,000 or more guests	RoyalCaribbean.com
CDF Croisières de France	Less-known line	Caters to the French market; part of Royal Caribbean	CroisieresdeFrance.com
TUI Cruises	Less-known line	Caters to the German market; partly owned by Royal Caribbean	TUIcruises.com

Another group of ships spend their time on rivers. Such lines operate in Europe, Asia, Canada, and the US. These vessels are small by necessity. Some occupy the luxury end of the market, and others are rather basic.

The experience on a river cruise is more intimate, with guests and crew in close proximity. Travel by river usually means you are in sight of land at all times. This is also the only way to get to inland destinations by water. Oceangoing cruise lines cannot proceed on most of the waterways that river ships traverse.

Here are links to some of the best and most popular river cruise companies.

Avalon Waterways	More than two dozen ships in China, Europe, South America, and Vietnam	AvalonWaterways.com
Blount Small Ship Adventures	Two very basic ships that can reach some narrow, difficult waterways in New England, Hudson River, Erie Canal, Saint Lawrence, and eastern Canada, Lake Michigan, Caribbean, and Central America	BlountSmallShipAdventures.com/cruises/
Crystal River Cruises	Luxury cruise line promised a fleet of upscale river boats in 2017 after its first ship sailed in Europe	CrystalCruises.com/river
Uniworld River Cruises	A fleet of more than 20 vessels in China, Egypt, Europe, and Russia	Uniworld.com/river-cruise
Viking River Cruises	A fleet of about 60 ships in China, Egypt, Europe, and Russia	VikingRiverCruises.com

Compare Ships

Before examining price and quality, look at a couple of totally objective ways to measure a ship.

- **Passenger-space ratio.** The higher the space ratio, the less likely you'll find a stranger in a bath towel in your personal space by the pool or be assigned a seat at a dinner table for 12. Look at the ship's size (usually expressed as gross tonnage) and divide that number by the total passenger capacity. *Tonnage* refers to its capacity to carry passengers or cars or containers.

About passenger capacity: If a ship has 1,000 cabins, that could mean 1,000 single guests, or if there are two in a room, 2,000 guests. And many cabins are equipped with a sofa bed or can accommodate an extra bed, so the total number could 3,000 or even 4,000 people in that same ship.

You'll find statistics on gross tonnage and passenger capacity on ships' websites, or by searching Wikipedia listings for individual vessels. For example, enter *Wiki Oasis of the Seas* to find the numbers for that vessel.

- **Cabin square footage.** Read the brochures for the cruise line, or consult its website, and find the square footage for the exact cabin you are considering. In addition to the cruise line's website, you might also want to check CruiseDeckPlans.com or a site from a cruise travel agent. Remember that the total size quoted *includes the bathroom and any closets*. Also determine if the stated size includes a balcony or veranda, or if the size of that outdoors space is in addition to the cabin footage. Any cabin less than 200 square feet is small. A decent size for a basic cruise ship cabin is in the range of 225 to 250 square feet. That is large enough to include a double bed or two twin beds, a desk or vanity, and a table with chairs.

Want to live large? The Owner's Suite on a new luxury ship has 1,260 square feet plus a veranda (or balcony). Is it worth paying a premium for a veranda, or a small fortune for a top-end suite? It depends. Are you expecting to be spending a great deal of time in your cabin, or will you hang around the pool, faithfully attend lectures, stay out late for dinner, head to the theater for the nightly show, visit the casino, and go out for late-night drinks at the bar?

Motion of the Ocean

Are you prone to motion sickness? Consult your physician about prescription or over-the-counter medications, which you can get in pill or patch form. (If you're not sure if you get motion sick, pack some over-the-counter Dramamine, Bonine, or Benadryl with you just in case.) Some people believe a pressure point bracelet around the wrist helps stave off nausea, but a 2004 National Center for Biotechnology Information study found them ineffective (NCBI.nlm.nih.gov/pubmed/15018290). If you are sensitive to motion, reduce or eliminate alcohol, caffeine, and fatty or spicy foods. Drink lots of water. And you can reach back into maritime history for a natural calmative: ginger. Most ships offer candied ginger in the dining room. Ginger ale helps, too. Cabins that are located midship (and lower rather than higher) will reduce the amount of motion you feel at sea.

Shop Like a Cruise Pro

Booking passage on a cruise ship is not at all like choosing between two shirts sold online. There are many variables in a cruise vacation. Direct comparisons are extremely difficult. The following sections have tips for cruise shoppers. You can do all the work yourself, or you can enlist a travel agent's help. I suggest educating yourself either way, so that you can judge any recommendations you receive.

Cruise the Web

Start your search by visiting websites for cruise lines. Establish a baseline of information. Within each website, research a few specific itineraries and ships that interest you. Make notes about the list price and special offers available.

Be sure to do the following…

- **Compare apples to apples (or rowboats to rowboats).** Prices will vary depending on the length, time of year and, on some cruise lines, from ship to ship.

- **Know the true bottom-line price.** That includes the cruise, additional fees including port charges and taxes, and any upgrades or discounts. Read the fine print. Many cruise lines advertise 50% off or buy-one-get-one-free specials. Don't assume that the prices will be later reduced. The prices may have already been cut. If the cruise line includes air transportation, make sure flights from your nearest major airport are included. Does the cruise line provide transport from the airport to the ship, and the ship to the port at the end of the cruise?

Call the phone number listed on cruise line websites to ask questions if you want to, but try to avoid giving your name (or your real name) and phone number. Not only will this reduce the chances of bothersome follow-up calls, but in some situations a cruise line might consider you "their" client now and cause problems for travel agencies if you decide to book with them. On the other hand, you might want to register your email or street address with a cruise line to get mail about special deals. You can expect to receive quite a few.

Check Cruise Travel Companies

Check out four or five online websites of cruise travel companies and check the price for the same ships and itineraries. Again, be sure you get the bottom-line price, including the cruise, fees, taxes, and airfare, if it is part of the package.

Here are a few of the larger travel agencies with cruise expertise…

American Express Travel	Part of the credit card company, often able to offer special deals or all-inclusive air, hotel, and cruise bookings	Travel.AmericanExpress.com/home
Cruise Compete	A travel aggregator that can compare prices across multiple sites	CruiseCompete.com
The Cruise Outlet	A long-established agency specializing in cruises	TheCruiseOutlet.com

Major general travel websites, including Expedia, Orbitz, Priceline, and Travelocity, also offer cruise bookings. You can compare prices that you received elsewhere against listings here. You can also find travel agencies associated with major club shopping sites like Costco at Costcotravel.com and BJ's Wholesale Club at BJS.com/travel. (Note that Walmart and Sam's Club closed their travel affiliate in late 2017.)

This kind of website should offer the same sort of discounts offered by the cruise lines directly. Look for exclusive or similar special offers by these agencies. The price for the cruise itself is supposed to be the same everywhere you buy, but that doesn't mean that an agency can't offer some sort of rebate or upgrade of its own, such as money back in the form of a gift card or free transportation to or from ports through an independent supplier. Be sure you fully understand the terms of the offer, and make certain it is reflected in any booking form or contract you sign.

Check Lines You've Sailed

If you have sailed with a particular cruise line, look into loyalty programs that offer discounts or upgrades. Most lines automatically induct you into their clubs and contact you regularly. Most cruise lines also maintain an office aboard ship where you can initiate the booking for your next trip, with a special discount. Some cruise lines require you to book a particular cruise, while others allow you to put down a deposit to guarantee a discount but do not require you to select a particular cruise immediately.

Get the Best Price

The price of a cruise can vary greatly depending on a number of factors. *Here are a few…*

- **Luxury versus mainstream cruise lines.** Do you want a butler, 1,800 thread count linen bed sheets, and five-star furnishings and dining options? They don't come cheaply. If you choose to pay for luxury, make sure you receive value for your dollars.

- **Prime season versus off-season.** A cruise in the Mediterranean is usually at top price in July or August, but discounted earlier or later in the year. The same goes for the Caribbean, Alaska, and most anywhere else. Check the weather records. The Mediterranean can be almost unbearably crowded in August, much less so in October. The Caribbean is as warm and welcoming in September as it is in January, but the chances of a hurricane are much higher although still relatively rare.

- **Old ship versus the newest model.** The same cruise on a line's latest and greatest vessel may cost much more than the same or similar itinerary on a company's older ship. Here you need to decide whether it is the ship or the journey that excites you more. And older ships are almost always smaller than new ones, which is a plus for some cruisers.

- **Repositioning cruises.** Most cruise lines move their ships at the end of a season, for example, from the Caribbean to Alaska at the start of the summer and the other direction in the fall. Some cruise lines offer great prices on this repositioning. These cruises usually have six or eight (or more!) days at sea, which some guests treasure and others may dread.

- **Your agent.** In most instances, cruise lines sell trips at the same price whether you buy directly from them (only a few companies do this), from a travel agent, from an online travel discounter, or from a wholesale club. But—and this could be a big but—certain sellers include incentives. For example, an agency or an online travel site might be able to offer a special price on air travel to the port of departure and back. A wholesale club (like Costco, BJ's Wholesale Club, and the like) might sell you the cruise at list price and then kick back a discount of hundreds of dollars in the form of a debit card you can use for shopping. Alumni associations, auto clubs, and other groups may also have special offers. Pick the cruise you want and then

TIP

Make a Chart

Get a computer spreadsheet program like Excel (which you can get on PC and Apple machines, as well as in versions for smartphones and tablets) or an equivalent like Google Sheets (which you can get free online). These tools let you make notes on various offerings from cruise lines and travel agencies. You can easily update prices as they change, and directly compare the bottom lines.

put your business out to bid to several potential sellers. Don't feel bad about seeking the best deal. It's your money you're saving. *Consider asking for these perks…*

- An upgraded cabin
- An airline upgrade
- A hotel upgrade before or after the cruise
- Onboard spending credits for specialty restaurants, shore excursions, and bar tabs.

• **Use loyalty clubs.** Most cruise lines reward past customers with discounts, upgrades, or both. Try booking your next cruise while aboard ship. You may be able to use your club status from dry land as well.

• **Use memberships.** Are you a member of an alumni association, auto club, or wholesale club? Any of these or other groups may offer special deals that are based on a group purchase for a particular cruise.

• **Own stock.** Several of the largest cruise lines are publicly traded entities that quietly offer some special benefits for shareholders. The offer may require you to own the shares of stock for a particular period of time in advance of the booking. Check the investor relations website for cruise lines for details. If the shares go down just a few dollars, you will lose more than the possible benefit is worth. Over time, though—and this is not investment advice—the major cruise lines have performed well in the stock market. *As this book went to press, here are two such offers…*

- Royal Caribbean. If you own at least 100 shares of stock (ticker RCL), you can receive as much as a $250 onboard credit per stateroom for sailings of fourteen or more nights. The credit is lower for shorter cruises. The deal is good on the company's Royal Caribbean, Celebrity, and Azamara Club ships.
- Carnival. The largest cruise line has a very similar program for its lines, including Carnival, Princess, Costa, P&O, Cunard, Holland America, and Seabourn.

Lower-price cruise lines are more likely to offer deep discounts because they need to sell nearly 100% capacity to make money and because they hope to make profit from all guests for services, special meals, and drinks sold onboard. Luxury lines, which charge much more for their trips, are generally less likely to offer deep discounts because they usually can break even with fewer passengers.

Very much like carmakers, most cruise ships have all sorts of prices for the same cabin. The couple across the passageway may be paying half as much as you are for the same cabin. You will find a list price if you consult a cruise line, and in many instances a discounted price (it might be a percentage reduction, or a buy-one-get-one sort of free, or they might offer free air travel or an upgrade to business class for the price of an economy ticket).

If you are determined to buy a particular cabin or suite on a specific date and ship, you may have to pay top dollar. In general, the first accommodations to sell out are the fanciest and largest suites as well as the least expensive cabins. You are almost certain to get a much better price by being more flexible.

It's not easy to ferret out the best price, but there are some things you can do to try and get the best deal. *Start with these basic strategies…*

• **Be flexible on when and where you cruise.** The highest demand (and top prices) are in peak season, which is not the same everywhere at the same time. The *shoulder season*, which is the

Travel Agency Fare

Cruises are among the relatively few forms of travel still primarily served by travel agencies. Commissions generally range from about 10% to 16% on the cruise itself, with fees and certain services excluded from the calculation. Larger agencies generally receive higher commissions, but they also may have greater expenses. Hotels and car rental agencies generally pay about 10% to the agent. Airlines have almost completely stopped paying commissions except as part of larger packages including hotels and cars.

What does this mean to you? First of all, the travel agency can't rebate a large amount of money to customers, although the higher the bottom line, the more commission the line will pay. Large travel agencies may be very large cruise line customers, so they may be eligible to receive bonuses or other forms of endearment that they can pass along to you. However, don't expect a large rebate from a travel agency unless you are booking an expensive suite or purchasing a group of cabins for a family reunion. Regardless, ask for a better deal. The worst that can happen is that they will say no. More likely, they'll find some way to convince you to use their agency instead of one of their competitors.

Do your research online before visiting or calling a travel agency. Once you are quoted a price, politely ask if they can do something special for you. A reduced price? An upgrade of some sort? A rebate in the form of a cash-value debit card or gift certificate?

Know the price of necessary car rentals, hotels, and airline tickets before you contact the travel agency and ask them to come up with a package deal. They should be able to carve a little bit out of each element to make you happy.

time leading up to or following *just after* peak season often offers the best prices. If you can, travel to the Mediterranean in the spring or fall. Pick an Alaska tour after Labor Day. Go to the Caribbean in October or May. Consider taking a repositioning cruise (described earlier).

- **Look for sales and promotions.** They can come almost any time, but the most common are early in the year, starting in January for cruises later that year, and at the end of winter and summer when companies try their hardest to fill up ships.
- **Wait until the last minute.** Nearly all cruise lines will drop the price on empty cabins starting two to three months before the sailing date. On the downside, cabin selection will be limited—and you may not want an undesirable cabin (near lobbies, elevators, laundry rooms, bars, and showrooms, for example). And the least expensive cabins on most cruise lines are *inside*, meaning they have no portholes, windows, or balconies. Waiting too long to book could end up costing you more money (on airfare to the port of departure), although some cruise lines can include flights based on negotiated fares.
- **Book using a credit card that gives you a cash rebate.** Cruise lines can offer discounts without reducing their price. They can allow credit card companies to boost their rebates for certain types of travel, including cruises. If the card issuer has its own travel department, you may save more if you bundle other elements of the trip, such as car rental, airfare, transfers, and hotels at the start or end of the cruise.

Know Your Package Deals

Cruise ships come in different flavors, and so do package deals. You might run across an unbelievably cheap deal—but will you pay extra for every cup of coffee you have on the ship? What about all-inclusive deals—are they worth it? And finally, package deals may show up on your travel radar, and that could mean saving money on a specific aspect of your trip, such as alcohol. (Sometimes—not always—an all-inclusive cruise is less costly than a low-price line if you intend to live large aboard ship.) Different deals come from different cruise line levels, so keep that in mind as you're reading.

> **TIP**
>
> Low- and midrange cruise lines generally do not pay hotel staff (including room attendants, waiters, and other personnel) very well. They are very much dependent upon your gratuity for their income. Tipping them is simply the kind thing to do, and it greatly increases your good karma. If you're upset about the weather or the couple next door, don't take it out on your room attendant or waiter by refusing to tip.
>
> If something goes wrong on your cruise—a problem with your room, the food, or the entertainment, for example—discuss it with the reception or concierge desk or ask to speak to the hotel director aboard ship. They may be willing to do something to make you feel better about your vacation experience. Lodge your complaint early in the cruise, while there is still time for them to rectify the situation—change your cabin, provide a free pass to a specialty restaurant, or the like.

Very Inexpensive Cruises

Have we got an offer for you! How about a seven-day cruise in the Mediterranean for $777! How can you turn that down? Transportation, food, entertainment, and a place to sleep for $111 per day. It's a great deal.

Offers like this, mostly from midrange and lower cruise lines (according to the rankings I gave earlier in this chapter), seem too good to be true. If you are very careful about what you purchase on board, that great deal can remain spectacular. Here's the real deal: Those low, low prices are almost always offered by cruise lines that are willing to nearly give away their cabins in hopes of vacuuming out of your wallet hundreds or thousands of dollars in extra charges.

Under this sort of deal, your cruise ticket includes transportation from port to port, a cabin, meals at the basic restaurants on board, and most shows and other entertainment. *Here is what isn't included in a basic cruise ticket…*

- **Shore excursions.** The ship will take you to port, but what you do on shore is up to you on most cruise lines. Shore excursions, including bus or small boat trips, guided walking tours, visits to museums and other attractions, and other offerings are sold onboard the ship at prices that might range from $50 to hundreds of dollars per person. Later in this chapter I'll discuss ways to arrange for your own excursions at greatly reduced prices.
- **Beverages.** That includes mealtimes and in bars and specialty venues aboard ship. A soda might be $5 plus a tip, which is automatically added to your bill "for your convenience."
- **Other beverages.** That includes coffee and specialty drinks at most dining venues, usually with the exception of restaurants.
- **Bottled water.** You might need it when you go ashore.

- **Alcohol.** Wine, beer, and alcoholic drinks at dinner or at bars or shows are in this category.
- **Tips.** The recommended gratuities on major cruise lines range from about $12 to $15 per person per day—and it is usually added automatically. You can give a higher tip, if you like. If you go to the reception or concierge desk *before the last day of the cruise*, you can ask them to lower the gratuity or remove it from your bill.
- **Luxuries.** This includes spa treatments, exercise programs, certain enrichment programs like art, computer, or cooking classes, and the like.
- **Specialty restaurants.** Many cruise lines offer smaller and perhaps higher-quality dining places for extra charges that may range from $25 to $50 per person per meal. It isn't all that much, but think about the fact you are foregoing a meal you have already paid for at the regular restaurant.
- **Premium entertainment.** Want to use the rock climbing wall or the ice skating rink or attend a special performance in the theater? There's a charge for that.
- **WiFi internet and phone calls.** Although the price of using the internet aboard ship has come down, it is still quite easy to run up a large bill. Plus, service is usually much, much slower than at home and may not be available in some parts of the world. Most ships also have an onboard cellular system that will work with most cellphones for voice calls, although the rates are often shockingly high. There is also satellite phone service, the most expensive communication service aboard ship, but usually available almost anywhere.

TIP

Cellphone Roaming

Consult your cellphone provider and find available international roaming packages that allow you to make phone calls, use data services, and access the internet (for phone services like Skype). These services are only available when the ship is in port and when you are ashore, away from the onboard offerings.

All-Inclusive Cruises

Some cruise lines have *all-inclusive* offers. What is included with all-inclusive? It depends on your cruise line, so find out the full terms. These packages usually are available on luxury and upper-midrange cruise lines, which means that prices will be higher.

Do the math. In some instances, the price for an all-inclusive premium cruise line may be close to that of a lesser line that charges for almost everything other than a place to sleep.

Here is *one* definition of all-inclusive…

- **Free beverages, including wine and other alcoholic drinks, at bars and restaurants aboard ship.** The list of wines

Travel Companies Catering to Singles

Some travel companies are looking specifically for singles—for cruises and other kinds of trips. Search the internet for single travel offers or ask a local travel agency you have dealt with in the past. Here are a few to explore for package deals, singles matching, or both.

- **Best Single Travel** at BestSingleTravel.com
- **Singles Travel International** at SinglesTravelIntl.com
- **SinglesTravel Getaways** at SinglesTravelGetaways.com

and beverages is usually quite extensive, but if you insist on spending more money, there is usually a selection of premium wines and spirits available for purchase.

- **Gratuities included.** You can always add a bit more or give a cash-filled envelope to a favorite server, butler, or room attendant. Some guests prefer to give a contribution to a "crew welfare fund" maintained on many cruise lines for special perks offered to the entire crew. Inquire at the reception desk to see if such a fund is maintained on your ship.
- **No extra charge for premium restaurants.** Except for super-premium restaurants, that is.
- **Free WiFi.** No charge to use the ship's WiFi system to check email and consult the internet. You might *not* be able to make internet phone calls using services like Skype, and you probably will not be able to use streaming video services to watch movies or television. And some free services are limited to a few hours per day.
- **Free shore excursions.** Some lines include one or more basic shore excursions in each port, and many are perfectly adequate, but if you want to take a more adventurous or intensive tour, you'll likely find them available with extra payment. Some cruise lines allow you to deduct the list price of the basic tour from that of a more expensive tour. If you choose not to take a shore excursion in a particular port, you are unlikely to receive a credit or refund.
- **Some cruise lines include free airfare to the ship and back home.** Of course, as a savvy consumer, you understand that nothing comes free. Do your own research and find out the cost of airfare and transfers if you were booking them yourself and then subtract that amount from the cruise fare to see if you're truly receiving a bargain.

Special Package Cruises

Midrange cruise lines that charge sometimes-exorbitant prices for soda, beer, wine, and alcoholic drinks may offer an unlimited drinks package that softens the blow for some travelers. Once again, you've got to read the fine print (for example, most cruise lines insist that if one guest in a cabin purchases a drinks package, anyone else in the cabin has to add the same deal; they don't want you to share), and I suggest reading it before sampling a martini by the pool.

A typical drink package might cost $50 to $80 per day, per person. However, it does not fully cover the cost of drinks priced at $15 or more. (In that instance, think of the package as deductible coverage.) And there is a service charge of 15% to 18% that automatically is added to your bill, which means about $8 to $15 per day for your free drinks. For example, on a ten-day cruise, that drink package could add $800 plus $150 in service charges. That's per person.

Increasingly, cruise lines have begun offering free incentives at the time of booking, and the drinks package is commonly offered. When they say *free*, what they mean is free drinks below a certain price level, plus a 15% to 18% service charge based on the price of the package (if you were purchasing it). Free means at least $8 to $15 per day per person.

One more thing to remember is that nearly all drinks packages exclude bottled water. There's a separate package you can purchase for that, or you can buy bottled water ashore.

No BYOB

Most cruise lines that charge for drinks also *do not* allow you to bring aboard ship wine, beer, spirits, or bottled water purchased ashore. Some cruise lines will permit you to bring one or two bottles of wine but impose a *corkage fee*, which is nothing more than a charge to recoup their lost profit. Other lines allow you to buy wine off the ship, but insist on storing it in a locker and only returning it to you at the end of the cruise.

Cruising Solo

If there is just one person in a cabin, there is less cost to the cruise line for meals. And other expenses—moving the vessel from place to place, ship maintenance, and entertainment—are unaffected. Some cruise lines add a 100% *single supplement* to a room that is booked just for one person. In recent years, some lines have acknowledged that not all their expenses are the same when there is one in a cabin, and have reduced the supplement to 75% or 50%.

And some cruise lines have decided to directly court the singles market by offering either reduced-price small cabins specifically designed for individuals or without any single supplement. Cruise lines that have these cabins on some of their ships or on some of their sailings include Holland America, Norwegian Cruise Lines, P&O, and Royal Caribbean.

A few luxury cruises lines, which charge premium rates to begin with, offer sharply reduced single supplements on some trips. At the high end of the market, you may find such arrangements from Silversea or Seabourn.

As a single traveler, then, you have four options...

- **Pay the full singles supplement—as much as 100%.**
- **Find a special singles deal that might reduce the singles supplement to 50%, 25%, 10%, or to nothing.**

Share Contact Info

If you plan to venture away from the port on your own, make sure the ship's reception desk has your smartphone number and email address in case they need to contact you. For the same reason, make sure you carry the ship's phone number with you in case you need to get in touch.

You should be able to obtain the ship's satellite phone number when you are booking your cruise. If not, the contact number should be provided to you as you embark, and is often on room keys or schedules. The satellite number is, in theory, accessible anywhere in the world the ship travels.

- **Sign up for a singles-matching service that will seek to fill a cruise cabin with another person of the same gender and, within reason, of similar age.** Some such services say they will try to accommodate early birds with other early risers, and night owls with others who like to party hard. Snoring? Politics? Not so much.
- **Find your own traveling companion through local organizations, friends, or family.**

Save Money on Shore Excursions

Why would you want to pay the cruise line to arrange a shore excursion for you in any (or all) of the ports of call on a trip?

There is one very good reason: The ship's shore excursions are coordinated with the arrival and departure time, and the operators are in contact with the ship. If the shore excursion is delayed in its return, nearly all cruise lines guarantee that the ship will wait for its guests.

Why would you want to make your own arrangements in a port? Because you want to do something the cruise line isn't offering, or you can save money, or both. My wife and I have never hesitated to head out on our own by metro, train, or boat all over the world. When we do, we always plan to return to the ship two hours before departure to avoid problems.

A few minutes' searching on the internet will turn up the website addresses for a number of companies that offer shore excursions to cruise passengers who want to book independently. Some even offer a package, at a discount, that matches major ship itineraries. The independent companies promise to return you to the ship in time for its departure, but that is *not* the same as a guarantee by the cruise line to wait for your return.

Hiring a local guide for the day is another option I have used in places where both the language and alphabet are a bit daunting. On our first visit to Saint Petersburg, Russia, my wife and I contacted an agency that provided a local university student who traveled with us for the day, helping us understand how to get around.

CHAPTER 31

Choosing a Place to Stay

What's the difference between a $225 standard room and a $125 standard room at the same hotel? If you answered $100, you're a savvy consumer. Most larger hotels sell the same room for a range of prices—starting with a rack rate, which is the full list price, and going down from there to discounts based on the time of year or day of the week, special rates for members of associations or attendees at conventions, and rooms that are sold at deep discounts to hotel consolidators.

Before booking, consider how long you'll stay. How much time will you spend at the hotel and what are your specific needs? You want a safe, clean place to sleep, of course, but consider other things. Will you arrive at 10 p.m. and leave the next morning early? If so, does it matter whether the room has an ocean view or a glimpse of the parking lot? If you intend to use the hotel as your base for multiple days in a city, it is probably worthwhile to stay in the heart of town. If you will explore places elsewhere, it might make sense to stay in a less-expensive hotel outside of the city. If you have a car, either yours or a rental, consider the cost of parking in town. Some people fall head-over-heels in love with hotels that provide breakfast. I can save $50, forego the so-called "free" meal, and find a place to grab a bagel and coffee in the morning.

In this chapter, I show you some ways to get the lowest rates.

- **Set up for the best deal.**
- **Ask for the best room in the house.**
- **Fight if you are bumped from a reservation.**
- **Get a room at a sold-out hotel.**
- **Find special deals online.**
- **Try hotel auction sites.**
- **Try AirBnB.**
- **Safeguard your possessions when you travel.**

Set Up for the Best Deal

Here's how to get the best deal on a hotel.

- **Take advantage of special discounts.** Most hotels offer special rates for members of AAA or its Canadian equivalent CAA, as well as certain other groups like AARP. You may also find senior rates and other categories.

- **Book early or late, directly with a hotel or a hotel chain.** Many companies offer discount codes or special offers such as free breakfast or upgrades, especially in advance of off-season and shoulder season periods. (*Shoulder season* is a travel industry term that means the times leading up to or following just after peak times, and this sometimes represents the best deal.)

- **Book a non-cancelable room.** A recent trend among hotel companies is to offer a discount to guests who agree to accept a penalty of one day's booking, or the entire length of stay, if a guest is unable to use a reservation. I'd recommend you be very careful here, especially if your travel is weeks or months off. On the other hand, if a few days or a week ahead you are *certain* you will use a reservation, you can find some of the best rates by using this option.

  Some travel sites or hotels allow you to protect yourself by purchasing cancellation insurance, which reimburses you in certain circumstances. You may also be able to purchase cancellation insurance for an entire trip, including flights, cruises, and hotels, from third parties. Search online for *trip cancellation*. Be sure to read and fully understand any such policy before trying this sort of plan, and compare the cost of the non-cancelable room plus insurance to the cost of a cancelable room.

- **Consider a package deal.** Some hotel-booking websites, as well as airline and car rental sites, offer packages that put together hotel plus a rental car, or airfare with a hotel. Be sure to compare the package rate to the best price you can find by shopping for elements of your trip as separate bookings.

- **Try a different approach.** Follow these steps and see if you can get the room you want.

Get the Best Hotel Rates

1. **Visit one of the many online travel booking sites and see their offerings for the location and date you want to stay.** There are many such sites, and they generally show the same hotels at the same price or within a few dollars of each other. Determine the bottom-line cost, which is the price of the room plus any taxes and resort fees. Two major players have gobbled up many competitors and started other sites. Their various sites draw from the same database and generally operate in the same way. I'll discuss the slight differences that might help save you money in a moment. Expedia owns Expedia, Orbitz, Travelocity, Hotels, Hotwire, Trivago, and Venere. Priceline owns Priceline, Booking, and Kayak.

   Another major player is American Express, which has a travel booking site available to people who have that company's credit card, as well as to the general public. You'll find similar offerings from other credit cards companies as well as indirect connections offered by airlines. (I have found American Express travel services to have excellent customer service. On one occasion, they negotiated a partial refund from a hotel after I had to cancel a "non-refundable" reservation because of a family emergency.)

2. If you find exactly what you are looking for on one or more of the sites, compare before booking your room. Compare at least two sites that are not owned by the same company. And then, call or visit the website of the hotel you have chosen. The prices you see on a travel booking website are supposed to be the lowest possible, but that does not mean that some hotels do not have special offers reserved for customers they deal with directly. Go for the best price (including taxes and fees) at whichever site you choose.

3. If you still don't like your options, call the national reservations desk for a hotel chain. Sometimes you can get a lower rate by calling a particular hotel directly, and sometimes they can point you to a chain that is part of the same company and provide a lower price that way. (For example, Hilton owns Hilton, Conrad, Canopy, DoubleTree, Embassy Suites, Hampton Inn, Homewood Suites, Tru, and other brands.) Ask the reservations clerk for the best available rate, being sure to mention any special discounts you may be eligible for, including AAA, AARP, and hotel clubs.

Being Direct with Your Requests

Overall, calling the hotel directly is the best way to make special requests, from choosing a particular room or floor to asking for a rollaway bed or other special furnishings. A national reservation service will almost always tell you that they will pass along your special desires but not guarantee them. If you call the hotel directly, ask for the name of whoever makes a promise to you and keep that information with your confirmation number.

You can make your reservation using the hotel's national reservation desk and then call the hotel directly for special requests. And in most situations, you can do the same for reservations made through a hotel website.

Ask for the Best Room in the House

I live on a resort island, and one of my favorite pastimes involves reading the real-estate listings. One shady real-estate agent sometimes bills a piece of property as having "possible ocean views." What does that mean? I figure it means that if you build a two-story house with a roof walk and stood on that platform with a ladder and a telescope, you might be able to see the Atlantic—if the fog has lifted and your neighbor's house isn't in the way.

It's the same sort of thing with hotel rooms. Don't pay a nickel more for a room that says *ocean view* or *mountain view* or *premium* or any other level without knowing exactly what you are paying for. You wouldn't buy a suit without trying it on, and you wouldn't (at least you shouldn't) pay for a meal if you're not satisfied with the quality. Why, then, would you pay for a hotel room if you find it unacceptable?

Keep these hotel hints in mind.

Sleeping Single in a Double Bed

Single travelers who would like to save money on trips, fear not. I have tips that can help make your "Is that just...one?" trip less expensive than it otherwise would be.

Hotels will tell you they have essentially the same cost if there is one person or two people in a room. They have to pay for laundry, cleaning, and temperature regulation. All of that is true, except that a hotelier also understands that an unfilled room for any particular night is money they will never recover. Some hotels have begun offering slightly discounted rooms for singles. It is sometimes couched in a different manner, with the base rate set at one guest and a small price rise for a second person in the room. If you don't see this sort of pricing on a hotel or travel booking website, call directly and ask.

If you're willing to give up some privacy, take a chance on a singles-matching service. (This is not a dating service. You'll be paired with someone of the same gender who wants to save the cost of a hotel room or cruise cabin.) Or, you could try to put together your own travel party among friends, family, and other people you know (and are willing to share living space with).

- **Ask the reservations clerk for a definition of terms.** You'll get a much clearer picture if you call the hotel directly rather than asking a national service in Omaha about the view out the window in Boston.
- **Request a specific room number.** If you are told of a particularly wonderful room, ask for its number and find out if you can request it specifically. Again, this is much more likely to be honored if you call the hotel directly, and you'll stand more chance at a small, locally managed operation.
- **Learn about *room series*.** In many larger hotels, room classifications are identified by the numbers on the door. All of the 02 rooms, for example, may be alike: 1202, 1002, 902, and so on may all be larger corner rooms overlooking the lake. The 03 rooms, across the hallway, may be budget rooms with views of the back alley. If you've stayed in 1507 and like it, call to determine if all 07 rooms are the same and then ask for one when you make your reservation or show up at the check-in desk.
- **Tell them what you like.** Even if you don't have a particular room in mind, make known your preferences at check-in. *Here are mine*: I want a quiet room, away from the elevators, vending machines, and the all-night lounge. If I'm on an extended business trip, I ask for a room with a desk I can work at. And don't be shy about marching back down to the front desk if you don't like the room you've been given.
- **Check it out before checking in.** If you have any doubts about the hotel's or room's quality, ask to see a room of the quality you will be renting before you sign the register. If you have already checked in, don't be shy about going back to the front desk and asking for a new room or your money back.

Fight If You Are Bumped from a Reservation

When is a guaranteed room not a guarantee of a room? Although most hotels honor their promise of a room when you have a reservation, from time to time you may find there is no room at the inn when you arrive. How is this possible? Sometimes hotels make mistakes, renting too many rooms. Sometimes hotels deliberately overbook, expecting that a certain percentage of people will fail to show. And sometimes hotels are victimized by guests who refuse to leave at the time they promised when they checked in. (In many states, it is a difficult, time-consuming process for a hotel to dislodge a guest who doesn't leave on time.)

Here are some tips...

- **Take your reservation's confirmation number to check-in.** If you have booked your room from Expedia, Priceline, or another third-party website, bring the contact information for the reservation with you as well just in case they have no record of your reservation.
- **Confirm in advance.** Call the hotel directly to confirm your reservation a day or two before you arrive.
- **Be firm.** If you show up at the check-in desk and find a problem, stand your ground. Politely but firmly tell the clerk you want to speak to the manager. Don't step aside to let the clerk tend to other customers. Make it clear that the only way you'll leave the desk is with a key to an acceptable room.
- **Listen carefully to what they say.** If there are "no rooms at the rate you booked," tell the clerk you will accept a better room—a suite, a concierge-floor room, a luxury room—at your original reserved rate.
- **Read the fine print.** That includes the hotel booking site and at the hotel chain's website. Some offer a guarantee against cancellation or a promise to rebook you into a nearby hotel of equivalent quality and provide transportation if necessary.
- **Call customer service.** If you have been bumped from a hotel where you had a guaranteed reservation and don't feel you are being treated properly, call the customer-service department of the hotel company and enlist their assistance.
- **Call a travel website or your credit card's customer service.** If you booked through a travel website, call customer service at that company and insist they help you. If you booked your hotel through your credit card company's hotel site, call them and enlist their help.

Get a Room at a Sold-Out Hotel

There are six major conventions in town, it's spring break, two weddings are going on...and the national reservations desk of the hotel chain you want to stay at has the nerve to tell you they are completely sold out.

If you are absolutely determined, here are some ways to not take no for an answer...

- **Call the hotel directly.** Many chains do not release their entire inventory to national services, keeping some rooms for local rental only.
- **Try, try again.** Let the manager know what you're looking for and leave your name and phone number. And keep calling every few days to see if rooms have become available.
- **Confirm the protocol.** If you are calling weeks or months in advance, ask about their policies. Is there a date after which you can't cancel reservations without a penalty? Call again just before and on that date to see if any rooms have opened.

Take Ratings with a Grain of Salt

I treat ratings the way I view the judges' scores at Olympic games: throw out the top and bottom scores and then examine everything in the middle for kernels of truth. Needless to say, I am skeptical. Do you see page after page of "customer reviews?"

If you want something genuine, explore the official tourism websites for the places you want to visit. Also explore travelers' unofficial websites and blogs. For example, I have my own blog at CoreySandler.com. *The New York Times* and many other fine newspapers and magazines have detailed descriptions of places to visit and things to do on their websites.

- **Find out the guarantee time for reservations.** If someone with a reservation must cancel before 6 p.m. to avoid being charged for the room, start calling that afternoon just after 6 p.m. to try to snare a last-minute cancellation.

Find Special Deals Online

There is a pair of sometimes contradictory promises that coexist in our computerized travel world. Hotels that list with online booking sites generally cannot offer rooms at a lower price directly to the customer. At the same time, many websites for hotel chains or individual hotels promise that they offer the lowest available rate. Sometimes those two promises do not conflict, but sometimes there is a bit of space between them.

For example, you may find occasional special offers on hotel websites. Also, most major chains have a frequent guest points program that allows you to earn free rooms or upgrades. And finally, you will often find rebate or points programs offered on websites. Be on the lookout for special credit cards offered by some companies that offer cash rebates to users.

If you book using certain credit cards, you can look for opportunities to double dip, earning points from the airline as well as the hotel and sometimes airline or other programs. Here's a double-dip example: book a hotel using an airline affinity card, which will earn you points with the airline and with the hotel if you are a member of their loyalty club.

Consider Hotel Auction Sites

You can try your hand at one of the online auction sites where you make an offer to a group of hotels, telling them the amount you are willing to pay for a room on a particular date. You should be sure of your plans before committing to one of these services. If your offer is accepted, your credit card is billed for the entire reservation, and the payment is nonrefundable. (You may be able to purchase cancellation insurance.)

The pioneer in this type of hotel shopping was Priceline, which offers standard rates where you know the exact hotel you are booking, express rates that offer a discount without telling you the hotel name, and name-your-own-price rates where you bid on a room for a particular night (or whatever your length of stay) and general location.

I have successfully used Priceline a number of times, but I am hesitant to use it when I need a location that is convenient to a particular place. And I have found that the best deals are usually available for the higher-quality hotels. That means you may be paying a greater amount than you ordinarily would pay, although you may end up at a five-star hotel. Going the other way, offering $25 for a one-star hotel is an invitation to spend the night in a place that is well below the quality you are willing to accept.

Try AirBnB

AirBnB (AirBnB.com) is a pioneer in online homesharing, which is—for some—an attractive alternative to a hotel. Homeowners (and sometimes renters) register on the site, pass a vetting procedure, and allow people to "borrow" their homes or even single rooms. Some of the places are very modest and modestly priced. And then there are some pretty fantastical homes offered as well. Check out Casa Caracol (the Seashell House), Underground Hygge, or any number of tree houses.

You visit the website, enter where you want to stay (including international sites), and indicate how long you'd like to stay and how many people are joining you. It's pretty much like booking a hotel reservation so far. You can search by place or even excursion type, which allows you to enjoy events while you stay at the house you wind up choosing. You can choose an excursion centered around any number of events or themes, including nature, nightlife, and food. You can see the inside of the house, accommodation details, and the per-night price.

Most locations require a minimum number of nights for a reservation. Prices vary greatly according to location and type of accommodation. You pay through AirBnB, not directly to the proprietor, so there is a level of protection provided. Be sure you understand the cancellation and refund policies listed there as well. If you show up and the place is not as advertised, you have to file a complaint—complete with photographic evidence—within 24 hours.

You can read customer reviews, which sometimes provide feedback about the person whose place they used (the *host*). Good communication skills from your host are important. However, as I note throughout this book, take amateur ratings with many grains of salt. Some positive comments may have been planted, and some complaints are pretty unreasonable.

Finally, you have to be willing to put your trust in individuals you almost certainly do not know. Most reports about AirBnB reveal positive experiences, but consider the fact you are entering into a private home, apartment, or condo—not a hotel that (in theory) has to stand up to government and corporate scrutiny.

Safeguard Your Possessions When You Travel

How can you guard against theft of your property from a hotel room? And how do you guard against pickpockets and robbers when you are a stranger in a strange land?

The best advice: Don't bring with you anything of great value. *If you have no choice, follow this advice...*

• **Before your trip, buy a sturdy travel wallet.** I use a zipper pouch that attaches to my belt and sits inside my pants. I can't imagine a situation where a pickpocket could get at it unnoticed. I keep a small amount of cash and one credit card in a small folder in my front pants pocket for small purchases and only go into my hidden travel wallet in the security of a store or hotel. And—this is important—if I were approached by a robber who poses a real threat to me or my family, I would quickly hand over anything I have with me. No amount of cash or other personal possession is worth more than our health and welfare.

• **Use the hotel's in-room safe or vault in the front office.** Many hotels offer a small safe in room closets, which provides a basic level of security against some levels of crime. In it, put items such as essential paperwork, extra credit cards, small amounts of cash, and other small items. (Make sure you have copies of the papers and the numbers of your credit card stored elsewhere, such as photos on your smartphone. And make sure your smartphone is protected by a complex password or swipe code.)

For more valuable items, including passwords, laptop computers, and professional-grade cameras, ask to use the safe deposit boxes that are in the office of most hotels. Be aware, though: in most instances, the hotel's liability for theft from its safe is limited by state laws or company policies. Some hotels may voluntarily accept more liability, perhaps for a charge. Ask for a written copy of the hotel's policies and get a signed receipt for any deposits you make.

• **Know the hotel's liability.** You want to know their liability for any bags you leave with the bellhop, as well as any property you leave in a car that is parked by a valet or left in the parking garage or lot. The hotel may accept no liability at all for your property. If you are given any assurances about the security of your property or liability, be sure you have it in writing. Check claim checks and receipts to make sure they accurately reflect the number of bags and a description of each, for example.

• **Call your agent.** Consult your insurance agent to find out how well covered you are under your homeowner's or renter's policies. If you do a lot of traveling and regularly bring expensive cameras, computers, or jewelry, inquire about a special rider for your policy to increase your coverage on the road. A rider is a policy add-on that comes at additional cost.

In the event of apparent theft, most insurance companies insist you file a police report at the location. You should do so as soon you realize these types of items are missing. As with suitcase contents that you check with an airline, spend a few minutes taking photos of your most valuable items with the camera of your smartphone before you let them out of your sight.

PART VII

Insurance Essentials

CHAPTER 32

Shopping for Vehicle Insurance

We may not be happy about paying the bill, but we all understand the need for automobile insurance. We merely have to look around and notice bad drivers, bad roads, and scary situations we face on a daily basis. There's also the pretty bad job most insurance companies do when it comes to explaining their coverage. Many companies don't really mind if you pay too much and receive too little for your money.

The good news is this: the auto insurance market is extremely competitive, and it is easy to do your research, compare prices, and purchase insurance online. For most of us, the only reason to use an insurance agent is if he or she can offer competitive prices and superior service over internet sources.

Here are some tips on getting the most for your auto insurance dollar…

- **Take a crash course in auto insurance.**
- **Cruise the web to buy auto insurance.**
- **Research insurance companies.**
- **Reduce your auto insurance bills.**
- **Steer your driving child.**
- **Save on auto insurance before you buy a car.**
- **Don't pay twice for coverage.**
- **Know what to say at the auto-rental counter.**
- **Get under your umbrella.**
- **Kickstart your motorcycle coverage.**

Take a Crash Course in Auto Insurance

Understanding all the parts of an auto insurance policy puts you at an advantage. *Here are some of the common essential elements…*

- **Bodily injury liability.** This element pays legal defense costs and claims against you if your car injures or kills someone, up to the amount of coverage you purchase from the insurance company. Most policies also cover family members living with you and others driving your car with

> **TIP**
>
> **A Non-Owner's Policy**
>
> What if you do not own a car but rent regularly? Call your insurance agent or insurance company and find out the rates for a "non-owner's policy." It may be a wise investment both in terms of protecting against loss to a rented (or borrowed) vehicle and shielding you from liability for damages or injuries to others.

your permission—whether or not you are with them at the time of an accident.

• **Property damage liability.** This component pays legal defense costs and claims against you if your car damages someone else's property.

• **Collision.** This part is the insurance company's promise to pay for repairs or replacement of the vehicle because of damage caused by a collision with another vehicle or any other object, regardless of who was responsible.

Many experts advise you to cancel collision coverage on an old car if the premium amounts to 10% or more of the car's value. Collision covers repairs, but your insurance company is not likely to pay to rebuild an old hulk, no matter how well it used to run or how attached you were to it. That's one of the problems with owning a well-maintained older car.

But before you cancel collision coverage, consider this: If you do not have collision coverage, you are putting your finances at risk when next you rent a car. The fine print on most rental car agreements requires drivers to have that coverage or to buy the overpriced daily insurance they offer. If you don't have the coverage or don't buy the insurance company's daily cover, damage to the car is your responsibility. Find out how much it costs to have collision coverage for your own car and then figure out how many days per year you expect to rent a car. Daily rental car insurance can cost about $25.

Call your insurance agent or insurance company and discuss the ins and outs of collision coverage. Chapter 28 talks in depth about car rental.

• **Comprehensive physical damage.** The comprehensive policy pays for damages to your car resulting from theft, fire, hail, vandalism, and a number of other causes other than by collision.

• **Medical payments and/or personal injury protection.** Medical expenses for you and others riding in your vehicle injured as the result of an accident are paid by this coverage. Most policies also pay for injuries to you or family members while riding in another car, and some also cover you for injuries received if you are a pedestrian hit by a car.

• **Uninsured or underinsured motorist.** This coverage pays expenses related to injuries or property damage to you, your family members, and guests in your car with losses caused by an uninsured or underinsured driver, or as the result of a hit-and-run accident.

Before you dismiss your need for coverage in the instance of an uninsured or underinsured motorist, consider the fact that not all states require drivers to purchase automobile insurance. Instead of a policy, drivers may declare to the state that they have cash or property that could be used to pay expenses. However, rarely would an uninsured or underinsured motorist have enough resources to pay medical costs in the event of a serious injury.

Cruise the Web to Buy Auto Insurance

You can easily shop for auto insurance at multiple websites. You'll need your driver's license number and your car's VIN. (In some states, the insurance company can obtain that from your driver's license.) It might help to have your current policy in front of you. You'll be offered different levels of coverage. Once you make selections and obtain a price, save that quote for later reference. Some sites allow you to save your quote (after you register a username and password) or send the information to you by email. Or you could also print out a quote or go really old school and take notes about what you see on the screen. Move on to another company for a comparison, being sure to answer questions in the same way and make the same coverage choices.

Many websites claim to offer side-by-side comparisons and at least one insurance company (Progressive) says it will do that as part of its own quote to you. Aside from Progressive's comparison tool not being available in all states, in my experience you are better off doing your own company-by-company shopping to make certain you are doing an exact comparison.

Depending on your state, the insurance company can complete the entire transaction online, including payment by bank transfer from your checking account or payment by credit card. In some situations, you may be told to contact an agent to complete the purchase. Also, most insurance companies will offer a small discount if you pay in full rather than

Keep on Trucking

Insuring a truck (or an SUV) is usually a lot more expensive than insuring a car. Some reasons that insurance companies point to for this increased rate is a car's smaller size (which causes less damage and is less expensive to repair, all things being equal), a truck's higher horsepower, and how much thieves tend to steal these kinds of vehicles.

Like other vehicular insurance, however, your age and location (among other criteria) also determine your rates. Something companies take into account that you can control? Your driving record.

pay by month or quarterly, or alternately, they may charge if you spread out payments instead of paying in full.

In some states, you may be offered a six-month policy rather than a 12-month policy. Ask for a full year. That will guard against a rate hike during the policy's term. If they offer only six-month policies, and another company quotes a 12-month policy, unless the price differential is substantial (divide the 12-month quote in half to compare), choose the 12-month policy. Think of any extra cost as insurance against a jarring increase in costs halfway through the year.

Your insurance policy is a contract. Unless you have violated it by not fully disclosing your driving and personal history, or you have committed fraud or other crimes, the company is not ordinarily allowed to raise your rate or cancel the policy during the term of the agreement.

Research Insurance Companies

Auto insurance rates are bad enough—why pay more than you have to? Even in states that tightly regulate insurance companies to ensure equal rates for identical coverage, the savvy consumer can save money. You do so by carefully choosing particular types of coverage.

It is not improper to ask an agent at an office or online for the company's A.M. Best or other financial rating. (A.M. Best offers insurance credit ratings and other information. You can find it at AMBest.com.) You want to hear a rating in the A range: AAA, AA, A+, or A. And don't forget to consult the trusted *Consumer Reports*. You may also find comments by current and past customers online by searching for reviews of the insurance company but again, take those with a grain of salt.

Reduce Your Auto Insurance Bills

Here are some ways you can lower your auto insurance bill.

- **Choose the right car.** An expensive luxury car with a high value, expensive repairs, and a high rate of theft is going to cost a whole lot more to insure than a more modest vehicle that will get you to the shopping mall just as efficiently. Your insurance agent should be willing to offer advice when it comes to choosing between various cars. The latest model cars come with some advanced safety features (some standard, some are optional) like rearview cameras, lane change warnings, and automatic collision avoidance. Having such features may lower your insurance cost. Insurance companies should be able to figure out the features of your vehicle based on its VIN, but don't hesitate to discuss safety features with the agent.

- **Live in the right place.** Rates tend to be lower in rural areas than in big cities. The difference is probably not enough to influence a decision about where you choose to live.

- **Drive less.** If you expect to drive less than the typical 10,000 to 15,000 miles per year, ask for a low-mileage discount. You may be asked to sign an affidavit, provide information from auto inspections, or otherwise prove your statement.

- **Allow the insurance company to monitor your driving.** Several companies are experimenting with monitors that record the speed you drive, how hard you apply the brake, and other factors that may indicate the type of driver you are. The monitors plug into a socket available on recent model cars and either transmit the information or require you to send back the device to the company for analysis. It might be worth trying—if you are a careful driver.

- **Consider higher deductibles.** Deductibles are the amount of money you'll have to pay out of your pocket for an accident or loss before the insurance company must write a check. Put another way, deductibles reduce the insurance company's exposure. Increasing the deductible on collision and comprehensive coverage can sharply reduce your bills; an increase in deductible from $200 to $500 could lower that portion of your bill by 15% to 30%. Everyone has his or her own level of pain. Compare your savings to your own exposure, and factor in your driving history. As always, in many instances there's a Catch-22 that benefits the insurance company: if you've been unlucky enough to have had a number of claims in recent years, your insurance rates are probably sky-high and the insurance company may have insisted on a high deductible level to protect against repeated losses.

- **Consider dropping Collision and Comprehensive coverage on older, low-value cars.** If you have a $1,000 deductible on a car that is worth $1,000, you are paying money for nothing. Your insurance agent, a loan officer at your bank, or a car dealer can give you an idea of the value of your vehicle. I warned against this earlier in this chapter, with the additional warning about not having proper coverage for rental cars. No matter how old your car, though, you do want to maintain a high level of liability coverage to protect yourself against damage you might do to others.

- **Don't pay twice for medical coverage.** If you have health insurance, you are probably already covered for any injuries you might receive in an auto accident. Two policies do not mean you will collect twice for the same accident—your medical policy will most likely take precedence over any coverage on your auto policy. Rules vary from state to state, but in some places the driver who is determined to be at fault is responsible for medical payments. Consult with your insurance agent about both policies, and if you do have duplicate coverage, cancel the medical coverage on the automobile policy. Doing so may lower personal injury protection (PIP) costs by as much as 40%.

- **Look for special discounts.** Ask about discounts offered to alumni of certain colleges and universities, members of clubs, current or former military, and other offers. Also ask how much you can save by insuring multiple cars with the same company.

- **List the least-expensive primary driver.** If the car will be driven regularly by more than one person, the insurance rate will be based on the primary driver. Young drivers and elderly drivers may be charged more in some states, but a middle-aged driver with a good driving record may be offered a lower rate. You can consult your agent or insurance company about specifying the primary driver to your advantage, but I am in no way suggesting you commit fraud or make a misleading statement to save a few bucks.

- **Be defensive.** In some states, drivers can reduce their rates by taking a defensive driving course. You can take some courses online, while others require you to show up at a few sessions of driver education school. The National Safety Council offers an online defensive driving course (NSC.org/learn/Safety-Training/Pages/defensive-driving-course-online.aspx), but again, make sure any course is in compliance with state laws and your insurance company's requirements.

Insurance Agents

If you choose to deal with an insurance agency, choose one who is willing to compare several insurance companies and policies and will work with you to get the most for your insurance dollar. In some states, insurance rates are set by a government agency, but that does not mean you should not search for a company that offers better service or has a better reputation for paying claims fairly and promptly. Your agent should also be able to provide information on companies' financial ratings. You want a company that is able to stand behind its promises. To do some legwork yourself, check out insurance company ratings at Ambest.com.

Having a good insurance agent who you can call or visit is a fine thing, especially if you ever have to put in a claim. But there shouldn't be a huge price differential between an insurance agency and an online insurance seller.

Don't overlook the fact that agents have a built-in conflict of interest. You may be the client, but the insurance company is the one who pays them their commissions or salary, unless the agent is independent (in which case the agent's employer pays his or her salary). Check with friends and coworkers to find an agent who has performed well in the past.

- **Bundle your insurance.** Many companies offer discounts to customers who also insure their home or apartment with them. They may also offer better prices if you have other types of insurance such as an umbrella policy.

- **Comparison shop among insurance companies and insurance agents.** If you buy coverage from an insurance agency, ask for the best rate from the various companies he or she represents. Compare the best price from the agency to the best price you find from an online company.

Be sure you are checking prices for identical coverage, with the same optional elements, the same deductible levels, and the same payment terms.

Steer Your Driving Child

One of the lesser joys of being a parent is the day when your youngster announces that he or she wants to start driving. Oh, the pain. Of course you love your children and worry about them being safe on the road. And then there is the hurt that you will feel when your policy reflects the fact that a young driver will be driving. In some instances, rates can more than double. And your youngster's driving record can impact the family's policy for years to come.

You can lessen the pain.

- **Find a family-friendly policy.** Research online or at an insurance agency for companies that have the best policies for families that include younger drivers. Some companies will forgive one or two minor infractions, while others may boost rates or cancel policies.

- **Monitor closely your child's use of the car.** Do you see dangerous habits or improper behavior? As a parent, as a fellow driver, and as the one who pays the bills, you need to be involved.

- **Have them help.** Speaking of paying the bills, one way to get a youngster's attention is to get him or her involved in paying some or all of the insurance bill. Also make it clear that a ticket or accident will boost those costs even higher.

- **Register to an older person.** If you give a car to a youngster and it is registered under his or her name, you can expect the highest possible rates. In some cases, it is less expensive to register the car in the name of an older, more experienced driver. Seek the advice of an agent or online company in this case.

- **Enroll kids in class.** If your children take a comprehensive driver education and training class, not only are they likely to become better drivers, but most insurance companies will apply a discount to graduates.
- **Check into discounts for good grades.** Many insurance agencies offer this benefit to youngsters. The discount is usually available to students maintaining an average of B or better.
- **Apply with care.** If you have more than one car in the family, make sure your insurance company applies the increased premium to the car the young driver will actually use. If you drive an expensive car to work and the family car is more modest, you're probably going to assign the lesser car to your child. Be sure the insurance company knows this.
- **Have Junior ride the bus.** Does your child drive the car to school? Some policies apply a higher premium for such use, or may offer a discount if Junior uses public transportation to get to school or work.
- **Choose the right policy.** Make sure you have appropriate coverage, especially in collision or comprehensive deductibles on an older car with a low value.
- **Model safe driving.** Be a good model for your child by driving responsibly, always using seat belts, and never driving under the influence of alcohol or drugs.

Save on Auto Insurance Before You Buy a Car

If you're not already in love with a particular model of car, consider calling your insurance agent or insurance company with your list of finalists and ask for the cost of a policy for each. You may be surprised to find wide differences in rates between different models. Sometimes a more expensive vehicle warrants a lower premium than a less expensive car. This is because insurance companies base their charges on information including the expense of repairing particular cars and the rate of theft for that model.

Cars with higher crash safety ratings and advanced features are also rewarded with lower liability and medical coverage prices. Rates vary based on the car's value, its history of theft, safety in an accident, and the cost of repairs. Some options, like a fancy stereo system or chrome wheels, may end up costing you extra money on your auto insurance bill each year. Others, like car alarms, forward collision warning, and other safety and security options, may reduce your bill a few percent per year.

Don't Pay Twice for Coverage

Eliminate duplicate coverage. Don't pay for an auto insurer's towing coverage if you are also a member of AAA. Or drop AAA and include towing in your auto coverage. Do the math and see which is of most benefit to you. Remember that services like those of AAA follow the driver wherever he or she is in the US, while most auto insurance towing plans are attached to a particular car.

What does that mean for you? If you rent cars often, the AAA coverage may be of some benefit. Similarly, if you are a passenger in someone else's vehicle (a carpool, for example), your AAA card could help summon services even if you are not driving. (Be sure to confirm your coverage with your local auto club.)

Don't buy a small life-insurance policy as part of auto coverage if you have a larger life-insurance policy through another insurer. Similarly, ask your insurance agent to see if your health insurance coverage is comprehensive enough to remove the need for medical insurance as part of an auto policy.

Know What to Say at the Auto-Rental Counter

You've been driving for years without an accident. You're very careful. And you made it to the airport this morning completely without mishap. So why not take a chance and skip the extra insurance coverage on your rental car when you arrive at your destination? After all, you'll only be using it for a short time.

It's a bad idea to go completely without insurance on a rental car. To begin with, the average cost of a new car is moving past $30,000. Besides, your rental is likely to be a different car from the one you drive, with a different response to the brake, gas pedals, and steering wheel. And then there's the fact that you're an out-of-towner with unfamiliar places to go and pressing things on your mind. Finally, you're likely to be tired after a day of travel.

I do not recommend paying the generally outrageous daily rates for insurance that the rental car company will offer to tack on. Except in some unusual situations, you are better off making other arrangements for coverage. First, your personal auto policy coverage extends to a rental car. Check with your insurance company whether coverage is different between cars rented for pleasure trips or business.

If your employer provides you with a car, your business auto policy should cover its use on a business trip. Check with your insurance agent to find out about its applicability to personal trips. If you are traveling on company business, see if your employer has any special coverage for employees on the road or arrangements with auto rental companies.

If you don't own a car but rent frequently, look into buying a non-owner auto policy, which typically costs a few hundred dollars a year. Compare the cost of this specialized policy to the daily rate charged by rental companies.

One of the best added features of some credit cards is a specialized form of coverage for most auto rentals charged to the card. Be sure you understand the coverage type and pay attention to exclusions. Many of these policies do not cover exotic and luxury cars, and some do not extend coverage outside the US. Call your credit card company and discuss its auto rental insurance coverage. In most cases the policy is secondary, meaning that you are reimbursed for any expenses not covered by your personal auto insurance (if you have any). But some credit card companies allow you to purchase a higher level of primary coverage, almost always at a significantly lower cost than the coverage offered by rental agencies. That means your personal policy should not be affected by any claims.

If you do end up at the counter without a policy of your own, read carefully the rental agreement put in front of you to sign, paying special attention to the sections about extra-cost insurance options. *Here are a few pointers about the coverage offered by rental companies...*

- **Collision damage waiver (CDW).** This is actually not insurance. It is a promise by the rental company that it will not charge you for any damage sustained. It does not provide liability coverage or provide for medical expenses. The CDW may be voided if you are found to have caused an accident by reckless driving, speeding, driving while intoxicated, or other actions, including taking a car on unpaved roads. In some states, insurance for collision damage is already included in the rental price. CDW rates can range from about $10 to $20 per day, and sometimes more. Think of this charge as an annual rate and you'll get an idea of just how bad this coverage is: $10 per day is the equivalent of $3,650 per year and $20 is $7,300 per year, just for collision coverage.

- **Personal accident insurance.** You shouldn't need this coverage if you have a health insurance policy or an automobile policy with personal injury protection. Again, the daily rate works out to the equivalent of a very high annual rate.

- **Personal effects coverage.** This policy covers you if someone steals personal items from the car. Your homeowner's or renter's insurance should include coverage for off-premises theft. (You will have to pay any deductible in that policy, though.) The rental company's coverage might make sense if you are traveling with anything of very high value not otherwise covered by your own policy, especially if you will be leaving your vehicle unattended for a period of time. Read the coverage details to see if there is a deductible and determine if anything specific, such as cameras, computers, or jewelry, are excluded from coverage. Better yet, don't leave anything of value in your car. In any case, be sure you have copies of receipts and full descriptions of all possessions in your suitcases and other bags. You'll need that information for any claim.

- **Additional liability insurance.** This policy protects you from other drivers' claims. You would do a lot better carrying a personal umbrella policy (explained in the following section) that costs a few hundred dollars a year and extends your home, auto, and personal coverage.

Get Under Your Umbrella

If you own any property, drive a car, earn a decent income, or have any prospects of ever having a decent net worth, you should have a good umbrella. A *personal umbrella policy* is a way to protect you and your family from large liability claims that might result from an auto accident (and from many other types of claims). In a worst case, an umbrella policy may protect your home and other assets from seizure in a claim.

Personal umbrella policies are among the best buys in insurance and something most people should consider. Umbrellas provide extended coverage—typically $1 million or more—if you must pay damages from a lawsuit or if you incur costs to fight such a suit. They often include coverage for things that standard homeowners' policies don't cover, such as libel and slander suits and automobile liability coverage for international driving. Some policies, such as high-value homeowner's coverage, may require you to add an umbrella.

Insure Your Other Wheels

Bicycles have come a long way since the $25 Schwinn bikes many of us grew up with. Today, fancy racing bikes and off-road cycles cost several thousand dollars. Not surprisingly, they have become tempting targets for theft. Follow these tips in addition to the insurance coverage advice I offer here.

- **Properly apply a good lock.** Be sure the bicycle frame and at least one wheel are secured to a metal rack or post. Don't run the cable through the wheel alone—a thief with a wrench could leave the relatively inexpensive wheel behind and take the rest of the bicycle.
- **If your local police department has a bicycle registry,** report your new bike's serial number and description. This may help recover a stolen bike or help you file a claim with your insurance company.
- **Keep your receipts for purchase and keep a photograph of your bike.**
- **If your bicycle is stolen,** promptly file a detailed report with the appropriate local police department.
- **Wear a helmet.** Keeping your noggin away from the ER (or the ICU) is a huge money saver. A 2015 study in *The American Journal of Surgery* (Blinc.Media/2wX59AZ) reports that bicyclists who wear helmets are 51% less likely to suffer a traumatic brain injury.

Here are some two-wheeler insurance tips.

- **Bicycles are usually covered by your homeowner's or renter's insurance,** although you may have a deductible of several hundred dollars or more. If you own an expensive bike, tell your agent you are considering a rider to extend and improve on your coverage. (The rider is sometimes called a *floater* or *scheduled coverage*.) The rider may also include the cost of repairs in case of an accident.
- **Your homeowner's or renter's policy provides a specified amount of liability coverage in the event of a collision that results in injury to another party.**

As with any claim, insurance companies may have a way to deny coverage if they decide the bicycle was not properly protected or locked when it should have been, or if the rider was being deliberately unsafe.

With an umbrella policy, you are protecting yourself against most claims that could take away your assets and even your future earnings. Umbrella policies typically cost only about $150 to $300 for $1 million in coverage and are usually to extend your coverage in existing auto or home policies. The policy issuer may require you to maintain a particular level of liability coverage on those underlying policies. The cost of an umbrella policy may rise if you present particular risks, such as owning a boat or swimming pool, or owning property used for hunting.

The umbrella coverage is secondary, meaning that initial payment comes from other policies you may have, such as auto, home, or renter's insurance. This sort of insurance is a relative bargain. Consult your insurance company or agent for advice.

Kickstart Your Motorcycle Coverage

If you have a motorcycle, buying liability coverage is nonnegotiable (and some states require a motorcyclist to carry additional medical insurance coverage; you can ask an insurance agent what your state's law is). Beyond that, depending on how valuable your motorcycle is, you may want to boost your coverage with comprehensive or collision. So many variables factor into the cost (your age, driving record, and so on) that you should get at least three estimates from different companies before deciding on a company. Some companies offer a discount if you take a Motorcycle Safety Foundation (MSF-usa.org) driving course.

Ask for a motorcycle discount (though coverage usually costs less than car insurance), and mention a multivehicle discount of you have other transportation that needs insurance.

Finally, always, always wear a helmet. Head injuries are more common (and often more serious) in riders who don't wear them. Wearing a helmet actually decreases medical costs according to the National Highway Traffic Safety Administration (Blinc.Media/2wWP8v9). You know what they call a motorcyclist who doesn't wear a helmet, right? An organ donor.

CHAPTER 33

Shopping for Homeowner's and Renter's Insurance

As the great philosopher and comedian George Carlin observed, your home is the place you leave your stuff when you go out to buy more stuff. And when you leave your house, you have to worry that someone doesn't break in and take your stuff. That's one of the reasons homeowners and renters buy insurance. Another reason is to protect themselves against losses caused by catastrophes, from storm damage to theft. And renters, though they're not responsible for the house or apartment itself, may want to protect their stuff, too.

In this chapter, I show you how to assess the stuff you own and then find the proper insurance coverage for your home, apartment, or condo and all the stuff within.

- **Protect yourself against insurance insufficiencies.**
- **Schedule valuable possessions.**
- **Prepare for the flood.**
- **Understand renter's insurance.**
- **Lower homeowner's and renter's insurance costs.**
- **Alarm your home.**

Protect Yourself Against Insurance Insufficiencies

Before the fire, before the storm, before the burglary, before the electrical power surge, ask yourself these questions…

- **What do I own?**

- **How much are all my possessions worth put together?** What would it cost to replace them? (A camera you bought for $3,000 three years ago may have a *depreciated value* of $1,000, but it still might cost you $3,000 to buy a replacement.)

- **Can I prove to the insurance company that I own this stuff?** Do I have receipts, credit card statements, warranty registrations, or other evidence?

- **Do I have enough insurance coverage to pay for a loss of some or all of my possessions?** And does that coverage promise to pay for the replacement cost, or merely the *present value* or depreciated value?

Survey Your Home or Apartment

You can save yourself a tremendous amount of trouble and possibly many thousands of dollars by conducting a survey of your possessions. *Here are some suggestions…*

• **Do a detailed inventory of your possessions.** Make an itemized list of everything of value, including the price paid and purchase date, if possible. Hold on to any receipt to help substantiate claims. Better than a written inventory—and one that your insurance company may find irrefutable proof—is a video tour of your home. Use a video camera like the one in nearly every smartphone to make a running commentary on every room. Stop in front of a flat-screen television set, for example, and announce the manufacturer and model number plus its serial number. If you have a copy of the receipt at hand, read it to record the information, including the store name, date, price, and any identifying number on the receipt. You can also do the same thing with a still camera, taking pictures and making notes on a room-by-room tour.

Make a copy of the digital file from the video or camera, and create copies of any paperwork you produce. You can send copies of the file electronically to yourself or to someone in your family. Most smartphones also store files in the *cloud*, which means somewhere in a big computer far away. Store paper inventory records in a fireproof safe, a bank safe-deposit box, or somewhere away from your home or apartment.

• **If you don't have receipts and details of some possessions—furniture or clothing, for example—estimate their cost and get replacement values other ways.** You can search online for purchase prices. The more details you have, the stronger your case if you ever have to make a claim. It is difficult to put a value on every piece, including family heirlooms. Provide as much detail as you can in your description.

• **Have valuable items, including works of art and antiques, appraised by a reputable expert.** You'll probably want to purchase scheduled insurance for these sorts of items. I'll discuss that later in this chapter.

• **Consult with your insurance agent or insurance company.** Ask for any suggestions they have for this sort of accounting, and ask if they will accept your inventory and keep it on record. An insurance agent with whom you have a personal relationship should be happy to accept a written or electronic copy of your file, and in doing so you are putting your information on the record. And add a note on your calendar to update your list at least annually, and update it any time you add a new expensive item to your stuff.

Survey Your Insurance Coverage

Schedule a review of your insurance coverage at least once a year to assess the amount and type of coverage you have. If you purchase your policy over the internet, call the company and ask to speak with a licensed agent for the same purpose. Your goal should not be to increase your insurance bill. You want to know if you are adequately protected and understand your policy's exceptions and exclusions. Are you covered against flood damage? Does your policy include extra provisions for modern-day threats like identity theft? Is your coverage for possessions intended to pay you the depreciated value of items or their replacement cost? What about acts of God?

Insurance components sometimes change from year to year based on the economy and local conditions. Make sure your coverage accurately reflects the cost per square foot for construction where you live. If you live near the ocean, be sure you understand the amount of coverage you have for damage caused by wind or flood. Make sure the underwriter has the latest information on the proximity to fire stations and fire hydrants. If you have installed a burglar, smoke, fire, freeze, or water alarm, make sure you are receiving proper credit in your policy.

If you no longer own that expensive camera, or have sold off your coin collection, have your scheduled items list (and its associated cost to you) adjusted.

The purpose of homeowner's insurance is to protect from theft, fire, damage from certain events like burst pipes and other perils (not including flood, war, and a few other exclusions). The policy's value should reflect the replacement cost of the house and attached structures, and most policies apportion a percentage of coverage to landscaping as well. It does not ordinarily include the value of the land itself. That is projected to survive most covered catastrophes.

Your Dwelling

Your insurance agent or company should be able to give you an estimate of construction costs for a home like yours. There are also a number of real estate websites that display information about your property (whether you like it or not). Update your insurance agent on any improvements or additions you have made to your house since you last talked about your insurance policy. If your home is an unusual design or has historical significance, you may want to hire a professional appraiser. Keep a copy of the report you receive, and discuss it with your insurance agent or company as part of your annual review. Many insurance companies require your home to be reinspected by their own appraiser every few years.

For a rough estimate of rebuilding cost, figure the square footage of the house and multiply it by the average building costs in your area. In some parts of the country, home construction may cost $100 per square foot, while in other regions, the rates can cross $200 or $300 per square foot. (Search online for *construction cost surveys*.) My wife and I live on an island, in a tough climate, in a place where buyers demand top-quality construction: $350 per square foot is a starting place. Colder climates, for example, require sturdier construction, better insulation, and larger heating systems. Additional cost items include basements, fireplaces, decks, and custom design features. Builders talk about things like a *contractor's kitchen* or *contractor's bathroom* versus a *custom luxury* version (which is much more expensive).

Make certain that your insurance policy keeps up with increases in local building costs. Ask your insurance agent or company representative whether your policy includes an *inflation-guard clause* to automatically adjust the dwelling limit. That clause should reflect current construction costs in your area. Most insurance companies recommend insuring your home for 100% of the cost of rebuilding it, in which case inflation guard is usually built in to the quote. Inflation guard coverage cost is related to the expected rate of inflation in construction. If the coverage is not included in your policy, you will need to boost your home's replacement value. How much will it cost? It depends on how undercovered you are and the estimated cost of replacement for your home.

If you accept a policy that puts a specific value on your home, you may find it insufficient in the event of a total loss. Few homes are totally destroyed, but why take that chance? If you have a mortgage on your home, the lender will have something to say about the amount of coverage you purchase. They want you to have at least enough coverage to pay off your loan if the house is destroyed.

Most insurance policies offer replacement-cost coverage for structural damage, and you should seek nothing else. However, some companies will not offer that sort of coverage for very old houses because of outdated construction techniques and because of the great expense of recreating old wood and plaster elements. They may instead offer a modified replacement-cost policy that reconstructs a similar house using contemporary techniques. It is also possible that building codes will not permit reconstruction of a noncomplying structure.

The standard policy (called an HO1 policy in most locales) provides the structure's replacement cost. An HOA policy is an actual cash value policy, which may (or may not) be enough to rebuild a ruined house. An HO8 policy insures a home for market value—the amount of money it could have been expected to receive if sold. This sort of policy might be appropriate for historic homes or those with unusual design features. This is where a good insurance agent is essential. Most homeowners are properly covered with HO1, but ask if that's the case when you apply for or renew your policy.

In some places, building codes may have the effect of raising or lowering average construction prices. If your home is in a historical district or an area with other forms of restricted zoning, local requirements have to be followed in construction or reconstruction.

Stuff Inside Your Dwelling

After figuring out your home replacement costs, consider the coverage you have for personal possessions including furniture, clothing, and appliances. The limit of the policy is usually shown on the Declarations Page under Section I, Coverages, Personal Property.

A standard HO1 policy sets coverage for possessions at 40% to 60% of the amount of insurance on the structure. Some states may set different minimums or maximums for basic coverage. If your house would cost $500,000 to rebuild and possessions are covered up to 50% of that amount, the maximum you could collect for your possessions is $250,000. Compare the amount of coverage to your own estimate of replacement costs.

Most policies include named perils that are covered partially or in full. Standard policies protect from theft, fire, lightning strikes, explosions, volcanic eruptions, water damage from pipes, and the like. It is also common to protect against riot or civil disturbance, but not zombie invasions. Although standard policies do cover damage caused by wind, in some areas companies apply a very high deductible because of the risk of hurricanes and other weather perils. See this chapter's "Prepare for the Flood" section for details about flood insurance.

Like with the insurance for the structure itself, a replacement-cost policy pays the dollar amount needed to replace a damaged item with one of similar kind and quality without deductions for depreciation. An actual cash value policy pays the amount needed to replace the item, minus depreciation.

TIP

How solid is the insurance company itself? A policy from a company that cannot pay claims is useless. Simply ask an agent or check online for a company's A.M. Best or other financial rating. (A.M. Best offers insurance credit ratings and other information; check AMBest.com.) Don't buy coverage from any company that has a rating less than in the A range (including AAA, AA, A+, or A).

Schedule Valuable Possessions

To *schedule* personal property means listing specific items on a policy to ensure coverage. A scheduled item, or one listed in a floater, is one that is specifically named and assigned a value. Most policies offer only limited coverage for expensive items such as jewelry, fur, artwork, and specialized equipment. Those policies also are unlikely to cover your personal collection of stamps, Beanie Babies, or baseball cards beyond a certain level. If you have items like that, consult your insurance agent about scheduling specific items within your homeowner's or renter's policy, or about purchasing what insurance companies call a special endorsement or floater to add coverage for those items.

Make sure to provide full information about scheduled items: Manufacturer, model number, serial number, purchase date, and the price you paid. Most insurance companies will require a receipt or a professional appraisal value before adding it to a policy. And once again, make sure you understand whether the coverage is for actual *cash value* (the depreciated value of the item at the time of loss) or *replacement value* (the price to obtain a substitute).

Some items, such as paintings and jewelry, may go up in value over time. Other valuables, such as expensive cameras or electronics, may go down. Check your scheduled items each time you renew your policy to make sure the values are accurate, and don't pay for coverage you don't need.

Prepare for the Flood

Homes that are in a flood zone or near bodies of water usually cost considerably more to insure (or require separate flood insurance), or you may find that some companies simply won't write a policy for that situation. If your home is in a designated flood zone, the insurance company or your local government should point you in the direction of a federally backed flood insurance policy that provides specific coverage for that named peril.

If your home is in an area designated as a flood zone, you can—and should—purchase federally backed flood insurance through the National Flood Insurance Plan. You can find out more about this through your local government, or by consulting FEMA.gov/national-flood-insurance-program or Floodsmart.gov.

If you have a loan from a federally regulated or insured lender, you may be legally required to purchase this insurance if you live in a designated flood area.

Note that the flood insurance is a supplement to your standard homeowner's policy, which covers the other perils your home, apartment, or condo may face.

Homes that are near the ocean (or even a few miles away) may have higher rates because of the possibility of hurricane damage. In my part of the country, many insurance companies have simply dropped out of the market, forcing homeowners to either pay exorbitant premiums to remaining companies or seek special policies from out-of-state or foreign insurers.

Understand Renter's Insurance

A renter's policy is similar to that of a homeowner's policy, except that in most cases you are not buying protection for the structure itself. If an apartment building or rented house burns down, the building owner, not the tenant, loses. But the contents of each housing unit are your possessions. One exception is for policies that cover condominiums, co-ops, timeshares, and other such specialized housing arrangements. In those cases, there may be a shared liability for the structure itself and the grounds, as well as liability for accidents or claims that might occur in shared spaces or property.

A typical policy protects you against losses due to fire, smoke, lightning, vandalism, theft, explosion, windstorm, and water damage from plumbing. The liability portion of the policy offers protection if someone slips and falls in your home or is injured by any of your possessions and then sues.

If you have any particularly valuable possessions, from artwork to jewelry to electronics, consult your insurance agent or company to make sure you have enough coverage. You may need to add a floater that *schedules*, or expands coverage limits, on specific possessions. Hold onto receipts and other documentation for pricey possessions (or, if it's worth that much and you have no receipt, seek an appraisal if the insurance company requires one). A photographic or video inventory like that described earlier in this chapter can also be valuable.

Backups of Your Backups

When personal computers were fairly expensive, I scheduled coverage on mine. Today, PCs and tablets are much less costly, and may be fully covered by your basic policy. But what is the value of the data on your machine? If you run a business from your home (something you should disclose to your insurance company), it might be valuable to purchase coverage for the potential loss of that data by theft or as a result of a named peril. Your other option—and a generally good suggestion—is to make several copies of your data and store them in different places. Having multiple backups in different locations will save you the cost of buying a rider that deals with data recovery.

I have data backups on external hard drives that I store in a fire-resistant safe and I also regularly upload much of my data to cloud-based storage systems. Because I travel often, I have a scheduled item section for our homeowner policy to provide replacement-cost coverage for cameras, lenses, and a laptop that goes with me. (I'm using the laptop right now, writing this chapter on the island of Santorini in Greece.)

Most homeowner's and renter's insurance policies do not cover data loss (if you have to recover data from a dead computer, for instance). Again, your insurer may offer riders for this type of coverage if you think you need it. Some high-tech companies offer data-loss insurance, but they're loaded with conflicts of interest—data recovery companies and hard-drive manufacturers, for example. They obviously benefit from such events.

Lower Homeowner's and Renter's Insurance Costs

Homeowner's insurance is an essential coverage. It is required by mortgage lenders to protect their interests. Make certain your own assets are covered properly, as well. The insurance industry has generally standardized its coverage types, and in many states, policy types are stipulated by government agencies. But prices vary. One company may put a different value on your home. Another may offer different discounts or price increases for certain situations.

Insurance companies should automatically take into account the type of home construction in use. Brick homes are considered less likely to be destroyed in a fire than wood, for example. Companies also look at the distance to the nearest fire station and fire hydrant, and in some locales also rate the quality of fire protection service.

Newer homes, with modern electrical, heating, and plumbing systems and other improved structural features, can typically command discounts of 8% to 15%. Insurance companies also look at the age of the roof and major systems like furnaces and boilers.

Make certain you are comparing the same coverage and features when you look at various prices. *Here are some ways to get the most coverage for the least cost...*

- **Shop around.** Call more than one insurance company. If you are dealing with an agent who represents multiple companies, insist on getting quotes from several companies. Ask friends and neighbors about their experience with insurance companies. The most valuable experience is from someone who has filed a claim in recent years.

Lots of websites offer to compare rates across multiple companies, or to shop your policy for the best rate. Although these *might* save a bit of time, I am not a big fan of them because they almost always result in a heavy level of telephone and email sales contacts. I prefer to seek quotes from a local agent who will shop on my behalf, or to visit websites for individual companies that offer policies in my area.

If you do want to try an insurance comparison site, you might start with these.

- Everquote at Home.everquote.com
- Universal Direct at UniversalDirect.com

- **Look into special discount programs.** Some companies give discounts as high as 15% if you buy your home and auto policies from the same insurer. Some insurers grant discounts to longtime customers. Underwriters will also base their quote on your history of filing claims over the past three to five years (or more, if they choose); they are looking for potential clients who represent the least risk to *them*. Ask if the company gives a discount if none of the residents in the home are smokers (on the assumption that this reduces fire risk). Some insurers offer 10% discounts to retired seniors (on the assumption that they are at home more and can guard against fire and other loss). Look into discounts offered by insurance companies to members of certain associations or groups, such as alumni of certain colleges and sometimes to employees of major corporations.

- **Consider removing extra risks.** If your home has a swimming pool or a trampoline, many insurance companies will assess higher liability premiums. That is because of the possibility of claims by family members, visitors, and uninvited guests. Having certain types of dogs or other animals on your property may also raise your rate.

• **Check the effect of increasing the deductible.** Deductibles on homeowner policies generally start at $250. By increasing that deductible to $500, an insurance industry group estimates you could save up to 12% on damage coverage, which represents just a part of the total bill. Going to $1,000 could save you as much as 24%. A deductible of $5,000 could reduce insurance rates up to 37%. Ask your agent or insurance company to do the math and show you the numbers.

There is no hard-and-fast rule to calculate the relative value of a reduced premium versus a larger deductible. You have to decide whether saving about $100 by changing from a $500 to a $1,000 deductible is worth an extra $500 of exposure. And then there is this: if you have a $500 deductible and suffer a $1,000 loss because a tree shattered a patio door, would you be better off just paying the expense yourself and not risk having your insurance premium rise in the following year? Ask your insurance agent to go over all the deductible ins and outs, and determine your personal threshold of pain. In my experience, it is generally better to avoid making small claims against an insurance policy and paying lower premiums, while maintaining a high level of coverage against a major disaster.

Alarm Your Home

Most insurance companies will give you credit for smoke detectors, carbon monoxide detectors, and other alarm systems, including low-temperature monitors and burglar alarms. In general, you get a higher discount if the alarm is connected to a central station or to the police department.

If you have a burglar alarm, be sure to use it and maintain it. Don't give an insurance adjustor any excuse to reduce the company's payback to you in the event of a theft.

If you do not already have a qualified burglar alarm system in your home, ask the insurance company or your agent how much you would save if you installed one. Compare the cost of the alarm (and any monthly or annual monitoring and maintenance fees) to the amount you might save and choose accordingly. A large discount may be offered for a fire-sprinkler system, although the cost of such a system may outweigh its value in terms of insurance savings.

Chapter 15 discusses home security systems, as well as smoke and other kinds of detectors.

CHAPTER 34

Shopping for Life Insurance

A life insurance policy doesn't protect anyone from dying. Why should you buy life insurance, then? To provide for your family while you have young children or to provide an estate for your significant other. You can run the numbers many ways, but most financial experts agree that the best use of a life insurance policy is to safeguard your family's lifestyle while you (or you and your partner) are in your prime earning years.

In this chapter, I'll give you a tour of the basics of life insurance, and offer some tips on saving money and getting the most out of your policy, including a way to enjoy some of the fruits of a policy while you are still above ground.

- **Understand common life insurance policies.**
- **Determine how much life insurance to buy.**
- **Decide whether to sell your life insurance while you're alive.**
- **Know what life insurance to avoid.**

Understand Common Life Insurance Policies

Here are some reasons to buy life insurance…

- **To protect a family in case one or both breadwinners dies before dependents can provide for themselves**
- **To pay off the rest of a home mortgage for the surviving spouse or co-owner**
- **To cover funeral expenses and other end-of-life costs**
- **To pay off estate taxes and funeral expenses.**

Here are some things you should not expect from life insurance.

- **It is not an investment.** The best of whole-life policies rarely perform better than the worst of money-market mutual funds. The rate of return on a life insurance policy is generally well below that of other investments.
- **The old financial planner's mantra is still correct:** Buy term insurance and invest the rest.

- **It does not guarantee insurability at a later age.** You either need life insurance now or you don't.

Life insurance comes as two basic types, and the following sections explain each.

- ***Term* provides coverage for a stated number of years.** If you buy a 10-year term policy and die on the first day of the eleventh year, your heirs get nothing.
- ***Whole life* is coverage for your whole life, provided that you keep making payments for as long as the contract demands.**

Term Life

A term policy is the simplest way to buy. It covers a specific period. The coverage expires at the end of the specified period, and if you haven't cashed in your chips (in a metaphorical sense), the insurance company keeps the change. Rates for term policies start out low for younger clients and go up as you get older. (It's all based on the actuarial tables that lay out the statistical chances of a person of any particular age surviving to the end of the term.)

Term insurance makes it easy to compare one company's policy to that of another. (The key difference between offerings may be the financial health of the insurance company itself. I explain that later in the "Odds on Insurance Companies" sidebar.) You can easily get quotes online for term insurance, either directly from a company or through a website that compares multiple companies. Examples of those include IntelliQuote (IntelliQuote.com) and SelectQuote (SelectQuote.com).

You may have to provide medical records from your personal physician or submit to a simple examination by a nurse who represents the insurance company before the policy is issued. This is called *evidence of insurability* (or *EOI*). You can be declined coverage if the company thinks the risk of providing insurance to you is too high. (But not all companies deny coverage for the same reasons, so shop around. An independent life insurance broker isn't bound to any one company.)

Depending on the state in which you reside, you may be able to purchase low-cost term insurance through a savings bank or through various websites of Savings Bank Life Insurance (SBLI—search online for *SBLI Your State* and check online at the sites recommended in this chapter's "Odds on Insurance Companies" to make sure the bank you're contacting has an A rating or better).

Term rates are based on your age, sex, and health. Younger people are presumed to have a longer life ahead of them, women generally live longer than men. Smokers and those with certain other health conditions will be charged much higher premiums. There are also certain hobbies (skydiving, anyone?) and certain professions (miners, pilots, steeplejacks, offshore drilling technicians among them) that are considered high risk and charged much higher rates.

Term life insurance premiums are set for the agreed-upon term, and may include your right to renew the policy without reapplying (although the premium will likely increase for the new term because you are older).

Something called *level-premium insurance* is very similar. It is term life insurance written for a longer period of time—perhaps 10 or 20 years. Once again, the premium will not increase over the policy's term, but the annual cost will be higher at the start than it would be for a shorter-term policy. However, by the end of the contract, the fixed annual premium would be lower than it would be for a short-term policy. Ask your insurance agent or company for a cost comparison of each policy for various scenarios, including keeping the level-premium policy for its full period and renewing a shorter-term policy. Sometimes a longer-term level-premium policy is less expensive, and sometimes there is little or no difference.

Once a policy has been issued, the rate will not increase (or decrease) because of changes to your health or life circumstances. If you purchase term insurance, the premium will remain level for the number of years you agreed to in the contract. When you come to the end of the term, chances are very high you will have to re-apply and answer medical and risk questions again, and your new rate will be based on those updated answers.

On the other hand, if you no longer have a risky occupation or hobby, consult with your insurance agent about the possibility of canceling an existing policy and reapplying. It may or may not make economic sense. Regardless, do not cancel a policy you need until you have a replacement contract.

The only exception here is if an applicant commits fraud or otherwise gives a life insurance company an excuse to cancel a policy for cause.

Whole Life

Agents are anxious to sell life insurance because these policies are good moneymakers for them and their companies. Whole-life policies are the most profitable—profitable for those who sell them, that is.

Whole-life policies—in versions that include universal and variable plans—are based on a permanent concept rather than on term. In other words, if you have a whole-life policy and you keep it current by paying all of your premiums, you own something of value. It will pay off the stated amount when you die, and it also builds a cash value while you live. An important gotcha about it, though: the cash value exists only for as long as the policy is in force. If you die, the policy's face value goes to your beneficiary—the cash value goes back into the insurance company's paperwork. As with term insurance, rates will vary based on age, health, and occupational risks.

Whole-life coverage is more expensive than term for two reasons.

- **Almost all policyholders (rather, their survivors) end up collecting benefits.** By contrast, most term-insurance policies never pay off benefits because holders either move from company to company or stop buying coverage as they reach an advanced age.
- **Whole-life policies build up a value, which you can borrow against or cash in.**

However, you may be in a situation where whole-life insurance makes sense. For example, if your child has special needs, you may want to provide for your child longer after you are gone. Some tax advisors who recommend whole-life insurance as part of estate planning for wealthy clients.

Here's an example of whole life at work: say you had a $250,000 whole-life policy that built up a $50,000 cash value after you paid your premiums for perhaps 20 years. (Ask your insurance agent or company for a calculation. The value will vary based on your age at the start of the policy, your health, and other factors.) You could close out the policy and receive $50,000 to spend on

Odds on Insurance Companies

A great price on an insurance policy is irrelevant if the company can't pay claims. Several organizations rate the financial strength of insurance companies, so you know who is more likely to be around in the long run (sort of like life expectancies on life insurance companies). These rating organizations include the following, among others. You'll have to sign up, or register, for these sites before they'll give you their information. Basic information, which is often all you need, is generally available without a fee.

- **A.M. Best** at AMBest.com
- **Fitch Ratings** at Fitch Ratings.com
- **Standard & Poor's** at StandardAndPoors.com

The strongest insurance companies get an AAA rating, with close cousins AA, A+, and A. Don't use a company that has a rating of B or lower.

Most insurance companies or insurance comparison websites prominently display their financial rating. You can also ask an agent for the rating. If something seems fishy about a company, you have many other places to take your business.

All insurance companies have to follow the same state and federal regulations, and prices for identical forms and terms of life insurance are usually very close from one source to another. You may find slightly lower rates from online and telephone direct-sellers (because they do not have the overhead of retail offices or have to pay commissions). On the other hand, you may find it worthwhile (and sometimes no more expensive) to seek the guidance of a professional agent who can compare quotes from multiple companies.

your retirement. Before you jump up and down with excitement, consider the fact that you may have spent $100,000 in premiums over the years to reach that point. Alternatively, you could borrow the $50,000 in cash value from the policy and spend it any way you want. Now you'd have a loan to repay with interest. What happens if you die soon after the loan? Your beneficiaries would receive only $200,000—the face value *minus the cash value that was given out as a loan and the interest on the loan*.

By comparison—and remember that rates differ depending on your age and other factors at the time of application—a 40-year-old male could purchase a 20-year-term $250,000 policy and pay a total of about $5,280 over the full term. (A woman ordinarily pays a bit less.) At the end of the term, your policy will be worthless, but the outlay of cash would be much less.

A Vanishing-but-Permanent Option

Some other forms use various complex formulas. One type of policy scares many financial experts—especially in a period when interest rates are low. So-called vanishing-premium permanent or whole-life policies claim that the interest earned on a policy's cash value can be used to pay the premiums in future years. That's a big if. It is usually based on some pretty optimistic estimates of earnings.

Personally, I wouldn't touch this sort of policy with a 10-foot stack of insurance salespeople. At the very least, I recommend seeking advice from a trusted financial advisor who works for you—not for an insurance company.

Overall, just be very cautious about buying deals that seem too good to be true—most are.

Determine How Much Life Insurance to Buy

There is no simple hard-and-fast rule about what you should buy because everyone's situation is different. The old classic advice was to buy a policy worth 10 times the policyholder's income.

Ask yourself some questions before adhering to this advice…

- **Is your family particularly young?** If so, might it make sense to buy as much as 20 times your income to extend a policy through the college years, or the marriageable years, or other family events?
- **Does your child have special needs that require continued financial help after he or she is grown?**
- **Do you want to include enough coverage to pay off a mortgage?**
- **Do you have any other major debts to pay off so your surviving family can get along?**

One interesting solution is to layer policies. It is similar to a strategy some investors use when purchasing bonds or other long-term notes. To layer, for example, you could buy a large policy with a 10- or 15-year term, and a lesser policy with a 30-year term, to cover different periods in your family's expected life.

In most cases, a committed romantic couple will name each other as the beneficiary of any policy. Things become more complicated if the *beneficiary*—the person who will receive the money—is a minor child at the time the policy pays out the benefit. An alternative is to create a testamentary trust, revocable living trust, or other form of trust as the beneficiary. Seek the advice of an attorney or financial advisor about any questions here and to properly create and maintain a trust.

Decide Whether to Sell Your Life Insurance While You're Alive

Depending upon your medical, financial, and familial states, viatical settlements of life-insurance policies are either a godsend or an extremely ghoulish sideline in modern business. A *viatical* settlement, also called a *life benefit* (as opposed to a death benefit), is selling a still-valid whole-life insurance policy to a third party. The amount of money paid for a whole life policy will be more than its cash surrender value, but less than its death benefit.

The third party becomes the policy owner and the beneficiary. If there are any outstanding monthly or annual premiums, the new owner is responsible for making them. The new beneficiary seeks a medical estimation of life expectancy, and the premium is adjusted based on the anticipated interest cost of the money paid out before death plus any premiums that must be paid to keep the policy in force.

I have to point out that the company or individual who buys your policy will sit around and wait for you to die. (There have been more than a few murder mystery novels based on the premise that a beneficiary just might try to hasten someone's death in order to collect. I am not suggesting that would happen with a viatical settlement. But try not to think about it too much.)

Before entering into a viatical agreement, do the following...

- **Determine if there are any tax consequences for receiving payment for the policy before death.** Federal law generally exempts the proceeds of a viatical sale for people who are chronically or terminally ill. At the state level, tax consequences vary. Consult a qualified tax advisor.
- **Determine if this income affects your eligibility for public-assistance programs,** such as Medicaid, that are based on financial need.

Put your quest for a viatical settlement out to bid. The payment amount can vary greatly from one company to another, depending on its medical and financial calculations. Modern medicine has transformed many formerly deadly conditions like AIDS into treatable conditions, and there has been overall improvement in medical treatment, extending many lives. That makes it less appealing to viatical companies to bet on a short lifetime for many applicants. And back to the ghoulish side of the equation: the buyer can conduct its own medical investigation and even check in with you from time to time to see how you're feeling. Buyers value policies from highly rated insurance companies—especially those that do not have large amounts of outstanding premiums to be paid.

You can find viatical settlement companies by searching the internet, but it is probably to your benefit to involve a professional such as your life insurance agent or financial advisor. Begin by asking, "Does this make sense for me?" Then, if you proceed, ask for help finding the best deal and payout options.

The Viatical Less Traveled

The term viatical comes from the Latin via, which means road. Viatical has come to mean an allowance for travel expenses (or, in the Roman Catholic church, the last rites for a dying person). It has come to mean the sale by the owner of an existing life insurance policy to a third party for more than its cash surrender value, but less than what it would have paid out on the death of the insured.

Know What Life Insurance to Avoid

This is what you came here to avoid—scams.

Don't Buy Life Insurance for Children

To make it short and sweet, most experts say purchasing a life insurance policy on a young child is a sucker's bet or worse. A term life policy doesn't benefit the child in any way—he or she has to die for the policy to pay off. A whole life policy with a cash value is a poor way to invest for college. A better route is an early regular investment plan in mutual funds or stocks or a 529 savings account that allows tax-free earnings. Consult a financial planner and be sure to check for any changes to federal or state policies. (You can read more about the latter at the IRS's website at Blinc.Media/2vxLYu0.)

Remember that the real purpose of life insurance is to provide living expenses for surviving family members.

Don't Buy Credit Life Insurance

Credit life insurance is a bad deal. It promises to pay off your outstanding credit card account balance and certain other loans should you die. The rates are high, and if you're doing things right, you shouldn't have large personal credit obligations. Instead, just make sure that your term life-insurance policy coverage—which costs much less per thousand than a credit-life policy—is large enough to pay off any outstanding debts and provide for your family in the event of your untimely demise.

CHAPTER 35

Shopping for Health Insurance

Although many of us concentrate on life insurance as a way to take care of our loved ones at the time of our death, two policies are arguably more important over the course of our own lives: medical insurance and disability insurance. Both can be complex, with greatly varying coverage and prices.

The Affordable Care Act (ACA) in the US made progress toward establishing minimum levels of coverage for health care insurance and standardizing policy classes offered by state exchanges. The ACA also ensured that no one can be turned down for health insurance because of a pre-existing condition (such as diabetes or cancer), and extended the period of time that young people can continue to fall under the umbrella of their parents' policy.

However, the ACA, at the time of this writing, is in limbo. Health insurance plans are all but certain to change in coming years. Whether these changes are for the better or worse are a matter of political judgment. My number-one tip is to spend time researching health insurance policies and the companies that offer them *before* signing up for one.

As this book goes to press, about half of Americans receive health insurance through their employers. About 25% receive coverage through a government plan such as Medicare, Medicaid, military, or veterans benefits. The remainder buy individual plans or have no insurance coverage.

If your employer offers a health insurance policy, set up an appointment with your personnel or benefits office and ask for an explanation. Ask about deductibles and copayments, and ask how you can make the best use of the coverage. If you have to purchase health insurance on your own, interview several insurance companies to find one that explains policies to your satisfaction. Your goals are multiple: to obtain the best level of coverage with the doctors and hospitals you prefer to use and that offer the best price for you, and to find a company that holds the potential to offer you the best customer service.

- **Buy the right health insurance plan.**
- **Don't pay for duplicate medical insurance.**
- **Extend your Medicare coverage.**
- **Choose a disability insurance policy with care.**
- **Find long-term care coverage.**

Buy the Right Health Insurance Plan

Health insurance, like most forms of insurance, is a relatively expensive purchase we make and hope never to use. If you are not provided a plan by your employer or a government program, an hour or so of research might end with you and your family having significantly better coverage.

Many details of health insurance plans purchased by individuals (and on behalf of their spouse and family) are likely to change in coming years as the result of political maneuvering in Washington, D.C. as this book goes to press—but the basic principles of being a savvy, careful consumer still apply.

Under the ACA, there were exchanges in participating states that allowed consumers to compare the prices of standardized plans. Some states chose to leave the sales function to the federal government. As this book goes to press, it is likely that the ACA's structure will stay in place for a period of time—either until a replacement system arrives or the existing system is modified. Some sort of change is likely. The nature of long-range planning by insurance companies and government funding plans would suggest that replacement or improvement will require at least several years.

If you are going to buy an insurance policy, follow this research plan:

1. Educate yourself on the details of policies, including types of coverage, deductibles, and copays.

Companies that operate in your state will have websites. There are also government and private websites that may allow you to compare policies from numerous companies in one place.

2. If there are multiple insurance companies in your state, call the sales department for several of them. Ask a few questions about how the policy will work for you.

I do this when I am preparing to make a major purchase. If a company does not provide me with good customer service *before* they have my money in hand, why should I expect better results *after* the check has cleared?

3. Call or visit your personal physician's business office or visit a hospital. Ask which plans they accept. Also ask if they have any thoughts to share about working with particular health insurance companies.

You're not likely to get a specific recommendation, but you just might learn—as I did when I made such a call—that two or three companies I was considering seemed to be providing good service to their customers, while one company was very difficult to work with.

Don't Pay for Duplicate Medical Insurance

If you and your spouse are both employed, you may each have medical coverage that can extend to each other and to your family. Study the provisions of both plans—it might be worthwhile to meet with the benefits administrator at each of your workplaces—to see which plan offers better coverage at a better price. In some cases, it might make sense to keep each independent policy, or you might be better off declining one insurance and bringing your family together under the other. You cannot collect twice for the same medical incident or treatment, so duplicate coverage has no value. You may be able to receive cash payment from an employer if you decline its health coverage because of coverage from a spouse's plan.

Extend Your Medicare Coverage

In the US, if you are 65 years of age or older or have certain medical conditions, you are eligible for the federal Medicare plan, which provides a very good level of coverage at a very low price, but not without a few gaps. You can find out more about Medicare at the Medicare.gov website, as well as on other sites offered by groups serving older people.

I strongly urge you to consider purchasing a supplemental Medicare policy (called a Medigap policy by some). These supplemental policies, offered in most states in one or two levels of coverage, automatically coordinate with your Medicare plan to reduce or eliminate some deductibles or copays. You can find out about available supplemental plans through the Medicare website.

Neither Medicare nor Medigap will pay the cost of prescription drugs and other medically necessary items except for those dispensed to patients who are hospitalized or in certain other situations. Because of that, also consider buying a Medicare Part D plan from private insurers for medication coverage. Make a list of medications you are currently taking, and then consult the websites for these prescription insurance plans to find out which is best for you.

Run the numbers or ask one of the companies to help. You might find a plan that is $50 less per month, but will cost $1,000 more per year for medications that you know you will need. That's a bad deal.

Choose a Disability Insurance Policy with Care

It's not something most people give a lot of thought about, but disability insurance may be one of the most important policies you buy. Think of it this way: Life insurance pays your family if you die, while disability pays your family if you live but are unable to work. And don't think this is something that you're

Employer Plans Post-65

If you are still employed after age 65 at a company that provides health insurance, spend the time studying the details.

Once again, this is an area that may change because of alterations to or replacement of the Affordable Care Act. But as this book goes to press, companies with 20 or more employees are required to offer their older workers the same coverage as younger ones. That means, under the ACA, this is "primary coverage" that may be superior to Medicare. Smaller companies are (or were) not required to provide such coverage. For many older workers in that situation, Medicare would probably be superior as primary coverage.

You can read about the dividing line (as it existed as this book went to press), in an article from Bottom Line, at BottomLineInc.com/money/health-insurance/health-insurance-alert.

too young to worry about. According to industry statistics, one out of three people between the ages of 35 and 65 will become disabled for at least three months, and one in ten will become permanently disabled before age 65.

If your employer offers a generous benefits package, you may have disability coverage already. Check with the benefits administrator for details. If not, contact a competent insurance agent.

Here are some tips on shopping for disability coverage…

• **Understand the distinction between short-term (STD) and long-term disability (LTD) coverage.** A long-term policy will replace your income for your entire life (or until a specified age, such as 65, when you would be presumed to retire from work). A short-term policy may promise to pay for only a few months or years. This is better than nothing, but not much benefit to a young breadwinner with a family.

• **Go for as long a payment term as you feel comfortable paying for.** Seek as high a disability payment as possible. Typical policies promise to replace about 60% to 75% of your income. (They don't want to pay 100% because that doesn't give you much of an incentive to go back to work.) In any case, the income from a disability policy that was paid for with post-tax income is not subject to taxation if you draw on the policy. Therefore, you should be able to get by on a reduced portion of your previous income. On the other hand, if you or your employer purchased a policy with pre-tax money and the benefit was not included in your gross income, then the benefits are taxable when you receive them. In any case, discuss this with your accountant and benefits manager before making any decision.

• **Read the policy's fine print about your occupation.** The best sort of disability policy promises to pay you for as long as you are unable to engage in your *own* occupation. A much less valuable version pays you only if you are unable to engage in *any* occupation. You don't want some insurance adjuster expecting you to work at McDonald's after you are forced by accident or illness to leave your occupation as a rocket scientist, right?

• **Adjust the cost of a disability policy by accepting a longer *elimination period*—**the length of time after an accident or illness before you begin to collect. If you choose, for example, a less expensive policy with a six-month elimination

Check Your Calendar

Most Medigap and Medicare Part D plans have a limited enrollment period each year. You can enroll in Medicare in the month in which you turn 65, but (with some exception for special circumstances) you can only change your plan during the open enrollment period, which runs between October 15 and December 7 of each year…unless the rules are changed.

Be sure you understand when you are allowed to change from one plan to another, and check your policy every year to make sure you have the best coverage for you. Some events allow you to reassess your plan outside that period. Those kinds of events include moving to an address that's outside the plan's service area or moving into or out of a nursing home or a similar institution. Medicare.gov (Blinc.media/2vxpadU) addresses exceptions.

Medigap plans have their own open enrollment period, and Medicare Part D (prescription drug coverage) has an additional wrinkle: a penalty for not enrolling at the time you first signed up for Medicare. You can find further information on these plans and deadlines at Medicare.gov. There, you can find information from advocacy groups like AARP and state agencies for the aging.

period, the insurance company is gambling that you'll return to work before that period elapses. From your point of view, you should compare the cost savings in a long elimination period against your ability to do without income during those months.

- **Seek a noncancelable and guaranteed-renewable policy if you can get both features.** The insurance company is bound to keep the policy in force as long as you make payments, and the premium is locked in place for the agreement's entire term.

A less-desirable plan is a *guaranteed renewable policy*, which prevents the insurance company from singling you out for a premium increase. The rate can go up only if an entire class of policyholders faces the same boost. What kind of classes? An entire state, or an entire occupation, or every policy holder.

- **Get a good insurance agent on your side when you seek a plan, and do not rely on verbal promises.** Get everything in writing. And don't hesitate to seek assistance from an attorney if an insurance company attempts to deny payment to you for a covered disability.

Find Long-Term Care Coverage

Private health insurance and Medicare each will provide a basic amount of coverage if you find it necessary to receive long-term care in a nursing home or rehabilitation center, or if you need help at home performing basic needs. But the coverage period or amount of money spent is limited.

This is a situation most of us dread ever having to consider, but you might have to spend your personal and retirement savings to be able to qualify for government-assisted Medicaid coverage. One way to guard against that is to purchase a long-term care insurance policy. Long-term policies are not inexpensive, and the cost rises sharply the longer you wait before enrolling. The annual policy charge for a 40-year-old is much lower than that for a 60-year-old, even if you consider that the younger person has paid for a longer period of time.

Many experts say the sweet spot to purchase an LTC plan is about age 50, when you are likely to be established in your career and before insurance prices begin to rise steeply.

You will have to pass a medical examination before being approved for this policy, and you must continue making payments. If your policy lapses because of nonpayment, you will lose all the money you paid over the years.

The number of companies offering LTC plans has diminished as health care costs have risen. Some companies do not offer new policies, but continue to service their existing clients.

Buying a long-term-care policy ideally involves assistance from a capable, independent financial advisor. Don't hesitate to consult with more than one, and be sure you understand all the types and levels of coverage and how each applies to you. Also ask about the company's financial rating. Remember that you are literally banking on an insurance company remaining financially solvent.

And remember that you will have to continue paying premiums in retirement until and unless you need to use the policy for your care. In certain circumstances, some insurance providers allow you to reduce the monthly or annual premium for an LTC policy if you accept a lower coverage level. That's not a great situation, but is probably better than dropping the policy completely and receiving nothing for the thousands of dollars you have paid over the years.

Index